The Banquet

THE COMPLETE PLAYS, FILMS, AND LIBRETTOS

KENNETH KOCH

The Banquet

THE COMPLETE PLAYS, FILMS, AND LIBRETTOS

FOREWORD BY MAC WELLMAN & INTRODUCTION BY AMBER REED

EDITED BY KAREN KOCH, RON PADGETT, AND JORDAN DAVIS

COFFEE HOUSE PRESS :: MINNEAPOLIS
2013

COPYRIGHT © 2013 by the Kenneth Koch Literary Estate
BOOK DESIGN by Allan Kornblum
COVER DESIGN by Linda Koutsky
COVER IMAGE © Corrado Bonini

COFFEE HOUSE PRESS books are available to the trade through our primary distributor, Consortium Book Sales & Distribution, cbsd.com or (800) 283-3572. For personal orders, catalogs, or other information, write to: info@coffeehousepress.org.

Coffee House Press is a nonprofit literary publishing house. Support from private foundations, corporate giving programs, government programs, and generous individuals helps make the publication of our books possible. We gratefully acknowledge their support in detail in the back of this book. To you and our many readers around the world, we send our thanks for your continuing support.

Good books are brewing at coffeehousepress.org

LIBRARY OF CONGRESS CIP INFORMATION
Koch, Kenneth, 1925–2002.
[Works. Selections]
The banquet : the complete plays, films, and librettos / foreword by Mac Wellman ; introduction by Amber Reed ; edited by Karen Koch, Ron Padgett, and Jordan Davis.
p. cm.
Includes bibliographical references.
ISBN 978-1-56689-328-2 (trade paper)— ISBN 978-1-56689-329-9 (trade cloth)
I. Wellman, Mac. II. Reed, Amber. III. Koch, Karen. IV. Padgett, Ron, 1942– V. Davis, Jordan. VI. Title.
PS3521.027A6 2013
812'.54–DC23
2012043733

FIRST EDITION | FIRST PRINTING
PRINTED IN THE U.S.A.

Table of Contents

ONE THOUSAND AVANT-GARDE PLAYS

Foreword

The poetic plays of Kenneth Koch offer us a poetry that is profoundly playful and comprise a teasing theater that we can or cannot take at face value. For although the material of his plays is simple, the plays themselves are never simple-minded (in the manner of so much face-value art that characterizes our time: what you see is what you get. Period.) Simplicity resists mere explanation in a way simple-mindedness would never dare. What is simple exists in the moment, and in the words of Jonathan Edwards "is altogether equivalent to an immediate production out of nothing at each moment"; whereas simple-mindedness would have us go no further, look more closely, think no further. The effect is numbing. Koch's method enlivens.

Formally the plays of Kenneth Koch resemble the minimal and almost fragmentary minuscules of drastic theater writers of earlier times, notably the Sintesi of the Italian Futurists and the very short plays of the so-called Last Soviet avant-garde, the Oberiu group, notably Alexander Vvedensky and Daniil Kharms. Brevity is the most striking aspect of this kind of work, along with a refusal to explain with exposition or familiar theater psychology, usually a watered down and dated Freudianism. Very short plays tend, obviously, to the aphoristic. They amount to judgments rendered without the meandering of a jury devoted to the conventional truths of realism or its yet more serious country cousin, naturalism. Brevity sees, in short, nothing natural in naturalness, and prefers the oddness, the weird locatedness, of one throw of the theatrical die:

Incident on the Street

(MAN *comes up to another man,* HARRIMAN, *on the street and offers him a rather large box.*)

MAN:
Harriman, I have brought you this box of balls—
Wooden balls and steel balls, and balls with gold upon them,
Acorn balls, nylon balls, balls of porphyry and of ancient silver,
Every kind of ball you can imagine that is of human make.

(MAN *leaves.*)

*   *   *

Here and elsewhere, Koch's plays display aspects of the Camp aesthetic so nimbly adumbrated by Susan Sontag in her 1964 essay "Notes on Camp." She points to, among other things, a fascination with the concept of boredom and the place of boredom in our lives, and in the art we employ to understand who we are, where we come from, and where we are going. Indeed, most of Koch's plays have the feeling of being brief way stations on a journey that both begins and ends in mystery, a journey that can be redeemed by the merest instant of an awakening, as in the following play (in its entirety).

The Yangtse

(The stage represents the entire length of the Yangtse River, or at least both ends of it.)

KI FO: *(a young man)*
    A branch falls into the Yangtse.

TI FAI: *(a young woman)*
    The water pushes it on. And here at the end
    It washes onto the bank.
    It is wet, and there is a white blossom
    On this one tip of it.

KI FO:
    Now I shall head for home.

TI FAI:
    I will take this branch in my hand.

OLD WOMAN:
    However, no one can move
    Because the king has all the stage directions.

OLD MAN:
    Then how did the branch move? and the Yangtse River?

(JAI FU *appears.*)

JAI FU:
    It is only the people who are controlled.

*   *   *

If there is a unifying theme in Koch's work, as there seems to be in that of the earlier masters of brevity, it is not so much of themes as of practice—that of *the tease.* In this case I would define the tease as a continuum of separate points running from *taunt* to *charm,* with many microscopic and nuanced intervening degrees. These are works that play with the practice of play writing and play *making,* which, taken altogether as a body of work, pose a rather substantial challenge to standard dramaturgy, or what I have referred to elsewhere as Geezer Theater. But if a tease is a challenge, then there is another aspect to the game: the implied offer of a seduction. These miniature theater devices offer a challenge that is also an erotic *come hither*. Reading Koch, I keep thinking of Shuzo Kuki, the Japanese philosopher (and an important acquaintance of both Sartre and Heidegger). Central to his thought is the notion of *Iki*, which is an erotic component of all elements of design and culture in traditional Japan; He writes "While detachedly breathing neutral air, *Iki* purposelessly and disinterestedly engages in self-disciplined play. It is, in a word, coquetry for the sake of coquetry." Indeed, to the literal-minded and humorless (not to mention clueless), this apparently antitheatrical manner, almost a Camp manner, seems a slap in the face of the "better class" of mainstream drama.

The antitheatrical tradition is long—at least as long as that of the theatrical. As Jonas Barish, a noted Ben Jonson scholar, has pointed out in his book *The Antitheatrical Prejudice,* all significant advances in the theater come from a ferocious, unrepentant antitheatrical passion. Witness Ibsen on the well-made play, Brecht on the melodrama of his time, Rich Maxwell on the shibboleths of Method acting. Living theater feeds off dead theater the way plants feed on manure.

Just as the work of the Italian and Russian Futurists grew out of dissatisfaction with mainstream bourgeois theater, so did the many plays of Kenneth Koch. But the mockery of a dated and *passéist* aesthetic is certainly not all they are about, nor is it certainly all they amount to. They are also formally exact and rigorously wrought, elegant and spare, the works of a mature craftsperson. One likes to look at them, on the page and in the mind, as well as on the stage.

Some of Kenneth Koch's plays are reminiscent of Elizabethan and Jacobean masques. They either embody a political event or comment on one, but one possibly forgotten, as though the plays were lost fragments or lost dialogues of someone very much like Plato, or like Noh plays from a lost possible world of an American Shangri-la.

The sheer oddity of many of their sources (medieval Morality plays, Asian theater, anecdotal asides from the lives of great philosophers, Futurist and Surrealist theater, and pop culture) point to the amazing and frequently annoying richness of real human behavior, history, and artifice, which rarely makes it to the well-appointed domestic rooms of mainstream drama, resplendent in plush sofas and sofa speeches. Plays like Kenneth Koch's are the classic antidote to all this sofa business! Odd, miniature, unbreakable, and forever young at heart.

*   *   *

It needs to be pointed out that the ghetto of Poets Theater, however splendid in its own terms, remains a ghetto. Young playwrights, in my experience, know very little about the world of poetry in general, regarding it as hardly more than a *literary* (hence suspect) hobby. This is regrettable, especially considering the rich historical interplay between the two arts over the centuries. Indeed, one could say that it is only quite recently—since the end of World War II—that poetry and theater have, in our country at least, become totally distinct. (Remember that both Gertrude Stein and Ezra Pound wrote operas, and the original title of *The Wasteland* was *He Do the Police in Different Voices*.) Likewise, young poets avoid the theater altogether in favor of cinema, the hipper sorts of television, or spoken word performance. To them, all theater is by definition Geezer Theater, to be avoided at all costs.

This is where the plays of Kenneth Koch come in. I would love to see them produced by serious (though not solemn) professional theater actors, directors, and designers, as work to be explored and produced in our major theaters. Perhaps we have all accepted too easily the assumption that this work is for a small, sophisticated coterie of those in the know. There is no need to rest in the assumption that they might not prove as theatrically durable as, say, the plays of Samuel Beckett and Sam Shepard. Taking the strange and wonderful little plays of Kenneth Koch down from the shelf and dusting them off might awaken us to a whole new theatrical landscape, one that was there all the time.

—*Mac Wellman*

Introduction

Kenneth Koch, whose fresh, irreverent, expansive, and wise poetry constitutes one of the great legacies of America's twentieth century, also wrote for the theater from almost the beginning to nearly the end of his life. He took up the form boldly and easily, because a friend had a venue for a week and needed something to do in it, or because he was curious about whether one could still bring the whole world onto the stage. Although his dramatic work's charm and vigor often reflect the same, recognizably Kochian attitude toward art and life as his poetry, his plays, films, and libretti were not mere extensions of his poetic practice. Koch's technical virtuosity and passion for the stage's specific potentialities ensured the creation of a distinctly dramatic body of work that re-imagines, as deeply as almost any other, what theater can be and do. To read Kenneth Koch's plays is to inhabit his excitement as one improbable, delightful possibility opens after the next.

In an interview with Jordan Davis published in *American Poetry Review* (APR), Koch recalled his beginnings in theater:

> I started writing "plays" when I was eleven, they were satires of our extended family life, all fairly benign caricatural stuff—Uncle Nate was "nervous," Uncle Leo ate too much, etc. No one varied from his character in these early dramatic works and nothing ever happened. It was fun, I remember, writing ENTER and EXIT and ENTER AUNT MARIAN IN A RED COAT.

He loved Shakespeare early and well, "speaking in blank verse at a rather early age," and while at Harvard on the GI Bill would read verse dramas tirelessly as he searched for the secret of writing a play "in poetry"; it seemed to him "a delicious mystery, that Shakespeare could do it, so perfectly, and that there was no way to do it now." He read plays by Lorca, Eliot, Yeats, Auden, Delmore Schwartz, and William Vaughan Moody; by Byron, Keats, Shelley, and Beddoes; by Marlowe, Webster, and Shakespeare. He even tried his hand at Yeatsian symbolic drama with a play called *Little Red Riding Hood* that was "full of gongs, slow-downs, freezing in position, and iambic pentameter."

But Koch would find that he was most compelled by something more than, and other than, versified dramatic speech. Something like Ubu Roi entering, announcing, "I am going to kill everyone!" and walking off the stage. A children's production of *Peter Pan*. Or a play whose entire action consisted of the lights being turned on after ten minutes of darkness (*Luce!*, by the Italian futurist Francesco Cangiullo). He loved the sweet, slight shock of each word's absolute unambiguity in medieval mystery and morality plays: "I am Mary fair and dear. I will do a dance now here." He found Japanese Noh astounding, and spent hour after hour being happily mystified at the Chinese theater under the Manhattan Bridge. Anything, he would later say, that got him away

> from the dreary Broadway-type plays I'd been taken to see in Cincinnati and was still menaced by in the pages of the Sunday Times, artificial and stilted arrangements of stale persons and staler ideas; people who carped at one another, discussed issues, were false, were true. Who would ever want to write plays? —APR

*   *   *

The earliest plays with which Koch remained happy, among them *Pericles, The Merry Stones*, and *Guinevere, or The Death of the Kangaroo*, were written around the same time he was working on the poem "When the Sun Tries to Go On," a cacophonous epic in which one word follows from the next in a way determined less by syntax and reason than by Koch's sense of each word as an object of peculiar characteristics. With words denied harbor in their expected contexts, the language of his early plays takes on a shining, almost tactile quality.

CHIEFTAIN:
> He is falling toward me like the charm bracelet
> I saw laughing out of the window. At this minute a giraffe
> Knows the cow who is offering night my atlas.
> The wind, curving from Chinese charm bracelet
> To charm bracelet, seems to counsel me, "Dollars,
> Feenamint, dollars, gunsmoke." After one night
> With Dolores, I visited the Huguenot people.
> —from *Guinevere, or The Death of the Kangaroo*

This is theater in which each sentence is a small occasion. To this clear, hard brightness of language, Koch's early plays marry a corresponding brightness of action: events follow each other crisply, in a manner that neither offers nor requires explanation, and when they stop, the play is over.

Also tucked among the early work is *Six Improvisational Plays,* a little-known treasure encompassing, among other things, an academic murder mystery in which a professor drops dead after declaring his preference for Jung over the Zen masters, a minutely detailed description of Mexico City, repeated twice, and an improvised resurrection. One play, *The Gold Standard,* whose challenge Koch would later take up in a longer work, begins in this way:

> A Mountain Shrine, in China. Two monks enter, and try, without the slightest success, to explain the gold standard to each other, for four hours. There should be nothing comical whatsoever in anything they say.

Even by a conservative reckoning, a faithful production of this nine-page suite would last at least twelve hours and require an ensemble of three dozen children, actors, and opera singers, a symphony orchestra, and unlimited means. But though it is one of his few plays that seem written more for provocation than production, this sextet stands out as an early exemplar of Koch's conviction that everything was potentially dramatic. His plays are animated by the same spirit in which the ceilings of the stages of Shakespeare's time were painted with the sun, moon, and stars; looking at a stage, he saw not only a living room but also the world, which included not only the kinds of human relations that seemed to preoccupy much of the drama of his day but also philosophy and religion, the birth and death of civilizations, existence in time and space, and the blessedly dumb and trivial, too.

At the same time that his poetry was moving into a more narrative style (beginning with *Ko, or a Season on Earth* and *Thank You and Other Poems*), Koch began writing plays that attempted to conjure what he termed a third theatrical tradition: neither commercial nor avant-garde (at least in the sense of being absurdist), but epic, imaginative, heroic, and high-spirited. He had been struck by a British production of Marlowe's *Tamburlaine*—"the conquest of Asia taking place on the stage, in action and in that marvelous poetry"— and by Luca Ronconi's staging of *Orlando Furioso*, an epic Koch had long admired for the way one action followed another without pause for reflection. "In the American theater there is no tradition of the epic, noble, heroic, operatic," Koch remarked to a *New York Times* reviewer in 1979. "There's no patience with the old apparatus of that tradition. But I don't think the desire to experience grand emotions grandly ever goes away."

His plays invoking this third tradition included *Bertha*, a spirited dash through the life and death of a Norwegian queen (which Ned Rorem would set as an opera), and *George Washington Crossing the Delaware*, which would become a kind of underground classic. Inspired by Larry Rivers's celebrated painting of the same subject, *George Washington* is a heroic romance that seems unable to resist goosing itself. A daring nighttime raid on the British camp is followed by a scene in which Washington decides to cross the Delaware after dreaming about how he swam a river to escape his father's wrath after cutting down the infamous cherry tree (in its utter inanity, a jab at the thin psychological gruel then dished up as "motivation" in theater). Earnest expository speeches that would seem equally at home in an Elizabethan chronicle play or a school pageant suddenly give way to doggerel thieved straight out of "'Twas the Night Before Christmas":

GEORGE WASHINGTON:
  So pack up your shyness, your shame, and your fear,
  And throw them away, and come meet me, all, here,

At twelve o'clock midnight, and off we shall go
To the camp of the English that lies down below!
And we shall return in their splendid attire,
And every man present shall have his desire.
So, come, get you ready—go blacken each face,
And meet me at midnight in this very place!

But it would be a mistake to view this or any other Koch play as merely paro-
dic. Rather than negating Koch's heroic, romantic enthusiasm, the comic element holds it aloft, out of the morass of the familiar. Even the most solemn,
portentous events in this and Koch's other epically styled plays seem lit from
within by his personal excitement that such things happened, or could be imag-
ined to have happened, and that we are alive and able to write and think about
them. Serious things are not treated unseriously, but joy and life's richness of
possibility are counted among them, allowing us to laugh at our cake and eat
it too; when one old man says to another, "The men and horses on the other
side of the river are shaking themselves free of water," at the end of "George
Washington," the feeling is one of awe.

Although his plays are pleasures on the page, Koch himself nearly always
wrote for production; *George Washington,* for example, came about when Larry
Rivers asked for a play to be performed at his son's elementary school in
Southampton. (Sadly, the school's auditorium collapsed, and the play premiered
Off Broadway instead.) "I almost always write plays for special occasions," Koch
once said. "Sometimes they take place, sometimes not." To him, it felt like a lost
opportunity when he saw the contemporary theater directors he most admired—Robert Wilson, Peter Brook, Ariane Mnouchkine, and Luca Ronconi,
among others—using old texts, such as Shakespeare or the Mahabharata. He
believed that theater at its best was one of life's great joys, loved the process of
staging a play even more than its performance, and was concerned by the fact
that few of the young writers he had taught were interested in theater:

> In the thirty or so years I've taught writing at Columbia, I had as stu-
> dents quite a few good, even brilliant, poets and fiction writers, but only
> one who wanted to write plays. Hard to want to if you don't see them—
> it's like wanting to build a temple to Isis in Idaho. "This one will be really
> good!" —APR

Koch, on the other hand, seemed happy to build temples to Isis anywhere and
on the slightest provocation. He wrote plays quickly and often, amassing an
astonishing body of work for someone whose main pursuits were writing and
teaching poetry. Some of his plays were truly occasional; *The Moon Balloon*
was dashed off for just one night, New Year's Eve 1969. Performed at Bethesda
Fountain in Central Park, it launched some of the worst aggravations of 1960s

New York—smog, Con Edison, Nixon—into space with all the pomp of a Jacobean civic entertainment (unfortunately, *The Moon Balloon* didn't get far). Koch's theatrical work also provided opportunities for collaboration with his artist friends. Red Grooms designed the sets and costumes for *Guinevere, or The Death of the Kangaroo;* for *George Washington Crossing the Delaware,* Alex Katz painted life-sized cutouts of British soldiers and Washington's famous boating party. There were more complex collaborations as well. *The Tinguely Machine Mystery,* presented on one night at the Jewish Museum in 1965, featured three motorized machines made by Jean Tinguely in important roles—moving, speaking, committing crimes—in Koch's wonderfully odd mash-up of Noh and police detective mystery. In *The Construction of Boston,* Tinguely, Niki de Saint Phalle, and Robert Rauschenberg built the city of Boston onstage to the accompaniment of Koch's text, which was written in heroic blank verse and narrated the city's history and the artists' actions. Rauschenberg chose to bring people and weather, in the form of a couple of extras and a rain machine; Tinguely was responsible for the architecture, building a wall of sandstone bricks that, by the end of the performance, completely obstructed the audience's view of the stage; and Saint Phalle provided the art, entering from the audience with three soldiers and shooting a rifle at a copy of the Venus de Milo, causing it to bleed paint. The whole thing was satisfyingly colossal and unsubtle and spectacular, in the manner of an Elizabethan court masque; a cannon was fired but did not go off. Koch would later adapt this text into a libretto for the composer Scott Wheeler, adding a prologue explaining the circumstances of that unrepeatable night.

Perhaps the climax of Koch's theatrical collaborations with artists would come with the 1978 New York production of *The Red Robins,* which Koch adapted from his novel of the same title. Inspired by the purity and intensity of boys' and girls' adventure books, the story concerns a group of healthy, passionate young Americans who all have their own planes and fly around Asia. The story, which involves a tiger hunt, the search for a famous mythical city, and Santa Claus and the Easter Bunny, is irreducible and exhaustingly intricate. In an interview with Allen Ginsberg, Koch rebuked him for trying to probe beneath the surface of his work:

> GINSBERG: What's the deep plot of *The Red Robins?*
> KOCH: I'd rather tell you the superficial plot.
> GINSBERG: Why?
> KOCH: That's what the plot is. There is no hidden meaning.
>
> —Allen Ginsberg, *A Poet Writes for the Stage, New York Times,*
>   January 8, 1978

Koch went on to quote Frank O'Hara's insight regarding the artist David Smith's work: in Smith's steel sculptures, O'Hara had said, "unification is approached by inviting the eye to travel over the complicated surface exhaustively, rather than inviting it to settle on the whole first and then explore certain details." The play's sets by Red Grooms (Shanghai, the jungle, an island), Roy Lichtenstein (a silver-and-blue airplane), Jane Freilicher (a garden), Rory McEwen (another island), Alex Katz (robins in flight), Katherine Koch (the Capitol), and Vanessa James (sky, mountains), underscored the whirl of changes of location and emotion in the play, and became part of its intricate surface. *The Red Robins* is that rare, plot-driven adventure in which the audience never finds itself waiting outside of the work, ahead of the action, having sensed where everything was tending the moment the protagonist appeared (if not before). If we are to attend at all to *The Red Robins*, we must do so completely, moment by moment; even if we could guess what happened next, the thing after that would be no less of an enigma. Perhaps because of the unusually close demands on us and the lack of the usual escape hatches through which our attention is wont to flee, we feel by the end of *The Red Robins* as happily fatigued as if we ourselves had flown over the North Pole, around Shanghai, and back, in search of Tin Fan.

*   *   *

There are actually 112 plays in *One Thousand Avant-Garde Plays*. They are not long; in their first production, seventy-two were staged in a single evening. Koch, who tended to speak more freely about his dramatic work than his poetry, connected their brevity to a couple of simple observations. First, there was his recognition that after the first minute or two, the initial excitement of the strangeness of being in a theater, in the presence of people we are supposed to pretend to believe are other than they are, tends to wear off quickly as one essentially "gets" where things are going. Second, and more crucially, he perceived that most of the dramatic moments in our lives are short and would probably seem unrelated if plucked out of our lives and placed side by side:

> The emotion I feel on the Grand Canal in Venice seems unconnected to the emotion I feel when a poem of mine is published, or when I'm with someone I love, or when I win a game of tennis. These don't seem to be connected, and they also don't seem to be connected with all the thrilling moments that I read about when I read about the past. But in a way they are connected because they make up my life.

> —from a 1989 interview with John Tranter, published in *Jacket* 5 (1998)

In *One Thousand Avant-Garde Plays* Koch offers, excised from their history, what seem like a thousand dramatic, climactic moments—from the present, from his imagination, from things that happened in the past and were momentous then or proved momentous later. (Koch was particularly taken by the great French historian Fernand Braudel, drawing many ideas for the plays from his books on the Mediterranean world in the second half of the sixteenth century and material life in the fifteenth through the eighteenth centuries.) In these 112 plays there are leitmotifs, recurring characters, and odd little groupings—six different Hamlets, two returns of Odysseus—but if anything unites them, it is a sense that experience extends far beyond the borders of the self and excludes neither the tectonic (AFRICA: "Madagascar, why are you leaving?") nor the fleeting and minuscule:

SPECK OF FOAM:
    Out of all being
    I come,
    A tiny speck
    Of white
    Foam—t

    Oh!
    You
    Forgot
    Me, and
    I'm
    Gone!

*   *   *

In one of his last plays, *Edward and Christine,* Koch took two lovers who had cropped up here and there in *One Thousand Avant-Garde Plays* and set them loose in a landscape in which time, geography, and identity shift and spin kaleidoscopically. Now in medieval England, now in Tokyo, donning fresh guises more often than Orlando, *Edward and Christine* embrace, separate, eat, have children, and buy vases, lending their forms to scenes that flash by with the intensity and specificity of memories. (Some vignettes appeared in different form in *Hotel Lambosa,* a collection of short fiction inspired by Kawabata's *Palm-of-the-Hand* stories.) "I mean to put experiences together the way memory and passion and reflection do," wrote Koch in his introductory note, "and to present the result as ordinary reality so as to make it visible." That the experiences put together here appear, unusually, so personal to him makes the play one of his most poignant.

*   *   *

Koch once said that he thought the perfect job for him would be as a court librettist responsible for creating at least three opera libretti a year. He liked opera "because you can celebrate anything. You can open the window and say: 'The window is open. The sun is shining. My hand is on the window, and I love you.' And somehow the music can make that beautiful enough." Some of

Koch's libretti, among them *The Gold Standard,* were plays later taken up by composers. He also wrote libretti from scratch for his friends: *Bertha* for Ned Rorem, *A Change of Hearts* for David Hollister, and *Garibaldi en Sicile* and *The Banquet: Talking about Love* for Marcello Panni. The last couldn't be simpler in structure; at a banquet in Paris toward the end of the war, Picasso, Stein, Marinetti, Satie, Cocteau, Marie Laurencin, and Apollinaire take turns speaking of love, until the future in the form of a great crowd breaks in and joins the celebration.

APOLLINAIRE:
>   Marie I've seen this century turn and change
>   I've seen this century's art become as strange
>   As any ever was in history
>   There never was so beautiful and strange
>   A moment as this present century

This collection leaves no doubt of Kenneth Koch's irreplaceability in that beautiful and strange moment. He has laid out a banquet, to be sure, and we had better come in and sit down. As one of his latecomers sings, "Our revels now begin."

—*Amber Reed*

Editors' Note

We have assembled Kenneth Koch's plays, film scripts, and opera librettos into a single volume for the general reader, grouping the pieces by genre, and then within each genre sequencing them mainly in chronological order. The dating was complicated: Kenneth's manuscripts did not always include the date of their composition, he often revised, certain plays were published long after their composition, and he adapted certain plays to be performed as operas—only *Angelica, A Change of Hearts, The Banquet (Talking about Love)*, and *Garibaldi en Sicile* were written from the outset as librettos. We have added a date at the end of each piece; the production notes appendix provides additional details. In all cases we have used Koch's final versions.

Our aim has been to assemble a collection that is as complete as Kenneth would have wanted. His purely occasional sketches and unfinished drafts have been omitted. We have also omitted his poems that were set to music—by Ned Rorem, Virgil Thomson, Mason Bates, William Bolcom, Mike Nussbaum, Paul Reif, and others—though sometimes those have been described as operas. In one instance we intentionally abandoned the chronology by reversing the order of the final two works in the book, in order to have a nice big finish.

—*Karen Koch, Ron Padgett, and Jordan Davis*

PLAYS

Pericles

Scene 1

FRIEND:
I stop and go, Pericles.

PERICLES:
Because we have come to find this land

FRIEND:
In the midst of truth,
climates, guitars

PERICLES:
This breeze is smaller than my mouth.

FRIEND:
O Pericles
what is a leader?

PERICLES:
How we have grown, dears, since we've
been from Greece!

FRIEND:
How tall a music

PERICLES:
Lies wasting on the shore.

Scene 2

ANOTHER MAN:
Here I sit.

Scene 3

A WOMAN:
Not that the gnat of smallness itself
has anything to offer the beach
with and through, without our tears
as if some tea had raised a blind
into the concussion of nonsense,
and a coughing death.

In Athens I saw twenty-nine old people
and the sidewalk was faery.
Oh everywhere the rats struck down ribbons,
heaven. A slave ship hides my ears.

O friends
amid the fornication of signposts
I saw a new Greece
arise!

Scene 4

FRIEND:
 You know. And yet
 he is bothered by the misery of pebbles
 which hat the lovely show
 in which he dies and does appear.
 He: "Take me back to the faucets
 of truth; my mind is a mass."

PERICLES:
 Here is freshness and the shore's timeless teeth!

Scene 5

FRIEND:
 There's no midnight mystery
 and no coconuts here to see,
 nothing but the ocean's sea
 which will wash history's tattoos from me;
 I hope to live satisfactorily
 like a capon that's struck by a tree
 and does die gladly
 bereft, O large, of his sexuality.
 Oh as honey fills the bee
 while the waves' orchestra's business spree
 sticks its night in your head like a country,
 and as the madman throws the flea
 to music, helplessly,
 here always shall I be
 and not in idolatry,
 but yet superfluous as a ski
 in a barge; while the withered air
 reduces baneful boughs to everywhere.

PERICLES:

Good-night, the parachutes have gone to sleep.

FRIEND:

I stop and go, Pericles.

Scene 6

PERICLES:

The air is Chinese!
I felt so strange
the days after tomorrow.
The stops have been removed
and the bottle is filled with leeks.
In the forest a sparring partner
whispers, "We grow."
O maidenhead of today
O maidenhead of yesterday

FRIEND:

My lord, I found this face in the sand.

PERICLES:

Drop it!

FACE OF ANOTHER MAN:

Help!

FINAL CURTAIN

EPILOGUE

(spoken by the conductor of the orchestra)

And would it not have been too late
The gas goes on the gas goes off
And we stood there with pure roots
In silence in violence one two one two
Will you please go through that again
The organ's orgasm and the aspirin tablet's speechless spasm.

—1953

Little Red Riding Hood

AN ENTERTAINMENT IN ONE ACT

Scene 1

Curtain rises on a small, simple room, the home of LITTLE RED RIDING HOOD *and her* MOTHER. RED RIDING HOOD *is lying on the floor reading a very large picture book. In this scene she is a little girl, about five or six years old.*

RED RIDING HOOD: *(sings, slowly and happily)*
    Apple—Bear—Cherry—Dog—Eat
    Fish—Giant—House—Island—Jar
    Katherine—Lion—Miller—Neat
    Ocean—Pig—Queen—Rabbit—Star
    Table—Ukelele—Violin—
    Wolf—Xylophone—Yard

    Mummy, do I have to stay in? / Mummy, if I read real hard / Can I play?

MOTHER:
    Not today. No—today, dear, you have to stay in.

RED RIDING HOOD:
    Even if I study real hard?

MOTHER:
    Even if you study very hard.

(RED RIDING HOOD *pores over her book while* MOTHER *sits down in chair right-front and knits. After a few moments* RED RIDING HOOD *gets up; she holds the book in front of her and does little dancing steps back and forth. She speaks delightedly.*)

RED RIDING HOOD:
    Mummy—if I gave an Apple to a Bear
    Would he care? Would he take me anywhere?

MOTHER:
    A bear would eat you up.

(*Throughout this next little scene,* RED RIDING HOOD's *dancing becomes slower and slower as she becomes frightened—she experiences fear for the first time; she moves slowly toward her* MOTHER *as her fear increases.* RED RIDING HOOD's *voice is emotional; her* MOTHER's, *deliberate and rather slow. Tension should be steadily built up until the clash of the cymbals.*)

RED RIDING HOOD:
  Would a Dog?

MOTHER:
  A big dog would.

RED RIDING HOOD:
  Why would a big dog? No—
  A nice big dog would let me go.
  I'd give a Cherry and he'd let me go.

MOTHER:
  A dog would eat you up.

RED RIDING HOOD:
  Would a Giant? Would a Fish?

MOTHER:
  A big fish would.

RED RIDING HOOD:
  Would a Lion?

MOTHER:
  Yes he would.

RED RIDING HOOD:
  Even if I were good?

MOTHER:
  Bad or good—a lion would.

RED RIDING HOOD:
  Not a Pig?

MOTHER:
  If he were big—

RED RIDING HOOD:
  Well, a Rabbit wouldn't ever eat me up.

MOTHER:
  No—a rabbit *couldn't* ever eat you up.

RED RIDING HOOD:
  Would a *Wolf*?

(MOTHER *starts suddenly in her chair, says nothing.* RED RIDING HOOD *is now very close to her, extremely frightened.*)

RED RIDING HOOD:

Would—a—Wolf—?

MOTHER: *(quickly, angrily almost)*

Yes he would!

RED RIDING HOOD: *(crying)*

Mummy—why would everybody eat me up?

(RED RIDING HOOD crawls onto her MOTHER's lap and starts to put her arms about her neck. Her MOTHER makes a gesture of slapping her sharply—the slap is symbolized by a clash of the cymbals. RED RIDING HOOD slips to the floor, and now the players freeze in their positions and do not move.)

MOTHER:

I didn't want to strike you, dear—and maybe even that's a lie—but it had to come sometime. That's just the way things are. . . . You don't know why anything would eat you up, but you can be pretty sure you're going to face being eaten sometime, and soon at that. Most everything ends up as a mouth; you lie awake crying about mouths: they kiss you and then they swallow you and you lie in the dark dreaming of mouths and being afraid. I could swallow you—but don't be afraid—I know myself too well: I have to leave that to somebody else.

RED RIDING HOOD:

To somebody else?

MOTHER:

To somebody else. Listen—you have to know what to do. You have to know what to do. . . . It's warm in here—and pleasant. Anybody knows it's warm and pleasant in here, but that doesn't do anybody any good. Every day people look in the window and scratch the glass till their fingers bleed—don't you think I know how it is? Bleeding fingers: that's another thing—bleeding fingers and mouths—it's not pleasant: crying like summer rain, you lick the blood off your hands and turn around to be swallowed. Everybody thinks it's a dance. Well, dancers have to work for a long time to be able to strike the lovely curve, the accurate pose—

RED RIDING HOOD:

Mother—can *we* dance?

MOTHER:

No. No, dear, it's not worth the risk. You pose for an image in the mind and end up with your eyes like shattered glass. . . . No, if you dance, you'll go crying down the April weather. I want you to be—safe—and—warm. I can't help myself. Listen, dear—you have to go away. You have to go away.

RED RIDING HOOD:

Will you come too?

MOTHER:

No. You have to go alone. . . . Do you think I *like* this job? I took it because it's the only one I could get—the only one you don't need any experience for . . . I do the best I can. Look—I don't like this any better than you. I do the best I can. I don't like this any better than you.

RED RIDING HOOD:

Where do I have to go?

MOTHER:

To . . . Grandmother's.

(Another sharp clash on the cymbals; the players slip out of their rigid poses.)

RED RIDING HOOD:

Oh, is *that* all? I'd like to go to Grandma's.

(RED RIDING HOOD *rises and dances around room, singing.)*

Going to *Grand*-ma's! Going to *Grand*-ma's
I'll wear my hood and play in the wood . . .
(frightened) No—a bear would eat me up.

(RED RIDING HOOD *runs over and throws her arms around her mother.)*

Oh Mummy—I'm afraid to go alone.

MOTHER:

You have to go alone.

RED RIDING HOOD:

Suppose a—a Thing should eat me up before I get to Grandma's?

MOTHER:

Nothing will eat you up if you are good.

RED RIDING HOOD:

You said before they would—?

MOTHER:

You had no fear before.

RED RIDING HOOD:

Oh Mommy—I'll be *good.*

MOTHER:

You have to fear now, but you don't know how to be good. Come stand by me and listen.

(RED RIDING HOOD *walks over and stands by her* MOTHER; *as she listens to her instructions, her body becomes rather tense, and her movements are less spontaneous and graceful.*)

MOTHER:

I have to give you these instructions. Listen carefully and nothing will happen to you before you get to Grandma's. . . . First—Go straight to her house: don't take any side roads or detours. Go straight to her house. Second— I'm going to give you a basket. You are to take it to Grandmother, so don't let anyone else open it. Do you understand?

RED RIDING HOOD:

Yes, Mother: go straight to her house and don't let anyone touch the basket.

MOTHER:

You are beginning to understand. Three—don't let anyone delay you on the way: tell them you have a place to go and that you are very sorry but you have to go.

RED RIDING HOOD:

I can't stop with *anyone*?

MOTHER:

It depends on whom you meet. . . . *No—listen*—don't stop with anybody. It's too much of a chance.

RED RIDING HOOD:

Nobody?

MOTHER:

Nobody. Four—Avoid wolves.

RED RIDING HOOD:

Oh—*that* will be easy: I don't like wolves.

MOTHER:

Wait till you've been on the road awhile. . . . *No—listen:* avoid wolves.

RED RIDING HOOD:

Go straight; guard the basket; don't stop; avoid wolves; is that all?

(MOTHER *turns away quickly; she obviously does not want to answer the question.*)

RED RIDING HOOD:

Mother—is that all?

(MOTHER *remains with her back toward* RED RIDING HOOD *who walks close to her and puts her arm around her.* MOTHER *gets the riding hood and with great affection slips it on* RED RIDING HOOD; *then she takes the basket and hands it to* RED RIDING HOOD. MOTHER *kisses* RED RIDING HOOD *and turns away.* RED RIDING HOOD *leaves slowly right; she turns around as if to ask a question, but she sees that her mother has gone. Then she too turns and goes.*

CURTAIN

Scene 2

Curtain rises on a forest scene. There is a stump on the right, in front of the curtain.

RED RIDING HOOD *enters* LEFT. *In this scene she is a lovely, seductive young woman. The* WOLF *who has been backstage-center sees her and leaps in the air. He should be a tall slender man dressed in brown with some sort of mask suggesting a wolf. Throughout the first part of this scene, the* WOLF *dances behind and to the side of* RED RIDING HOOD *who stands still after she reaches center stage. She is uncertain and a little frightened until the* WOLF *speaks; he examines her closely.*

WOLF:
　A pretty maiden! Oh, a pretty maid!

RED RIDING HOOD:
　A churlish wolf.

WOLF:
　I beg your pardon, maid. I only meant to say a lovely maid.

RED RIDING HOOD:
　A churlish churlish churlish churlish wolf. I'll go my way.

WOLF:
　No, stay. Say "churlish," maid,
　Another time and it will melt away.
　Already it is limber on your lips;
　Your lips are limber on your fingertips . . .
　I'll burn the lovely lumber of your lips.

(RED RIDING HOOD *starts to go offstage right.*)

WOLF:
　Stay, my peevish girl—
　The summer is too brilliant up above
　Not to be seen with the sensitive eyes of love:
　The forest brushing dull before our eyes
　When we have loved may well begin to blaze.

RED RIDING HOOD:

    The sympathetic fallacy—how dull.

WOLF:

    Do not be metaphysical, my gull.
    Our eyes will be enchanted, not the trees.

RED RIDING HOOD:

    You have no thought above a woman's knees.

WOLF:

    I were a wolf perverse if that were so.

RED RIDING HOOD:

    You are a witty wolf, but I must go.

WOLF:

    A witty woman would not wish it so.

RED RIDING HOOD:

    Well, womanly, wit-wanting, I must go.

WOLF:

    Pray do not leave the W behind.

RED RIDING HOOD:

    I have more vital matters on my mind
    Than waxing witty with a wayward wolf.

WOLF:

    Does it concern the basket, pretty lass?

RED RIDING HOOD:

    Far must I travel over stone and grass
    And wood and grass and stone—

WOLF:

    Alone?

RED RIDING HOOD:

    Alone.

(RED RIDING HOOD *starts to go off again.*)

(*In the following short scene the wolf follows* RED RIDING HOOD *across the stage and back, doing little dancing tricks for her.*)

WOLF:

    And where?

RED RIDING HOOD:
   Why should you care?

WOLF:
   I care.

RED RIDING HOOD:
   Swear?

(*Here* RED RIDING HOOD *is at extreme right, almost offstage. Now she turns and goes slowly back to center stage as she speaks.*)

WOLF:
   I swear I care.

RED RIDING HOOD:
   I care not either way.
   I swear I care not if you swear you care.

WOLF:
   Then where?

RED RIDING HOOD:
   I *swear*—I'd rather meet a bear.

WOLF:
   Bear meat is very rare.

RED RIDING HOOD:
   No *bear* would care.

WOLF:
   A bear who cares is very very rare.

RED RIDING HOOD:
   I'd rather meet a bear.

WOLF:
   But bears are rare . . .
   Yet you and *bare* would make a pretty pair.

RED RIDING HOOD:
   I swear—the rarest bear would barely care.

WOLF:
   The rarest bear would never care to swear. *(tenderly)* What
   lovely hair! I'll take you anywhere.

(*He touches a strand of her hair.*)

RED RIDING HOOD:

   No thanks—I'll go alone.

(RED RIDING HOOD *starts offstage right quickly but stops at a sudden pounding of drums. At sound of drums, both abandon their dancing postures and freeze where they are standing, facing each other.*)

WOLF:

   Listen: enough of this foolish rhyming. It's all very well to be carelessly happy when the outcome is assured, but here nothing at all seems to be assured. You have a basket. Where are you taking it?

RED RIDING HOOD:

   To my grandmother.

WOLF:

   Why didn't you say so?

RED RIDING HOOD:

   I didn't think you *cared*—

WOLF:

   Don't start *that* again.

RED RIDING HOOD:

   What?

WOLF:

   Never mind. So you're taking the basket to your grandmother. . . . Well, you've plenty of time to get *there*.

RED RIDING HOOD:

   I *don't* have plenty of time.

WOLF:

   Never mind. So you're taking the basket to your grandmother . . .
   Well, you've plenty of time to get *there*.

RED RIDING HOOD:

   Now *you're* doing it.

WOLF:

   Nevertheless, you have plenty of time. Listen—the whole day
   is bursting for us. No more dancing now till we get this straight.

RED RIDING HOOD:

   Who's dancing? I've got to go.

WOLF:

   Wouldn't you like to get back into iambic pentameter?

RED RIDING HOOD:
   I don't *care.*

WOLF:
   We could rhyme.

RED RIDING HOOD:
   All the time?

WOLF:
   All the time.

RED RIDING HOOD:
   I don't care. I've got to go somewhere.

WOLF:
   See?

RED RIDING HOOD:
   What?

WOLF:
   You're back into it already, just thinking about you and me.

RED RIDING HOOD:
   Back into what?

WOLF:
   Back in the sun, back in your dancing slippers. . . . What the devil is the difference?

RED RIDING HOOD:
   It's beginning to come clear.

WOLF:
   What?

RED RIDING HOOD:
   The sun, the dancing slippers. . . . What *is* the difference?

WOLF:
   Now—

(*Another sudden pounding of drums. The players abruptly relax into loose, graceful poses, and go into an erotic dance; the* WOLF *however, is never able to touch* RED RIDING HOOD *or her basket: she always manages, just barely, to elude him. . . . After a few minutes,* RED RIDING HOOD *stops suddenly and tries to race offstage right. The* WOLF *leaps ahead of her, however, and stands in front of the exit, blocking the way with outstretched arms.*)

RED RIDING HOOD:

Let me *go*! Let me *go*! I have no time for this.
I have a place to go. You've got me all confused.
Oh, you've got me all confused.

WOLF:

It's the least that I could do.
Why did you so abruptly leave the dance?

RED RIDING HOOD:

I'm better now—I'll get away from you.

WOLF:

You may not ever have another chance.

RED RIDING HOOD:

To get away?

WOLF:

To stay.

RED RIDING HOOD:

The dance is through
Why should I stay and waste the day with you?
I have a job to do.

(Thunderclap. Most of the lights go out.)

RED RIDING HOOD:

Oh I'm afraid! I'm afraid. What shall I do? What shall I do? I'll go home to
Mother. Oh I was so comfortable and *sure* till *you* came along—and now
this terrible old storm. Why did you have to bother me?

WOLF:

You were too beautiful to go unbothered.
Besides—I didn't cause the storm.

RED RIDING HOOD:

I suspect you had something to do with it. I'll go home.

(Exit RED RIDING HOOD *left.)*

*(*WOLF *looks after her, shakes his head, lights a cigarette, and goes and sits on a
stump which is right front, in front of the curtain.*

After a few moments, RED RIDING HOOD RE-ENTERS *left. Stage lights go on again
and thunder stops. For the rest of the scene* RED RIDING HOOD *can neither see nor
hear the* WOLF *who remains sitting, smoking, and apparently not even watching her.)*

RED RIDING HOOD:
    Oh I can't find the way. So the rain *has* stopped. What good does that do *me*?
    The rain has washed the path away—I can't go home.

WOLF: (*casually—speaking to no one*)
    I could have told you that.

(RED RIDING HOOD *goes extreme right and looks at the ground.*)

RED RIDING HOOD:
    Thank heavens it hasn't rained here! The path to
    Grandmother's is still clear. But I wanted to go home. That wolf . . .

WOLF: (*as before—casually*)
    You can't go home; but, in your condition,
    going to Grandma's will amount to the same thing.

RED RIDING HOOD:
    I'll find my way. I haven't any time to lose.

(EXIT RED RIDING HOOD *right.*)

WOLF:
    It's a damned shame, baby, a damned shame . . .
    But then—this happens almost every day.

(WOLF *stands up, stamps out his cigarette, and walks resignedly* offstage right.*)

CURTAIN

Scene 3

Curtain rises on a room with grey walls, grey floor—it is GRANDMOTHER's *house.*
The only piece of furniture is a bed right center.

GRANDMOTHER *is lying in bed with covers pulled up over her; her face cannot be*
seen by audience. After a few moments RED RIDING HOOD *enters left. In this scene*
she should be played as an older woman—not hobbling & crotchety, but somewhat
tired and despairing—at times, however, her virginal girlishness may appear, es-
pecially when she is frightened by GRANDMOTHER.

RED RIDING HOOD:
    Grandmother. Grandmother.

(RED RIDING HOOD *does not see* GRANDMOTHER; *sinks wearily to the floor, set-*
ting the basket at her side.)

Yes, I seem to recognize the place
As though its weather were indelible
And formal in my mind. Though long ago
I thought the walls could be a well of colour
Deep reds and darker blues—the crazy quilt
Of comfortable old age—they have of late
Seemed greyer in the mirror of my mind.
I recognize the place—the grey fatigue
That hoods the journey's end.

GRANDMOTHER:
Red Riding Hood?

RED RIDING HOOD:
Grandmother?

GRANDMOTHER:
Yes—I was expecting you—
            But not so early. Was your travel smooth?

RED RIDING HOOD:
It was.

GRANDMOTHER:
No incident delayed you on the road?

(*Throughout this part of the scene* RED RIDING HOOD *does not see* GRAND-MOTHER's *face.*)

RED RIDING HOOD:
One—one—it seems that there was one—
That I was tempted in a crazy dance
And broke the rhythm for an emptiness
I followed to this place. . . . It seems to me
That there was one such—

GRANDMOTHER:
And no more?
I know the answer: and no more . . .
A wolf who sang you were a lovely maid
And spun you in the heat of afternoon
Until you saw your shadow as a poem
Delirious on the grass—

RED RIDING HOOD:
Small and careless on the grass . . .

I saw my shadow careless on the grass
Wound in a sudden dance, unraveled then
To filter through the summer afternoon ...
How did *you* know?

GRANDMOTHER:
    Such thoughts come easily
    To an old woman who has known the rise
    And fall of water in the sea at dusk
    And watched the lights go moving on the water
    To end their dance in dark ... I know the world
    Through metaphor, reflection—coins of light
    Moving on the smooth dark sea—

RED RIDING HOOD:
    As though there were
    No lights at all, only the shadow of a light
    Which shudders in the mind. Yet I remember
    A dancing blood as positive as light—
    I fled the dance; the storm had washed away
    The road to home; I followed to this place
    A shadowed path, as though my memory
    Would blossom into sorrow in the light
    As it does now—heavy and sudden.

GRANDMOTHER:
    Your memory?

RED RIDING HOOD:
    As shadowy and strange
    As a gong sounding in the wilderness—
    Something—uncertain: a blaze in emptiness
    That I had smothered in an empty dream.
    My hands feel old and empty where they gripped
    This basket close ...
    Oh how could I forget?
    This basket is for you; my mother said
    I was to bring it here, untouched.

(RED RIDING HOOD *rises and carries the basket to* GRANDMOTHER *who turns her face upward toward her.* RED RIDING HOOD *opens the basket and speaks— terrified.*)

RED RIDING HOOD:
    Empty—

GRANDMOTHER:

Empty.

(*Now* RED RIDING HOOD *for the first time sees the face of* GRANDMOTHER. *As this next movement, the questioning, goes on,* RED RIDING HOOD *grows more and more frightened—and steps slowly farther and farther away from the bed until she is* extreme left.)

RED RIDING HOOD:

Why is your face so strange?

GRANDMOTHER:

The better for you to notice me, my dear.

RED RIDING HOOD:

Why are your eyes so bright?

GRANDMOTHER:

The better for *me* to notice *you,* my dear.

RED RIDING HOOD:

Why do your hands shake so?

GRANDMOTHER:

I am old, my dear.

RED RIDING HOOD:

Why do your hands shake so when I am near you?

GRANDMOTHER:

Visitors excite me. I am eager to touch you, my dear.

RED RIDING HOOD:

Why is your voice so rough and deep?

GRANDMOTHER:

I am unused to speech.

RED RIDING HOOD:

Why do your lips quiver so?

GRANDMOTHER:

I would like to kiss you, my dear.

(RED RIDING HOOD *is now* extreme left. *She starts suddenly, and becomes excited almost to the point of frenzy.*)

RED RIDING HOOD:

No. No. You cannot. No-one has ever—said that to me. . . . Someone—once—once—only once. . . . I do not believe you: your face—your eyes—

your hands—your voice—You cannot—you must—you knew—you knew what happened to me in the wood. . . . Oh, it's not too late! To dance! Oh the dance—the end of shadows—You are—you must be—Oh my darling!—the *Wolf* . . .

(RED RIDING HOOD, *her exhaustion lost in a blaze of violent emotion, runs to the bed and throws herself onto the body of* GRANDMOTHER.)

GRANDMOTHER:
You'll make a good meal, you empty-headed fool! The Wolf never comes *near this* place.

(*As* GRANDMOTHER *says this, she rises on the bed and strangles* RED RIDING HOOD. *All the stage lights go out and the audience sees* GRANDMOTHER's *face for the first time: it is a glowing death mask. A small terrible sound—almost childish—bursts from* RED RIDING HOOD's *throat—and*)

FINAL CURTAIN

—1953

Bertha

Scene 1

Oslo, the ramparts.

NOBLE:

    The walls of our castles no longer withstand
    The barbarian attack!

COUNSELOR:

                  Seek BERTHA in her haven!

NOBLE:

    Bertha! We are at the barbarians' mercy.

BERTHA:

    Give the signal for attack!

NOBLE:

    Attack? Attack? How can we attack?
    We are at the barbarians' mercy, they have surrounded our walls!

BERTHA:

    Let me commune with my special gods a little.
    Meanwhile, ATTACK!

NOBLE:

                BERTHA commands attack!

COUNSELOR:

                                    Oh, the queen is mad!

NOBLE:

    Mad, yes—but queen still. Never had Norway fairer or more brave.

OFFICER:

    To the attack, as commanded by Queen Bertha!

OLD MAN:

    To the attack, as commanded by Queen Bertha!

OLD MAN:

    Unhappy pagans! Soon the wrath of Bertha will be wreaked on them!

(BERTHA *appears, clothed in a ring of white eagles.*)

BARBARIANS:

    Help, help! Back! We are defeated!

(They scurry.)

ALL:

Bertha has saved us from the barbarian menace.

(BERTHA *retires.*)

Scene 2

A study in the castle.

TEACHER:

Yes, it's a very interesting tale, that one you tell of the battle.
But why do you think you and your people yourselves are not barbarians?

BERTHA:

Off with my teacher's head!

WHACK!

Let higher learning be disreinstated!

(Banners are sent up all over the kingdom.)

Scene 3

BERTHA:

Ah, how sweet it is to take the Norway air
And breathe it in my own lungs, then out again
Where it again mingles with the white clouds and blue Norwegian sky.
For I myself, in a sense, am Norway, and when Bertha breathes
The country breathes, and it breathes itself in,
And so the sky remains perfectly pure Norway.

MESSENGER:

Bertha, the land is at peace.

BERTHA:

Attack Scotland!

Scene 4

A little Scotch frontier town, on the battle lines.

SCOTCHMAN:

They say Queen Bertha's men rage to win all of Scotland as a present for
their mad queen.

SECOND SCOTCHMAN:

No one has ever had Scotland defeated for very long; let Queen Bertha try
what she may!

THIRD SCOTCHMAN:
Here come the armies of Bertha, Queen of Norway!

BERTHA: *(at the head of her army, in a red and blue uniform; plants a banner)*
Here shall Bertha stay, nor all Scotland conquer!
Just to this flag's wave shall Bertha of Norway's kingdom reach!
No greed urges the just Norwegian nation to further spoils.

ALL SCOTCH:
Hurrah for Queen Bertha!

COMMON NORWEGIAN SOLDER:
She is mad!

(Trumpets, and dispersal of all troops; the flag alone remains standing on the snowy stage.)

Scene 5

The Council Chamber.

COUNSELOR:
Queen Bertha, we are tired of useless wars.

BERTHA:
Useless! Do you call it useless to fight off an invader?

COUNSELOR:
I was not speaking of the Barbarian Wars.

BERTHA:
Well, I was! The council is dismissed.

(Everyone leaves, including BERTHA.*)*

Scene 6

A rose garden.

GIRL:
If Queen Bertha knew we were here!

MAN:
She'd chop our two heads off, chip chap chop. There's no doubt about it.

GIRL:
Why does she forbid us young lovers to meet in the garden?

MAN:
A diseased mind, and the horrid fears of encroaching old age.

(They embrace. Explosion. Both fall dead.)

BERTHA: *(from the castle window)*
Let there be no more garden meetings.

Scene 7

BERTHA *on her throne.*

BERTHA:
I am old, I am an old queen. But I still have the power of my childhood
Contained in my office. If I should lose my office, no more power would accrue
To my aged and feeble person. But even supposing I keep my power?
What chance is there that anything really nice will happen to me?

(She plays with a flag, musing.)

The flag of Norway! Once its colors drove my young heart wild
With dreams of conquest, first of the Norwegian flag, then of all the other
nations in the world . . .
I haven't gotten very far—yet still Bertha is great!

(ringing a bell)

Call in the High Commissioners!

Scene 8

The Throne Room.

BERTHA:
We must give up the country to the barbarians!
I wish to conquer Norway again!

COUNSELOR: *(aside)*
Bertha's mad! *(To* BERTHA*)* Yes, your Majesty.

(Clarions are sounded.)

Scene 9

A public place.

NORWEGIAN CITIZEN:
They say Bertha will give us up to the barbarians!

SECOND NORWEGIAN CITIZEN:
Impossible!

(The barbarian armies march in, with red and white banners.)

BARBARIAN CHIEFTAIN:
    On to the Castle! Norway is barbarian!

(Sounds of cannon.)

Scene 10

The Throne Room.

MESSENGER:
    Bertha arrives, at the head of teeming troops!
    On her arrival from Scotland all Norway has rallied to her banner!
    Millions of Norwegians surround the castle shrieking,
    "Bertha, Queen of Norway!"

BARBARIAN CHIEFTAIN:
    Let us be gone! We cannot withstand such force. Quickly, to the tunnel!

(They disappear.)

(BERTHA appears in regal splendor and walks to her throne, followed by applauding citizens. She ascends the throne.)

BERTHA:
    Norway!

(She falls from the throne and lies dead in front of it.)

NOBLE:
    Bertha is dead!

CITIZEN:
    She was a great queen!

SECOND CITIZEN:
    She conquered her own country many times!

THIRD CITIZEN:
    Norway was happy under her rule!

(trumpets and sirens)

FINAL CURTAIN

—1953

The Election

Scene: 1960

The AUTHOR *is lying in bed, to the rear of his disorderly pad. Enter his* FRIEND.

FRIEND:
　Man, I hear you've written a new play, called *The Election.*

AUTHOR:
　Don't bug me, man. I'm waiting for the producer now.

FRIEND:
　The *producer?* Have you copped out, man, gone commercial? You mean
　you're going to *produce* one of your plays? Wow!

(looking around at the pad)

　Is this the theater?

AUTHOR:
　Of course this is the theater, man. What did you think?
　Wait a minute. This must be the producer now.
　Hold it!

*(*AUTHOR *jumps up. Enter* JOHN F. KENNEDY, LYNDON JOHNSON, *and* KENNEDY
AIDE; JOHNSON *and the* AIDE *are trying to hold onto* KENNEDY *to keep him from
falling down.)*

JOHNSON:
　Come on, man. That kind of posture does not befit the President of the
　United States.

KENNEDY: *(pepping up a little)*
　Has the VOTE come in? Is it in yet? is it over?

JOHNSON:
　Has *what* come in yet, man?

KENNEDY: *(groans)*
　The VOTE, man, the vote. . . . Oh, man, let me down again. I can't make it! I
　(spelled out) C-A-N-T M-A-K-E I-T, if you know what I mean.

KENNEDY AIDE:
　I do.

JOHNSON:
　And I do too.

(Now JOHNSON *comes forward center stage, facing the audience. While he is speaking, enter the* BAND—*which may be from one to four persons—which softly tunes up a little.)*

JOHNSON:

And I do too. I understand that John F. cannot make it, M-A-K-E I-T. Man, life is jes one big campaign, and when you does that, I mean when you ACTUALLY campaigns, then you is doublin' in life's bit—you aint "doin it," you tryin too hard, and, man, that mean trouble. Evvybody talkin' 'bout how unnatural and ambitious we is, jes waitin around all the time for the votes, all day long jes trying to GIT it, jes all day, and even effen you jes conneck wif one vote, man, then you is made for that day—it stand out: you say, "Well, there is one vote that ole man Nixon aint gonna git," and you feel good, sometime like you shake all over! And, man, it's them days you doan git no vote that you is in trouble, I mean TROUBLE—and then they's all that trash you got to associate with, all that trash that doan care WHO you is or WHAT you is, they jes waitin for you to say somethin that they like or they doan like, and then they say I gonna vote for *him* or for *him*—*and* you better sure hope that they say it's for YOU, too. And sometimes you feel you aint gittin the VOTE, you jes gittin the vote OUT, for the other fellah! Then you feel all bad, cause you doan like them and they doan like you, but you wants the VOTE, is, an they aint gonna GIVE it to you, nuther, and the worst is is you still up there at the same time hatin' them and wantin' IT—that's bad, that's very, very bad.

KENNEDY: *(reviving)*
Like whose pad is this? . . . Where's Jackie?

KENNEDY AIDE:
We don't know, man. We thought this was Democratic National Headquarters. Listen, do you want to get some chicks?

KENNEDY:
Yeah, man. Call up like Jackie.

FRIEND:
Wow, man, you got like actual political candidates in your play! Like!

AUTHOR:
Cool it, man, cool it. This is, wow, I didn't write this for them. Like—what are they doing in my pad?

BANDLEADER:
When do de vote come in, man?

KENNEDY AIDE: *(at the telephone)*

Hello, Jackie. We're at J.F.'s. Yeah, sure. What? you're with another chick? sure, bring her along. Yeah, man.

AUTHOR:

Listen, you guys, who told you to come here, anyway?

BANDLEADER:

Mistah Republikam, dass all who, ole man Nixie hisself. Ain dis Republikam Headquarters? Where am de vote?

AUTHOR:

Oh crazy! Listen, no, man, like! Listen, I've got to see a producer here. It's important to me, to my life. So like cut, man, beat it. This is a big moment for me. I don't want you guys to spoil it.

KENNEDY AIDE: *(to KENNEDY)*

She says she's coming over with another chick.

KENNEDY:

Oh, man, I can't make it.

(He passes out again.)

Where's the vote?

BANDLEADER: *(to the AUTHOR)*

Ain you innarested in de eleckshum, man? Pitty soon de eleckshum goan come in, and de vote. Den we gonna blow real nice. My Country Uh Liberty, an all dat. Ain you innarested in de eleckshum, Man? . . . Here. Take a look at dis poll. See . . . Nixon he favored in fo out of sebben key states, man.

AUTHOR:

Man, are you flipped? I don't care about this election one way or the other, and I'm not planning to get fixed on it, either. ELECTION? Oh no, man, I'm not a kid! . . . Let's have a look at one of those polls. . . .

(He takes a poll and reads it fascinatedly.)

JOHNSON:

That's the same poll I been lookin at since I stopped my long diatribe, which now I goan continue again.

(As JOHNSON comes forward center stage, BAND plays four bars of "Deep in the Heart of Texas.")

Man, once you git fixed on the vote, they aint nothing else ever gonna bother you, nosirree. Cause there aint no kick like it. Lemme tell you something. One day I tried gittin out of it an back in my old life in de Senate (or de House, I forgits which), and I was there standin outside while big posters was going up all red white and blue, and sayin "Nixon and Lodge" on em, and I realize I'm IN, cause I doan want THEM in—and then I walks down Broadway, and there they is goin up more of them red white and blue banners, and this time it says "Kennedy" and "JOHNSON," and, man, I praxickally gits down on my knees, prayin them to take me in—Man, I tell you, I was hooked, but plenty, and—

KENNEDY:

Lyndon, do you really think what you're saying is in the public interest? Cool it, man, cool it. Like, where is the VOTE? I got to have that vote.

(KENNEDY *passes out again, as do his aide and* LYNDON JOHNSON. *The* BAND *plays. There are repeated knocks on the door.*)

JOHNSON: *(half-awake)*
Maybe that's Jackie and the other chick.

KENNEDY:

Oh, man, I gotta have that vote . . .

(*Both pass out again.*)

(*Enter* RICHARD NIXON *and* HENRY CABOT LODGE; LODGE *is wearing an elephant mask.*)

LODGE:

No answer, Tricky Dicky. I guess we can go in.

NIXON:

Okay, Cabot, can the comedy. And why don't you take off that goddamned elephant mask? We haven't won this election yet, and it doesn't look as though we're going to. Oh, man, I'm just sick, s-I-c-K.

(LODGE *comes forward center stage facing first* NIXON, *then, after his first sentence, facing the audience. As he turns from* NIXON *toward the audience the* BAND *plays a flourish.*)

LODGE:

You caint have it no other way, Tricky.

(*flourish here*)

Ef you in business, then you got to make it wif bread; and here in guvmint de bread come too, but you got to cool it, an first git ELECTED, man, if you know what I mean. But in business, after you git de bread, DEN you got it cool to pick up de influence, man—like you can step right into a CABINET

POST, wiffout even one vote. They got you both ways, man; here in dis racket we first got to git de VOTE, en come de bread cool, where dere you got to first git de bread, den come de vote cool, or de INFLUENCE. Yeah, man, it's de same thing, it's de same thing. They got you both ways. We in guvmint is got to sweat out de vote, and dey in business is got to sweat out de bread. It's de same thing, man, it's the SAME thing.

BANDLEADER:
Yeah, man, you're right!

NIXON: *(collapsing)*
Oh, man, cool it, cool it! When is the ELECTION, man? When is the election? Oh, man, I'm sick. I got to have that vote . . .

(NIXON passes out. After a moment of silence, the band plays eight bars of "Hail to the Chief." When they have finished, NIXON jumps up.)

Oh, God, man! Like I just had the most horrible DREAM!

LODGE:
What was it, Tricky? Tell us. Was it about de VOTE?

NIXON:
No, man, no, or, like, yes, maybe—I don't know.

(NIXON steps forward.)

My dream was this. I was standing up on television facing Senator John F. Kennedy, and I was speaking, when suddenly . . .

(Lights go off. While lights are off, KENNEDY and NIXON put on KENNEDY and NIXON masks. KENNEDY rises and stands facing NIXON stage front.)

BANDLEADER: *(while lights are off)*
De DREAM of Richard Nixon.

(Lights go on.)

NIXON:
I believe that the mothers of America should . . . God . . . glub . . . glub. . . .

(He chokes.)

LODGE and AIDE: *(confusedly)*
Help! Hey, Nix, what's the matter? Hey! We'd better get a doctor! What? No! Yes! Yes! No doctor! Get IKE! Get IKE!

(AIDE goes backstage to get IKE, who is wearing IKE mask and carrying a large golf club and a big golf ball. IKE hands the golf ball to AIDE, who comes forward and

swats the golf ball into the audience. IKE *then immediately goes over to* NIXON *and thrusts his hand violently into* NIXON'*s mouth.* NIXON *chokes even more horribly. During* IKE'*s entrance and golf game the band plays "Hail to the Chief.")*

AIDE:

Mr. President, General Ike, sir, what are you doing? What on earth is the MATTER?

IKE:

Son of a bitch has got my golf balls in his mouth is what's the matter. I been looking for them all over the like White House, man. Didn't you ever notice how big this bugger's jowls are? Well, now you know why! He's got ONE

(IKE *extracts a golf ball, as* NIXON *screams.)*

TWO

(extracts another, another scream)

of my golf balls hidden in there. Son of a bitch if it doesn't make me feel like running again myself.

(to audience)

Would you trust a golf ball stealer in the White House? Would you like to give him the vote?

(When the BANDLEADER *delivers the next speech, which he does with great sentimental and patriotic fervor, the characters in the dream form a tableau,* NIXON *and* KENNEDY *kneeling each to one side of* IKE, *who remains stage center.)*

BANDLEADER:

Man, EVvybody got a right to de vote. If you is a human bein an you wants it, den you is got a right to de vote.

(The dream is over. Lights off, then on full. KENNEDY, JOHNSON, *and* AIDE *are unconscious.* NIXON *shudders, and speaks in his own person again from the floor, to which he has collapsed.)*

NIXON:

Oh, man, I can't make it. How much vote does that cat WANT?

LODGE:

It was only a dream, Tricky. Pitty soon WE gonna git de vote.

NIXON:

Listen, cool it with "Tricky," man. Don't call me that. America doesn't like it.

AUTHOR: *(leaping forward—anxious, excited, hooked)*

Listen, man, I want the VOTE! I'm announcing myself as a candidate for the PRESIDENCY OF THE UNITED STATES OF AMERICA!

(The band plays a flourish.)

I didn't understand before. I want the VOTE. I've got to have it. I didn't understand.

LODGE:

You're too late, man. Got to wait another four years. Maybe in two years, when congreshfumal elections come up. Maybe you can start out that way, then.

AUTHOR:

Man, I want the highest office in the land! Like man, I mean I'm an ar-tist-ic type, and I don't want any like second bests. I want the P-rezzy-denncy! Yeah, like!

BANDLEADER:

Maybe you could first be a gubner.

AUTHOR:

No, man, listen, don't get me mad. Man, I'm for President. Oh, where is the vote?

KENNEDY: *(waking up)*

Who is this kid? Where am I? I was just dreaming about myself deciding to run for the Presidency. Hey, kid, who are you?

LODGE:

Cool it, John F. That's the author of this play. You wasn't dreamin, you was listenin to him!

KENNEDY:

Oh, man, man, I got to have that vote.

LODGE:

Maybe Jackie will come, man.

ALL: *(except LODGE)*

Oh, cool it, man, cool it—WHERE AM DE VOTE?

(Everyone passes out except BANDLEADER, AUTHOR, and FRIEND. Enter, wildly, JULIAN BECK.)

JULIAN:

My name is Julian Beck.

(BAND *plays four bars of "There's No Business Like Show Business."*)

Hello, Garry, everybody. Ladies and gentlemen, good evening; ladies and gentlemen, tonight we are going to present to you—QUIET out there! Really, you will have to be—present to you a very significant play by a young—I may say in years but not in ideas, as you shall so abundantly see—playwright . . .

(BAND *starts playing.*)

Quiet, please! You boys—who the hell ARE you, anyway? can play after I finish my opening speech—on the subject of VOTE ADDICTION . . .

AUTHOR:
Julian, the play has already started, but like with real characters. And, like, listen, man, I'm a candidate, like I myself am a candidate for President!

JULIAN:
Garry, shut up!

(JULIAN *accidentally kicks* KENNEDY.)

Say, who the hell are all these people anyway? What do they think this theater is, a flophouse? JUDITH! Somebody! Get these creeps offstage!

(*Enter* JUDITH *and* STAGEHAND *who start to lug off* KENNEDY, JOHNSON, AIDE, NIXON, *and* LODGE.)

JULIAN:
Good! There, there, you don't have to be *too* gentle with them, GOOD-night, GO! No, leave the band. We can use it.

AUTHOR:
Man, don't you have any pity? All they wanted was the vote! I want it too, man.

JULIAN:
Garry, will you get the hell off the stage! Your personal life is entirely yours, it is no concern of mine—but your *play* is—now GET OFF the stage, and—

BANDLEADER:
Man, supposing we doesn't want to stay and be in your play? We is waitin for de vote.

JULIAN:
You'll stay, you'll stay—just be patient. Garry, shut up!

AUTHOR:
Julian, I'm a—

JULIAN:

And get OFF the stage.

AUTHOR:

I didn't FEEL it right before, I was—

JULIAN:

Ladies and gentlemen, yes, yes, we've already tried your patience more than enough, yes, I know that, but now, now I'm sure you're going to be satisfied, now when you see this play you're going to feel that all you've been through is certainly worth it, you can be sure of that. This is not an ordinary play, it's not a play ABOUT reality, it's a play that IS reality, that gets right to the heart of reality itself. This play—

(hoots from the audience)

Yes, yes, all right, yes, I know, we've—yes, all right, yes, yes, I won't say a word more. LIGHTS! The ELECTION!

(Complete darkness, then lights on quite dim. Band plays two "Boops." A number of men come in through the door in the semidarkness and pass out immediately. Finally, in comes a man wearing a waist-length NIXON MASK.)

NIXON MASK:

Man, man . . .

ALL OTHERS: *(gasping, flipping, etc.)*

What is it, man? what is it? Like what's the matter, man? What's wrong?

NIXON MASK: *(collapsing in joy)*

Like, man! I just got the VOTE! I'm the next PRESIDENT of the UNITED STATES!

(BAND starts to play "My Country 'Tis of Thee.")

ALL OTHERS: *(from the floor)*

Cool it. Oh, man, cool it.

AUTHOR:

Oh, my God! Nixon won!

(AUTHOR runs up on stage wildly, finds a pistol, shoots himself in the head, staggers, and dies. JULIAN bends over him.)

JULIAN:

Garry! Garry! That wasn't the REAL election! That was your play!

(There is knocking at the door. Enter JACKIE KENNEDY and PAT NIXON.)

JACKIE:

    Are Jack and Dick here? We wanted to tell them that they can relax—it's all been called off. IKE has decided to hold on to the reins of power for another twenty years. Isn't that wonderful?

JULIAN: *(terrified—loud and clear)*

    Garry! Garry! Wake up! Was that your PLAY

(JULIAN turns full face toward audience.)

    or THE TRUTH?

FINAL CURTAIN

                                                 —1960

The Merry Stones

Scene 1

A room in a house by the sea. ROY, *a young man, is lying in bed.* INGELIL, *a young Swedish nurse, is standing at the bedside.*

INGELIL:

Lay down and be slumbering. A cabinet is kind. The music is full of fishes. Have some liberty. Eat colds. Don't be neglected. Board up the hose. Thank the rip tides. Lose collectedness. Break, break the ramps.

ROY:

I went to smiling wrists.

INGELIL:

Govern the deciding wasps. Age new badness. Sign Lohengrin. Be out on the Caspian.

ROY:

Locks were coming in bananas.
Furniture is necks.
Sacrilege is leaning on tiny horse.
A lamprey, oh, has begun to kiss
The sea.

INGELIL:

Use the deigning colors of this cabinet for your windows; only don't, when the winter comes, complain of the cannon-fare of the horses; for as surely as hay is tucked into the orphan straw, time will have guess his last lust in the ephemeral killing bottle. I am a laziness that comes from a nuttier country; I see to not understand your flailing indecrepitude. May the blue star of yesterday pink its liberal summit to that head, this yours, which, like a re-volvement, fats the walls with lowing circumvention. Oh good-by, normal!

ROY:

Farewell, moral, and may the neckerchiefs of humming be kind cousins to your gloom. The illiterate flowers are incompatible with shows.

Scene 2

A room. JIM, *a young man, is lying in bed.*

JIM:

If I should die, myself,
Give me the wallpaper

And wrap me up around the ceiling,
As if sky to an ornament.
Oh how fitting is my known
Beneath the dense whack of the sheet;
If mattress covers in truth
Were known, ah, steel would be riven!
But I am back to my back
On flowers, like the Chinese river
Sink-you-and-go-long-go-she-go,
And music is everywhere.
I wonder if this knife
Would not slay me like an imbecile
If I let it fall, down snow-light
In registered rocks from here—

(He seems to stab himself.)

Oh, lie steep as a swan!
Exaggeration of comments, then help me!

Scene 3

A bare stage.

MASTER OF CEREMONIES: *(about forty-five years old)*
Here are the starriest chain-weaving starvers
That ever an eyeball sees, O chasing frankness with sleds!

(Exit M.C.*)*

FIRST SHOWGIRL:
I am the music bell of doughnuts, ruthful ball,
Beds at night in the Sierras, the beach of brass
That an annoyedly soft breast dims,
And my revealing counsels are foolish with sonnets.

SECOND SHOWGIRL:
The least of time's molluscs, and the last of the golden hinters
Am I, come down to Seventieth with my scants on!
I am teas
Without formulas! London!

THIRD SHOWGIRL:
I am the bashful banditress of beans,
Irritants, Coca-Cola, and steaks.

I lie beyond the built-in Sierra of plates
To see our cares mated to a roach in oblivion!

MASTER OF CEREMONIES: *(re-enters; he is much younger)*
So seize your hats,
Be merry as a phone,
And cry out at the graying night,
"Oh thou high pajama of happiness!"
Last week
I felt it know you care so cold.

Scene 4

In the Sierras.

ELDERLY MAN:
A season is my birthright; for which reason
Winter is very indebted to hats. We are
Condemning you to
Breath under water.

BOB:
But I am a mountain lad! my whole bearing and being
Calls out for freedom from Fordham.

ELDERLY MAN:
Nevertheless, go under;
And when you rise, the flowers of heat
Will open your eyes,
And you shall see this Sierra
As the beautiful door to the bust
Of the highly chlorinate female wind
Who hides the masculine hills in her boxes;
The magic of forceful steam
Will be yours, and the shying parts of airplanes,
The linked romance of degustation
And paralysis, to lie on, in the nights of tragic green.

BOB:
I am asea with lust!

ELDERLY MAN:
Yet no more forgotten
Than a cast-iron ring.
We are bored by the midday of flowers,

The Romeo riling amid the wildflowers,
And the beggar the boar smiling into the flowers.

Scene 5

A hotel room.

AL (A YOUNG HUSBAND):
There is another scene than this hotel room!
Where the boy tries to take his life!
O monsters, my wife!

NELLIE (HIS WIFE):
He is walking the floor in rings!

AL:
I once saw a Swedish stand amid the flowers, and throw blood upon dancers, while a sick man, roving up on the bourgeoisie, held in his hats the swan of their hands, as though a telephone rings.

(Ring. It is a doorbell. Enter BOB.*)*

NELLIE: *(throws her arms around* AL*)*
Did you send for the bugles of Lancaster?

FINAL CURTAIN

—circa 1960

Without Kinship

Scene 1

Somewhere on the lawn of Longfellow's House, in Cambridge, Massachusetts. A nightingale leans over her ironing board.

NIGHTINGALE:
It is small and white.

IRONING BOARD:
Over the pill and far away
I hot a vision of white
So mental, that where carpets kneel.

NIGHTINGALE:
Loon, pyramid, shine-shine,
O bark that has suds' little keel
In the gemlight, O bibarkcycle—

IRONING BOARD:
Am I then, lady's head,
Which you have tied unto a knot?

PEBBLE:
Kenneth stands for constancy,
Roommate for regret;
Our Christian society for clemency
To the dancing Sundays of seas' frenetic egret.
Janice stands for Japanese
Mapletrees, which stream about this yard
As though a mariner'd come here
To find his ocean hard.

GIRL PEBBLE:
O Melvin!

PEBBLE:
Charmian!

(They go together and form a driveway.)

Scene 2

The Nurse.

NURSE:
These modern gems have laziness;
My hat is his. This Denver sun
Shines on and down
What grassy slopes?
Season! here is the soap factory;
There is the charged balloon.
My grandfather at eighty offered
The stanza a million dollars
That could make him feel as though
He were really a lagoon.
His face is now seldom
More than unscientific explanation
For a rug. Oh, carry me, impossible slug!

(She lies down too and becomes driveway.)

Scene 3

Roadway, driveway. PATIENCE *and* HANDY *are in their car.*

HANDY:
Harrisonville to Spokane
In nine thousand three hundred and sixty-seven
Days, it doesn't seem impossible!

PATIENCE:
A storm moderates me this end.

NIGHTINGALE: *(from below, as she and her ironing board are now part of the driveway)*
Gazing with hope

PEBBLE:
This morning upon the

NURSE:
Foolish capers in the sun

GIRL PEBBLE:
I understood for the last time

IRONING BOARD:
   How the fanshaped crisscrosses,
   Which speak to everything, are done.

FOOTBALL: *(comes flying through)*
   I gave, for love, my terrifying heart.
   Ah, that laughing, papery summer, when we kissed
   The leaves of every down, that showed the field
   A prayer, and at evening a park.

HANDY:
   Please, Patience, take this green dress!

PATIENCE:
   O branches! where is the collie of happiness?

EVERYONE:
   Woof! Woof!

CURTAIN

Epilogue

GIRL:
   If you can fail to understand
   I have been formed to represent where
   Canada actually begins to understand
   Herself as a country and where carfare is the red postage stamps
   For freedom. When the oranges come in to stand
   For a cafeteria, I will be here to kiss you then.

FINAL CURTAIN

—circa 1960

Rooster Redivivus

CHICKENS:
>Chickens, when they first discover light,
>are not afraid of it. Nor does
>Light fear the chickens. Light is
>A very calm customer indeed. Fear
>Is usually not associated with light
>But with darkness. When you can see something
>You do not need to be afraid of it. I . . .

(scream)

>What has happened to the Homeless Rooster?

>The light has choked him, alas alas!

>We, the chorus of homeless chickens
>Mourn the death by light of the rooster.
>He was a good rooster, famous among barns
>And attentive near henhouses. He was
>A happy rooster except for the light

HEN 1:
>Which killed him for no reason
>That I can understand

HEN 2:
>He was the best rooster around. We
>Hens loved him. He gave to our lives
>That extra essence without which nothing
>Has the savor and the drama of the kind of life

HENS 1 & 2:
>We sense when at first dawning the loveless bluebells
>Attain to a dewy minimum
>Of joy, and the Queen Anne's
>Lace suffers its white limbs to
>Turn to autumn for remembrance and subtlety. Then the sun
>Rises high among the cloudbeds over us chickens,
>Us hens really in this case, since we are talking

CHICKENS: *(one at a time)*
>then pouf! blue

```
            then plam! red
        then goop! orange
            than clank! blue again
        plonk! green
            red
                yellow grey
        blue
And finally the golden sun
The ball which gives us all colors
```

But why did light kill the rooster?

No. Look! He is coming back to life. Oh who are you?

ROOSTER:
I am Rooster Redivivus.
Now I have new powers.
I shall tell you all
The story of Aeneas.
Aeneas sailed into the lights
Of dawn. There he met God and Abraham
Riding on a donkey.
Oh the purple now that feeds us
Cried he
And by the orange light of dawn
Who are you two? They replied
We are red and white.

Blue evenings
Sensations over the Mexican border
Yellow orange blue white and red
These are my seeds
Now I shall plant them
In each of the hens

HEN 1:
We love you Don

HEN 2:
We do love you too

ROOSTER:
I know and now I go on
To tell you about some things that are new
Do you see these flaming spears?

Do you notice those streams?
Roosters both dead and alive
Now come to the forefront of consciousness
Of people everywhere
Look Look Now white begins to arrive

CHICKENS & ROOSTER:
Hail White to your sweet buccaneering.

HEN 1:
Good morning everyone says white
But why doesn't he arrive
Actually?
    We will wait for him until he comes?
Orange is coming and greens in legions
And violets and yellows and purples
But I do not see white
        Yes here no there he
    Was is
  Now no yes well in any case

It is time for us chickens to take command!

Yes we are tired of taking orders from everyone
We are tired of letting the farmer put us to flight
We are tired of being stolen by the fox and eaten
We have found that we are the natural fountains of light

        to the whole universe

So I say

    Light Chickens! Rise
    and Unite!

HEN 2:
And they did. Why is why today
Everything is nothing and nothing is everything.

ROOSTER:
Now let us begin our march on the world.

Listen listen listen
Now everything is orange!

    That owl looks red
We are back in the egg again

Don't be funny
       eggs eggs everywhere nothing but eggs
The word egg and the word everything are united
   I mean we are related
They, orange and green, are the same thing

  And what about the word De Light
  That is everything too—and egg as well

 So we chickens pass away
        And Light endures
Then we chickens come back at evening
      And morning
  Hello blue red green blue
And so on and so forth.

FINAL CURTAIN

—1960

Youth

A baby is shown, then a child of five, then a girl of eleven, then a boy of fifteen, then a boy of nineteen, then a woman of twenty, then a young man of twenty-five, then a beautiful young woman of twenty-nine, then a vigorous-looking young man of thirty-three, then a beautiful young woman of thirty-four, then an extremely young-looking man of forty, then a woman of forty-six who has kept all her youth and beauty, then a very young-looking man of fifty-two, a very young-looking woman of sixty, an extraordinarily youthful-looking man of seventy, an oddly beautiful young-looking woman of eighty, and then a chorus of wind instruments playing slightly off-key as all the characters previously shown race toward the camera. Everything rather blacked out as they all get too close. Then large title again: YOUTH. Then the camera moves back just a little so one can just vaguely make out this mass of people, and on top of this shot comes on the large title: YOUTH NEEDS YOUR HELP. GIVE NOW TO MEDICAL SCIENCE TO KEEP YOUTH ALIVE. Everything turns to green and purple, then the whole blank screen to red, as the band continues to play. Various people who have been in the film come out on stage now and go down into the audience to collect money in envelopes. The envelopes are marked in large blue or violet capital letters: YOUTH.

FINAL CURTAIN

—circa 1960

Guinevere, or *The Death of the Kangaroo*

Scene: A street, a plaza.

GUINEVERE:
Oh solids!

GIRAFFE: *(moving along the sidewalk)*
Yes, and you know, last evening there were junctures of drunken breath's dear pink flowers on my lariat. He put around me. They said, "Denmark and the vitrines! nameless one!"

WEISSER ELEFANT: *(crossing the street toward the* GIRAFFE *at right angles)*
I remember.

GUINEVERE: *(sings)*
With soles on her shoes,
She takes the gyroscope
Between her fingers,
And, quietly, it spins.

KANGAROO: *(waiting at point where the paths of the* GIRAFFE *and* WEISSER ELEFANT *cross)*

The. O the the. The. I gave the pillow a cussing sandwich. America said, "A tree." The manager lay dead. Cuff links.

GIRAFFE: *(pausing)*
Listen, darlings, don't be so sassy. Do you remember when Chicago was only fingertips?

ALL: *(sing)*
Though circumstances may collect our iced man!

MAN: *(who enters)*
Unpin these benches that you may descry
The leafs beneath them. Lovers know my voice
As that which is or was most at the docks
Before they stopped shipping roses to say "*vivre,*"
O macadam. A child sicklier than restaurant
Waits for the marrying blue of a stiff morning.
We seem to go to run about in a stiff roustabout,
Cuter is the pear of string. Common last touch
Is to die at the nest. Roommate, charm bracelet,
Oh I swear, this is Mexico City.

CHIEFTAIN:
> He is falling toward me like the charm bracelet
> I saw laughing out of the window. At this minute a giraffe
> Knows the cow who is offering night my atlas.
> The wind, curving from Chinese charm bracelet
> To charm bracelet, seems to counsel me, "Dollars,
> Feenamint, dollars, gunsmoke." After one night
> With Dolores, I visited the Huguenot people.

CAPTAIN:
> Anchors aweigh!

(The plaza with all its occupants floats away; VENUS *rises from the waves.)*

VENUS:
> Listen. Listen to the bouquet.
> Baby, that placing powder in the pistols,
> Married, and placing pistols in the bouquet,
> Left me to be long ago at this moment,
> Lively, the goddess, a headache. A market
> Of fleas!

(It is Paris, a Place. VENUS *disappears.)*

FIRST FLEA:
> Let go of my left elbow.

SECOND FLEA:
> That's your pot belly!

A PINK GIRL:
> I chanced to find these two
> Arguing. There were sadly smoke,
> Giant cow-guns, shoguns; and, it appears,
> A glass page blonder as a neck of blue jeers.

GIRAFFE & VENUS: *(entering together)*
> Aren't we a stray couple
> From No Land? Oh when
> Will catching diseases fly in our plane?

PILOT:
> Never! Take everyone a box.

(He passes out little boxes, which, when they are opened, reveal white pieces of paper.)

WEISSER ELEFANT: *(reads)*
"The bench you are sitting on is made of orange boa constrictors which have been treated with piratical chocolate Georgia-bannisters. The Maryland of your face. Despite what you have been, ho ho, the incinerator is not a call girl. Depart before the ice cream melts." Mine is about food!

GUINEVERE: *(throwing herself on* WEISSER ELEFANT*)*
O my lover, my lover!

PILOT:
Wait a minute. Read yours.

GUINEVERE: *(gazes into* VENUS's *face)*
"Your head may be paralyzed by lint." Orchids! buzz saws!

ORCHIDS:
This is not blood. This is an orchard.
Through which you may walk. Like a bug.

BUZZ SAW:
Everybody: one, two, three!
Plywood!
Goldsmith!
Sunglasses!

(The plaza splits in two like an orange. WEISSER ELEFANT *eats one half of it. On the other half,* GUINEVERE *is playing a guitar to the* KANGAROO, *and playing cards are falling from his pocket. In the slight breeze one can just make out the chorus of neckties. It seems as if the Old World had become the New. A* MOUSE *enjoys this séance.)*

MOUSE:
God plays the guitar
And Religion listens.
The weary squash
Lurks beside the lotus.
See! the glass buildings
Decide nothing.
We are the sobbing world,
Just as they are in the nude.

GUINEVERE: *(very loud)*
Photomatic bad living
Gigantic prisms. Beaued. Gee. Leaves!

KANGAROO: *(softly)*
Pretty Geneva, pretty Southland, beloved orchestra!

GUINEVERE:

    I am pink in the nude.

KANGAROO:

    Yes yes.

GUINEVERE:

    O Joy!

KANGAROO:

    Listen. Baccalaureate. Is that
    Prometheus?

MAN: *(he is wearing a large mouse head, and plays the guitar)*
    Only the bathroom knees would care
    And the table of good red air
    Seriously affronts the car
    With the yellow daffodils of today.
    Somnolent I see an amethyst
    Clearing the way for future
    Eons, the ragged hoop
    And the dippy Fragonard of fluffier days,
    Played to the tune of our pablum violin.

GUINEVERE: *(throws herself, kissing, against a statue)*
    O you, concede that I am the airport!

MAN WITH MOUSE HEAD:

    America is like an elephant whose baseballs
    Are boundaries
    Of sunlight. *This* is peppermint,
    That billiard shore. Now she gets,
    Like horror, the main idea, a stove that is
    Brilliant as the curling raspberries and move to his heart.
    O olives, I know your reputation for fairness,
    And every pipe dreams of a shirtwaisted kimono
    Beyond the callow limousine of the funnies; but Nugent
    Drank the Coca-Cola, and Allen left the boudoir
    Where Jane lay thrown like a saint, the music of a thumb
    Daring the elate, childless strings.
    O mothers, weevil, market-place of the Sixties,
    What is the road to Gary, China?

GUINEVERE:

    Should industry delay,

Or mice parade? Is that a youth group
Signing: "Daft, weird, kind pennons,
Yo-yos and hills, shirts and displays"?

MAN WITH MOUSE HEAD:
O Germany of sofas,
Are we so clear
As beer is harmless?

GIRAFFE:
A shoplifting land of railroad pajamas
Passed my door, evil filmstars.
Huguenot! evil girls of filmstar plantation!

HIPPO:
Yes because we meant to spend the summer;
But now we see the human element
Is merely a white bear, tipping stars
By the briefcase of a violet hand
Meant to inform and believe concatenated
The surface of a wheel-lake, or "Morgen"
Meaning "morning" in German. Yes I meant
To thumb a ride along the Champs Elysées,
But the sunny negro
Of handsome stars
Bid for the fingers of my door, and lo! I lay,
The Hippopotamus, sweating as if funny
Water may come true even in the summertime
And—

(*Bang! The* HIPPO *falls dead.*)

SOMEONE:
Pure Pins the lobster!

(YELLOWMAY *comes in and takes off all* GUINEVERE's *clothes;* GUINEVERE *puts her clothes back on.*)

GUINEVERE:
The shortest way to go home yesterday
He always called the best way.
There's no suffering in a limeade
Of clearer captains, carpenters, and shipwrights
From brain solidly
In the pier. O the white shore, the red sea—

(YELLOWMAY takes her hand; they walk along the seashore.)

YELLOWMAY:
    And the works of pineapple.
    I have often been a shipmaster
    But never a ship. The blow from Tangiers
    Never came.

GUINEVERE:
    Soldiers waiting at my hammock
    Counseled me, "Be as back as soot."
    Oh nuts, the chairs have gone away.

YELLOWMAY:
    Paintings of the sea, I won't reveal to you my name is Yellowmay.

MAN: *(without mouse head)*
    Or the lobster
    That oval
    Which I often noticed.
    I think,
    "Is this a cigar
    Or, baby! maybe
    The license for a white cigarette,
    Given by the shields."
    And when the frog becomes a bicycle,
    Dear days of pineapple,
    Lilac where the giant ripple
    Rushes, as past a kangaroo.

KANGAROO:
    O mournful existence within the matchbox
    With a sullen cockatoo
    Whose brain beats its own division
    And dandy "wawa"—

OCEAN:
    Oh Sweden is endless! the earliest time to drink.

YELLOWMAY:
    Are we drinking in chairs like a column?

GUINEVERE:
    Oh yes, master. Come jinx with the merry columbine!

(Suddenly it is spring. The HIPPO appears, solus, covered with garlands of flowers.)

HIPPO:
Decency of printemps O
Knocks on my pillow!
Houses without a door!
Suitcases which miss my sleeves!
O bears, you too, on the misty shore
Of the sea, in whose elbows
I hear a moth beginning
To mourn on a blue, beautiful violin.

(*The* SKY *descends, covering all with blue; from the empty stage comes a song.*)

VOICE FROM EMPTY STAGE:
Who cares about them
In a grouping again
Or the poking amethyst
And delicious anthem?
The bread in the butter box
And a dictionary—
The day fears to tell me
Of white screams. Oh, don't you know it,
The marriage of blue
Bells, America, generous, as white screens
Failing, the magazine basement
Of archways. Water
Then generous magazines!

Summery blue daylight,
The manner of machines,
Daguerrotype, cigarette store.

(*The dead body of the* KANGAROO *is dragged across the stage by a two-horse cart.*)

FINAL CURTAIN

—1961

George Washington Crossing the Delaware

To Larry Rivers

Scene 1

Alpine, New Jersey

GEORGE WASHINGTON:

General Cornwallis, you cannot stay here in the trails of Alpine, New Jersey. The American army will drive you away, and away! Americans shall be masters of the American continent! Then, perhaps, of the world!

CORNWALLIS:

What tomfoolery is that you speak, George Washington? You are a general, and generals are supposed to have a college education. No man with any sense would see a victory in this conflict for any power but GREAT BRITAIN!

GEORGE WASHINGTON:

General Cornwallis, I am a mild man, but you had better not say that kind of thing to me. I tell you, America shall win the Revolutionary War!

FIRST AIDE TO CORNWALLIS:

Do you dare to speak to General Cornwallis, impudent Yankee?

FIRST AIDE TO GEORGE WASHINGTON:

Aye, I am an American, and I fear to speak to no man.

GEORGE WASHINGTON:

My aide is expressing the philosophy we all have. It is bound to triumph over your own British authoritarian and colonial system. My men all see eye to eye on this point.

CORNWALLIS:

I caution you, General Washington, that many of them will never see eye to eye with anything again if you persist in this useless, cruel, and wasteful battle.

GEORGE WASHINGTON:

Come, my loyal men. We waste our time in entreaty with the English lord. He mocks us and all we believe.

FIRST AIDE TO GEORGE WASHINGTON:

Aye, General, I follow you.

OTHER AIDES:
Aye, General, we come.

(They leave.)

CORNWALLIS:
There goes the greatest man who will ever live in America! If only he could come over to the English side, I could bring myself to give up my command to him. He is a perfect gentleman, excelling in manners as in speech. His dress is perfect, his buttoning neat, and his shoes of a high polish. He speaks frankly and freely, and will say straight out to his most bitter opponent that which is in his mind. There is nothing he could not accomplish, would he but set himself to it. What task, indeed, could ever challenge that general of the Revolutionary Army? He rides as he walks, with perfect grace; and when he reclines, one imagines one sees the stately bison taking its rest among the vast unexplored plains of this country, America, which now in foul and lawless revolt dares to lift its head against its English nurse and mother. What is more unnatural than that this man, Washington, who is one of God's gentlemen, should so defy the laws of right and wrong as to raise his hand against the breast that gave him suck, against the tender maternal care of England? O England, England! We who are your subjects are the most fortunate men on earth, and we shall struggle boldly to defend you, on land and at sea, no matter where we shall find ourselves, in whatever tempest or time of trouble that may come—we shall be, as we are, loyal to the end, and triumph we shall, for love makes our cause right . . . But that man Washington!

(Cornwallis leaves.)

FIRST AIDE TO CORNWALLIS:
Our general is troubled.

SECOND AIDE TO CORNWALLIS:
The sight of the Yankee general has quite o'erthrown him.

FIRST BRITISH SOLDIER: *(Cockney accent)*
A did not think 'e was such a great man but I could 'ave ho'ertopped 'im wi' me little musket 'ere. 'Tis bare gaddiness that our general be disturbed.

SECOND BRITISH SOLDIER: *(Cockney accent)*
Aye, but disturbed 'e is.

THIRD BRITISH SOLDIER: *(Irish brogue)*
Come off now. What is it turns your heads so low, and the sun beatin' back against them, and your steps draggin', and no light of day in your eyes, and here it bein' God's own glorious time, when His Majesty walked in

the Garden of Eden, in the cool of the day, and the glorious messenger of Zeus almighty and the eye of friendly Apollo ashinin' and aglistenin' in yonder famous West, where so many of our victories has been? What is there to make a man sad in a time of day such as this is, when all is gold as far as the eye can listen, and where the buzzin' of a thrillion insects shines through the ear? If a man were not happy at such a moment, he were but half a man, and that half not much good neither, but only for changin' and blackin' the pots while old Mother helps herself to some kidneys. It is a glad song I would be singin' but for some that would have it that all men must be sad in the time of the American War. Saw you not General Washington?

FIRST BRITISH SOLDIER: *(Cockney accent)*
Sawr'im plain, I did, just as big as your 'ead there; troubled a bit, our general is, 'aving seen 'im 'isself. Gaive a nice speech habout Hengland though.

SECOND BRITISH SOLDIER: *(Cockney accent)*
Aye, troubled 'e is, and deep, too. I see no good of this meetin'.

(They all leave.)

Scene 2
The American camp.

FIRST AMERICAN SOLDIER:
The general returns, and surely he will tell us much that he has seen.

SECOND AMERICAN SOLDIER:
When the general goes abroad, he never fails to tell each private soldier, though he be lowest in station in the Revolutionary Army, what he, the general, has seen, and what his thoughts have been upon the subjects of his contemplation.

THIRD AMERICAN SOLDIER:
Thus, each and every man in the Revolutionary Army shares in the secrets of the High Command, and every man knows exactly why he is fighting.

FOURTH AMERICAN SOLDIER:
This is democracy in action, actually being practiced in a military situation. The method of our struggle exemplifies its end—freedom for every man from the English.

FIFTH AMERICAN SOLDIER:
Here comes the general!

(GEORGE WASHINGTON enters and mounts a podium.)

GEORGE WASHINGTON:
Friends, soldiers, and Americans, lend me your ears!

(Laughter.)
I have seen the British general, Cornwallis—
Brightly he shines in regal uniform,
And brightly shines his sword—but she will cut
No better, boys, than ours!

(Draws his sword, amid the thunderous cheers of the soldiers.)

He said that we
Had not a chance at all to win the war . . .

(Laughter.)

Let's show that Englishman how wrong he is

(Growls.) And conquer them as quickly as we can!

(Cheers.)

A RAGGED SOLDIER:
General Washington, how can we conquer the Englishmen when we have no
guns, no ammunition, no clothing, and no food?

*(Loud murmurs from the soldiers of "Shhhh shhh," "Strike him," "Why does he
want to spoil everything?" "Kill him," etc.)*

GEORGE WASHINGTON: *(unruffled)*
We must make raids—raids, raids,
Raids on the English supplies. We must make raids!
Raids for clothing and raids for food
To do the Revolutionary Army good;
Raids in the morning and raids at night,
Raids on our stomachs by candlelight,
Raids on the tea chest and raids on the mill,
Raids on the granary that stands by the hill;
Raids on the clothing tents, beautiful raids,
Raids on Cornwallis, and raids on his aides.
For stealing is licensed if for a good cause,
And in love and in war, boys, you know there're no laws.
So pack up your shyness, your shame, and your fear,
And throw them away, and come meet me, all, here,
At twelve o'clock midnight, and off we shall go

To the camp of the English that lies down below!
And we shall return in their splendid attire,
And every man present shall have his desire.
So, come, get you ready—go blacken each face,
And meet me at midnight in this very place!

Scene 3

An English home.

ENGLISH GIRL:

You mustn't cry, Mummy. There's absolutely nothing we can do. We are in England, and he is in America. Your tears are going to waste. Has he written?

MOTHER:

The poor little fellow. I remember the first step he ever took. His father, may his soul rest in peace, was holding on to his tiny hands; and, when he began to step forward, all by his little self, his daddy let him go. And he took such a tumble! How I kissed him then—oh!

ENGLISH GIRL:

I don't see why you keep having these morbid thoughts. Many soldiers return from wars unhurt, only to engage in some peaceful occupation in the pursuit of which they are killed by some unforeseeable accident.

MOTHER:

Oh!

ENGLISH GIRL:

Hugh is as safe in the army of General Cornwallis as he would be right back here at home. After all, General Washington's army is made up only of seedy criminals and starving bootblacks! They have neither food nor equipment, and everyone says it is not possible that they shall hold out for more than a few weeks against the skilled and well-equipped troops of our English army. In all probability the war has already ended in our favor, and but for the slow and sluggish meanders of the ships bringing the news, we should be cognizant of it this day, this very hour.

MOTHER:

Child, Artella, you are kind. But, dear, when a people fights for its freedom, even though its army be composed of little children bearing branches, that people will never stop until it has attained that freedom; so that it seems that, inevitably, that people will win, and Hugh, if he stay long enough, be, of necessity, wounded or killed. And that is why I weep—for my only son.

ENGLISH GIRL:

But, Mother! the Americans cannot possibly win—they have no supplies!

Scene 4

The British camp at night. Complete darkness.

FIRST AMERICAN SOLDIER:

Jim?

SECOND AMERICAN SOLDIER:

Yes, Jack?

FIRST AMERICAN SOLDIER:

Jim, are you there, Jim?

SECOND AMERICAN SOLDIER:

Yes, Jack, I'm here, right here. What did you want, Jack?

FIRST AMERICAN SOLDIER:

Have you got some tobacco?

SECOND AMERICAN SOLDIER:

Yes. Here.

FIRST AMERICAN SOLDIER:

Thanks, buddy. It sure tastes good.

SECOND AMERICAN SOLDIER:

Isn't it delicious? I'm glad you like it.

FIRST AMERICAN SOLDIER:

It really is good.

SECOND AMERICAN SOLDIER:

I get a lot of satisfaction from hearing you say that. Why don't you take a little more so you'll have some for after the raid?

FIRST AMERICAN SOLDIER:

Aw, I don't want to—

SECOND AMERICAN SOLDIER:

No, go on, really, take it. I want you to have it.

FIRST AMERICAN SOLDIER:

Well, if you insist.

SECOND AMERICAN SOLDIER:

I do.

FIRST AMERICAN SOLDIER:
Thanks, Jim. You're . . .

SECOND AMERICAN SOLDIER:
Don't try to put it into words, Jack. Let's just forget it.

FIRST AMERICAN SOLDIER:
No—I . . .

SERGEANT: *(Cockney accent)*
Quiet up there! This is supposed to be a sneak raid.

GEORGE WASHINGTON:
What's the trouble here, Sergeant?

SERGEANT: *(Cockney accent)*
God save Your Honor, hit's a couple of the men, Sir, 'as been talking more
than what they ought to 'ave, and I was for putting them in line, Sir.

GEORGE WASHINGTON:
How long have you been in this country, Sergeant?

SERGEANT:
Two months, Sir. Not long. But I feel hit's as much my own country as if I'd
been 'ere fifty years, Your Lordship.

GEORGE WASHINGTON:
You wouldn't be a spy, by any chance, would you, trying to tip the enemy off
by making noise?

SERGEANT:
Bless me, no, Your Lordship, by all that's sacred and 'oly. I am but a poor
soldier would do 'is best to make this a land for free men to live and trade
in.

GEORGE WASHINGTON:
Very good. Continue with your work.

FIRST AIDE TO GEORGE WASHINGTON:
General Washington?

GEORGE WASHINGTON:
Is that you, Fitzdaniel? Haven't I told you not to use my name?

FIRST AIDE TO GEORGE WASHINGTON:
Begging Your Worship's pardon, Sir, but I think we may have come upon
something, Sir. Here are many heads, arms, and legs, and if it is not the English camp, I know not what it might be.

GEORGE WASHINGTON:

Excellent. Every man on his stomach. Get away with everything you can. Food is most important. Next, ammunition and clothing. Whatever you do, make no noise. Kill no man unless absolutely necessary. Is that understood?

ALL: *(whisper)*

Yes, General Washington.

(Sounds of crawling about and scuffling.)

CORNWALLIS: *(in his sleep)*

What's that? Ho!

FIRST AIDE TO GEORGE WASHINGTON:

What was that noise?

SECOND AIDE TO GEORGE WASHINGTON:

The voice had a familiar ring.

FIRST AIDE TO GEORGE WASHINGTON:

Yes! It was Cornwallis.

SECOND AIDE TO GEORGE WASHINGTON:

Where does the English general lie?

FIRST AIDE TO GEORGE WASHINGTON:

Near us, most likely, since we heard him so clearly.

SECOND AIDE TO GEORGE WASHINGTON:

Let's go into his tent. It is likely to be rich in booty!

THIRD BRITISH SOLDIER: *(waking up; speaks with an Irish brogue)*

Ooo-ooooooh me! *(pause)* Agh, it's little sleep I can be gettin', what with the cold wind blowin' against me head, and me all the time thinkin' of those that are near and those that are far away. And I did imagine as I lay thinkin' that I heard almost a ruslin,' a kind of noise almost, as if the winds themselves had come to bring some news into our Irish camp. It's a little air I'll be needin', and out of my tent I'll be steppin' and lookin' at the fair face of the moon with all her tiny stars.

FIRST AMERICAN SOLDIER:

What's this?

SECOND AMERICAN SOLDIER:

It's a Limey, Jack.

FIRST AMERICAN SOLDIER:

Shall we drop him?

SECOND AMERICAN SOLDIER:
  The general said no.

FIRST AMERICAN SOLDIER:
  Then what shall we do?

SECOND AMERICAN SOLDIER:
  Wait, and listen.

THIRD BRITISH SOLDIER:
  Ah, 'tis a fair dark night, and such as it would be wrong to sleep through.
  There is beauty in the blackness of the sky, which bears not one tiny star.
  'Twould be a fair night for a murder, and that's certain, for a man cannot see
  his hand before his face, even though he hold it up. A man could jump on
  another on a night such as this and sink a blade in his back without bein'
  noticed so much as a puff of smoke on a cloudy day. It's glad I am that the
  camp is guarded well by stalwart Irish soldiers and that we are safe from all
  harm.

SECOND AMERICAN SOLDIER:
  Quick, into his tent!

FIRST AMERICAN SOLDIER:
  Supposing he comes back?

SECOND AMERICAN SOLDIER:
  Then we'll have to—

FIRST AMERICAN SOLDIER:
  No!

SECOND AMERICAN SOLDIER:
  Yes! But he may not come. Come on, Jack!

FIRST AMERICAN SOLDIER:
  Lead the way!

GEORGE WASHINGTON:
  Sergeant, tell the men that the object of the raid has been accomplished.
  We have more than enough supplies for the campaign. Have them reassem-
  ble here, and we will then depart for our own camp.

SERGEANT:
  Yes, Sir. Yes, Sir. Oh, yes, Sir!

(much crawling and scuffling)

GEORGE WASHINGTON:
  Men, the raid has succeeded. We return to the American camp tonight!

ALL:
Hurrah for General Washington!

Scene 5

The English camp, next day.

CORNWALLIS: *(running out of his tent)*
Help! I've been robbed! My guns, my clothes, my food supplies—everything is gone!

FIRST AIDE TO CORNWALLIS:
And so have I! Everything is gone, everything!

SECOND AIDE TO CORNWALLIS:
And I.

THIRD BRITISH SOLDIER: *(Irish brogue)*
And I.

COOK:
The kitchen tent is completely emptied of supplies!

QUARTERMASTER:
All our equipment and ammunition are gone!

ASSISTANT QUARTERMASTER:
And our clothing!

FIRST AIDE TO CORNWALLIS:
What shall we do?

SECOND AIDE TO CORNWALLIS:
Who has done this deed? It is impossible—

CORNWALLIS: *(suddenly enlightened; is his calm self once more)*
Men, return to your quarters. Do not be alarmed. I shall issue instructions for your further conduct. Demoda and Bilgent, come with me.

(All leave, save for CORNWALLIS *and his two* AIDES.*)*

FIRST AIDE TO CORNWALLIS:
If it please Your Grace, how—?

SECOND AIDE TO CORNWALLIS:
If Your Lordship knows—

CORNWALLIS:
Precisely. It is very simple. The man Washington has duped us. In the dead of night, he and his soldiers must have crept into our camp and stripped us

of supplies. It is the only possibility. The man is a genius! If only we could win him over to our side . . . I've got it! Bilgent, you were once on the stage. Go to my tent. There is one trunk there they did not steal, because it was anchored to the ground. Take this key and open it. Inside you will find the uniform of an American officer. Put on this uniform and present yourself to General Washington, saying you have been sent to him by General Stevens, in Haskell. Then, when you have won his confidence, convince him of the justness of our cause. Washington is a righteous man, and if he is convinced we are right he will join us without hesitation. The future of England may depend on your mission! Take this key, and go!

(FIRST AIDE TO CORNWALLIS *leaves.*)

Now, Demoda, we must figure out a plan to obtain supplies. Our rear section is only three hours' march away, and we can easily reach them and resupply ourselves unless one thing happens—unless Washington is able to cut us off; and that he can do in one way only, by crossing a river—I forget its name. At any rate, there is little danger of his doing so, for he and his men are probably asleep after their strenuous night. Let's organize and march!

SECOND AIDE TO CORNWALLIS:
Aye, aye, General.

Scene 6

The American camp. George Washington's tent.

GEORGE WASHINGTON: *(sitting on his bed)*
I am tired, and I need sleep. Good-night, America.

(lies down and sleeps)

(A placard is now displayed, which reads

THE DREAM OF GEORGE WASHINGTON

Throughout the dream, GEORGE WASHINGTON *the man remains sleeping on his bed, and the part of* GEORGE WASHINGTON *is played by a child actor.)*

GEORGE WASHINGTON:
Where's Daddy, Mommy?

MOTHER:
He'll be here in just a little while, dear. He's bringing you a present for your birthday.

GEORGE WASHINGTON:
Oh, Mommy! A real present?

MOTHER:

Yes, and you must thank him for it and be nice to your daddy, as he loves you very much. Here he is now!

(Enter George Washington's FATHER. *He is carrying a young cherry tree, which he gives to* GEORGE.*)*

FATHER:

George, little George! Happy birthday to my little son!

*(*GEORGE WASHINGTON *cries.)*

MOTHER:

Why, baby, what's the matter?

GEORGE WASHINGTON:

Oh, Mommy, you said it was so nice, but it's all dirty and covered with roots!

FATHER:

What's the matter with the little crybaby? Is he afraid of getting his hands dirty?

MOTHER:

Oh, Elbert, you promised! Be nice to the child. It is a little one yet.

FATHER:

Humph! He'll never amount to a hill of beans, I can guarantee you that. All right, Sister, give me back the cherry tree! I'll give it to some other kid in the neighborhood, one who's a real man!

GEORGE WASHINGTON:

Oh, Daddy, don't! Is it really a cherry tree?

FATHER:

Come on, let go of it!

MOTHER:

Let the child keep it, dear. He wants it. He was only frightened at first, because it was so dirty and covered with roots.

FATHER:

All right, all right, he can have it. But give it to me! You don't think it's going to grow in your hands, do you, you little squirt? These things have to be planted, you know.

MOTHER:

Elbert, don't be so sarcastic. George only wants to be sure that you will not give the tree to another child.

FATHER:

No, of course I won't! I got it to give to him, didn't I? I only said that about another boy because he acted like he didn't want it before, like it was something that was no good, something dirty.

MOTHER:

George, go with your daddy and help him plant the tree.

GEORGE WASHINGTON:

Yes, Mommy.

(GEORGE WASHINGTON *and his* FATHER *plant the cherry tree, and both leave. Then* GEORGE WASHINGTON *comes back with a little axe and chops down the tree. The tree is carried offstage, and once again all three members of the family appear.*)

MOTHER:

Oh, I'm so sorry to hear about that! I wonder who could have chopped it down?

GEORGE WASHINGTON:

I did, Mother. I cannot tell a lie.

MOTHER:

Oh, my darling! *(Hugs him.)*

FATHER:

What? You chopped down the tree I slaved for, you little brat? I'm going to give you the beating of your life!

MOTHER:

Elbert, please!

FATHER:

I'm going to give you such a thrashing such as the world has never seen before!

GEORGE WASHINGTON:

I cannot tell a lie, but I can run! I can flee from injustice! The tree was mine, to chop down as I pleased!

FATHER:

I'll give you such a beating . . . !

(GEORGE WASHINGTON *runs off, his* FATHER *following him.* MOTHER *remains.* FATHER *returns.*)

FATHER:

He foxed me. He swam across the river. It was the only way he could have done it. The ONLY WAY!

(MOTHER *and* FATHER *vanish, as the "Dream" placard is removed.*)

GEORGE WASHINGTON: *(waking up suddenly)*
Father! you help me now! Quickly, assemble the men! We march at once
for the Delaware River!

Scene 7

A grayish-blue, flat area in front of the Delaware: the river cannot be seen.
GEORGE WASHINGTON *enters at the head of his troops.*

FIRST AIDE TO GEORGE WASHINGTON:
We have marched quickly, and we have marched well. But what is the
general's plan?

SECOND AIDE TO GEORGE WASHINGTON:
He has not confided it to me, but I have gathered from little things that he
has said that it is to cross the Delaware and cut off Cornwallis's army in its
search for supplies.

FIRST AIDE TO GEORGE WASHINGTON:
Washington is a genius! The army with supplies is the army that wins the
war. Washington has planned everything just right. First our night raid,
which took away all of their supplies; and now this forced march, to cut
them off in their attempt to renew their supplies.

SECOND AIDE TO GEORGE WASHINGTON:
You speak well. Washington has planned our every step. See how nobly he
marches at the head of our troops!

GEORGE WASHINGTON:
Halt! Here let us stop and dismount and prepare the boats.

(Busy activity—dismounting, boat-building, etc. Enter FIRST AIDE TO CORN-
WALLIS, *disguised as an American officer.)*

FIRST AIDE TO CORNWALLIS: *(to* GEORGE WASHINGTON*)*
I come to you from General Haskell, Sir, who is hard pressed at Stevens. I
mean Stevens, Stevens, Sir, Stevens who is hard-hask at pretzelled, hart had
at Prexelled, Sir, General Stevens, Sir, hart-passed at Haxel—

GEORGE WASHINGTON:
Tenwillet, remove this man at once to the medical tent, and place him under
armed guard. He seems dangerous.

SECOND AIDE TO GEORGE WASHINGTON:
Yes, Your Worship.

FIRST AIDE TO CORNWALLIS: *(being led away)*
  The man is a genius! It is impossible to deceive him.

GEORGE WASHINGTON:
  Fitzdaniel, what news is there of Cornwallis's army?

FIRST AIDE TO GEORGE WASHINGTON:
  He advances quickly, Sir, but by crossing at once, Sir, we shall be ahead of him by half an hour.

GEORGE WASHINGTON:
  Then let us go! For only if we go swiftly shall we have victory! And only victory is sweet! Come, men, battalions, uniforms, weapons, come, across the Delaware—we have nothing to fear but death, and we have America to win!

(They go. Two OLD MEN *enter. Both stare in the direction in which* GEORGE WASHINGTON *and his army have gone.)*

FIRST OLD MAN:
  What do you see?

SECOND OLD MAN:
  I am old, and I see nothing.

FIRST OLD MAN:
  I hear something, as though the sound of splashing.

SECOND OLD MAN:
  I hear nothing. My ears are dead things.

FIRST OLD MAN: *(suddenly very excited)*
  Why do I ask you what you hear and see, when now I hear and I see. Do you know what I hear and see?

SECOND OLD MAN:
  No.

FIRST OLD MAN: *(rapt)*
  I see General George Washington crossing the Delaware, with all his troops and horsemen. I see him standing up in his boat, but I cannot make out the expression on his face. The men and horses on the other side of the river are shaking themselves free of water.

SECOND OLD MAN:
  Go on! Do you see anything else?

FIRST OLD MAN:
  No. Now everything is dark again.

SECOND OLD MAN:
What you saw was enough.

(Cannons boom.)

FIRST OLD MAN:
The American army has crossed the Delaware.

FINAL CURTAIN

—1962

Six Improvisational Plays

THE ACADEMIC MURDERS

A Play of Detection, with Improvisations

Scene 1

The office of Department Chairman AUERHEIM, *a stout tweedy man in his late forties. His secretary,* MISS FUND, *sits typing in the office just outside. Enter a tall young man of about twenty-five; not seeing him at first,* MISS FUND *is a little startled.*

MISS FUND:
 Ah—!?

FETHERING:
 I'm George Fethering. I have an appointment to see Professor Auerheim.

MISS FUND:
 Oh—yes—of course. Just a moment. *(to* AUERHEIM*)*
 Sir, there's a young man to see you—Mr. Fethering.

AUERHEIM:
 Oh yes—uh—show him in.

MISS FUND:
 You can go right in, Mr. uh—

FETHERING:
 Fethering. Yes. Thank you.

AUERHEIM:
 Well, Mr. Fethering, what can I do for you?

FETHERING:
 I would like to apply for a job in your department, sir.

AUERHEIM:
 Yes. I understand from your letter that you are quite a Yeats scholar.

FETHERING:
 That's right, sir. I don't want to boast, but I dare say there's nothing about W. B. Yeats that I don't know. Nothing except what may be contained in the "secret letters," of course.

AUERHEIM:

The "secret letters" . . . ? Hmmm. I don't know anything about those. What are they?

FETHERING:

They are a group of letters kept in the possession of the heirs of Lady Gregory, sir. Yeats's will contains a stipulation that they are not to be opened for a thousand years.

AUERHEIM:

That seems rather a long time to keep something secret.

FETHERING:

Yes, sir. But apparently they contain information which Yeats thought might be harmful in our time. He believed that if the world was hardy enough to last for another thousand years probably nothing could harm it.

AUERHEIM:

It seems an ingenious idea . . . Well, let's get down to business. You have your degree, do you not?

FETHERING:

Yes, sir, a PhD from the University of Minnesota. I worked there with Hocking T. Nott on my dissertation on A.E., George Russell.

AUERHEIM:

The letter from Nott praised you very highly indeed. I vaguely remember reading the abstract of your dissertation, but I don't remember too well what it was about. Could you refresh my memory?

FETHERING:

If you put your memory on the table, sir, I may be able to refresh it.

AUERHEIM:

Mr. Fethering! What on earth do you mean?

FETHERING:

I'm sorry, sir. I—I guess I'm just a little nervous. When I am, I often make clumsy remarks of that kind. I have been reading a lot about Zen Buddhism, sir, and that sort of remark just naturally comes to my mind when I am nervous.

AUERHEIM:

I see. I see. Do you know Jung's splendid introduction to Suzuki's *Introduction to Zen Buddhism*?

FETHERING:

Yes, sir. I think Jung rather misses the point, sir. He tends to make Zen awfully Jungian.

AUERHEIM:

Ummm. Yes. Perhaps. It may be that I simply prefer the thought of Jung to that of Suzuki and the Zen masters.

FETHERING:

Sir, you should never say a thing like that!

(AUERHEIM *dies.*)

(*improvised speech by* FETHERING *on the danger of attacking Zen*)

Scene 2

The same office, twenty minutes later. Enter Police Officer STRAITER *and his assistant, Patrolman* BUDGE.

STRAITER:

So this is the murderer!

FETHERING:

Sir, I didn't touch the victim. Miss Fund can testify to that.

MISS FUND:

I didn't see a thing. I was busy here in my office with my typewriter.

FETHERING:

Sir, if Miss Fund won't admit that she was spying on us, you are free to examine the body for fingerprints.

MISS FUND:

Oh! poor Professor Auerheim! What have you done to him, you horrible person?

STRAITER:

Young lady, don't become hysterical. If this man is the murderer, we shall certainly see that he gets what he deserves. As yet, however, we really have no evidence.—Very well, Budge, you stay here and see that no one disturbs the body. I am going to phone our scientific squad to get over here on the double and examine this body for fingerprints.

BUDGE:

Yes, sir.

Scene 3

A political hall.

STRAITER:

Since there is no evidence of the body having been touched, it looks as though you're free, Fethering. But don't leave the city. We shall be wanting to have you within reach at all times for questioning.

FETHERING:

Sir, is that legal?

STRAITER:

You're damn right it is, Fethering. If we wanted to, we could hold you as a material witness indefinitely. In fact, I have half a mind to clap you in jail right now for your improper question.

FETHERING:

Oh no, sir. Yes, sir. I understand. I was just asking. You see, I know nothing of the law.

STRAITER:

Very well, Fethering. You are dismissed.

Scene 4

Fethering's furnished room.

FETHERING:

It would have been foolish to tell the police officer what I think actually killed Auerheim. My own problems, meanwhile, are only redoubled by this whole affair.

(improvisation by FETHERING *on the difficulties of his life, his unpleasant childhood, his need for a job, etc., and his determination to go to Japan to try to get to the root of the mystery)*

Scene 5

Japan.

(Improvisation of a busy day of turmoil in the Tokyo streets. At the end, enter FETHERING.*)*

Scene 6

The prison room of a ship, sailing to the United States. FETHERING *behind bars.*

POLICE OFFICER:
We told you not to leave the city, Fethering.

FETHERING:
But sir, I did it only to try to get to the heart of the mystery—

POLICE OFFICER:
If you expect us to believe that, then you are a greater fool than we thought!

Scene 7

Above, in the ship's bar. POLICE OFFICER, *other policemen, and other passengers.*

(Improvisation: Discussion of how great a fool FETHERING *is to expect them to believe such a story. At the end, enter* RADIO MAN.*)*

RADIO MAN:
Look! Look! Listen! There may be some truth in what the boy says after all! The University of Blenheim has just exploded!

POLICE OFFICER:
Blenheim!? What in tarnation has Blenheim got to do with this case? Constantia University, where Professor Auerheim was murdered by this boy, is in New York.

RADIO MAN:
But wait—wait—listen to this—Blenheim, my dear police officer, is the city in which Dagobert von Auerheim was born!

SAILOR: *(rushing up from below)*
And listen to this! The ship has been disemboweled, and young Fethering has mysteriously escaped. He can't be found anywhere!

POLICE OFFICER:
But then we must be sinking!

ALL:
Help! ho! Man the lifeboats! Abandon ship! Ho!

Scene 8

A lovely dusky garden in Japan. FETHERING *and a beautiful young Japanese girl,* TACOCA.

FETHERING:

I hope you don't mind my telling you this tedious story?

TACOCA:

I don't find it tedious at all, my darling. I don't find anything that you say tedious.

FETHERING:

To think, that I once planned to be a teacher!

TACOCA:

Yes—and that now you know what your true destiny is—to be a MAN!

FETHERING:

Yes, but I would still like to know who killed Professor Auerheim.

TACOCA:

We can ask at the shrine after we have performed our ablutions. But meanwhile, here comes my father, the famous Japanese businessman.

(Enter TACOCACOM, *a huge burly man.)*

TACOCACOM:

Hello, son! Been hearing a lot about y—

(He drops dead.)

CURTAIN

(improvised EPILOGUE *by* TACOCA*)*

FINAL CURTAIN

* * *

EASTER

Scene 1

A large lovely lawn filled with Easter eggs. Children rolling the eggs, etc. Improvisation by children on why they like Easter. The scene ends with a symphony orchestra playing something well-known from *Parsifal*.

Scene 2

A cave in the mountains. At the mouth of the cave stand a number of very large Easter rabbits. Improvisation: they discourse on the pleasures and burdens of Easter from the rabbits' point of view. The scene ends with a very thunderous music, probably from Berlioz.

Scene 3

A church. A number of priests are gathering informally about the altar and the lowered area in front of it. Improvisation: they discuss the meaning of Easter to church and to churchman, their love of the ecstatic aspects of the holiday, their eagerness in awaiting it, but also their displeasure at the pagan aspects of the popular Easter myth as well as at the general commercialization of the holiday by stores and popular media of communication. The scene ends with a number of grand opera bassos and baritones singing popular songs.

Scene 4

Empty stage. Improvisation: a murder is committed. The police arrest the criminal and electrocute him. The scene ends with low, solemn death-march music.

Scene 5

The resurrection. Entire improvisation. After the resurrection the stage fills up with the actors, who discuss the meaning of the play. Finally they are drowned out by extremely loud noises of coughing.

CURTAIN

* * *

MEXICO CITY

An elderly American homosexual tries to describe Mexico City to an illiterate
and extremely ugly Finnish farm girl who has never been in any city whatsoever. He should try to be as complete in his description as possible, including
such things as streetcars, buses, hotels, markets, and so on, as well as the life pattern of ordinary persons of the various social classes in the city. When he has
finished (his description should take from fifteen to forty-five minutes), the
farm girl should try to repeat everything he has said to her with as much ex-
actitude as she can manage. When she has done so, the elderly man should tell
her to what extent he feels she has truly captured the spirit and mood of the
city.

* * *

THE LOST FEED

Seven actresses, impersonating hens and chickens, should, while retaining their
human modesty and dignity, act out in as chicken-like a way as possible the
drama of the lost feed. The feed for the day is missing. None of the hens or
chickens present is responsible for the absence of the feed, but each one sus-
pects that some one of the others onstage may be the culprit. Whatever the
hens and chickens do, they should make no strictly *personal* remarks when
they accuse one another. Their accusations should be rather flat and rather
general, accusations that could be leveled at anybody about just about anything. Chicken life is not thought to be very differentiated. After the chickens
and hens have been arguing for a long time, the feed should be brought in and
given to them.

* * *

THE GOLD STANDARD

A Mountain Shrine, in China. Two monks enter, and try, without the slightest success, to explain the gold standard to each other, for four hours. There should be nothing comical whatsoever in anything they say. The drama should be allowed as a "field day" for the lighting technician, who should be allowed, and even encouraged, to make as many changes of lighting to show time of day, season, atmosphere, and moods as he deems fitting so as to make the play as beautiful and meaningful as it can possibly be. The play should end with a snowfall and with the exit of the monks.

* * *

COIL SUPREME

Eight or ten actors come onstage, being anyone they want. They speak for thirty minutes. The only requirement is that every sentence they utter must contain the phrase "coil supreme." They may distort the language in any way they wish in order to do this. They should try to generate as much excitement as possible by what they say and do, and the play should end on a note of unbearable suspense.

—1965

The Tinguely Machine Mystery
or The Love Suicides at Kaluka

This play was performed in an exhibition of motorized machines made by Jean Tinguely. Three of the machines have important parts in it: they move at certain times, and at other times they speak. ATTILA, *the most important of the machine characters, occupies a large part of the back wall of the stage. Sixteen feet wide and ten-and-a-half feet high,* ATTILA *is made of steel and machine parts mounted on wood; its metal part altogether looks something like the skeleton of an old horse; when the machine is activated, two of its steel parts begin banging together with a loud and regularly repeated sound.* MAY FAIR—*sixty-two inches long, forty-two inches high, twenty-eight inches wide—a machine on wheels, made of metal scrap and machine parts, resembles the bottom part of a big lawn mower. When activated, it rolls forward again, and so on, until turned off.* ODESSA—*a little over four feet tall and two-and-a-half feet wide at its widest point—is made of steel, painted grey. It looks something like a child's drawing of a man made with straight lines and circles. One of these circles is a chest-high cylinder about a foot and a half in diameter, which rotates and makes a whirring sound when the machine is activated. Other motorized machines stand on both sides and in back of the audience.*

The stage is bare, except for the machines. Shortly after the music begins, all lights go out. Then, while the music continues, spotlight on MAY FAIR, *then on* ATTILA, *then on* ODESSA, *then on various other machines. When music ends, complete blackout. The* MAY FAIR MACHINE *clangs five times. After the fifth clang, enter the* PRINCESS. *Dim light. A* CORPSE *is visible lying center stage. The* PRINCESS *discovers it and screams.*

PRINCESS:
A body! I've found a dead body! A body! It must have been
The May Fair Machine that did it! Oh I've told that gardener a thousand times
To get this vicious May Fair Machine out of my house—
For this is not the first time that it has snapped at people.
Now it has snapped at someone and he is dead.
Just think of that! and I'll be blamed! Horrible machine of May Fair!

(MAY FAIR MACHINE *clangs once. Enter* DETECTIVE.)

DETECTIVE:
I am Detective White.
I hear that you have a vicious May Fair Machine, a corpse here? Well! let us
see . . .

(He examines the CORPSE.*)*

No, lady, the May Fair Machine is not the killer.

(He sees the ATTILA MACHINE.*)*

Good Lord! what's this?

PRINCESS:
  That is my great-grandfather's portrait, which we call Attila.
  As long as I can remember, it has hung in this room, above my embroidered
      pillow.
  Each night as I sleep my great-grandfather's face gives me protection—
  But we must seek the killer and not idly waste away
  The hours from dusk to day.

(The princess has approached the DETECTIVE *in a seductive way, and now she is very close to him. He embraces her.)*

DETECTIVE:
  Oh lady, I do not care for any killer
  Or any corpse the way I care for you.
  From the first moment I saw you, with your back turned
  To me, at the Chandelier Ball, your back so bare and shining,
  I knew that when I met you privately, alone, I would be able to love you,
  And now it has come to pass.

PRINCESS:
  Yes, perhaps a promising life now lies before us,
  But first we must find the killer, whose hideous purpose
  How can we understand? Release me, detective.

DETECTIVE:
  Your word is my command.
  Oh, lady, if I could be with you in Odessa—

*(*ODESSA MACHINE *starts, then stops.)*

PRINCESS:
  What's that noise?

*(*ODESSA MACHINE *starts, and stays on while the character* ODESSA *is speaking. Up to this time the character* ODESSA *has been standing motionless in the dark beside the* ODESSA MACHINE, *with her back to the audience.)*

ODESSA:
  It is I, Odessa! I am a city that no one understands.
  And when everyone sits about with their bare backs turned to me

And their bare knees pointing in one direction and their fair bare calves in
    another,
I often think of my waterfront, and sometimes weep.

(ODESSA MACHINE *stops.*)

DETECTIVE:
    Have a care, Odessa,
    That you don't interrupt this criminal investigation.
    Let's see now, where were we?

PRINCESS:
    You were just saying that Attila—

(ODESSA MACHINE *starts.*)

ODESSA:
    All right, I will be silent; but mark my words:
    The killer's not always to be found in one direction.

(ODESSA MACHINE *stops.*)

DETECTIVE:
    Odessa, thanks. Now, Princess . . . this killer . . .

PRINCESS:
    Oh darling, your kiss was so wonderful. . . .

DETECTIVE:
    Wait, Princess, please. I am only a detective
    And only flesh and blood. But I must solve this case.
    Otherwise all our lives we would carry the burden
    Of guilt that, because of us, a killer went free.

PRINCESS:
    Yes. Your words are good. We must solve this case.

DETECTIVE:
    Tell me, Princess, tell me about this portrait, Attila—
    Does it ever change the expression on its face?

PRINCESS:
    Why er uh no, never. . . . Why do you ask?

DETECTIVE:
    I thought that it might be the killer. I thought it just might.
    A marvelous inspiration came to me as I
    Was standing behind your left shoulder more shapely than April

And looking at this picture Attila, It struck me it might
Be a "moving" or "kinetic" picture.

PRINCESS:

But there has not been
A picture like that for years. Old books tell us that in fifteen hundred
There was one like it in Venice—
But—

DETECTIVE:

Exactly—this Attila reminded me of a certain old Titian
Which was said once to have killed a man, also in Venice.
They found strange markings on his throat.

PRINCESS:

But this old picture
Has been in the family for years. And never moved an inch.
It's a dear old portrait and I have grown very fond of it.
If I had ever thought it could move or attack people I'd have thrown it out
Subitamente.

DETECTIVE:

What's that you said?

PRINCESS:

That I would have thrown it out
Er, right away . . .

(ODESSA MACHINE *starts.*)

ODESSA:

I Odessa must now voice my earnest hope
That Detective White will get the hint and end this tragedy.
Attila it seems to me is obviously the killer
And that woman spoke Italian.

(ODESSA MACHINE *stops.*)

DETECTIVE:

Be quiet, Odessa. One more move and I'll poke you,
And then you'll be back in the atlas where you belong.

(ODESSA MACHINE *starts.*)

ODESSA:
No! not in the atlas!

(ODESSA MACHINE *stops.*)

DETECTIVE:
  Then, calm! and be still!

(ODESSA MACHINE *starts.*)

ODESSA:
  I was only wishing . . .

(ODESSA MACHINE *stops.*)

DETECTIVE: *(threateningly)*
  Odessa! . . .

(*to* PRINCESS)

  You said "*subitamente.*"

PRINCESS:
  Kiss me, my darling!

DETECTIVE:
  No. Princess, no.
  I suspect Attila is our killer!

PRINCESS:
  No! why?

DETECTIVE:
  You said "*subitamente*"
  And then denied you'd said "*subitamente.*"
  "*Subitamente*" is an Italian word
  Which is used very frequently in Venice—
  In the rest of Italy it is used rarely.
  And yet you said it naturally, "*su-*
  Bitamente"—

PRINCESS:
  What's that? what does that prove?
  May not a person say "*subitamente*"
  And not be thrown in gaol? Are we free still
  Or have we now gone back to barbarous ages
  Where men were thrown in gaol at tyrants' will?
  What if I said, or say, "*subitamente*"?

DETECTIVE:
  The world is but a wheel,
  And on this wheel new persons every day
  Go sailing through their lives. Sometimes from far

Come words that have no meaning and no resonance
And sometimes they may come from farther still
And mean more than they say. I think you wished,
Because you loved me, to confess to me
That you suspect Attila as I do.
Princess, you are Venetian. That straight nose,
That glistening black hair, that back of backs
Which makes my heart grow still even to think of it,
Those eyes like brimming pools—Princess, don't cry.
Tell me you are Venetian. I do not
Suspect YOU of this crime—

PRINCESS:
But you suspect
My great-grandfather, which is the same thing
As far as I am concerned. I love the old man in this picture
And I have always loved him. I wonder that you do not see the regal
    qualities
And the charm he has about him. Ah, you are vulgar!

DETECTIVE:
But Princess! Princess!

(PRINCESS *falls to her knees and addresses the* ATTILA MACHINE.)

PRINCESS:
You dear old man!
Forgive me that I bring into your presence
A being vulgar enough to think that you
Could do a thing so wrong as kill a man.
Forgive me, father! Oh shrive me, great-grandfather!

(*strange lights on the* ATTILA MACHINE)

VOICE FROM THE ATTILA MACHINE:
Oh I forgive you, child. Long have you loved me.
Long love deserves long praise. Yet now you see
There is some truth in what the detective said.

(*strange lights off*)

PRINCESS:
Grandfather, is that all? Great-grandfather?

DETECTIVE:
The message that he gave was very short

And yet it seemed to me it was significant.
It is incredible with what wily skill those old Venetians
Constructed their machines. This, obviously, is a "talking" picture,
Not a machine that moves. And it said things with a certain
Gentilezza, to use an Italian word. It is obviously not
And cannot be the killer, for it cannot move. The which leave ME
With a terrible dilemma. I must find the killer soon
Or be fired from the force.

PRINCESS:

Farewell, sweet Detective.
I'll leave the corpse exactly as you found it
So that you may come again tomorrow morning
And pick up clues from it. And now good-night.
Fain would I pass the long hours in amorous banter,
But already glowering Arcturus has sped beyond the Northeast Crescent,
And Diana's horns are amaranth with light. Farewell, sweet pleasant
Man—I'll see thee on the morrow's swell!

DETECTIVE:

Good-night, sweet Princess.
Fain would I stay and chase away the night
Hugg'd in your warm embraces, but I must
Go to my precinct station and report.
Our chief is a tough man, too tough I think—
He is unfair and thinks that others are:
He is so suspicious that he is always testing
The very men he works with, night and day.
Sweet love, good-night.

PRINCESS:

Adieu, Detective White.

(DETECTIVE *leaves, right, and as he does so the character* ODESSA *slips offstage, left. The* CORPSE *rises from the floor. It is the* POLICE CHIEF.)

POLICE CHIEF:

What did he say, that idiot? What were his last
Few words? What did he say about me?

PRINCESS: *(astonished)*

Why, Chief! What a strange man you are!

POLICE CHIEF:

Tish tush, my dear, let's drink away the night!

Oh now will you believe me when I tell you
How stupid is our entire detective force?
Now can you understand what imbecilic
Persons I have to work with all day long?
Now can you, love, forgive me sometimes when
I come to you all harsh and out of spirits?
Oh now can you see why? I have two hundred
Men of the exact same caliber as this one,
And they are the fruit and the flower of the police.
The rest are more stupid still.

PRINCESS:
Well, he was clumsy. But was he stupid as all that?

POLICE CHIEF:
Do you need proof of it? For one thing, he did not see that I wasn't dead
And that therefore no crime had been committed. And for another
He thought that machine was the city of Odessa,
Whereas in fact I taped a voice for it. But stupidest of all
Was his attitude toward this portrait, which he concluded
Could speak, therefore not move.

PRINCESS:
It did speak, didn't it?

POLICE CHIEF:
It was I who spoke.
I leaped up quickly from where I lay on the floor
And stood behind it and spoke, then I quickly returned to
My place as the corpse on the floor. . . . Oh let us riot
And drink the whole night long!

PRINCESS:
I will, hale spirit. Oh let us carouse till dawn!

POLICE CHIEF:
And speak . . . of love . . .

(*They lie down, stage left. Complete darkness.* ATTILA MACHINE *goes on for ten seconds, then off. Enter* JAPANESE PRIEST.)

PRIEST:
Here am I, a Japanese priest, Hogasoki by name,
And I am weary from all the traveling I have done.
On this one night I have come a fearfully long way,
And now it is time to repose myself in sleep.

(He starts to lie down; then he sees the ATTILA MACHINE.)

Ah! What is this emblem, this great piece of architectural phantasm?
It is the ruins of Kaluka bridge
Where so many young lovers who found their love impossible
Have ended their days. Old legends state
That when a traveler sleeps by Kaluka bridge
Sometimes the spirits of the dead come out
And re-enact their ancient tragedy.
Well, we shall see. But now I must lie down.

(He lies down to sleep where the CORPSE *was before. Enter the* SPIRIT OF THE
NIGHT, *with stars and a wand.)*

SPIRIT OF THE NIGHT: *(indicating the priest, then the princess and the police
chief)*
Gently sleep, and may the Spirit
Of the Night look over you!
May the butterfly and emmet,
Bee and wasp stay far from you!

(to the MACHINES*)*

Come, my sisters, join in chorus
And assure their peaceful sleep—
Fields of daylight stretch out before us,
But, for now, make slumber deep—
Oh voices of the forest,
Awake, and give them dreams!

(The SPIRIT OF THE NIGHT *now points to the machines one at a time, beginning
with* MAY FAIR, *and continuing clockwise. As she points to each machine, it goes
on, then off. After the last machine has gone on and off, all the machines go on
at once, then off. The* SPIRIT OF THE NIGHT *leave. Enter a* JAPANESE LOVE-
SUICIDE COUPLE.)*

MAN:
Wa San, we have walked all night, and still we are far from the cemetery
Of forgetfulness.

GIRL:
Yes, still the freezing panoply
Of nonexistence seems pitifully far from us.

MAN:
We were not happy in life; thus for death we come
To the Kaluka bridge.

GIRL:

My heart is embroidered with snow
And my hands tremble. You must hold the knife, beloved,
And kill me first.

MAN:

My heart trembles at the thought of it
And my hand is chilled with snow. If we could but live—
Yet your family will not permit us to live together—
You are highly born, and I am a mere apprentice.

GIRL:

It is better we should be dead than to live despised
And unhappy.

MAN:

Yes, here is the bridge.

(He indicates the ATTILA MACHINE. Then he takes out the knife and raises it above the GIRL's chest.)

Now, Wa San—

(Simultaneously, there is a complete blackout, the GIRL screams, and the ATTILA MACHINE goes on. Then the MAN screams. Lights on. The ATTILA MACHINE goes off. The lovers have vanished. Enter, hurriedly, POLICEMAN.)

POLICEMAN:

Quickly! Everyone out! Attila is on the rampage!

PRIEST:

I have dreamed of the Wa San lovers! Their end was so tragic!
I feel very stirred by what I have seen. I am now convinced in my resolve
To end my life, just as these two have done.

(PRIEST approaches the ATTILA MACHINE. POLICEMAN intercepts him.)

POLICEMAN:

Mister, watch out! You can't go fooling around with that
Attila machine, or it will kill you!
Detective White informed the department tonight
That it was only a talking machine, but it is obviously a killer—so watch
  out!

PRIEST:

But I wish to die . . .

POLICEMAN:

Well, you can't do it here!

*(*PRIEST *retreats to stage right center, where he kneels in silent prayer. Now* POLICE-MAN *discovers the recumbent forms of* POLICE CHIEF *and* PRINCESS.*)*

What? Chief! Is he dead? Has there been foul play?
Oh, monstrous Attila!

(Enter ADMIRAL.*)*

ADMIRAL:
I am looking for two deserting sailors,
Both of them assigned to the battleship *Remorseless* of my fleet.
These two sailors, actually one is a chief petty officer
And the other one a ship's first mate, have escaped within the last few
Days, and I wish to apprehend them.
They are both very clever at disguise. One is an alcoholic
And the other a transvestite of low degree.
I am sorry to disturb you here so early,
But one of my outposts said he saw some suspicious-looking people come
    in here!

POLICEMAN:
Admiral, there's been a tragedy! What,
How can we find your men? Look,
The Police Chief, perhaps he has been murdered!

*(*POLICEMAN *and* ADMIRAL *walk slowly around* POLICE CHIEF *and* PRINCESS *and look at them.* PRIEST *gets up and follows them. He looks at the sleeping couple with amazement.)*

PRIEST:
It is the love suicides of Kaluka!

(Once again PRIEST *heads for the* ATTILA MACHINE *with the intention of killing himself but is stopped by* POLICEMAN.*)*

POLICEMAN:
I told you to stop that! Don't we have enough trouble?

PRIEST:
I've got—I must get away!

ADMIRAL:
Officer, who is this man?

POLICEMAN:
He seems, sir, to be a Japanese priest who was spending the night here—
Naturally, if the chief is injured, we are holding this man as a suspect,
    though.

ADMIRAL:
A priest. . . ? Let me see . . .

PRIEST:
I . . . I . . .

ADMIRAL:
It's you! Cabroso! My prime escapee!

(*Scuffle.* PRIEST *bolts.* ADMIRAL *and* POLICEMAN *start to pursue him. Simultaneously, there is a blackout and the* ATTILA MACHINE *goes on.* ATTILA MACHINE *goes off. Then, from behind the* ATTILA MACHINE *comes the* SPIRIT OF THE NIGHT. *Her presence casts a spell over* ADMIRAL *and* MAN. *They are unable to move.* PRIEST *has already gotten offstage.*)

SPIRIT OF THE NIGHT:
Gently rest, your souls at ease,
Gently in the forest breeze,
And sing, creative spirits
Of the night!
Make such music as will pleasure
Modern man in modern measure
And will make the night
With all its burning fantasies take flight—
Now, spirits, play.

(*Music plays. When the music ends,* SPIRIT OF THE NIGHT *leaves, and lights come up. The spell has ended.* POLICEMAN *rushes offstage left in pursuit of* PRIEST.)

ADMIRAL: (*coming out of the spell*)
Damn! That voice! What? I've been in a
Trance—hyp-
Notized, almost!

(*to* SAILORS *offstage*)

Boys!

(*Enter* SAILORS.)

Get that man! I've
Heard that voice before, that one
Who's the spirit—that's
Hendersy, the other one,
The transvestite deserter from the navy!

(SAILORS *run offstage and come back with* SPIRIT OF THE NIGHT *and* PRIEST.)

ADMIRAL:
  Damn you! Deserting the navy! Away!

SPIRIT OF THE NIGHT:
  Oh gently rest!

PRIEST:
  I have traveled many miles and I am not tired.

ADMIRAL:
  Take them away!

(SPIRIT OF THE NIGHT *and* PRIEST *are dragged offstage. While being dragged off, they continue to repeat their last lines—"Oh gently rest!" and "I have traveled many miles and I am not tired."*)

  Oh, damn it! Oh I hate
  Deserters! Ah! I've given my whole life to
  The navy! And they desert! Ah
  Damn it! Ah, ah, the excitement, the
  Tension . . . my . . . my my my heart!

(ADMIRAL *falls dead where the* CORPSE *had been before. Re-enter* MAN, *on the run. He sees the* ADMIRAL's *body and runs over to the* POLICE CHIEF.)

POLICEMAN:
  Chief, Chief, sir, wake up
  Before it is too late! Chief, awaken!

POLICE CHIEF:
  No, no, God damn it, I'm perfectly all right!
  Can't you damned lower staff men ever let a person alone?
  After all, a police chief is allowed to sleep in a friend's apartment, no?
  What the hell are you doing here, anyway? Now, get out.

POLICEMAN: *(backing away)*
  But the love
  Suicides . . .

POLICE CHIEF:
  Get out!
  Ah, Princess . . .

(*His arm around her, he starts to go back to sleep.*)

(*to* POLICEMAN)

  And turn off the lights!

(Lights go off. POLICEMAN *leaves. After a while, dawn light.* MAY FAIR MACHINE *clangs once. More light. Enter* DETECTIVE.)*

DETECTIVE:
Ah, all night long I have puzzled over this terrible mystery.
And at last I understand it! I have been duped!

(Now he sees the corpse of the ADMIRAL.)*

No! Admiral Murphy! Can it be? Dead, dead as my heart! . . .
Hmmm. I think this is not the same corpse that was here before,
And yet it may well be. Before, I was distracted. But now I must find the
    killer . . .
Princess! Where are you, Princess?

PRINCESS: *(half-asleep)*
Ah, ummm . . . over here . . .

*(*DETECTIVE *discovers* PRINCESS *and* POLICE CHIEF.)*

DETECTIVE: *(softly)*
Ah, so THERE
You are! And there, THERE is the killer!

(He rushes to the couple and ties them both up, then draws back and aims his gun at the POLICE CHIEF.)*

No longer can you deceive me, you bloody maniac!
No longer will your stupid wiles beguile the police department!
Yes, you are the murderer! It is you have done all these crimes! Do not speak
    to me of machines!
Yes, you are the killer! Ah ha! And you
Were the corpse before, pretending to be dead—
A perfect alibi, being dead, for if you were dead
How could you murder the Admiral? You abominable slime! I know your
    methods!
And now you shall pay for them dearly! . . . Get up!

POLICE CHIEF:
This man is insane!

*(*POLICE CHIEF *and* PRINCESS *struggle up, and* DETECTIVE, *tugging at the rope that binds them and occasionally turning to menace them with his gun, with difficulty pulls them offstage as he delivers his final speech.)*

DETECTIVE:
Come now, come, don't resist me—I'll drag you into the daylight,

Which now breaks fresh and crystalline over our city,
A city of terror and dreams, but from henceforward
A city of pleasure and peace!

(*to* POLICE CHIEF, *tugging at him*)

Move, you idiot!

(*to* PRINCESS)

Ah, do not hold back, Princess!
Come, both of you, into the day!

(POLICE CHIEF *and* PRINCESS *are dragged off.* TWO SAILORS *come in and pick up the* ADMIRAL'S CORPSE *and hold it upright; each* SAILOR *has one of the* ADMIRAL'S *arms around his shoulder.*)

ONE OF THE SAILORS:
This is the story of the love suicides at Kaluka.
Rather than live apart they chose to die together.
And all of those who sleep near these machines
Will see them again, and forever, until the break of day.

Blackout. End.

After the blackout, music; lights up, and all the MACHINES *go on.*

FINAL CURTAIN

—1965

The Return of Yellowmay

(Enter YELLOWMAY.*)*

YELLOWMAY:
Oh I have surfeited so many borders
Seeking for an equitable light!

CROWD:
Welcome back, Yellowmay!

(A huge lightbulb is brought in.)

YELLOWMAY:
Here will I proclaim my new religion!
Guinevere shall be the Queen of April

*(*GUINEVERE *dances in.)*

And I myself shall be the God of May.

(Thunder and explosions. The seashore.)

(Enter KING LEAR.*)*

LEAR:
You see me here, you Gods, a poor old man
More sinned against than sinning.

CHORUS OF GODS:
Yes, we see you, Lear.

(Enter YELLOWMAY.*)*

And also we see Yellowmay!

(A dome is brought in.)

YELLOWMAY:
I here declare my new politick power.
Here shall I stay to manage all the state!

(Crowds cheer. The ocean is revealed. With a SEABIRD.*)*

SEABIRD:
I am worried about Yellowmay. I am wondering
If he should not practice more modest ambitions.
He is likely to get in trouble with

The real gods and political powers, behaving
As he's been behaving these days.

(the City of San Francisco)

(Enter a WALRUS, *with* YELLOWMAY.*)*

WALRUS:
San Francisco, welcome your new ruler,
And welcome to his queen of pretty May.

*(*GUINEVERE *is drawn in in a flowery cart.)*

YELLOWMAY:
I do believe she is my queen, my heart!

(Honolulu)

RULER:
Here in this new state,
Yellowmay, may you and Guinevere
Be happy, wearing the traditional Hawaiian lei.

(They put them on.)

YELLOWMAY:
Thank you, sir. And might we now
Visit that famous leper colony?

RULER:
You shall.

(They go off.)

(Leper Colony)

YELLOWMAY:
Lepers! I am Yellowmay!

LEPER WOMEN:
Kill him! kill him!

LEPER MEN:
No, preserve him, save him for our sanctuary!

RULER:
Be careful! What sanctuary do you lepers have, anyway?

LEPERS:
Our leprosy sanctuary! Now clear out of the way!
We want him!

(They capture YELLOWMAY *and lead him away.* RULER *rages, and* GUINEVERE *weeps.)*

(absolute darkness; four years later)

ELEPHANT:
  Rescue by the animals

GIRAFFE:
  Is hard but not hopeless—

KANGAROO:
  We will rescue Yellowmay

HIPPOPOTAMUS:
  If Guinevere permits us.

(Enter GUINEVERE, *wearing a dress and a crown of green flowers.)*

GUINEVERE:
  No, animals, do not rescue Yellowmay
  You only would yourselves be put in prison.
  And something is happening of great importance.
  Some day he'll be free.

(Her flowers fade. It is autumn.)

*(*YELLOWMAY, *crowned King of the Lepers, in a purple crown and on a yellow throne.)*

YELLOWMAY:
  King of the Lepers, I—
  Who once wanted to be king of the world.
  And yet I feel this kingdom is the essential one, I feel

*(*LEPERS *come in and do a ceremonial dance. They present* YELLOWMAY *with a young girl and he kills her. The* LEPERS *quietly carry her off.)*

  That this is the essential kingdom of our time.

(The jungle floats away, revealing YELLOWMAY *lying asleep on the beach.* GUINEVERE, *wearing the head of a seabird, leans over him.)*

GUINEVERE:
  Darling, wake up.
  Bad dreams of leprosy oppress the night—
  Wake up.

YELLOWMAY: *(still lying down)*
  Nothing that happens

Affects the human heart
But sadness.

GUINEVERE:
Now the curtain rolls away!

(It does—revealing the city of Paris and crowds.)

CROWD:
We declare Yellowmay King of the World!

(YELLOWMAY stands up. The LEPERS come in and he goes off with them.)

(silence, music, end)

FINAL CURTAIN

—1966

The Revolt of the Giant Animals

KANGAROO:
　Here shall we,

GIRAFFE:
　Revolting animals,

HIPPOPOTAMUS:
　Gather our forces by the sea

ELEPHANT:
　To war on Master Yellowmay.

(Enter YELLOWMAY *and* GUINEVERE, *in a royal cart.)*

YELLOWMAY:
　To thee I do bequeath these kingdoms, sweetest—
　May they lie upon your heart
　Gently as a peanut.

GUINEVERE:
　Yellowmay, look! turn around!

YELLOWMAY:
　It's the giant animals, in revolt!

FINAL CURTAIN

—1966

The Building of Florence

Florence.

GIRAFFE:
Come, lolly counselors, here are your plans.

ELEPHANT:
They say the competition for the Dome is fierce.

KANGAROO:
Tell me what competition is this.

HIPPOPOTAMUS:
It is a competition for the Dome of Florence,
Celebrated Duomo,
Which we are now building.

GIRAFFE:
Who's favored to win the prize?

ELEPHANT:
Michelangelo, of the brilliant blue eyes?

HIPPOPOTAMUS:
No, he's only a baby as yet.

GIRAFFE:
Though he'll design the Laurentian Library of great fame, you can bet!

KANGAROO:
And other masterpieces of enormous size.

HIPPOPOTAMUS:
I have been reading the Autobiography
Of Benvenuto Cellini . . .

GIRAFFE:
That's a good book—

ELEPHANT:
Here is Florence in its period of formation.

GIRAFFE:
And yet we live after Dante does.

HIPPOPOTAMUS:
Not if our creator wished to transform us
And transfer us to another period . . .

GIRAFFE:
Do you think he would do that?

ELEPHANT:
We're speaking of holier
Things perhaps than men should speak of—

HIPPOPOTAMUS:
Be quiet! I hear a cry!

(*It becomes darker. Enter the* ARNO RIVER—*it may be* YELLOWMAY *in disguise.*)

ARNO:
I am the famous Arno River
Which water to wonderful Florence supplies—
But have you thought of me at night, in dark,
How lonely and how odd I am . . . ?

GIRAFFE:
Good Lord! I hear a bird!
And you are the river of time as well!

(*Rush!! Everything is blown offstage, or gotten off somehow. Bright sunlight. The year 1266.*)

MAN:
They say a new baby's been born in our town—

SECOND MAN:
Yes, Dante Alighieri of famous renown.

MAN:
But who are these figures who walk toward us now

SECOND MAN:
Who seem of another age, bent the Lord knows how!

GIRAFFE, HIPPO, ELEPHANT, KANGAROO:
Oh alas alas!
We are that famous Arno, that flows unrecognized
In its true nature, and we
Are principally what isn't known about time,
And it's also true that death we are . . .

ELEPHANT:

Do you want information from the future? I have it now!

LORENZO DE MEDICI:

There's no time for that now! Here is Dante!

(Baby Dante is brought out on a silken cushion. Behind him, painted on a flat, is a Florentine crowd, principally ladies resembling those in the Dante and Beatrice "recognition scene.")

GIRAFFE:

Gosh, Elephant, it's Dante!

RULER:

Think of all this baby has to do!

(Enter, unobserved, YELLOWMAY, who shoots Baby Dante.)

YELLOWMAY:

Nothing that the future
Holds in store can be—

(YELLOWMAY is shot by Florentines. The Animals go to pick him up and take him off. They discover his River costume.)

ELEPHANT:

Why—it's the Arno!

KANGAROO:

From this day forth it will never be the same—

GIRAFFE:

On some future day

HIPPOPOTAMUS:

It will run dry.

(procession offstage)

FINAL CURTAIN

—1966

The Enchantment

An open place; it is dusk, a May evening. A young man, RINALDO, *enters.*

RINALDO: *(kneeling)*
    Oh winds that blow from left to right
    Make me an animal just for tonight
    I want to know how an animal feels
    I'm tired of jackets and of wheels
    I want to roam out of sight
    Lose myself in nature and so on
    Feel old godlike phenomenon
    Be me, in a new sense.

(GODS *appear above.*)

GODS:
    This one night shall we give to you
    Change to be any animal you wish
    And any animals.
    You may change the whole night through
    Being as many as you like.
    But if dawn find you any one animal
    That animal you must remain.

RINALDO:
    No fear of that
    Unless I find one that I so much like
    That it will be my choice
    Not only for tonight
    But every night.
    So I can be
    An animal for half a second or for ten long hours?

GODS:
    Yes. And now begin.
    There are some rules but they are ours.
    You'll feel them as you go along.
    Now start. What shall we turn you into?

RINALDO:
    A lion.

GODS:
A trite choice, but begin.

(RINALDO *becomes a lion.*)

RINALDO:
Rrrrroar. Ah help wait a minute
I'm in the middle of the city of Turin
How do I get out of here?

CITIZENS:
Capture the lion!

RINALDO:
Hmmm. I'm trapped. Don't want to kill
These people. Let me be a bird, a bald-headed eagle!

(*He turns into an eagle, and ascends to the skies.*)

Zoom! Here, flying through the skies
A lovely landscape I surmise
Below. On it human beings
With their human hearings and human seeings.
Ah! I'll head for that old cliff
Far from the Land of But and If. Oh this is freedom! ...
Now to a fish I'll change and dive—

(*He turns into a fish and starts to fall.*)

Wait a minute no, too late! I've got to arrive
At a stream. Let me be a sparrow

(*He becomes a sparrow.*)

Ha! straight as arrow
I'll go!
Now here below
Is stream—
An otter now I'll be. Splash.

(*He becomes an otter.*)

My motto now will be
Catch fish. Oh lovely water!

(GIRL *comes to edge of cliff before water.*)

GIRL:
Oh how sad I am and gloomy

My boyfriend it turns out is a big louse
He doesn't love me
Or in any case
He is untrue to me
That's the same difference, damn
Here in this lonely place
Where we used to make love
I will throw myself into the water!
But ho, what's this? An otter!

RINALDO:

Ah what a beautiful woman
Just like my sweetheart in my native land
Of Poland who died in an air crash!
I'll change myself—no not into a human
I would lose my magic night
But into something to attract her sight!
That's it. A peacock!

(RINALDO *turns into a Peacock and begins to drown.*)

Help! I'm drowning!

GIRL:

Good God that otter's turned into a peacock
All nature seems to be insane tonight!
My anguish makes me see things—it's not possible!
Still, I will wait and see.

RINALDO:

Glllg. Quickly. Let me be a dog, a swimming one!

(*He turns into a dog and swims out of the water.*)

Ah saved again. Now I'll swim back to shore
Change to a horse and let her stroke my sides
And ride me into the night!

(RINALDO *changes to a horse; he runs up and down the shore but can't climb the cliff.*)

GIRL:

I don't believe it! That which was otter then was peacock now
Is changed into a dog—and no, a horse
Now shaking water off runs 'round the shore
and seems to be trying to get up here to me!

RINALDO:

    I totally forgot a horse can't run
    Up a sheer cliff. I've got to be—a what?
    A gull to get up there! So, easily!

(turns into a gull and flies up)

GIRL:

    Oh no! I have gone crazy! What once was otter peacock dog and horse
    Now changes to a gull! Oh Benjy Benjy
    Look what your lying love has done to me!
    Now I'll jump off.
    What needs a crazy girl to stay?
    I might as well be dead!

(goes closer to edge of cliff)

RINALDO:

    Good Lord she's trying
    To kill herself again. What shall I be,
    A gull's not big enough, to make her stop?
    I know! A cow, and she may ride on me
    In fashion of Europa long ago!

GIRL:

    Oh destiny! What! a cow
    Blocking my way!

RINALDO:

    One that can speak . . .

GIRL:

    No no help I must get away!

RINALDO:

    Shall I be dove and follow? or be swallow?
    No matter what bird blue or white
    I'd only frighten her tonight.
    I've saved her from her death
    Tomorrow I'll come back when I'm a man
    Again.
    But let me now pursue my animal fate
    For I've done little and it's getting late!
    I've only dealt with human things so far.

(Enter starving deserted SOLDIER.)

SOLDIER:

My soul! a wandering cow!
And I a starving man, deserted from the war.
I'll milk it, straight.

RINALDO:

No, there are some things that are
Too utterly unfamiliar
And destined so to me to remain!
I cannot let myself be milked. Not pain
But strangeness makes me now determine
Thus to escape. Let me be an ermine!

(He becomes an ermine.)

SOLDIER:

The cow is gone. I'm dying of starvation.
Oh cruel nature! This was a delusion! Where gone? Moo moo.

(He wanders off, madly.)

RINALDO:

Oh I must bring him food. here, here's some berries.
I'll lug them at his feet. hey, starver, come!

SOLDIER:

My god a talking ermine or some little thing
Like that! But he's laid berries at my feet! Oh thank you God!

(He eats.)

RINALDO:

What a responsibility it is
To be an animal or bird, when people
Need so many things and act so insanely!
If I'm to experience total animal being
I must go to the jungle where no light
Of human intellect penetrates the total jungle night!
To get there I shall be
A hawk—vroom!

(RINALDO, now a hawk, rises into the sky. He is flying.)

Alas I see
The nearest jungle is too far from me
To get there in one night
And I only have this night

What can I do that most would give me
Outside jungles utmost animal sensitivity?
Being a mole
Deep into the earth. But first—I'm learning—
I'll land and find some suitable place for me
To dig into.

(He lands and becomes a mole.)

WOMAN:
Ack scream a mole!

RINALDO:
Well I shall be
An elephant then in some near zoo
But first a crow to take me there—
I don't like scaring people.

(He awaits his change from mole to crow. It comes, but slowly.)

WOMAN: *(horrified)*
Look at that mole!

(At last he is a crow, flying.)

RINALDO:
Ah ah that took a little longer time
Than all my other changes did I wonder
If night is ending faster than I thought?
Perhaps back into man I ought
To change but no I would not say
After this magic holiday
I had been nothing much—
Oh elephant legs sweet mine to touch
And elephant ears and eyes
Elephant trunk to twist around
And lift up to dark skies—
I want that once
Want that sensation once I want to be
A part of elephant earth! I go! O size
Gigantic! ivory tusks! why did I stay
In other forms on this huge night in May?

(RINALDO is now a crow flying over a zoo. At zoo wall stand two LOVERS.)

MAN (BOB):
> Look at that crow, love. Is it not a sign
> As Doctor Bodd predicted, that you always will be mine?

GIRL (SHEILA):
> Mmm. Hold me tight.

BOB:
> And there above the zoo peeps the first light
> Of ever-recurring dawn.

SHEILA:
> I love thee, Bob.

(RINALDO, *as a crow, flies into an empty elephant cage.*)

RINALDO:
> So now, climactic moment. In the dark
> Of this enormous indoors cage I shout
> To all my gods, make me an elephant! They do!

(RINALDO *becomes an elephant.*)

> My fate
> Is glorious! Huge legs, back straight
> Inclined. O earthy pleasure!
> Now you have come to me in full great measure!
> And I with deep content—

SHEILA:
> We must be going, Bob. See there!

RINALDO:
> Shall turn back to a man again—

(GODS *reappear.*)

GODS:
> TOO LATE!

RINALDO:
> Shall turn back to ma maeranheranh

BOB:
> I'll follow you. But if your parents find we're out, they'll kill us.

RINALDO: *(now completely and eternally an elephant)*
> Erooonh eroonh hegh hegh anktoongh aigh aigh

GODS:
    O Man, too late!

RINALDO:
    Eeroundg eeroundg

(full beautiful sunrise and dawn)

FINAL CURTAIN

—1966

E. Kology

ACT I

Scene 1

A field, with cherry trees. GAS MAN *runs along spraying the trees with gas.*

GAS MAN:
> Gassing the cherry trees here come I
> Perverting all nature beneath the blue sky!

(Enter E. KOLOGY.*)*

E. KOLOGY:
> Stop, mindless one!

GAS MAN:
> Who're you? What are you going to do? I am GAS MAN!

E. KOLOGY:
> E. Kology's the name
> I'm not assigning any blame
> But we're going to put you
> In a silver shoe
> And lace it up
> Then have a dachshund pup
> Sit on you and guard you
> Until you agree to give up
> Your everywhere pollution
> Which is a lousy solution
> To anything!

GAS MAN:
> You impudent young pup! Why, I'll—

E. KOLOGY:
> Don't ever speak in that style
> To E. Kology! Whoomp!

*(*GAS MAN, *about to hit* E. KOLOGY, *is felled by him with a magical wave of the hand.)*

> That will hold him for a while.
> Dears, put him in the shoe.

(Two GIRLS *come in and carry* GAS MAN *off. If available, a big silver shoe may be brought onstage and* GAS MAN *placed inside it, with a dachshund on top. Enter a lot of* GIRLS *and* YOUNG MEN.*)*

GIRLS:
   We're ten thousand lovely girls

YOUNG MEN:
   We are fellows, hair that curls

VOICE FROM OFFSTAGE:
   I'm the air, I'm such a darling

ALL THESE:
   Dear E. Kology, we're calling
   You!

E. KOLOGY:
   Of course. Hello. Well, what can I do?

MEN AND GIRLS:
   We've got a problem. We all exist
   By a river. At eve in mist
   So beautiful, but by day
   Sewage flowing away
   All filled with garbage.
   The name of the town is Star Ridge.

E. KOLOGY:
   Say
   No more. I'll be there in a minute!

Scene 2

A large plaza between the sanitation department building and the river. E. KOLOGY, SANITATION BOSSES, YOUNG MEN, *and* GIRLS.

E. KOLOGY:
   Sanitation
   Department, great fools, stop
   Putting garbage
   In Star Ridge Stream!

SANITATION BOSSES:
   What bus-
   Iness is it of yours?

E. KOLOGY:
    I am E. Kology!

(Music)

SONG, BY E. KOLOGY, YOUNG MEN, AND GIRLS:
    When the skies get full of smoke
    And to breathe becomes a joke
    Or when the water's full of gunk
    White meadows crowded with old junk
            It's time
    To get rid of all that slime
            Eliminate crime
    Against our Mother Earth
    For it's a trouble that she's worth
            By Calling E
        By calling me
            He's very real
        Not yet a part of mythology
        By calling me   By calling E
                E. Kology!

SANITATION BOSSES:
    We give in. The garbage will no longer be
    Dumped in the river.

YOUNG MEN and GIRLS:
    Hooray! For E.K.!

E. KOLOGY:
    And for you, too. Farewell!

(He goes.)

Scene 3

Dark gray sky of early dawn above a city. Nothing can be seen. Then a GODDESS *appears in the sky.*

GODDESS: *(from above)*
    I declare Ecology Day.

*(*GODDESS *vanishes. Now there is more light. It is morning, and the city is visible with people in the streets.)*

CITIZEN 1:
    They say E. Kology's going through the nation

Showing to everyone in no matter how high a station
How to fix things to preserve us, hey!

CITIZEN 2:
It's Ecology Day!

(*Evening begins. Darkness as of early dawn.* GODDESS *again appears in the sky.*)

GODDESS:
Ecology Day has ended and the nation's still full of junk.

(*Enter* E. KOLOGY.)

E. KOLOGY:
Well, I've started, anyway.

(*He leaves.*)

ACT II

Just outside a big paper mill.

PAPER EXECUTIVES:
Paper paper paper
We are making paper
We are making paper so the people can write
Then we go home at night
And stack up the paper
Money that we make by doing everything not right!

PEOPLE OF THE TOWN:
Fumes, what fumes, oh, pulp! What fumes!

(*Enter* E. KOLOGY.)

E. KOLOGY:
Gentlemen, you've got to change your methods
Right away, and I mean business!

PAPER EXECUTIVES:
Who are you?

E. KOLOGY:
E. Kology.

PAPER EXECUTIVES:
And why should we
Do what you want us to?

E. KOLOGY:

Because I'll make a giant fish
To place you on a silver dish
And gobble you away!

PAPER EXECUTIVES:

Ha ha!

(Forty YOUNG MEN *and* GIRLS, *in costumes suggesting fish, carry in a* BIG FISH *and hold it pointing at the* EXECUTIVES.*)*

BIG FISH:

Let me at 'em!

GIRLS, YOUNG MEN, and BIG FISH:

Fish we are whose every gulp
Poisons us with that damn pulp
They are manufacturing!
Let me eat them! That will show them,
They who kill the fish below them,
Better than all lecturing!

(During this speech the group has been advancing on the EXECUTIVES, *the* BIG FISH *still pointed at them.)*

PAPER EXECUTIVES:

No! no! We give in! Help!
We'll change our paper-making means today!

GIRLS, MEN, and BIG FISH:

E. Kology, come swim with us tonight
And you shall witness fishes' whole delight!

E. KOLOGY:

Not now, but thanks, great water creature!
I still have many tasks ahead, preserving nature!
And so, for now, farewell!

GIRLS, MEN, and BIG FISH:

E. Kology, farewell!

(He goes.)

ACT III

Scene 1

A big city, with CITIZENS.

CITIZENS:
> Our city is ruined
> By horrible gas
> And fumes!

OTHER CITIZENS:
> The automobiles
> Emit
> What seals our dooms!

(E. KOLOGY *appears, above, in a helicopter, or suspended from the sky.*)

E. KOLOGY:
> I'm designing a fume-free car!
> And soon you shall breathe all day
> As if Heaven's door were ajar,
> Which it is, O my loved ones!

CITIZENS:
> Hooray
> For E. Kology!

Scene 2

Big automobile office in Detroit, with three AUTO EXECUTIVES. *Enter* E. KOLOGY.

E. KOLOGY:
> I've perfected my car!

FIRST EXECTUVE:
> I won't do it!

SECOND EXECUTIVE:
> I won't do it!

THIRD EXECUTIVE:
> I won't do it!

E. KOLOGY:
> You'll do it, because—
> Arabella, come in!

(Enter a ravishing beauty attired as AIR.*)*

ARABELLA AIR:
  I am Arabella Air.

FIRST EXECUTIVE:
  Good God, Chrysler, she is fair!

ARABELLA AIR:
  I am fair and sweet to breathe—

SECOND EXECUTIVE:
  Chevrolet, gad! by your leave—!
  She's wonderful!

ARABELLA AIR:
  I am wonderful in how
  I caress your cheek and brow. . . .

(She lightly touches the faces of the three EXECUTIVES.*)*

THIRD EXECUTIVE:
  O Cadillac, I'm dying! . . .

E. KOLOGY:
  No, you are reviving!
  This is what fresh air can do for you.

THIRD EXECUTIVE:
  I want her!

FIRST AND SECOND EXECUTIVES:
  I do too!

E. KOLOGY:
  She can belong to all of you—
  Only the tiniest millionthest part
  Of her beauty was not in hiding.
  Come, girls blue!

(Enter a group of AIR GIRLS, *in blue gauzy garments suggesting air. They go to different places on the stage.)*

AUTO EXECUTIVES and E. KOLOGY:
  One for me, one for you
  Every one so fair and blue
  On the wall, behind your chair
  Out that window, everywhere!

E. KOLOGY:
Detroit itself's reviving!
Our earth shall have a long affair with blue!
Still work to do!

(He leaves.)

ACT IV

Africa. A HUNTER, *about to shoot a* KUDU *(a large, grayish-brown antelope with white markings)*. E. KOLOGY *enters.*

E. KOLOGY:
Hunter, stay your murderous hand!

HUNTER:
Fellow, I don't understand—
I *paid* to come out here!

E. KOLOGY:
Do not kill that kudu, friend,
Lest you make a species end
Or help to make it ending.

HUNTER:
Ah, I'm comprehending!
But aren't there lots of kudus?

E. KOLOGY:
They are very rare. Think if
There were but one red rose in all the world,
You wouldn't slice it up

HUNTER:
That's true.

E. KOLOGY:
Or tear
Its petals off.

HUNTER:
But roses are of beauty past compare—

E. KOLOGY:
And so, to truest vision, is the kudu—
Look at its eyes, its graceful motions there!

(The HUNTER *looks, and throws down his gun. The* KUDU *happily goes away.)*

HUNTER:

Sir, I will go with you and help you find
Ways to perform good actions for mankind.

E. KOLOGY:

Good hunter, thanks. Stay here instead
And help sweet Earth to move ahead
Fresh as in the earliest days. You'll have helpers!

(*Enter a lot of* GIRLS *and* YOUNG MEN *in costumes suggesting animals. They sing* "Lalala," *they surround the hunter and embrace him, and all go off together.* E. KOLOGY *remains for an instant, then leaves another way.*)

ACT V

An open place by the ocean. E. KOLOGY *alone.*

E. KOLOGY:

Well, now I have patrolled the entire world
And tried to stop pollution everywhere
And have had some success. At makers of detergents I have hurled
Thousands of plastic bottles and unfurled
A great blue flag with "PURITY" written there.
And I've worked also to preserve the world—
Its birds, beasts, fish, and plants beyond compare—
That they should not grow less. O lovely world,
You're better than we ever dared to guess. Well, I confess
I am in love with you.

(*Enter* TERRA, *the Earth, a beautiful young woman resembling Flora in Botticelli's* "*Spring.*")

TERRA:

And I love you as well, E. Kology!
You've brought mankind from almost killing me
To sometimes anyway thinking about me
And caring about me.

E. KOLOGY:

O beautiful Terra, you!

TERRA:

But should you let mankind see
That it is for love of me
You've done all this, E. Kology?

E. KOLOGY:

    Why not? Love makes the world go round
    Why should not love of world make me go round
    Doing my utmost for my love, the round-
    Ed utterly beautiful world?

(He takes her arm and they go to the top of a little dune or hill. Enter many YOUNG MEN *and* GIRLS *in clothes suggesting air, fish, animals, trees, plants, flowers, birds, and some dressed merely as people.)*

YOUNG MEN and GIRLS:

    We agree, E. Kology!
    May you and your lady be
    In our hearts forever!
    Portion out their smoky dooms
    To the dons of death and fumes
    And relenting never
    From our task until we all can say
    Oh happy Earthday, happy wedding day
    To everyone, but most, sweet earth, to you!
    Hooray!

E. KOLOGY:

    This show is but a prelude to that day!

*(*MEN *and* GIRLS *come and take* E. KOLOGY *and* TERRA *on their shoulders.)*

ALL:

    Let it come soon! Hooray!

(All go.)

Music and End

FINAL CURTAIN

—1966

The Moon Balloon

New York. A platform built around the center of Bethesda Fountain in Central Park. The Moon Balloon, an enormous plastic spaceship of balloon shape, with two MOONMEN, *is discovered, by spotlights, on one side of the fountain—stage right. On the other side of the stage are* MAYOR LINDSAY *and* COMMISSIONER HECKSCHER. *In the center a* BAND *is playing. It stops.*

MOONMEN:
    Pardon pardon pardon pardon could we see the mayor?

BANDLEADER:
    That is Mayor Lindsay, he is standing over there!
    But what are you strange people doing here on New Year's Eve?

MOONMAN:
    Human if I tell you will you promise to believe?
    We have come here from the moon

OTHER MOONMAN:
    From the moon, from the moon

MOONMEN:
    And we want to see the mayor!

LINDSAY:
    What's happening over there?

MOONMEN:
    Mayor Lindsay, we have come here from the moon.

HECKSCHER:
    Well, you can't park in Central Park! Get that thing out of here!

LINDSAY:
    No no dear Heckscher let them talk, let's hear what they will say
    And if they don't convince us, we will tow them all away!

(to MOONMEN*)*

    Moonmen, why did you come here?

MOONMEN:
    To help New York to have a good New Year!

ALL:

To help New York to have a good New Year!
But how can you do that?

MOONMEN:

Let us explain.
We have a special spray up there, called MOONGLOW
Which changes everybody for the best.
We saw the troubles you were having here
And knew that we could help you out, so here
We are. We'll take the worst you have and then
We'll magically transform them and send them down again.
New York will have a lovely lunar decade: the Seventies!
Thanks to MOONGLOW!

LINDSAY:

Well. . . . that *sounds* great. . . .

MOONMAN:

You'll see. Just wait!

(*Big noise from the* BAND. MOONMAN *goes to center stage and speaks as though addressing the whole city, in a high prophetic style.*)

Oh let the HORRORS of New York come forth!

(*Now a number of giant puppets, representing various bad things in New York, one at a time come up the ramp, move about on stage to show themselves to everybody, then stand center stage and speak to the audience. Each at some point in his or her speech notices the Moon Balloon and decides for one reason or another to get into it, and does so. The first of these creatures to come up the ramp is* SAM SMOG.)

SMOG:

I am awful hateful smog
More horrible than a raging dog!

(SMOG *sees Moon Balloon.*)

Ha! I'll leap inside this huge great ball
And who's inside I'll suffocate them all!

(SMOG *goes into Balloon.*)

HECKSCHER:

Well, that's good, John—our smog's gone to the moon!

LINDSAY:

I hope the Moonmen don't die from it. Soon,

Cough cough, I guess we'll know.

(Enter up ramp and onto stage LOUSY LANDLORD.*)*

LANDLORD:
  I a hateful landlord am, getting rich as Croesus!
  For you I do not give a damn, my buildings fall to pieces!

(sees Balloon)

  There's a piece of property I don't own yet!
  I will go inside and make it horrible, you bet!

*(*LANDLORD *goes into Balloon.)*

(Enter up ramp and onto stage CONNIE COCKROACH.*)*

COCKROACH:
  I am Connie Cockroach, a great big bug!
  I have lots of feelers and a horrible mug!

(sees Balloon)

  Here's an apartment I haven't yet seen—
  Ha ha ha I'll go into it, I'm so mean!

*(*CONNIE *goes into Balloon.)*

(Enter up ramp and onto stage NASTY NOISE.*)*

NASTY NOISE:
  Bang bang bang buzz honk shriek
  I am Nasty Noise, I hate for you to sleep!
  Crash crash bleep, honk bang scream!
  I am in your brainpan like a horrible dream!

(sees Balloon)

  Buzz shriek honk bang bang BOOM!
  I'll go drive people crazy in that funny-looking room!

*(*NASTY *enters Balloon amid a terrible din.)*

(Enter up ramp and onto stage HATEFUL HAG; *she carries a huge bag.)*

HATEFUL HAG:
  Ha ha all you people I'm Hateful Hag!
  All kinds of horrors I have in my bag!
  Pistols to shoot you with, tear gas, and knives—
  So give me your money and give me your lives!

I'll bang every one of you hard on the head,
Policemen and students and bakers of bread
And good guys and bad guys of white black and red
And leave you for dead, and leave you for dead
Ha HA ha ha HA ha, and leave you for dead—

(sees Balloon)

I'll go bop somebody in there!

(On her way to the Balloon, she turns again to audience.)

O New Yorkers, BEWARE!

(HAG gets into Balloon.)

(Enter up ramp and onto stage THE 1960S.)

THE 1960S:
I'm the Nineteen Sixties! Look at me!
You think soon that I will just be history!

(sees Balloon)

You think I'm leaving, but to fool you all
I am going to hide inside that great big ball!
Then, when you make your New Year's shout,
Instead of the new decade, I'll come out!
Instead of nineteen seventy you'll have a surprise:
Me, Sixties, coming back again, before your very eyes!
Ha ha Ho! What a dirty blow!
I am going to trick them all and nobody will know!

(THE 1960S gets into Balloon.)

(THE MOONMAN, believing that is all, goes over toward the Moon Balloon as though to close it up.)

MOONMAN:
Well, that must be the end.

(addressing the audience)

We'll take these awful creatures into space
And bring down lovely creatures in their place!
Now, OFF, then, to the moon!

VOICES FROM THE AUDIENCE:
Let us come too! Let us come too!
We're tired of life beneath the moon!

(Now a number of persons wearing masks come up the ramp from the audience. Unlike the previous six figures they know the Balloon is going to the moon, and each wants to go there for his own reasons. Each runs quickly up the ramp to the stage, faces the audience, speaks his lines, then runs into the Balloon.)

RUDOLF BING:
> I am Rudolf Bing, the Manager of the Met!
> I'll get in this thing and see how far I get!
> My opera's too expensive and too hard to get in
> So I'm going to the moon to drink a lot of gin!

TV ADVERTISING:
> I am TV advertising, how awful can you get?
> Whang bang zing! Have a cup of bloogle
> For white clothes—

FADED ROSE:
> And I, a faded rose!

MOONMEN:
> Hurry and get in! The ship is going to close!

VOICES:
> Wait! wait for me!

CON EDISON:
> I am Con Edison I want to expand!
> Making fumes in the air and making holes in the land!
> And now I want to dig up the moon!

TELEPHONE COMPANY: *(sugary voice)*
> I am your telephone, foe to your slumber—
> Ha ha you wake up, ha ha it's a wrong number.
> Brring I'm going to the moon
> To drive everyone crazy up there!

MOONMEN:
> All right, that's all!

THE DAILY NEWSMEN:
> Let us in! Oh don't refuse!
> We're writers for the *Daily News*!
> We want to spread our nasty feelings
> Wider than windows and higher than ceilings—
> New York is not enough—we want the moon!

MOONMAN:

Come. Whoosh! And now THAT'S ALL!

NIXON, AGNEW, and ROCKEFELLER:

Let us come too!

MOONMAN:

Well who are you, who come so late, to see the moon so yellow?

ROCKEFELLER:

The governor of New York State, Nelson Rockefeller!
Once upon the moon, I'd never need to spend a dime—
There, there are no CITIES wanting money all the time!

NIXON:

I am Richard Nixon, president of this land!
I want to spend some time among the Connie Cockroach band!
I think that I can use them—Lousy Landlord, Noise, and Hate—
To split America in two and keep me head of state!
New York will get no better, and only NIXON will be great!
Come, Spiro, you come too!

AGNEW: *(looking at the MOONMEN)*
Effete Blobs!

(All the MASKED PERSONS are now inside the BALLOON, and the MOONMEN stand outside it ready to close it up.)

MASKED PERSONS INSIDE BALLOON:

We're going to the moon, we're going to the moon, to the moon!
And nobody knows if we'll come back soon!
We've climbed into a rocket that is like a giant pocket
And we soon will be cavorting through the sky like a balloon.
We're going to the moon, we're going to the moon
And nobody will write to us or sing to us a tune
For we will be so far away, we can't come back till New Year's Day
We're going to the moon!

MOONMEN:

And there you all will change
As you shall soon discern!
You'll bring the nineteen seventies down
With you when you return!
Oh may it happen soon!
A New Year from the moon
A new year and new decade from the moon!

Ten years to make New York a place
As strong and clear as Outer Space—
A decade from the moon!

SMOG, COCKROACH, NASTY, LANDLORD, HAG, 1960S: *(from inside Moon Balloon)*
Help! Let us out of here! We don't want to leave
New York! Bang! Screech! Ouch! Horrible COCKROACH! Fume! Yecch! Ugh.
    Scream! Let us OUT! etc.

MOONMAN:
It's time to go!

(to the Moon Balloon)

Sweet sack,
Arise!
To the skies! To

BOTH MOONMEN:
MOONGLOW!

(As they say this, two MOONMEN *get into the Balloon. And it begins to rise into the sky. As it rises, the* BAND *plays and sings the song, "The Moon Balloon." The Moon Balloon vanishes. At the end of the song, however, it comes crashing back to earth. It lands where it was before, on the right side of the fountain.)*

BANDLEADER:
No! They've come back!

BAND:
Help! let's all get out of here!

BANDLEADER:
No—wait! It's very strange—
I have a feeling that they all have changed
Just as the moonmen said they would—

BAND:
It could be true. Let's wait and see.

(Each of the six HORRORS *of New York comes center stage to show and tell how he has changed.)*

(The former SAM SMOG *steps out.)*

(FORMER) SMOG:
Oh I the Smog have developed a flair—
Instead of all poison I've turned to Fresh Air!

So whether you're waking or whether you sleep,
Come, dear fellow citizens, breathe me in deep!

(dances and stands to one side)

(The FORMER LOUSY LANDLORD *steps out.)*

(FORMER) LOUSY LANDLORD:
I, Landlord, have returned from space
To make my land a lovely place!
I'm going to fix up all my property
Free of charge, and no more robbery!

(dances and stands to one side)

(The FORMER CONNIE COCKROACH *steps out.)*

(FORMER) CONNIE COCKROACH:
Formerly Connie the Cockroach, well I
Cocooned on the moon to a Blue Butterfly!
Instead of a house full of scurrying things
May your stairways be bright with my lovely blue wings!

(She shows her new blue wings, dances, and flutters off to one side.)

LINDSAY:
They really all have changed!
Moonmen, our thanks!

MOONMAN:
The change, John Lindsay's, largely due to you—
You gave us the idea you would welcome something new,
That's why we came. But here come more!

(The FORMER NASTY NOISE *steps out.)*

(FORMER) NASTY NOISE:
I who once was Nasty Noise
Now will bring you silent joys—
I left all my bangs and shrieks
On those lunar mountain peaks!
    I feel so good without them!
At just the stroke of midnight though
Let's make one last great noise to show
    How lovely silence is!

(dances and goes to one side)

(The FORMER HATEFUL HAG *steps out.)*

(FORMER) HATEFUL HAG:
    I, who once was Hateful Hag,
    Upon the moon have lost my bag!
        No more hate and killing!
    Now I am a LOVING MISS
    And will give you all a KISS,
        A great big hug and kiss is you are willing!
    Come, kiss me, everybody! Or kiss each other if you'd rather
    When it's the New Year!

(She dances and goes into the audience to kiss people.)

THE 1970S: (THE FORMER 1960S, *now* THE 1970S, *steps out)*
    Oh lovely lights! What have we here?
    Is this to celebrate me, the almost-born New Year?
    I who was once so sneaky was changed by moon moonshine
    To lovely nineteen seventy from nineteen sixty-nine!
    Soon it will be
    For you, I hope, as well as me, a ME—
    That is, a Happy New Year!

A VOICE:
    Happy New Year!

THE 1970S:
    No, not quite yet!

*(*THE 1970S *stands to one side.)*

(Now NIXON *and* ROCKEFELLER *come out, followed by the other* MASKED PER-SONS *who were in the Balloon.* NIXON'S *mask is now a yellow profile mask with a somewhat concave new-moon shape.* NIXON *carries two large sacks.)*

NIXON:
    The moon has turned my head around, I'm not at all the same!
    I think about the way I was and all I feel is shame!
    I brought the country war and darkness—now, to make it sunny,
    I'll give it peace in Asia, and I'll give its cities money!

(He hands one sack to ROCKEFELLER *and keeps one for himself. They reach inside the bags and shower gold coins on the audience.)*

NIXON:
    Oh spend it, Mayor Lindsay, on all that you need
    To make New York City a city indeed!

(NIXON, ROCKEFELLER, *and other* MASKED PERSONS *stand to the left and right.*
THE 1970S *now moves to center stage and speaks.*)

THE 1970S:
    Let us hope that these changes wrought by the moon's beams
    Are not just deceit and electoral schemes,
    And that what your words promise, you'll give!
    For we must have truth, and true peace, if we are to live!
    And now as a model to all of the nation
    Let's freely declare and dance our dedication
    To bringing a good life to everyone soon,
    Beginning in New York, and not on the moon!
        And so—this celebration!

(big fireworks display on the lake, in back of the fountain)

FINAL CURTAIN

—1969

The Gold Standard

A mountain shrine in China. Enter two MONKS.

FIRST MONK:

    Sit down. Now let us rest the burden here
    Of our exhausted mortal parts and speak
    Of things we do not understand. Commence.

SECOND MONK:

    Oft have I wondered when I hear men say
    That in their land the currency is solid
    Because it rests upon a base of gold.
    They call it . . .

FIRST MONK:

    The gold standard—

SECOND MONK:

    Yes, that's it!
    And often on some lonely winter night
    Which freezes traveler and his poor mount
    Who, wandering down some valley side, know not
    Which way to turn so as to find their rest,
    Oft have I heard men's conversation turn
    To gold and to that system too whereby
    The currency of any nation may
    Be given a solid base

FIRST MONK:

    By the gold standard.

SECOND MONK:

    Yes, "gold standard." But you who seem to understand
    Such fiscal matters, tell me now and briefly
    What this gold-standard fiscal system is.

FIRST MONK:

    That I shall try, though of success be never sure
    Till it has come unquestioned. Shall not I
    Use for example the United States
    For there I know the gold is in Fort Knox
    And all their currency is based on it?

SECOND MONK:
   It's well. Proceed.

FIRST MONK:
   Proceed to it I shall.
   But where shall I begin? Perhaps with coin,
   Yes that is where I should begin, because
   It's there the question rises. Let me see.
   If I have here a token in my hand
   Of wood or metal, and we say that it
   Is "worth five dollars," then what can we mean?

SECOND MONK:
   What is a dollar? Tell me that before
   You carry any further this great theme.

FIRST MONK:
   It is the coin of the United States.
   One says one dollar, two dollars, five dollars,
   Ten dollars, twenty dollars, ninety dollars,
   And so on to a billion. As for smaller
   Denominations, they are parts of dollars—
   A nickel, for example, is one-twentieth
   Part of a dollar, and a dime one-tenth.
   A penny is a hundredth part, a quarter
   A quarter part as one might well expect.
   There is among the coins also another,
   The half-dollar—and now my list's complete.
   So when I say one dollar now you will
   Know what I mean? or when I say a dime?

SECOND MONK:
   Perhaps I'd better have a record of it.
   Have you a plume? I'll write these figures down.
   Yes, now, that's it, I think I understand
   And if I do not I can look that up
   Upon the list which I forget to know.

FIRST MONK:
   Fine, now we have the list and have begun.
   Thus to more difficult matters. If I have
   A token in my hand of which 'tis said
   That is five dollars, in what sense can that
   Be said to have a meaning? That is to say,

Why should you give me, if I give you this,
This token that I say is worth five dollars,
Why should you give me rice, and fish, and ink?

SECOND MONK:

Because you are my brother, Cho Fu San,
And I would not deny you anything.

FIRST MONK:

I asked here for a monetary reason.
I know, Kai Fong, there is not anything
We'd not do for each other—but if I,
A stranger to you, held this token out,
Why should you give me meat or fish for it?

SECOND MONK: *(smiling)*

Why, I would recognize you, Cho Fu San—
That scar upon your hand which healed the cut
You got in gathering branches in last year
So we could make the fire at Ho Ku Temple
Where they had for a time run out of fuel.
You were much praised for that. Could I forget
A deed so noble or a hand so marred
By what it did for selflessness? Besides,
Even if you had no scar upon that hand,
What if I did not know your name or face,
What if you came to me and asked for fish
And held a token out—would I not give?
Is not our duty still toward all who need?

FIRST MONK:

I now perceive
How far the concept of all payment is
From your enlightened soul. Yet I'll explain
In a more fundamental way, so that
You may perceive it clearly—for, who knows?
Such knowledge may empower us some day
To do some good we do not know of now.
Attend! You know in the non-priestly world
That men instead of bartering, that is,
Giving a fish for rice, or trees for seed,
Or wives for cattle, or spun silk for tea
Have worked a system out in which there is
Some kind of general substance which is used

To represent the barter value of
Each kind of thing one needs.

SECOND MONK:
    I do not know
    Exactly what you mean by "value," brother.

FIRST MONK:
    Explain.

SECOND MONK:
    Well, if I give you green tea leaves,
    Say half a pound of them and you give me
    In fair exchange three pounds of rice, shall not
    We say then, that the "value" of a pound
    Of rice can be computed at one-third
    A half-pound of green tea?

FIRST MONK:
    That is, one sixth,
    Yes, one sixth of a pound of green tea leaves
    Would be the "value" of a pound of rice.
    You seem to me to understand the concept.

SECOND MONK:
    Wait! If another brother, passing by,
    Has urgent need of rice, and offers me
    Six pounds of green tea leaves for what I have
    What is the "value" of the green tea then
    And of the pound of rice?

FIRST MONK:
    The pound of rice
    Is worth six pounds of green tea leaves.

SECOND MONK:
    Then you,
    If you should wish to buy your own rice back,
    Would find that with your half a pound of tea
    You could buy but one-twelfth of a pound of rice.
    If then you wished some tea along with rice
    And tried to purchase some green tea from me
    At what we had agreed to be the "value"
    Of half a pound of tea, you would receive
    For all your rice but one-twelfth of one-sixth

Of one pound of green tea, which is, I think,
One seventy-second of a pound of tea.
Then if you tried to buy some rice from him
Who had the rice you sold him, and perhaps
By chance had now some more, for all your tea
You would receive, I must take plume and paper,
One seventy-two times six, four thirty-second,
One four hundred and thirty-second part
Of a pound of rice is all you would receive.
Then if you wished—

FIRST MONK:

Stop, brother! you are driving me insane!
I have not followed you. I am all lost
In these fine figurings. Let me begin
Another way, that all shall not be lost.

SECOND MONK:

Lost surely to you were much rice and tea
In what I figured out, which I imagine
Was accurately tuned to what you'd said.
Perhaps all currency is chaos—

FIRST MONK:

No,
Let me explain again. At least I'll try.
For night is going past.
And we, in this part of the subject, are
Still far from understanding what the "base"
Of currency may be, and how a standard
Of gold or silver can sustain its value.

SECOND MONK:
But "value"—

FIRST MONK:

Kai Fong, I said that I would try.
I know that "value" is not clear just yet
And yet it is an ordinary concept
Which I am certain we can understand
Together, let me but find the proper words.
In the example that you gave just now,
You spoke of two discreet ideas of value—
For me, the rice was worth less than the tea,
And so for you, at the time of our exchange.

SECOND MONK:

    Yes, I can vouch for that. For you gave me
    For three whole pounds of rice only one half
    A pound of green tea leaves.

FIRST MONK:

    But this was done
    By our agreement; we did not dispute
    The value of these things.

SECOND MONK:

    Yes, for the sake
    Of finishing our discussion, let us say
    That we agreed, although I do not remember
    How we agreed, or why.

FIRST MONK:

    Then let us say,
    That we agreed and that there was a reason
    We came to this agreement, which was this:
    That there is only a given amount of rice
    In China and a given amount of tea.

SECOND MONK:

    The man who can find out such vast amounts
    Must be some sort of Buddha at the least—
    For who could know such things?

FIRST MONK:

    Why, men may go
    To all the villages and ask each man
    How much of rice he has and how much tea.

SECOND MONK:

    But this would take a thousand thousand years.
    China is vast.

FIRST MONK:

    True—and perhaps there is no need
    To go to every village in the country—
    Perhaps it is enough to know how much
    Rice and tea there are in one's own village.
    Then, if one finds there are ten thousand pounds
    Of rice, and fifteen thousand pounds of tea,
    One can compute that for one pound of rice
    One should receive a pound and a half of tea.

SECOND MONK:

> Yes, I have checked it with my plume
> And paper, and I find you are correct.

FIRST MONK:

> Thus can each village figure for itself
> The price of rice in tea or tea in rice.
> Then if, say, Village Chu should be the one
> In which one pound of rice is worth of tea
> One pound and a half, and if in Village Cheng
> There were eighteen thousand pounds of rice and nine
> Thousand pounds of tea, so that for one
> Pound of rice one got one half-pound of tea,
> Then it would be in the interests of the men of Chu
> To take their tea to Cheng and sell it there;
> So men of Cheng would sell their rice in Chu.
> Eventually there would be established
> A common rate for rice and tea which was
> Observed in Cheng and Chu.

SECOND MONK:

> Which I suppose
> Would be—let's see—the total of the rice
> In both towns is twenty-eight thousand pounds,
> Of the tea twenty-four thousand—both can be
> Divided, seven to six. Yes tea would be
> Worth one and one-sixth pounds of rice per pound.

FIRST MONK:

> See what a brilliant light the moon throws now
> Upon our humble floor of straw and reeds!
> So man by guidance of superior light
> May understand his world.

SECOND MONK:

> And we may see
> How little we have fathomed yet of all
> We have set out to know. Distant still seems
> The goal of understanding this our subject.
> For what has gold to do with where we are now?

FIRST MONK:

> If it is decided
> That for one pound of tea one can receive

One and a sixth pounds of rice, then one can say
Let this wood token serve to represent
One-sixth of a pound of rice. With six of these
One can obtain a pound of rice, with seven
One can obtain a pound of tea.

SECOND MONK:
But why
Would anyone take that which "represents"
In change for that which is? A sketch in ink
May "represent" this mountain, yet I would not
Take it in fair exchange.

FIRST MONK:
Of "represent"
Two meanings are there—other is the one
I took than that which you have understood.
And yet it serves to introduce the next
Step in the argument that binds us here.

SECOND MONK:
I wished to know, since I cannot eat wood
But must eat rice, why I would take this wood
And give good rice for it.

FIRST MONK:
The reason is
That for "this wood," if given in trade
You could receive the same amount of rice
You traded for the wood. Or, if you wished,
Six-sevenths of a pound of tea.

SECOND MONK:
And yet,
What if I traded all my tea for wood
And all my rice for wood, then had much wood,
A thousand thousand thousand pounds of wood
And what if no one wished to have my wood,
Would I turn termite then to eat my wood
Or would I simply starve for lack of rice
And die of thirst for lack of steaming tea
Which fills the soul with purpose and delight
And reverence for all being? I should not,
I think, give any of my rice for wood
Or any of my tea.

FIRST MONK:
    The deepest shades
    Of ebony-black night by now are past;
    Some stars are gone; few others through the fog
    Are shining still; much time does not remain
    Till we once more, at dawning, must descend
    Into the hills and valleylands below.
    I wish, before that come, that on this night
    Some further understanding yet might be
    Generously given us by One above.
    Perhaps I see a way: what if this wood,
    Which I agree with you necessity
    Would not require to be desired by many
    And certainly not all, what if this token
    Were made, instead, of gold?

SECOND MONK:
    A thing of beauty!
    A rare thing also! I would gladly give
    Some tea or rice for it, for then I could
    Carve a sweet Buddha from it which I'd place
    In great Gautama's honor in some shrine!

FIRST MONK:
    We have not yet
    Arrived at this great argument's full course!
    New difficulties show at every turn
    And we must show brave hearts to carry on!
    What if you did not make a statuette
    Of all this gold you had, but if you kept it
    And used it, some perhaps for sculpturing,
    But other pieces of it to buy tea
    And rice and clothing, to acquit yourself
    Of every human need, nor be obliged
    To carry rice and tea around with you
    To barter for each single thing you wanted?
    Would that not be a great convenience
    And joy and boon to man?

SECOND MONK:
    I think I see.
    The gold would "represent" the rice and tea
    Yet also have a value of its own.

FIRST MONK:

   Yes, and all persons would agree on it.

SECOND MONK:

   What if some person should not care for gold?

FIRST MONK:

   Why, he would learn he could get tea for it,
   So he would treasure it as he did tea.

SECOND MONK:

   I think I see. So by a general process
   Of village into village, state through state,
   The general value of a pound of tea
   Is fixed, as is the value of an ounce
   Of gold; but how is gold distributed?
   What if a man have only rice and tea?

FIRST MONK:

   Why, he can sell some rice and get some gold.

SECOND MONK:

   But what if no one in the country 'round
   Have any gold? What would they use for money?
   Would they go back to bartering again?

FIRST MONK:

   I do not know. Perhaps the government
   Would have in every village people doing
   Governmental jobs for which they'd pay them
   In quantities of gold, then gradually
   This gold would be distributed about
   So that each person had some, and each town.

SECOND MONK:

   If gold were scarce, might not men hoard it then
   And melt it into ingots, from which they
   Might mold great Bodhisattvas fair as heaven?
   And if sufficient number acted so
   There would not be much gold about, and so
   Men would go back to barter once again.

FIRST MONK:

   Too true. The only answer then would be
   To find more gold and turn it into coins.

SECOND MONK:

> And these, in turn, when hoarders got to them
> Would vanish into Buddhas. And besides,
> The supply of gold, you said, was limited.

FIRST MONK:

> We may be closer than we thought we were
> To the chief subject of our argument—
> Which is how gold which is not used can give
> "Value" to coins and paper bills which are.
> Where we are now, it seems to me, is this:
> That there are serious reasons for not using
> Gold as currency; and one is hoarding.

SECOND MONK:

> What might another be?

FIRST MONK:

> Gold wears away.
> It is a metal generally soft.
> With constant use the wealth of any nation
> Would gradually decrease, a sorry thing.

SECOND MONK:

> So paper, then, and other things are used
> In place of gold—but since they have no value,
> Or do not have the value of the gold,
> Why do men count them as if they were gold?

FIRST MONK:

> That is the mystery of the gold standard
> Which now we must attempt to understand.

SECOND MONK:

> Cho Fu San, I had a thought.

FIRST MONK:

> What is it, dear Kai Fong?

SECOND MONK:

> It did occur to me that I have heard
> That the United States no longer used
> What we have called gold standard, but instead
> The silver standard for its currency.

FIRST MONK:

    Your words ring true.
    I do remember that that is the case.
    I had forgot. Yet still we have not lost
    These precious hours of night, for I perceive
    We have but one more step to understand
    Once we have seen what the gold standard is.

SECOND MONK:

    What is it, Cho Fu San?

FIRST MONK:

    To understand
    How the gold ingots buried in Fort Knox
    Can guarantee the value of the paper
    In silver, which I think should be quite clear.
    For once one knows how much a pound of silver
    Is worth in gold, then one can calculate
    How much a piece of paper backed by gold
    Embedded in the earth is worth in silver.

SECOND MONK:

    I take it that the silver is not buried
    Instead of gold because, being less precious
    They would need more of it, a great deal more,
    And thus would have to dig a larger cavern
    And labor terribly to carry down
    Into the cavern so much weight in silver.

FIRST MONK:

    And, besides,
    The huge amount of gold now buried there
    Would have to be transported to the surface—
    And what, exactly, would they do with it?

SECOND MONK:

    Why, they could give it in exchange to those
    Who gave the silver that they placed in earth.

FIRST MONK:

    Would people give the silver? I believe
    That they would bury governmental silver.

SECOND MONK:

    How would the government obtain the silver?

FIRST MONK:

    From silver mines belonging to the state.

SECOND MONK:

    Has it much silver now?

FIRST MONK:

    I do not know.
    In any case, the gold is buried still
    And it is used to guarantee the value
    In silver of the paper and the coins.

SECOND MONK:

    Dear Cho Fu San, some aspects yet unclear
    Are to my spirit. Why should I accept
    A piece of paper for a pound of rice
    Because some gold is buried in the earth
    Which I can neither use, nor hoard, nor see?

FIRST MONK:

    I think perhaps that you would have the right
    At any time to give the government
    The piece of paper and receive that gold.

SECOND MONK:

    What? would they dig it up? Suppose each person
    Should trade in all his paper bills for gold?
    Then there would be no ingots in the earth
    Nor any paper bills. Then we should have
    Gold coins again—

FIRST MONK:

    Perhaps this is the reason
    The country has gone on the silver standard.
    The gold remains to guarantee the value
    Of coins and paper money, but one cannot
    Obtain the gold in fair exchange for it,
    But only silver.

SECOND MONK:

    Where, if not in earth,
    If not in some voluminous Fort Knox,
    Is all the silver kept which would be needed
    To give to everyone in fair exchange
    If all decided to turn in their money
    For silver bars?

FIRST MONK:

Kai Fong, I do not know.
Besides, if all these silver bars existed
What need would be to have the buried gold?
For silver itself would guarantee the value
Of every coin and bill.

SECOND MONK:

Oh Cho Fu San,
Our cerebrations now must reach an end.
The morning rises, and the mist that clears
Reveals a lightsome snow which promises
A perilous descent. Come on, old friend—
Let those who need possessions puzzle out
The snaggles of this argument. For us,
Who live by other lights, what we have learned
This evening seems enough.

FIRST MONK:

I come, old friend.
The trail is difficult.

SECOND MONK:

Here, take my arm.
We shall find other shelter once below.

FINAL CURTAIN

—1975

The Red Robins

To Don, Kate, and Vanessa

DRAMATIS PERSONAE

THE RED ROBINS, *a group of young pilots, each with his or her own airplane. They have come to Asia in search of excitement and adventure:* BOB, JILL, BILL, JIM, LYN, LOUIS, BUD.

SANTA CLAUS, *a powerful middle-aged man who is now a sort of leader of the* RED ROBINS. *Some things about his appearance suggest he is the traditional Christmas figure, others that he is not.*

THE EASTER BUNNY, *also middle-aged, the powerful enemy of* SANTA CLAUS *and the* RED ROBINS. *His traditional holiday identity is as ambiguous as that of* SANTA CLAUS.

THE PRESIDENT *(of the United States), middle-aged, appears in two guises—as the Good President and as the Bad President.*

AIDE *to the* PRESIDENT.

THE MAN IN THE YELLOW COAT, *a retired Western diplomat living in Shanghai and devoting his life to philosophy.*

JILL'S FATHER *and* JILL'S MOTHER, *a middle-aged couple from Minneapolis.*

CAPTAIN *(of a ship)*

MEINHEER PUSHNER, *an old, retired Dutch-Irish colonial official who is spending the last days of his life on a small tropical island.*

FIRST *and* SECOND NATIVE BEARERS

NI SHU, *an old and very celebrated Chinese philosopher.*

MOTHER *and* CHILD, *characters in* JILL'S *dream and residents of Tin Fan.*

MARIAN, *an island girl, a love slave.*

MIKE THE TIGER, *a man-eating tiger.*

THE SLIMY GREEN THINGS

DOG

OCTOPUS

TERRENCE, *a treacherous ape.*

FIRST *and* SECOND APE, *political leaders of L'Isola non Trovata.*

BIRD, *a mysterious talking bird.*

THE STARS

JIM THE PLANT

PYOTOR, *a gland*

ROUGHIE, *a stone*

ELIA, *a possibility.*

Also, WAITER, APES, MONKS, SHARDS, COLD BACHELORS, *others.*

ACT ONE

Scene 1

The springtime morning sky above Asia. Birdsongs. Then the sound of airplanes. The RED ROBINS *appear in their planes.*

BOB:

 Jill, that's the place, I think—look over there!
 Mount Kin-to-pang! Those rocky, snowy slopes
 Lead down to Inner Malay, where we're going
 To hunt man-eating tigers.

JILL:

       Yes! I see it.

BOB:

 And after that, we'll go to Ching Tang Palace
 Where we will get the Map That Shows All Rivers,
 Including the Five Rivers of the Air—

BOB:

 Look, up ahead—

JIM:

 It's—Occhu Bocchu, Aplaganda Lake,
 That celebrated haunt of octopus!
 And, through that mist beyond those plains, Shanghai,
 The City of Golden Stairways!

LYN:

       I can't see it.

LOUIS:

 It's still in mist. We should start going down.
 The Hindu monastery where I stayed
 Two years, just flashed beneath us, on the left.
 I think that's Tiger Jungle five miles off.

BUD:

   You're right. Bob, do you want to lead us in?

BOB:

   Yes! Jill, stay here beside me. Bud, go back
   And steady our formation from the rear.
   Apprise us of all dangers. Let's descend!

BILL:

   We'll follow you.

Scene 2

A Plateau in Malaya, where the RED ROBINS *have landed. They are all there, except for* BOB, *who enters.*

BOB:

   Bill, get the guns! Let's go! I heard the tiger!

JILL:

   I think we really ought to wait some more.
   He said that he was coming.

BILL:

   We should wait.

BUD:

   We did receive the message yesterday
   That, after such long time, he'd meet us here
   And make the hunt with us.

BOB:

                              He's late!

JILL:

                              He'll come!

LYN:

   If he said he would meet us here, he will.

JIM:

   Well, I don't know! Some one of us could stay here
   To meet him, wait for him, the rest go on . . .

BILL:

   I gladly would.

BOB:

   Well . . .

(Sounds of a plane crashing. Enter SANTA CLAUS, *a bit staggered at first. He has just made a crash landing.)*

BOB:

Well, no one has to stay to meet him now!

JIM: *(to* SANTA CLAUS)

How good it is to have you back with us!
How are you? Are you well? We have been wondering.
We haven't been together since November!

SANTA CLAUS:

Had a hard landing! Robins! My sweet friends!
My bunch! Sweet collaborators, all,
In the adventures of the human heart!
God, but it's good to see you! I have been
Away so long, not out of choice, my friends,
But trapped in battle with that monstrous fiend
Who hates us, who brings shivers of revulsion
To all who care for life, that vile debris
Whose name you know so well.

BOB:

                    Battling with . . . HIM?

SANTA CLAUS:

The EASTER BUNNY! Yes, that mass of horror!
I thought him dead, at last—I had him caught
Inside the stony mass of Mount Kabongo,
But he punched his way out and followed me
Without my knowing, through the Burmese sky.
Just now he almost killed me, hit my plane
With fighter bullets strong as bolts of lightning!
But I hit his as well, and left him burning,
Unable to go on.

JILL:

                    Why does he hate us?

SANTA:

I've never known, but have supposed that he
Is jealous of my holiday celebrity—
Greater, he knows, than his. And then, again,
He envies our Red Robin happiness.
He is morose, alone.

BILL:
> Could something cure him?

SANTA:
> Perhaps. But perhaps not. In any case,
> I think that he will cause us no more trouble,
> Not for a long, long while. Of this enough,
> Of him enough. I come to bring good news.
> You got the letter that I sent you? Good.
> Well, there is something else. Within a twelvemonth
> The airways will be clear, and we'll be able
> To try to reach that place, to fly, and land there,
> Which we have so far scarcely dared to speak of
> It seemed so out of reach—And, if we can . . .

LYN: *(Excited)*
> You mean—do you mean—can it be—

SANTA CLAUS:
> TIN FAN!   *(A gong sounds.)*
> Yes, we perhaps at last may see Tin Fan,
> The legendary city of the East
> Where there is perfect happiness—TIN FAN!

(Another gong. SANTA CLAUS *pauses for a moment.)*

> But now, let's go to the jungle, and the heat
> Of hunting tigers! We have vowed we would,
> A long time past, come help the Malays kill
> The great man-eater, bane of all their lives!

(They go off.)

Scene 3

Jungle

(Enter BILL.*)*

BILL:
> I've tried it, but I can't. This hunting no.
> I'd hunt for anything, but not to kill,
> Not kill what never had done harm to me.
> I know this Malay beast has eaten men,
> But I don't think it's fair that twenty people
> Should follow him with guns. I'd gladly stand
> Against him one to one. But I can't hunt him.

(A thrashing sound in the brush. BILL *turns about, thinking it is the* TIGER, *and aims his rifle. But it is* LYN.)

LYN:

Bill! I am not the tiger! Listen! Listen!
I think they've found him. How are you? I wondered—

BILL:

There are no tigers any more. No tigers.
I hate this hunt. I wish that it would end.

LYN:

I'll stay with you.

BILL: *(much happier now)*

Intoxicating friend!
Say why we should kill tigers, or they us?
Let love be all, be our sole blunderbuss!

*(*BILL *embraces* LYN, *then they walk off.* BOB *enters, holding* MIKE THE TIGER *by the tail.)*

BOB:

I've got the tiger, caught him by the tail,
And now, by God, we'll find a way to shoot him!
Robins, help!

*(*MIKE *escapes. Enter* SANTA CLAUS, BUD, JILL, JIM, *and* LYN.*)*

BOB:

I had the tiger, but he got away!

SANTA CLAUS:

We'll find him!

BUD:

Damn! *(All run off. Re-enter* MIKE THE TIGER.*)*

MIKE:

My name is Mike, and I am a man-eating tiger. My kind stems from up around Kuannon, which is an old Indian word for "ring-face," and I guess that region must have gotten its name from us tigers who wear upon our brownish-red faces one and sometimes two or three medium-sized white rings. Sometimes, when the harvest is good and the sheep are fat, I like to pounce down into the valley and carry off some plump little lambs to my den and eat them. But whether the harvest is good or not, my favorite food is men. Men have a *je ne sais quoi,* I guess you could almost say it was an "intellectual" flavor, that kind of flavor you can only develop after you have spent a few years engaged in speculative thought. It's like the patina on some of the beautiful Chinese jars that some of these men have made. It's an "extra." As we tigers say, "Man is the only animal who is his own sauce." I don't blame them for trying to kill us! How would you like to have somebody after you who wanted to eat you?

(Enter JIM THE PLANT.*)*

JIM THE PLANT:

I am a tropical plant. My name, for you, is Jim. I have a more complicated name in plant language, a language which is completely unnoticed not to say undeciphered and which, even if it were discovered, would make the decipherment of Linear-B seem like child's play. At any rate, to continue. Now, I like tigers because tigers don't like plants. There are two ways of liking, obviously enough. I don't like to eat tigers or, really, to do anything with them, but I like the fact that they don't want to do anything to me. Do you like me? If so, which way do you like me of the two ways I have named?

(Enter PYOTOR, *a gland.)*

PYOTOR:

I am a gland, a part of a redbird's body. Without me the bird would not function normally but would flap wildly around on one wing, screaming its head off. In fact, it is doing that now, because I am not "doing my part" but am, instead, talking to you. My name is Pyotor (in gland language), I live in the jungle inside this bird, and I am the organ which gives him his sense of balance and his ability to control his actions.

(Enter ROUGHIE, *a stone.)*

ROUGHIE:

My name is Roughie and I am a stone. You have walked over me many times and not noticed me. I don't blame you at all. But when you need a stone, to crush a rattlesnake or an asp, then, then you run through the jungle shouting, "Where is Roughie? Oh where is a stone? I'd give anything to find a stone!" Why don't you stop to appreciate me now?

(Enter ELIA, *an as-yet-undiscovered possibility.)*

ELIA:

My name is Elia. I am a possibility which has not yet been discovered by mankind or by animals. I am ignorant. I don't even know whether I am a solid, a liquid, or a gas, an idea, or an emotion. I am motionless. The rattlesnake moves right through me, and the Tibetan monkey-bear. Yes, you are right, I do know about other things, but I know nothing about myself. Please find me. I will love you if you do—if I am capable of that.

(Darkness. All leave.)

Scene 4

A Malay hospital room. JIM *and* BILL *are there, and* LYN, *who is in bed, sleeping, feverish. She wakes up.*

LYN:

> Oh! ah! what? Help! Gland! Roughie! Jim! What?
> Tiger . . .

JIM: *(leans over her)*

> Lyn, Lyn, you have had a bad dream and that is all!
> Wake up! Wake up! There was no tiger hunt!

BILL:

> But, Jim—there was!

JIM:

> Better to let her feel
> That she was only dreaming, that it all
> Was nothing but a nightmare. She is ill.
> She needs to rest and sleep.

BILL:

> Well, I'll away
> To other precincts on this woeful day!

(BILL *leaves.*)

LYN: *(to* JIM)

> But—but, was it all a dream? I saw the tiger
> And HEARD HIM SPEAK. That was the worst of all.
> Do tigers speak? And then a redbird's body
> Or part of it, a gland. And there was Roughie
> A stone, and something unknown, named Elia . . .

JIM:

> You know, the jungle
> Is full of things that almost speak to us—
> Not ever, really. Now, it's best you sleep
> To get rid of the fever. When you're stronger
> Perhaps we two can puzzle all this out.
> I'll stay here while you're sleeping.

LYN:

> Well, good-night!

(LYN *sleeps.*)

JIM:

    Strange that back in America I was,
    True, a good student, but mostly interested
    In engineering and other applied science.
    That got me interested one day in airplanes
    From the mechanical aspect of the thing.
    Once I discovered them, I hardly slept
    But kept on working at them day and night,
    Tinkering with their engines and their wings.
    And there seemed to come to me in the night
    Visions of a surprising kind on which
    My body was an airplane, or my spirit,
    Whatever it is we think of as the soul,
    And that it flew me anywhere I wished.
    I met, that year, two people, Bob and Jill,
    Who seemed to me some way the way I was.
    They both loved airplanes. Jill liked poetry
    And got me interested in that. They spoke
    Of Asia as a place where we might find
    Some consummation, some amazing answer
    To everything, but what we'd see and do—
    It made no sense to go there—but we went!
    Soon there were more and we became a group
    And called ourselves Red Robins. And we stayed.
    And I met Lyn, who's lying here asleep,
    Dreaming of roses now, I hope, not tigers
    And frightful things from those unconscious depths
    Which plague us humans all our lives whenever
    Some little disk has slipped inside our minds.
    Yes, I met Lyn. And also there began
    A curious revolution of my spirit
    Which made me less and less an engineer
    And more and more a poet. I began
    To write! and, writing, felt I had discovered
    The secret motions of the soul and body
    Which were, precisely, those my self became
    When I went flying, nightly, in my dreams.
    These poems, they seem hardly a natural thing,
    Surely not natural they should seem so strange,
    So necessary, and so immanent—
    They are just notes on paper, after all!
    And yet to me they seem more permanent,

Inspiring proof of happiness than all
The mountainous sides of Asia's God-hewn summits
Which leave us grasping on their slopes. Well, each
Is part of what I feel and know we are . . .

(turning to LYN*)*

Sleep soundly. I shall come to thee anon.

(Now JIM *sits down at a table and writes. Enter* SANTA CLAUS *and* JILL. *Their words are what he is writing.)*

SANTA CLAUS:
The love I feel for you, Jill, is so deep
That I can scarcely understand its force.
I thought you were too young for me. I thought
That thirty years made differences too steep
For hearts to cross, but I see I was wrong.

JILL:
Whenever I awake, or when I sleep,
When silent, or when busy with discourse,
When sitting, lying, walking, I am caught
By feelings of a sort I cannot keep
From speaking of to you, they are so strong.
You know—I love you!

SANTA CLAUS:
You love me, too?
Fade, Mount Kabongo, in your circling mist!
Fade house! Fade, palm trees! fade, all I have known
Up to this moment, sacreder to me,
Than gold to misers, pollen to the bee,
Or Asia to us all!

(They embrace, then leave.)

JIM: *(looking up from his writing)*
I'll finish later. So far it's pretty good,
It seems to me a sort of play in poetry.
There is another part I have in mind
About an island and a war with apes.
She's waking up!

LYN:
Well, I feel better.

(SANTA CLAUS *runs in.*)

SANTA CLAUS:
    Hurry! Lyn, are you better? Ah, I'm glad!
    If so, let's hurry! There is news that we
    May soon have dealings with the President
    Of the United States!

JIM:
                How can that be?
    What's he to do with us, or we with him?

SANTA CLAUS:
    I don't know, but he's coming.

LYN:
                Oh how strong
    This feeling is, that I approach my fate
    And never can escape it!

(JIM *sees her consternation and goes over and embraces her. She trembles.*)

JIM:
                My sweet love!

Scene 5

The White House. A private chamber. The PRESIDENT *sits at his desk, re-reading a letter he has written.*

PRESIDENT:
    "Dear Lyn . . ." I wonder if she'll believe I'm writing
    To ask her for her hand. No, it's too ridiculous.
    I love her, but it's crazy. I'll tear this up!

(*He tears up the letter and then sets fire to it. Smoke. Enter, in haste, a White House servant—he is really the Red Robin,* BUD, *in disguise.*)

BUD: (*affecting a German accent*)
    Sir, Sir, vot is de trouble here? Vere from de smoke?

PRESIDENT:
    Oh, it's nothing. A letter I was writing.
    Here, young man, take these ashes off for me.

BUD:
    Dot I vill.

PRESIDENT:
Thanks much.

(He goes out.)

BUD: *(dropping the German accent and revealing his true identity)*
. . . And will
Survey their contents for I much suspect
(I am Bud, Red Robin of a long renown)
They have some matter relevant to us . . .
Ha! Here's the burned name "Lyn." "I love you"—What?
Our President loves Lyn? How curious!
He is a man I thought was too important
To care about such things. I'll take this letter
To Santa Claus. Away!

(BUD rushes off.)

PRESIDENT: *(re-enters)*
Curse! damn, damn, curse! that she's so young and I so eminent!
O would I were a worm upon the ground
Of foul Tibet, that I might touch her foot! Alas, no help!
My words rise up, but I remain below.
We Presidents were ever fettered so!

Scene 6

An airfield, on a plateau. BUD *runs to* SANTA CLAUS *with the letter.*

SANTA CLAUS: *(reading it)*
Thank goodness you got there in time!
Ho! everybody! The President isn't coming after all!

BUD:
Let us away, then, to Shanghai.

SANTA CLAUS:
Good!
I'll go there first to make sure all is safe.

Scene 7

A party, on a dark night in the jungle. All the RED ROBINS *are there except for* BOB. *Some are dancing. The atmosphere is hushed and romantic.*

(Enter in a great hurry, BOB, *in goggles and helmet, ready to fly.)*

BOB:

Come on, everybody! We've got to pack up our airplanes and go!

BILL:

What great incentive moves you on this night,
When we are all so gay at this mild party,
Friend Bob, to urge us to such sudden action?
Have all the apes got ready to attack?
Are octopus about to suck us down
Into the very bosom of the deep?
What is the reason for this hurry, friend?

BOB:

It's time to go to Shanghai. It is the time
When we must go. It is the ideal time
When morning's sunshine mirrored on the stairways
Can show another sky. It is the time
When Shanghai's mist has cleared and is the time
To fly there, and to be there, and to see.
Red Man has sent me word.

BILL:

                   I should have thought
That you would rather stay here now, with Jill.

BOB:

It's not that way. Jill's feelings are her own,
And whom she loves, she loves. It is not me.

JILL:

Oh, Bob. Dear Bob! I've loved you, I feel something. I don't know.
I feel, for Santa Claus, some other thing
Quite past control—a sort of exaltation . . .

BILL:

So, upward! To the Stairways of the Shanghai!

(*All leave quickly, to get in the planes.*)

Scene 8

The streets of Shanghai, with strange, beautiful unattached stairways.

(*Enter* SANTA CLAUS, *who climbs up one of the stairways. Enter* LYN *and* BILL, *who walk about looking at the city.* BILL *sees* SANTA CLAUS.)

BILL:

Santa Claus—greetings! Glad you came here first.
How is the city? Safe? All as we hoped?

SANTA CLAUS:

Yes, safe. We've come here in a time of peace.
And we are protected by a group of monks
Whose leader is Louis, on the southern wall
Which is the only place some crazy foe
Could even try to enter. The Easter Bunny,
I think, though, will not dare attack us here.
Ah, these old stairways! They are beautiful
Like nothing else on earth—some made of glass,
Some made of thinnest paper, some of gold,
Others of rubies and of emeralds!
Free-standing stairways for five thousand years
Have multiplied in Shanghai, until, now,
No matter where one stands, on King Ching Street
Or at the Pong Chai Gate, one's thoughts are upward,
As surely as one's eyes, in strangest ways.
Well, walk, see what you can. We'll reassemble
And speak some hours later. I must go
Elsewhere in Shanghai for a while. Good-bye!

(SANTA CLAUS leaves.)

BILL:

The stairways of Shanghai! (BILL sees LYN.) Lyn! Look at them!
Let's climb one—would you like to?

LYN:

                                        Let me see.
I have a guide to Shanghai. Let's begin
With here, this one, the Ho Ka Palisade.
This is the "Paper Stairway of the Gods"
Pity the man who set a match to this!

BILL:

For the gods would destroy him.

LYN:

                                I believe
They are entirely colored gold and silver.
Look at them in the noontime. How they gleam!

(They start to climb the gold and silver stairway.)

BILL:

Wait! what? Lyn, stop! oh, listen! I heard something,
Some sounds as if of shouting down below.

(Enter, agitatedly, some Buddhist MONKS.)

MONKS:

Ha ha ho! They have captured Louis! Help!
They have entered into the city and may doom
All the Red Robins who are on the stairs.
Where's Santa Claus? There's Bill and Lyn there—ho!

LYN:

What—?

BILL:

Don't be afraid!

(LYN and BILL run down stairs to the street. Re-enter SANTA CLAUS.)

SANTA CLAUS:

What's this? Got in? Well, so—
The Slimy Green Things are the only answer!

LYN:

What are the slimy green things?

BILL:

What are they?

SANTA CLAUS:

That Santa Claus commends them? You shall see!

(Enter BOB, then JILL.)

BILL:

What's up?

SANTA CLAUS:

I'm going to call the Slimy Greens!

JILL:

Good God, dear Santa, do it carefully!

(Enter BUD.)

BUD:

There's not much time.
The southern walls are all aswarm with enemies.

I've just come from there. Neal and I were on
The Chi Chung Escalier and saw them swarming!

SANTA CLAUS:
What are their names?

BUD:
                         Don't know. Cold Bachelors, mostly!
I recognized a few of them, I think.
Behind them rose a great white pair of ears
And there was bunny sniffing.

SANTA CLAUS:
                          That I knew.
Well, we must find the Slimies. Let's fan out—
Bud you to the east, Jill west, I to the south
Where most the danger is, Jim you to north
And with you Lyn and Bill—there in the north
Is where I think the Slimy Green Things are—

JILL:
How will we recognize them when we find them?

SANTA CLAUS:
Oh you'll know when you find them!

(SANTA CLAUS *gives all the* RED ROBINS *some seeds.*)

When you do,
Scatter this seed where you would have them follow.
Don't worry. They won't harm you. They are gentle.

BILL:
How will they help us in our fight?

SANTA CLAUS:
                       They have
A special poison gas which they exude
When they are close to rabbits. I've a mask
Which will protect me, but you should stay back
When they come near our foes. I'll hold them back
Until you get there with the Slimy Green Things.
Hurry, though! I cannot hold out too long!

(All go off.)

Scene 9

A beautiful city garden in Shanghai.

(LYN *wanders in, looking for the* SLIMY GREEN THINGS. *She is intrigued by the beauty of the garden. The* MAN IN THE YELLOW COAT *comes in absorbed in his thoughts; he is holding a cigar.* LYN *hides behind a tree.*)

MAN IN THE YELLOW COAT:
> And what is the answer? what can it mean that we are born into paradise or nothingness? and that we spend our earliest years in paradise or nothingness, though subject to pain, and that when we are twelve or thirteen we seem to be lifted into another sphere (a stratosphere or sexisphere) of paradise or nothingness. We are always filled with excitement over life as well as with the ignorance of all that it means—beset by passion, not knowing if we are loving a ghost, beset, beset . . .

LYN: *(appearing to him)*
> There were so many blue wasps that summer! so many young girls dancing in frocks at the hotel! so much orange! so many teeter-totters left abandoned in the public square!

MAN IN THE YELLOW COAT:
> What? Who are you? What?

LYN:
> The railroad train stopped. It looked like a smokestack.
> Then green spots started to appear all over its wheels and sides.

MAN IN THE YELLOW COAT:
> Lyn, you must find the ring!

LYN:
> What ring?

MAN IN THE YELLOW COAT:
> The Ring of Destiny! Yes, for with that ring, and only with it, you will be able to get to Tin Fan—the Country of Desire Fulfilled!

LYN:
> Oh! And the Slimy Green Things? I have to find those now.

MAN IN THE YELLOW COAT:
> They are just ahead of you a little ways.

LYN:
> And the ring?

MAN IN THE YELLOW COAT:

 I can't tell you any more about that.

(LYN *goes off left, where there is an increasing green glow. It is the* SLIMY GREEN THINGS. *The* MAN IN THE YELLOW COAT *starts off right.*)

LYN:

 The Green Things are here! But what on earth can that mean about the "ring"?

MAN IN THE YELLOW COAT:

 I must phone the President!

Scene 10

Shanghai—the Southern Gate and the Chi Chung Escalier.

(*Enter* EASTER BUNNY *and* COLD BACHELORS, *his henchmen.*)

EASTER BUNNY:

 Come! come! They are defeated. They cannot resist us any further.
 Come! come! They are defeated! Come away, come!

FIRST COLD BACHELOR:

 Master, one stands beyond and challenges
 Your mighty self to come do combat with him.
 He says his name is one that you well know.

EASTER BUNNY:

 Were he the greatest bully on this earth
 I should not fear him.

FIRST COLD BACHELOR:

 He is dressed in red,
 Has a white beard and very savage smile.

EASTER BUNNY:

 At last, that monster Claus. Give me my armour.
 Let these white limbs in steel be buckled up
 And I shall go against this worst of evils!

(*He arms himself.* SANTA CLAUS *appears.*)

EASTER BUNNY: (*to the* COLD BACHELORS)
 Stay here close hidden. If the advantage turns
 To that same bearded fool, take aim and kill him.
 I do not plan to toy with life this day.
 He'll die, no matter what.

FIRST COLD BACHELOR:

                             Yes, Master, yes.

EASTER BUNNY:

    Well, Claus, you fool, the great day's come at last!
    I'll kill you—*(aside)* or they will. *(to* SANTA CLAUS*)* Come, fight with me!

SANTA CLAUS:

    Aye, that I shall.

(They start fighting. It is a mighty combat, a fight between elemental forces. At certain moments the combat ceases and one or the other speaks.)

EASTER BUNNY:

    I have a feeling, fighting with this man,
    That I am fighting Death and Crime and Night.
    I sense an evil in his coming forth
    And in his moving back and to the sides.
    He terrifies me as none other does—
    But I shall fight him grandly, come what may!

SANTA CLAUS:

    This Easter Rabbit's Envy, Smut, and Bile!
    Nothing has ever been, than him, more vile.
    It makes me weak with evil even to stand
    To fight with him, it weakens my good hand.

EASTER BUNNY:

    He seems the natural force of all that's wrong.

SANTA CLAUS:

    He is the dirty words to a good song!
    Ah, Hatred guide my blows! and Justice, too!

FIRST COLD BACHELOR:

    How goes the fight?

SECOND COLD BACHELOR:

                          It's even as of now.

FIRST COLD BACHELOR:

    Our Lord will kill the old red bastard, sure!

SECOND COLD BACHELOR:

    If not, our guns turn him to bird manure!

(Enter the SLIMY GREEN THINGS.*)*

EASTER BUNNY: *(losing his strength)*
    What—what's that? Help!

COLD BACHELORS:
    Ah, help! help! help!

(The SLIMY GREEN THINGS *advance.* SANTA CLAUS *puts on his mask. The* EASTER BUNNY *and the* COLD BACHELORS *cough, grow faint, and sicken, then stumble or crawl away, followed by the* SLIMY GREEN THINGS. *Enter* LYN, *then* BOB.*)*

SANTA CLAUS:
    Lyn, dear, Lyn!

LYN:
                    Yes! Yes, I found them
    In the northwestern section of this town
    And me they followed hither.

BOB:
                            Bless your soul.
    Where are the other Robins?

(Enter JILL, JIM, BUD, BILL, *and* LOUIS, *all of them worn out from their search for the* SLIMY GREEN THINGS.*)*

SANTA CLAUS:
                        Here they come,
    And tired one and all, poor valiant stragglers!

(All embrace.)

    Tonight we'll feast on octopus *galant*
    Cooked by Wang Po, the best chef in Shanghai!

(They go off.)

ACT TWO

Scene 1

The terrace of the Coluhdson Hotel, a huge resort hotel in Asia. BOB, *alone.*

BOB: *(reading aloud)*
    And one day her parents came to Asia, to the great hotel—
    It was a long time past. And a long time past, the father,
    The father who did not know what he knew,
    The father who took a fancy to the freshness and the sweetness of his girl,
    And the father who said to her, the mother willing it, too,
    "Dear, you must come home . . ."

(JILL *and her* PARENTS *enter;* BOB *looks at them a moment, then leaves.*)

JILL'S FATHER:
We want to meet him.

JILL:
I don't know if that's possible. He's well—
He is a little odder than you think—
Or than you might think. He is rather fierce.

JILL'S MOTHER:
Jill, dearest child, we want you to come home.

JILL'S FATHER:
To this Coluhdson's walls from far away
By airplane, camelback, canoe, and horse
We've traveled, though we're middle-aged and weak-
Er in some ways than you young people are
Who call yourself Red Robins, just to say
Jill, that we want you back, we want you home.

JILL:
Dear parents, I do not think that I can.

COLUHDSON WAITER:
Some goopah, Ma'am?

JILL'S MOTHER:
What's that?

JILL:
It is a native drink.

JILL'S FATHER:
                      Mm, well, no thank you.
Well, yes, I'll have one, on the other hand.
Jill, dear, you must come home.

JILL:
                      Don't think I can.

JILL'S FATHER:
Would you like one of these cold goopahs, Mother?
They're very cool and good.

JILL'S MOTHER:
                      Well, yes, I'll try one.

JILL'S FATHER:
Make that two goopahs, waiter. And you, Jill?

JILL:
I'll have a goopah, yes.

JILL'S FATHER:
Then that makes three.

JILL:
I can't come home.

JILL'S FATHER:
You must come home.
Why should you have this senseless life out here
When there is such a good life in the States
Where you can live in peace and happiness,
Secure and not surrounded by the jungle
And apes and octopus and crazy birds,
And puzzling people speaking alien tongues?
Why should you have to live a life like this?
We brought you up to be a regular girl.
You can have anything you want, back home.
What holds you here?

JILL'S MOTHER:
People ask us. We're embarrassed.
We don't know what to say
Why should Jill Brules be flying around Asia
When other girls are getting engaged and married
And having babies, making grandparents
Of their proud, doting parents? We'd be happy
If your young man would come back home with you.

JILL:
Er—he is not so young. But to explain
A little bit. One thing is I'm in love
With Santa Claus—yes, yes, that is his name.
Oh he's not the traditional one, of course,
Not someone who goes flying off at Christmas
As one is told he does when one's a child.
He is a different one. At least, if he
Is the traditional one, then everyone's
Been misinformed as to what is his nature.
He's a man

So full of the excitement of his life
That he seems more than human, like a god—

JILL'S MOTHER:
That's sacriligious.
We have no right to speak of men like that.
Please do not say such things.

JILL:
I'm sorry Mother
I guess I'm just in love, like any girl,
And guess I have exaggerated feelings
As any other would. Well, that's not all, though.
It isn't all that I'm so much in love.
For I loved being a Red Robin when
I first came out to be one, and when he
Still roamed the savage North.

JILL'S FATHER:
But it all seems so strange, and unconnected
To you—and all you are!

JILL:
It isn't really.
Do you remember—I do—all through childhood
How much I loved to dance? And I remember
A night in high school when the time was May,
The term had almost ended, and, in white
I danced with William Sansom and we whirled
About the floor—we whirled, and whirled, and whirled—
And I had the sensation that my movements
Were like the movements of the waves and stars
And were the only motions of the earth,
Which, for our dancing, stopped. When in our airplanes,
Or when in jungle converse with my friends,
Or walking softly on the high plateaus
Of Asia, I have these same feelings now—
I feel, not a rejection of your life
And all that is back home, but something stronger
That makes me so much surer of *this* life.

JILL'S FATHER:
Do all your young friends feel this way about it?

JILL:

　　They all feel something.
　　Something perhaps for all not quite the same,
　　But strong enough to keep them here and happy—

JILL'S MOTHER:

　　Well, it is nice they're here
　　So you aren't all alone!

JILL'S FATHER:

　　I say, let's meet this man, this Santa Claus!
　　If he is worthy of you, we shall see.

JILL:

　　I'll—try to get him.

JILL'S MOTHER:

　　　　I'm sure that he will come.

JILL'S FATHER:

　　Why shouldn't he? Are you ashamed of us?

JILL:

　　No, Father, no. It's just that San—that he,
　　Well, as I said, he is a little strange.
　　He might be *violent.*

JILL'S FATHER:

　　　　　　Then so might I!
　　Goddamn, no man has rights over my daughter
　　By violence and shall not be with me—
　　No matter if he be Great Death Himself—
　　Brutal or threatening in the slightest bit!
　　I shall be violent with him, the clod,
　　If he—

JILL'S MOTHER:

　　　　Charles, stop. I'm sure that Jill's new friend
　　If he loves her, will love or like us too.
　　Go, get him, dearest. We will be waiting here.

JILL'S FATHER:

　　Yes, try to have him come here before lunch.
　　Then we can talk and then have lunch together.

JILL'S MOTHER:

　　Dear, it will be so nice.

JILL:

Well, well, I'll try.

(*JILL leaves her parents. As she is about to leave the Coluhdson terrace, she stops for a moment and speaks, as if she were musing, or reading aloud from a book.*)

A tender strain of violin music came floating to them on the steps of the Coluhdson as they sat there in the middle of the day, and Jill suddenly remembered it was spring. She remembered a May evening filled with frost-white butterflies and tulip-and-rose-bearing sticks.

(*JILL goes off.*)

JILL'S FATHER:

If I can talk some sense into his head,
And I do think I can, I think that we'll
Be going Stateside, dear, with a new son
And not have lost a daughter.

JILL'S MOTHER:

Well . . . I hope so.

JILL'S FATHER:

All shall be well.

Scene 2

JILL'S MOTHER *and* FATHER, *at a table in the shade on the Coluhdson terrace, where they remain, silent, during this scene.*

(*Enter a DOG.*)

DOG:

I am an animal, though civilized and domestic.
And I am not known. Yea, there is in my heart
That which is totally unknown to man.
Ah, Man, with his machines, his tools, his customs
Knows nothing of the generous, easy ways
We animals have nor knows he the nobility
That comes from being wholly without hope—
The secret of our being. And like a slave
Who follows a lord in haste and does not know
Where he is going, like a miser, too,
Who hurries after wealth which is his tyrant
And peace more quickly flees, so man pursues me,
Believes he tames me, takes me to his house

And chains me close, but does not know my heart,
And gives me food, but does not know my heart—
Wide open, generous, unsponsored, free—
And does not know, I think he does not know—
Believing that if, when called by him, I go,
He knows the best of me.

VOICE OFFSTAGE:
    Where's that damned beagle?
    Oh, Christ! He's gotten loose in the hotel!
    Here, Kahndor, come! Come Kahndor!

DOG:
                        Rrrf! I will!

(DOG *runs off.*)

Scene 3

Still the Coluhdson terrace.

(SANTA CLAUS *enters, greets* JILL'S FATHER *and* MOTHER, *and joins them at a table.* JILL *is not there.*)

SANTA CLAUS:
    I'm pleased to meet you, Sir, and hope that your
    Trip has been good and that you're liking Asia.
    There are so many grand things here to see.

JILL'S FATHER:
    Why, yes, in fact we did have a good flight,
    A good canoe trip and good camel ride.
    We came here to see Jill, as you must know.

SANTA CLAUS:
    Of course she told me. Yes.

JILL'S FATHER:
    This thing in Burma,
    This new political leader they have there,
    Sam Wando—what's his name

SANTA CLAUS:
                        Sanwandohfarris?

JILL'S FATHER:
    Yes, that's the fellow. Do you think he's good
    Or harmful? Did he win by an honest vote?

JILL'S MOTHER:
>   Dear, that's all fine, but don't you think we should,
>   Well, talk of Jill a little more?

SANTA CLAUS:
>   Miz Brules,
>   I see now where your daughter got her smile
>   And her blue eyes. They twinkle just like yours—
>   And like the blue Pacific's waves, when they
>   Are touched so gently by the summer dawn
>   They show us pink and pearl as well as blue.
>   Then daylight comes with his transforming hand
>   And turns those tints to one engulfing hue,
>   More various for so being.

JILL'S FATHER:
>   What? What's that?

SANTA CLAUS:
>   And I believe—
>   I see it in your eyes and so believe—
>   It may be true stout Sir, sweet Madame, that
>   It is a life, too, would go well with you
>   And you with it, could you but be persuaded
>   To be Red Robins like ourselves. I think
>   This broad expanse, these mountains' sides already
>   Have been persuasive, made you wish to stay.
>   You . . . have had such a thought?

JILL'S FATHER:
>   No, we'll go home
>   Not Robins, I should guess. You do seem confident
>   And Jill does too, and all the rest, you say,
>   This way of life is good.

SANTA CLAUS:
>   It is a way
>   Of life you may imagine and not live
>   And say such life is poetry, not life,
>   But once you've lived it for one day, one hour,
>   No other makes the slightest sense at all.

JILL'S MOTHER:
>   You, Sir, you really love her?

SANTA CLAUS:
Love, Madame, is my name.

JILL'S FATHER:
                              This Wandohfarris
You think he's a good man?

SANTA CLAUS:
                              He is all right.
We met last summer at the Hunters Club
Outside of Horror Burma's batwing region
And spoke of economics. He's first rate
In that. Don't know if he knows people, though,
As well as he knows finance.

JILL'S FATHER:
                              Hmm, that will
Be interesting to see, if he works out.
Mother, call Jill. She said she'd be downstairs
Near the front desk. It's time to have our lunch
And speak of something lighter.

(JILL'S MOTHER *leaves.* JILL'S FATHER *soliloquizes.*)

                              By my judgment
This is a good man. He'll be good to her.

(JILL *comes in, with her mother.*)

Jill, darling!

SANTA CLAUS:
May I order?

JILL: (*aside, to* SANTA CLAUS)
Is everything all right?

SANTA CLAUS:
I think it is.

JILL'S MOTHER: (*answering* SANTA CLAUS)
                              Yes, please.

SANTA CLAUS:
                              I know the restaurant
And know the chef. I would suggest the Burmese Badger
As a main course, with pickled octopus
As a first course. Then pilot's salad after,
Mousse Tour Eiffel for sweet, then Burmese Coffee.

JILL'S FATHER:
Sounds good.

(SANTA CLAUS *looks up and sees something alarming in the sky. He jumps to his feet, agitated.*)

SANTA CLAUS:
                    Alas, I cannot stay with you,
     For I have urgent business in the sky.

JILL'S MOTHER:
What? What?

JILL'S FATHER:
                    What's this?

SANTA CLAUS:
                              There is a sign
     Of light in that far stratosphere that shows
     The Blood-Filled Rakes are screaming through the air
     Of Lower Asia, heading for this place
     And I must up before them and bring down
     Their prideful feathers, leading to their doom.
     Sweet parents of my Jill, a warm farewell
     And my excuses. I have liked so much
     To meet you, and I hope you will be here
     When I get back. If not, good voyage home.

JILL:
Dear, must you? Yes, I see that you must go.

SANTA CLAUS:
Dear friends, farewell. *(He goes, swiftly.)*

JILL'S MOTHER:
                    He is a most unusual man.

JILL'S FATHER:
He seems a sensible one, and if you love him—

JILL:
I'm worried about him so, but yes, I do.

Scene 4

A beach in Asia, and the Pacific Ocean, with a steamboat. The RED ROBINS *are gathered on the beach, ready for departure.*

BOB:

Our next stop's Occhu Bocchu and its mountains,
Amidst which we'll find Aplaganda Lake,
With Congers Island in the midst of it
Where at this time—it's Maytime—of the year
The octopus hold solemn festival
And shriek and crawl about the savage rocks.

LYN:

How wonderful to see it! Jim and I
Will go there on the boat. We have our tickets.

BOB:

We'll see you there. The rest of us will fly.
Good luck. Good voyage. I know you love the ocean,
But do be careful as you're going there.
For octopus *en marche* from everywhere
Are gathering for fiesta.

JIM:

        We'll take care.

(ROBINS *go off to their planes;* JIM *and* LYN *go aboard the boat,* JIM *goes below;*
LYN *stands looking over the side.*)

LYN:

Happy I'll be to make this trip but happier
To make another one. Of my bad dreams
One is the chief, that I shall die before,
Or shall grow old, weary, or weak before
I see that fabled city of the East
Known as Tin Fan, which old philosophers hold
Is the external form of what is best
In this our universe. Its golden streets,
Or else not gold but asphalt, concrete, dirt,
Whatever they may be, they must be streets
Which lead to the fulfillment of desires
Before one even knows one has them, and
Its buildings, filled with feelings and ideas,
Its music and its statues and its forms
Of public celebration, and the life
Of its least citizen fill me with fire
To think of, and my chest and forehead burn
With the extreme desire to feel myself
Be there, and turn amidst its sights and sounds.

(Music plays, and a VOICE *speaks.)*

VOICE:

In the interior of China, I exist.
I am Cathay, Tin Fan, or what you wish
To call me by. I will not come. For you
Must come to me by sky and ocean blue
And over land, on rivers, come by mountains,
A million snowy mountains to the North,
Ten million snowy mountains to the South,
And a long winding river in between
With islands on it, on which can be seen
Small huts of grass and little chairs and tables
At which sit those who will not come so far
As you must come because some special feeling
Makes it the great necessity for you.
I am Tin Fan. I am Cathay. Extreme
The pleasures I propose. Extreme the dangers
You must go through to find me—chiefly, one:
That you will not believe that I exist.
At last, you'll not believe that I exist
And you'll give up the search. If you do not,
I'll make you happy for eternity.

*(*OCTOPUS *appear.)*

OCTOPUS:

We are the Octopus, and we are not known!
We're here to make you drown before you go!

LYN: *(not noticing the* OCTOPUS—*dreamily)*
That voice! I heard that voice! It was Tin Fan!

(Now she notices the OCTOPUS, *who are threatening.)*

Help! Octopus! They'll squeeze me till I'm dead
And leave me at the mercy of the sea!

(Enter JIM, *concernedly.)*

JIM:

Octopus!
Down! Stay your pods! Oh, Lyn! Are you all right?
Down, slimy, damn you, octopus! Disgust!

(The OCTOPUS *withdraw.)*

OCTOPUS:
　　We weren't really doing any harm—
　　Just wanted a little kiss!

JIM:
　　　　　　　　　　　That you shan't have!
　　Down, damn you, down! To Congers Island go,
　　Where sliminess is all the way of life!

OCTOPUS:
　　Ungrateful! You were saved by slimy things
　　That time in Shanghai of the Golden Stairs.

JIM:
　　That time is past. Besides, they were not you.

OCTOPUS:
　　How do you know they weren't? The prejudice
　　All human creatures have against the slime
　　That is the source of life, the space and time
　　Of embryos and all that vaunted lot,
　　Is vicious, unfair, and destructive as
　　A glass of Malay poison drunk at dawn.
　　We are but what you have forgotten once
　　You were, but grow away from every year:
　　Love's precious cold miasmic source of life.

JIM:
　　Perhaps. But you've no reason to hug Lyn!
　　God damn you, down! She is my girl, not yours!

OCTOPUS:
　　Well, we'll away. Remember us, though. Give our cares a though.

(OCTOPUS *leave.*)

JIM:
　　Their cares a thought! Good God!

LYN:
　　　　　　　　　　　Jim, I think I
　　Heard something from Tin Fan. Jim, we must go there!
　　Oh we must try to get there if we can!

JIM:
　　Lyn! Dearest! You're all right? Of course we'll go there!
　　We will do all we can!

(He kisses her. Enter CAPTAIN, *holding a letter.)*

Well—who are you? The captain—

CAPTAIN:

Of this boat.
I hate to interrupt you, but this note,
This precious note I have within my hand
Is from the ruler of a mighty land
And is addressed to someone he calls "Lyn."
Do you know such a person? Is it she,
As somehow I suspect that it may be?
If not, I beg your pardon. I any case,
I'm sorry to interrupt your private parley—

LYN:

My name is Lyn. You say a ruler. Is—

(a musical flourish)

CAPTAIN:

It is the President of the United States,
Whose dream you are. He bade me bring you this.

(He hands her the letter. LYN *starts to read it and is frightened.* JIM *takes the letter from her, starts to read, and he too is frightened. Suddenly, an* APE *leaps up to them and seizes the letter.)*

APE:

Ha! ha! Now mine!

*(*APE *jumps overboard and swims off.)*

LYN:

Got

JIM:

to get

CAPTAIN:

it back!

LYN:

Oh God! God! God!

(Blackout. Spotlight now shows APE *on shore with the letter.* APE *pulls off his mask. It is the* EASTER BUNNY.)*

EASTER BUNNY:
Ha ha! This letter so incriminates
Lyn and the President of the United States
That in it I can taste my full revenge
Against democracy and Robins both—
And this will be the DEATH of Santa Claus!

Scene 5

An airfield near Lake Aplaganda. Sky above. BOB *stands apart from the other* RED ROBINS.

BOB: *(thinking aloud)*
It is over.
The Octopanorama's at an end
Which we came here to witness. In the sky
Are many things I love. But here on land
It's Jill, and only she. Somehow together
In this odd place, I think we may have found
A reason, if there is one, to stay upon the ground!
And yet not quite
Has she been wholly mine. And now, too late!

(An airgram is delivered to BOB. *He calls to the other* RED ROBINS.*)*

Jill! Everyone! We're summoned
By airgram, by an Englishman named Terrence
Who promises to show us Unfound Island!

OTHER RED ROBINS:
Good! Away!

BOB:
I think the route that's best is that one over
Isola Pushner. Now—into the planes!

(All run off. Then, very shortly thereafter, BOB *reappears, in his plane, in the sky.)*

BOB:
In the sky, and this is something that has been noticed before, everything seems to be all right. Coming back to land, though, can often be a trial. Balzac wanted everything—fame, money, love, power, acceptance—and he was able to get them all. Yet he was tormented. Byron was born an aristocrat; he was wealthy, handsome—and a great genius. Yet Byron led a miserable life. Tennyson, too, was an unhappy man, in love with his landlady's son.

The most remarkable thing about the sky is that there seems to be nothing there, and this probably has something to do with the feeling of happiness (or perhaps it is only euphoria) which is produced in a person by being there. When Jill and I have our planes close together up high, that is a moment I love. Conversation is often impossible to hear but sometimes seems to have a celestial quality when one is flying.

I wonder if Napoleon was happy—and Homer. Nobody even knows where Homer was born. Here are three "Homeric birthplaces" in Greece. Nobody is even sure that Homer wrote *The Odyssey*. Apparently, he was blind. Like us, he was a sailor, though not a sailor of the sky.

Jesus Christ, perhaps the most influential man who ever lived, was almost certainly extremely unhappy. Socrates was unhappy. I guess you think Mao Tse-tung was a happy man. He was suffering from gastric ulcers and could scarcely ascend the ancient speaking mound. The fact that we are betrothed to old age and death is enough to make all people unhappy.

In the air, I feel occupied. There is the steering, there are the controls, There is that sense of being "above it all" yet participating in it in the most lively and exhilarating way. I wonder if "escape" is the right word, as someone once suggested when I talked of these things, for something which so wholly absorbs the beings and which requires so much skill, and which brings so much of life into one small span. The countries that float by down beneath me are like chapters in a book; and I feel them, and what is in the air above them, in my face, and in my heart, and in my mind.

Scene 6

A small Pacific island. MEINHEER PUSHNER, *an old colonial official, is there, with his two* NATIVE BEARERS.

FIRST NATIVE BEARER:
Meinheer Pushner, let me take you a little further in out of the cold. It's a cool morning this is after being for the jungle, and you no longer a young man, though a great man you have been after being and having been and a great one still are, to my lights and by those of all other living beings that knows of your name.

SECOND BEARER:
Of your existence and your name.

MEINHEER PUSHNER:
Yes, Manawa, and yes, Bonoro, thank you for what you say.
And thank you too for the concern you are after for being having just now
    for me.

(The RED ROBINS' *planes fly over. He looks up at them.)*

> But as the chilly waters of the blue Pacific swell
> And scratch with morning light, I want to see
> The birds as they fly overhead.

FIRST BEARER:
> Oh my God, Sir, those are not real birds!

MEINHEER PUSHNER:
> Manawa, who are we to say? and how are we to know?
> Have I, in all these years here on the island, taught you nothing
> But respect for me? I wanted to teach you also independent thought.
> These may or may not be birds.
> The important thing is that we do not know.

SECOND BEARER:
> Those are Red Robins, Master.

MEINHEER PUSHNER: *(musing)*
> And there is one among them
> Named Jill, whom I will always love!

FIRST BEARER:
> Ah, yes, Master. She of whom you have spoken so often, in the island evenings!

Scene 7

L'Isola Non Trovata, a beautiful Pacific island filled with flowers. JILL *is there alone with a bunch of flowers she has picked.* TERRENCE, *an Englishman, and the other* RED ROBINS *enter on the other side of the island, not seeing* JILL. *Also present is the* EASTER BUNNY, *whom no one sees—perhaps very far to one side, away from the action.*

TERRENCE:
> These giant flowers on your left are what
> Is most amazing on this Unfound Island—
> Isola Non Trovata to Gozzano,
> The Italian poet who first used its name—
> These flowers are said to be the origin
> Of colors and of the human alphabet—
> Somehow the vowels have been derived from them
> And consonants from their leaves.

LYN:
What beautiful flowers!

BOB:
They seem somehow to mean
More than a flower could mean . . .

JILL: (coming over to the other ROBINS: looking at the flowers in her hand)
A, black; E, white; I, red; U, green; O, blue. O vowels!
I see you now and now know where you come from—
Vowels are color, which I'll now explain.

BOB:
What? Jill!
You've picked some flowers? Jill—

BUNNY: (unheard by others)
I planned all this,
And this will bring them to a tragic doom.

LYN:
Is she all right?

BOB:
She seems to be in some sort of a trance!

TERRENCE:
It seems to be some magic of the island
That doth affect her thus—the Vowel Flowers.

(Now JILL gives people flowers, one at a time, starting with BOB. To BOB she gives
a black flower, to LYN a white one, to JIM a red one, to LOUIS a green one. She keeps
the blue flower for herself. Each person who has a flower looks at it and speaks.)

BOB:
A, Black. Chess pieces, licorice, funeral clothes;
Full note, half note, banana bruise, ape nose.

LYN:
E, White. Albumen, chiffon, blanks, cashmere;
White swimsuit-covered breasts; Tin Fan grown clear.

JIM:
I, Red. Nails, bitten lips, sunrise-tipped airways;
Deep re-created red of Shanghai stairways.

LOUIS:
U, Green. Eyelids, green ink, a praying mantis;
Costume of Pan, the opposite of Santa's.

JILL:

    O, Blue. Smoke, goggles, air reflecting things;
    Eyes, linen and silk shirts, engagement rings.

(JILL *runs off.*)

BILL:

    Jill! Come back!
    She's going too far inland.

(*Distant ape sounds are heard.*)

BOB:

                  What? That shout—!

(*Now huge grunts and groans are heard.*)

    Jesus Christ! It hink it is the Apes of Banzona!

BUD:

    Have we come to the wrong island?

TERRENCE:

                  I—I don't know—

BILL:

    You—!

(*He unmasks* TERRENCE, *who, beneath mask, turns out to be an ape.*)

BOB:

           Quick! Got to rescue Jill—

(BOB *runs off and runs back on, tugging* JILL, *who is very frightened. Now* APES *advance onto the stage. Their leader,* FIRST APE, *walks up to* BOB.)

FIRST APE:

    No one shall resist the Apes of Banzona!
    Whoever sets foot on this island must die!

BOB:

    We shall see, insane rodents
    Of human size, we shall see!

LOUIS:

    Yet, enemies, stop!
    Why should we groups do battle with each other
    And cause much harm to bodies, leave some dead
    And others maimed and bleeding? Can we not,
    Instead, make some agreements? I propose

We give each other tokens of esteem
And drink some heady beverage of the island,
Then we depart in peace.

BOB:

They want to kill us!

JIM:

Stay, Robins stay. The words that Louis says
Are true enough if the apes but accept them.

FIRST APE:

You have invaded
Our sacred island precincts. You must die.

SECOND APE:

But, Lord, these are fair words the stranger speaks.
Shall we not bend old custom to sweet peace
And friendly gestures?

BILL:

Part of which, for us,
Will be returning to you this same traitor
Who brought us here.

*(He pushes "*TERRENCE*" forward.)*

FIRST APE: *(recognizing him)*
Medoga Banzonino!
You! seeking power still! brought them to fight
On this most gracious Admiralty Island
Unknown to all but us!

FIRST APE:

I did and hoped
They'd kill you, after which I would take power
And use my fellow apes to conquer earth
And drive all other beings into Hell!

FIRST APE:

Take him to dungeon. And there let him be
Treated with cacao and betel juice
Till he return to reason. Then with trial
Severe but fair we shall adjudge his case.
Meanwhile, fair-haired strangers,
Pardon, and welcome to these ape-brushed shores.
Let ape musicians come, young ape and apess

184 🎵 KENNETH KOCH

The wreathe these strangers' heads with vowel flowers
A, E, I, O, and U. But Jill, who picked
These flowers, must spend five months upon this island
Each year, one month per flower.

BOB:

                                    She will not!

FIRST APE:
Why damn you, then!

BOB:
And you, goddamn!

(BOB and FIRST APE start to fight.)

SECOND APE:
Lord, stay your hand! Dear strangers, we wish nothing!
Combating so, you play into the hand
Of foul Medoga, who stands seething here
Awash with grins like an old pot that's boiling
Until its water's swirling. We cannot
Blame one for picking flowers here which have
On everyone a strange unknown effect,
Making them irresistible to hands.

FIRST APE:
All right. I humbly do apologize again.

BOB:
Which we accept. Now make we merry, friends,
For we must be in China by nightfall.

(The APES and the RED ROBINS drink and dance.)

EASTER BUNNY: (unseen and unheard by others)
So fails my plan! Dull peace has won the day.
I must destroy them in another way!

(He goes off.)

ACT THREE

Scene 1

A high place, with a small pavilion, in China. The RED ROBINS are together. JILL
is reading from a book.

JILL: *(reading)*

And a man in a yellow coat, a tall man holding in his hand an excellent green tobacco cigar, was standing in the boathouse doorway. Was saying, "I do not think the gulls will fly this year." Or was saying, "I do not think they will fly, will fly very high, so high above our sights, our heads, and heavens, that we shall never see them." And the blue dregs from his cigar like the ashes of the sea. "Shall fly high, and we shall never see them, so that to us it shall be as if they had never flown at all." That's beautiful!

(Enter LOUIS, excited.)

LOUIS:

Quickly! into the Seat House! Ni Shu has come,
The Chinese philosopher has come,
And with him Santa Claus and the President!

(Enter NI SHU with his retinue. Then enter SANTA CLAUS and the PRESIDENT. The PRESIDENT is holding the Ring of Destiny. LYN sees it.)

LYN: *(to herself)*
The Ring of Destiny!

PRESIDENT:

How hot it is, Santa Claus! Is it always this hot out here?

SANTA CLAUS:

It varies, Your Lordship. Sometimes the jungle is very cool.
Once we almost froze to death.

PRESIDENT:

I should be very very sorry to hear of that!

(Enter MIKE THE TIGER.)

MIKE THE TIGER:
My name is Mike the Tiger.

(SANTA CLAUS shoots Mike, and he is dragged off.)

PRESIDENT:
What was that?

SANTA CLAUS:
A man-eating tiger who's been bothering us.

PRESIDENT:
Good Lord!

LYN: *(coming up to them)*
Mr. President—

PRESIDENT:

My God, it's—Lyn!

LYN:

Mr. President, hand me that ring!

PRESIDENT:

No! Never! It contains the secret of life. I haven't had time to use it yet or even much time to look at or study it, really, but it's mine. I'm just too busy, so far, to devote my time to it. But I'm going to. I don't want to give it to anyone. After all, I'm the goddamned fucking President of the All States Whites and I have perfect right to every fucking thing in the universe that I wish!

JILL:

Which President are you?

PRESIDENT:

Oh my God! Fuck! I forgot I'm no longer President!

(He runs away into the jungle.)

LYN:

Follow him! We've got to get that ring!

(She starts to run after him, but SANTA CLAUS *stops her.)*

SANTA CLAUS:

No! Let him go. The sadomasochistic jungle will do him in, and we'll have that ring tomorrow or the next day.

LYN:

You don't understand how important it is.

SANTA CLAUS:

I think I may.
And I think you may not understand how unimportant it is.
Now all must go to sleep.

BILL:

Wait, Mr. Santa Claus. You forgot about Ni Shu's being here.
Isn't he going to talk with us? Isn't that what this visit is all about?

NI SHU:

Yes, that is so.

SANTA CLAUS:

Sir, aren't you too disturbed by what has happened?

NI SHU:

No, I am never so. I am not rattled
By such events. For this same life and death
We feel about us now and in us now
Will always be here, whether we are here
Breathing its salt and lilac, or are not,
Hearing its breathy splashing. And once we know
Our separation from and oneness with it,
We can endure whatever it may bring
And go on talking, go on functioning.

JILL:

How brave a thing it is to hear a man
Speak like an angel and render thin as air
The problems that destroy us every day!

SANTA CLAUS:

Well, then, my lord, sit down and speak to us.

BILL:

Let us dispose ourselves upon the banks
Of this high wide pavilion and take on
The wisdom of the universe.

NI SHU:

Well, thanks.

(NI SHU *is seated in the pavilion, the* RED ROBINS *and* SANTA CLAUS *on the rocks and grass around it.*)

NI SHU:

Let us proceed this way, that you ask me
Short questions and in brief I shall reply.
That way we'll deal with more and keep things lively.
You have a question, you?

JILL:

What is life?

NI SHU:

It is a combination of the future
With old regrets, chained to a grinding engine
Of body's truck, which clambers up a hill.

BILL:

What then is love in life?

NI SHU:

                Love is an essence
Which people think about in various cultures
In different ways, according to their views.
But always there is an element in love
Of selflessness or seeming selflessness,
Aggrandizement from giving of oneself—
Sometimes, it seems that one could say, a means—
To put it otherwise—of being free
Of what's most monstrous in the selfish self
By caring more for someone else. This can be
Attended by such shaking of the body that
One knows not what one is.

BOB:

                Do you believe
Love, as you have described it, puts a person,
From being outside himself, in a more true
Relation with the world? Since all about us
There are so many things—skies, jungles, apes—
Which are not we ourselves?

NI SHU:

                Yes, you could say so,
And said so I believe it were well said.

BILL:

Does our adventuring, then, here in the jungle
And in the skies and out upon the sea
To distant islands filled with strangest creatures,
Do our adventures bring us close to love
Or, failing that, close to the true estate
Of persons in the universe? Or would
A Stateside life be better—working hard
And raising children, acting out our part
In some already staked-out cultural plan?
That is, are we being fools to be Red Robins
And live the way we do?

NI SHU:

                No one can answer.
Final evaluation of the self
Or what seems to be but is not the self
Must rest with something past the powers of man.

And how you'd grow a soul to be your best one
I do not know. But I suspect you know,
As I do, for myself. This lofty jungle
With its o'ertopping sky, this sensual freedom,
In which like raspberries steeped in their juice
You may so love each other, seems to be,
Surely, the life you love. And, loving it,
You're parted from your selfish selves and brought
Back to the self you'd be, if you could choose.

LYN:

What of Tin Fan? Shouldn't we try to go there?
Some people say so.

NI SHU:

                    I can't speak of it.
I'm sorry but it seems I have to go.
I have a consultation in Shanghai
At seven thirty. Santa, can you fly me?
Dear young people, farewell!

LYN:

                    But I was asking—

BOB:

Shh. Lyn, he's obviously set against it.
He doesn't want to talk about it.

LYN:

                    But—

SANTA CLAUS:

Course I can, Master.
It's been a joy for us to have you here.

NI SHU:

And for me too. Your young people are trenchant,
Intelligent, and wise. They please me much.

BOB:

Thank you, Master. Thank you from us all.

SANTA CLAUS:

I'll fly Ni Shu to Shanghai. Meanwhile, dear ones,
You all should get some sleep. Tomorrow will
Be difficult and bloody, or else I
Am a poor prophet.

BILL:
                    Aye, aye, Sir, we shall.

(SANTA CLAUS *and* NI SHU *leave. It grows dark. The* RED ROBINS *lie down around the pavilion and go to sleep.*)

Scene 2

A high, rocky desert place in Asia. The EASTER BUNNY *summons and then addresses his followers, in this instance the* SHARDS.

EASTER BUNNY:
    Thanks, my good helpers, for assembling here.
    As you know, very soon the time will come
    When we must meet in battle with the Robins
    And totally destroy them every one.
    And we must do it quickly, for they are
    Every day drawing nearer to Tin Fan,
    Which they must never reach, or else the earth
    Will be a mass of rubble. It is believed
    That if they get there, life will be destroyed.
    Our victory will not be an easy thing—
    For they have elements extremely strong
    Among them. There's no air fighter like Bob
    In any other outfit on the earth
    Nor is there any girl as smart as Jill
    Nor any, save myself, like Santa Claus
    For pure ferocity of flesh and spirit.
    He is a monster of increasing size,
    A dreadful visitation on this earth
    Where human eyes, deceived, conceive him kind
    And generous, think he brings gifts to children
    At cold December's finish, while the truth
    Is that he is the cruelest to mankind
    Of any person ever—

(PRESIDENT *runs in with the ring.*)

                    What, you here?
    You, whom the letter clearly showed to be
    The ally of those Robins whom I hate?
    Take this, and live no more!

(*He shoots him. The* PRESIDENT *falls down dead.*)

Let him be buried
With greatest pomp. He was our President—
Or theirs—somebody's—or in any case
So he has been reputed. Wait—I think
I may have murdered the wrong man. I think
This may not be the President at all!

(EASTER BUNNY *is troubled.*)

Well, give this man some honors, that his spirit
May go wherever it deserves to be
In heaven or hell, and then come back to listen
To all I'll tell you here.

FIRST, SECOND, and THIRD SHARDS:
                    Aye, Mastering Lord!

(*They go off.*)

EASTER BUNNY:
Go off, you rest, as well. This thing upsets me.
I need some quiet with myself alone.

OTHER SHARDS:
Great Leader, yes.

(*All other* SHARDS *leave.*)

EASTER BUNNY:
                    What have I come to be
If murder, which is held the foulest crime
Of any in the universe, has come
To be my second nature, aye my first—
For I as soon would kill a man as not.
Is it my heritage from the animal world
Which I escaped by some Divine mistake
Or some Divine Intent unknown to me
Or anyone save Him who forms us all?
Oh I do not myself know what I am
And hate these moments of uncertainty
When I must speak of it. Better the life
Of violence and crime, far better a day
Filled with bright knives' sharp sides, the cannons' boom,
The leaden pellet splintering living bone,
The agony, the anguish, and the scream!
In such rough times I can forget my woes

And be the sacred rabbit of myself.
But, damn! Even I, because I'm part of life,
Although so freakish and so lost a part,
Must have self-doubts and weep at what I am!
Well, we must win! My Shards! Great Shards, return!

(SHARDS *come back.*)

What battle we from henceforth shall indite
Let all be moved to wonder by! These stones
Which form this chain of mountains shall erupt
In fiery particles, which hence spewn forth
Shall burn this red-winged evil and consume!
All Asia shall turn poison to them. Touch
Whatever is, they die. And you, sad pieces
Of the Eternal Law, which now is broken,
Shatter their wings as you are shattered here!
Bring them to desperation! Twist their dreams
So that they have no hope!

SHARDS:

Aye, fatal Lord!

(*They go off.*)

Scene 3

A clearing in the jungle. Late night. BOB *has been sleeping; he gets up.*

BOB:
It's true, although I've said that it was not,
Told Jill and Bud and Bill that it was not,
That I am more unhappy than I think
It natural I should be. I do not know
Exactly why, though most from loving Jill
And being afraid I've lost her. Those first days,
Flying through Asia, how we loved each other!
Whole nights would turn to days and days to nights
And we would still be kissing. Occhu Bocchu
Filled suddenly with roses from our love
And Burma with regrets, for what we'd lost.
Yet still sometimes we have it, it is there,
I feel it, it is gone. Oh that I might
Meet toward the end of this deep jungle night
Some new endearing Presence, that could guide

Me to new love or Jill back to my side,
Or else make me forget it all and be
Absorbed in this profound intensity
Of Asian jungle dark undecked with stars!

(BIRD *appears.*)

BIRD:

I am a bird, a jungle bird. I am
Bird's true condition, always voyaging.

BOB:

A talking bird! You are a talking bird?

BIRD:

Each person has, some time, a talking bird.
At just one moment of each person's life,
Old books say (I believe them), man or woman,
The person has an intimate encounter
With what's nonhuman in the natural world.
This time of yours is now and is with me.

BOB:

It is? It's true, I dreamed, when six years old
And thereabouts, that I might learn the language
Of birds and animals, and speak to them—
Especially I wanted that of birds.

BIRD:

What did you wish to say to us? or hear?

BOB:

I wanted to know what it would be like
To be nonhuman, to have colors, and
To spread myself about, by wings, in space,
But most of all to know some kind of freedom,
Some special lightness, being rid of legs
And chest and arms and back and knowing only
The feeling of the air on every part.

BIRD:

Have you experienced this at all as yet?

BOB:

I have, in dreams, when, often, I can fly,
Which I can start by running very fast.
But only then—and then I am asleep.

(SANTA CLAUS *appears, on a terrace, looking out at a river.*)

SANTA CLAUS:
> Look how the Ho Ching River gently breaks
> Its silver lines in moonlight to the east!
> Oh for such beauty I would, sure, surrender
> My criminality, and love the world!
> But where is beauty when the moonlight's gone?
> Aye, there's the rub! In wealth and robbery!
> Ho Ching, good-night!

BOB:
> Dear Bird, did you hear that?

BIRD:
> Hear what? Heard no
> One but yourself for I can only hear
> Your human words and not another's, no.
> But, what distracted you? What did you hear?

BOB:
> Heard Santa Claus, who's led us this far way,
> And who is loved by Jill—she whom I love—
> Speak of his criminality and evil,
> Which makes me fearful that some ill may come
> If we go on with him. Bird, you heard nothing?
> Something in how he said it made me fear—
> Could it have been a dream? My mind is troubled.
> Would you could tell me what this was and means!

BIRD:
> Gladly shall I inform you. Come with me
> Into this singing arbour, where we birds
> Are holding solemn colloquy tonight,
> A parliament of fowls, where we decide
> Each six-month all the most important questions
> Pertaining to our state. Come, follow me,
> And you may ask the question of us all!

(BOB *and* BIRD *go off. Loud singing of birds.*)

Scene 4

A clearing. JILL *is asleep.*

(Enter a young MOTHER, *with a* CHILD *five or six years old. The* MOTHER *and* CHILD *are dressed in a rather old-fashioned way. They are* JILL'S *dream.)*

MOTHER: *(as if continuing a story)*

But no one could ever really harm the Red Robins. You see, they had some kind of wonderful good luck, which always meant they'd come to no serious harm. Of course, that was not really the President that was killed, either. The real President was back in the capital, signing bills. The Red Robins! The Red Robins! Oh how we—I mean how they—loved islands! And the sky!

CHILD:

What were they like, Mommy?

MOTHER:

They were—Oh, I don't know, child, don't ask me. They were happier in a way than anyone else on the earth. *(She cries a little.)*

CHILD:

Oh Mommy! Don't cry. I'm sorry I asked you. Why is it so sad? Was it a long time ago?

MOTHER:

It seems a long time. But—it's all right. You can ask me anything you want. Come, what would you like to know?

CHILD:

I'm—I'm so sorry!

MOTHER:

You needn't be sorry, actually. I shouldn't be such a fool.
Why are you still beside me? Why aren't you off at school?

CHILD:

I'm not old enough yet, Mother.

MOTHER:

Oh, I'm sorry. Of course. Yes, we'd get into the planes, start the motors humming, and fly off regularly into the grey-pink evening sky!

CHILD:

Where would you land, Mother?

MOTHER:

Oh, in every sort of place! Islands, volcanic mountains, sometimes in fiery molten valleys hundreds of miles under the earth. Once there was a high place full of snowfalls, a terrace on which gulls served us lemonade, and high trumpets made a music out of stars.

CHILD:

Oh, if only I could see it!

MOTHER:

Do you want to go?

CHILD:

Go where, Mother? Go there, Mother? Oh Mother, I'd die to do it!

MOTHER:

You mustn't do that, child. Just stay. Grow older, a little older. Then we shall
see. I will, if I can, then take you back myself—Chim Dek, Chim Dek—

CHILD:

What, Mother? Oh tell me, what did you say?

MOTHER:

I—I don't know. I am a foolish mother, a stupid girl. Listen, darling, I'm
sorry. I don't know quite what I said.

CHILD:

I want to go!

MOTHER:

We cannot go, dearest. As far as being a Red Robin is concerned, either one
is one or not. There is no way to get to be one.

(MOTHER *and* CHILD *go off, and* JILL *wakes up.* BOB *comes in and sits on a stone.*
JILL *goes to him.*)

BOB: *(to himself)*
I saw last night that Santa Claus was evil
And the birds told me there was no Tin Fan!

JILL: *(her dream has made her very sad)*
Bob . . . let's go home.

BOB:

You, too? Yes, I've been feeling that we should.
Why do you want to?

JILL:

I don't know.

BOB:

I think it's probably the best thing after all—
Yes—I'll go tell the plan to everyone—
We'll rendezvous in Shanghai and, from there,

Take the long passage home. Jill, meet me here
In half an hour, and we'll fly.

JILL:

                I will.

(BOB *leaves.* JILL *now speaks alone.*)

Asia, good-bye! Travels, good-bye! And you,
Hope of my life, my love, my Santa Claus,
Forgive me, and good-bye! I don't quite know
What takes me back, but do know I must go.

Scene 5

The White House. Seated around a great table are the PRESIDENT, JILL'S FATHER,
the EASTER BUNNY *(disguised as* COUNT LAPIN, *a French nobleman), and* TERRENCE
(disguised as an ENGLISH LORD*).*

PRESIDENT:
It's a great pleasure, of course, to have convened
A group of such distinguished persons here.
Count Lapin, you are welcome, and you, Sir Terrence,
Lord of Northumberland and Counties east
And west of there. You, also, Henry Brules,
Of Minneapolis, a businessman,
The image and the model of what's best
In the American way. Our subject is—

EASTER BUNNY:
Sir, the Red Robins and the harm they've done
And do your country by their voyagings!

PRESIDENT:
Dear Count, what harm is that? It's always seemed
To me they were benign, good, lovely birds,
Both girls and boys, who seek the beau ideal,
The truth that lies beyond the sun and moon
Where luck and love are one.

TERRENCE:
                      Those are but dreams—
Proper to youth, perhaps—but only dreams!
The truth, dear Sir, is that when they're enacted
As they are by this foul, unlawful bunch,
They harm your nation's image—and the world.

PRESIDENT:
  So bad as that? I do not think I know
  What these proud boys and girls have done that is
  Of harm to anyone.

EASTER BUNNY:
      Sir, you must know it—
  They've done much wrong! Have taunted apes; have planted
  Rose seeds on Kinta Plain which grew so strongly
  They forced all other vegetation out
  And left the natives starving. This year, they
  Brought snowstorms and all kinds of winter weather
  Into the Burmese jungle, where before,
  Even apes did sweat to climb. These are your "Robins"
  You think so innocent!

TERRENCE:
  And they have broken Attanwandu Island's
  Enormous crystal eggs to look inside
  For clues to where Tin Fan is, which, once known,
  The earth will be destroyed!

PRESIDENT:
                          The earth destroyed . . . ?
  That doesn't sound to me like them at all!

JILL'S FATHER:
  I don't believe it! My daughter never would—

PRESIDENT:
  I do not think—

EASTER BUNNY:
                  Think! They have spoiled the image
  Of that good, sweet United States you love!
  I say this shame must stop!

TERRENCE:
                  And I agree!

JILL'S FATHER:
  Something of this that is too strong for me!
  I am Jill's father, come to claim her back—
  But you, goddamn, I'll not hear her reviled
  By such as you—and you—

(He angrily attacks TERRENCE *and the* EASTER BUNNY, *tearing at them, and thus reveals something of their true ape and bunny identities beneath their disguises.)*

EASTER BUNNY:

Why, damn you, I—

PRESIDENT: *(leaping to his feet)*
Stop! Instant! Peace!

(He rings a bell. Enter WHITE HOUSE POLICEMEN, *who seize* TERRENCE *and* EASTER BUNNY.)

Most furious officers, arrest these two!
(indicating the EASTER BUNNY*)*
Lock this one fast in prison. Heaviest chains
About him wind—for he is magical
And may have powers that go beyond those known
To human intellect. *(indicating* TERRENCE*)* This ape, once chained,
Load onto plane and fly to Unfound Island,
Where he'll be held by those who justly rule.
(to JILL'S FATHER*)* Sir, I am sorry. I am much distracted.
What was your suit to me?

EASTER BUNNY: *(aside)*

He knows too much!
How did he ever get to know so much?

(to PRESIDENT*)*

Believe me, President, you have not the power
To hold me here. The Robins all shall die!

PRESIDENT:
Take him away! Enough!

(The BUNNY *and* TERRENCE *are led off.)*

JILL'S FATHER:

I have a picture
Of Jill with the Red Robins. *(He hands a photograph to the* PRESIDENT.*)* I have come
To ask you if my baby might come home.
I want her home. Mother is sad and lonely—
Her life seems nothing to her without Jill—

PRESIDENT:
Dear Sir, you once agreed to let her stay—
On the Coluhdson Terrace you agreed—

JILL'S FATHER:
How did you know?

PRESIDENT:
I know. But is it fair—?

JILL'S FATHER:
Feelings are fair, my Lord, howe'er they come!

PRESIDENT: *(gazing at* LYN's *face in the photograph)*
True! True!
(aside) Oh, down, my surging heart! My pulse, lie still!
Lyn! Lyn! *(to* FATHER*)* Perhaps I'll go there with you—and we'll see!

(Great roaring, crashing, and flapping. Enter an aide, very upset.)

AIDE:
The East—the Easter Bunny has escaped
And with him Terrence, clutched in his white arm!
He broke the White House walls and all the roofs
And, with one kicking punch, destroyed the work
That all First Ladies ever dreamed and did!

PRESIDENT:
(aside) Good God! Dear Lyn! To think she is in danger
Takes all my thoughts from me! *(to* AIDE*)* Quick, Sirs, a plane!
I'll follow him!

AIDE:
All planes are grounded, Sir,
By some strange palpitation of the air
Caused by the Easter Bunny!

JILL'S FATHER:
Oh, Jill—

PRESIDENT:
Lyn!

AIDE:
And scientists are saying—this is worse!—
That any flights attempted in or out
Of the United States for thirty days
Will end in engine failure, and in death!

PRESIDENT:
Alert the nation!

(He goes off swiftly, followed by JILL'S FATHER *and the* AIDE.*)*

Scene 6

The streets of Shangai. JILL *has just arrived. At the top of one of the Shanghai stairways are the* MOTHER *and* CHILD *who were her dream.*

MOTHER: *(to* CHILD*)*
Well, we got here just in time! We're with the Robins!

CHILD:
I like it! How beautiful everything is!

JILL:
Shanghai!

MOTHER: *(unseen and unheard by* JILL—*to the audience)*
The Easter Bunny, when they were asleep,
Gave all the worst of dreams. Jill's was of me—
The rabbit's evil powers summoned me
From where I lived, to be in it, to be
Herself, a mother, living in the States
And not a Robin any more—remembering
The life she'd had, wishing it would come back.
And all the Robins were in fact the worse
For what the Bunny'd done. They all decided
Their life was useless and they should go home.

(Enter LYN, JIM, *and other* RED ROBINS, *separately.)*

LYN:
Should we go home? Bob, I feel something . . . *wrong*—
As if I were no longer sure, as if
We were by going home somehow endangered.
Do you suppose
It all could be an Easter Bunny's trick?

BOB:
How could we know? We have to do what we
Are able to. I feel I can't go on.

(The EASTER BUNNY *appears. Only the* MOTHER *sees him.)*

EASTER BUNNY: *(jubilantly)*
Victory! Victory is mine!

*(*EASTER BUNNY *leaves.)*

MOTHER: *(aside)*
Not yours but mine,

May be this victory, Bunny, after all!
For I shall right whatever wrong I did
And save my younger self, whose dream I was,
And thus reverse the time.

(*To* JILL—*only* JILL *can see or hear her.*)

Jill, can you hear me? Jill, call Santa Claus!
It can be your salvation if you do.
Call Santa Claus.
Have you forgotten him? He has some powers
You've known, and loved, but he has others, too,
Some holiday power he has not used as yet,
With which I think that he can save you now.
Jill, call him! He's not far.

JILL:

Didn't I see you last night in my dream?

MOTHER:

You did. And you will never see me more
Unless you do arrive in Tin Fan, for
There I reside , in a white-silvery building
Which looks out on the River of the Doors—
And *there* is Paradise. Beautiful Shanghai,
City of golden stars—but as a cloud,
A shadow, or a memory, to Tin Fan!
Till you come there, farewell!

(MOTHER *and* CHILD *go off.*)

JILL:

Santa Claus, can you help us? Oh where are you?

BOB:

Jill, it is too late! We must go home!

(SANTA CLAUS *appears at the top of the stairs. While he speaks,* SANTA CLAUS *scatters snowflakes over the* RED ROBINS, *reviving them both with the snowflakes and with his magical words.*)

SANTA:

It's not too late. Because—
Get up everybody, we're going to go
To a place where there's sunshine and soft white snow—
To a place that's been perfect since time began—

We're going to take a journey to fabulous Tin Fan!
Tin Fan, Tin Fan, the old people say
Is the only place on earth that is also a Way!
So . . . ARISE!

(*The* RED ROBINS *are themselves again.*)

BOB:
What happened to us? What?

JIM:
Shanghai! The stairways!

JILL:
How strange! I can't believe that we gave up . . .

BOB: (*to* SANTA CLAUS)
Santa Claus, I . . . apologize. I dreamed . . .
I dreamed last night . . . I thought . . . that you were evil.

SANTA CLAUS:
Sometimes I think it myself. You've done no harm.

BOB:
And there was something else as bad—or worse—
I was with birds and understood their language.
In some strange way they seemed to know the truth.
I ask them things. They answered me. They told me
That there was no Tin Fan!

LYN:
N-no Tin Fan!?

(*sounds of birds*)

The birds, though, may be lying after all
Out of wishing to keep Tin Fan for themselves!

BOB:
I never thought of that—that birds might lie.
But is that possible? Do birds and animals lie?

LYN:
I want to go and see!

JIM:
Of course we will.

(Now a VOICE *is heard, the* TIN FAN VOICE *that* LYN *heard in Act* II, *Scene 4, when she was on the boat.)*

VOICE:

> I am Tin Fan. I am Cathay. Extreme
> The pleasures I propose. Extreme the dangers
> You must go through to find me—chiefly, one:
> That you will not believe that I exist
> And you'll give up the search. If you do not,
> I'll make you happy for eternity.

(A MESSENGER *arrives and hands a letter to* JIM, *who opens it.)*

VARIOUS RED ROBINS:

> Jim, what is it?

JIM: *(dramatically)*

> > It's—it's a letter from Dr. Pep,
> Inviting us all to come and visit him
> At his plantation on the Azhakansee!
> It is important. The President will be there
> And other men and women filled with power
> And fortune, who would fain investigate
> The nature of our being on this earth.
> So we should go.

BOB:

> Then, quickly, into the planes!
> Toward Dr. Pep—and all that mystery!

(They fly off.)

Scene 7

The banks of a Jungle River.

(Enter MARIAN, *a native girl.)*

MARIAN:

> I am Marian, the native girl who is a sort of love slave to Dr. Pep. It was I who sent the message, which is mostly lies. But my God, I hope they come! My life here is unbearable. It will end. Only they can save me! Oh, I hope they will come!

(She goes off.)

Scene 8

The sky above Asia. It is late afternoon, changing to dark, and, with BOB'S *entrance, dawn. The characters appear in the sky one by one—first,* SANTA CLAUS.

SANTA CLAUS:

> I am Night. I am Death.
> I am the place where no one can follow.
> They cannot know it.
> My face and form do not show it.
> I am Crime. I am Death.
> I am Night. I am what never can be found.
> Chim Dek.
> I am master of all, of the day,
> Of the year, of the hour.
> Only at Christmas is my power seen,
> And then it is misunderstood.
> I am incapable of good
> (Or of evil). I am Power.

(Enter JILL.*)*

JILL:

> I am Life.
> I cut the Christmas cake with a keen-bladed knife
> And give it out unequally to the casual guests.
> I am involved in everything that is best
> And worst. I set standards for what I try
> But my only negative judgment is to die.
> Neither good nor evil am I,
> In Boston or in Shanghai,
> For I am Life.

(Enter LYN.*)*

LYN:

> I am Desire. I am Enchantment and Desire.
> Whenever, wherever I go there, there is fire.
> I burn and will consume. I startle the President in his living room,
> The hawk, and the acrobat on his high wire. I am Desire.

(Enter JIM.*)*

JIM:

> When will I find the peace of great experience?
> Where is the star I can follow

That is not hollow, that brings me home again?
I am Intellectual Desire, Aspiring Mind.
I fly, criss-crossing earth and humankind.

(*Enter* EASTER BUNNY.)

EASTER BUNNY:
I have infested these airplanes
With a kind of dream gas
So that no one will ever clearly know
Exactly what things mean.
By this, I expect to prevent
Them from reaching their destinations!

(*Enter* BUD.)

BUD:
Foolish as usual, our enemy miscalculates
The nature of our mission—to mediate, to communicate
To bridge the state between earth and the sky!
Oh tell me, Apollo-Buddha,
In what week are you fixing to linger
In the white bony church of our feet?

(*Enter* LOUIS.)

LOUIS:
In the peace of the night
I am the thought of the day
That is there, but cannot be seen.

(*Enter* BILL.)

BILL:
I am the missing page of the magazine
That prefigures light.
I am the body, when it is strong as a stone.

(*Enter the* PRESIDENT, *walking slowly, holding a letter.*)

PRESIDENT:
Forever alone . . . Well, maybe now . . . I'll find her with this letter.

(PRESIDENT *walks off. Enter the* STARS.)

STARS:
We are the Stars, and we are not known.
Only at midnight is our power shown

And then it is misunderstood.
We do no evil, no good. We stay here to show
As the ocean stays below to show
That what is not known
Shows many ways to be, although it seems,
Sometimes, that there is but one way alone.

(STARS *leave. It begins to grow light. Enter* BOB.)

BOB:
Why do you seek me, god of the sickly wail
And uneuphonious song? Is it that I and my kind
Have offended you in the temples of hillocks?
Of pillows? In the sky, everything is the controls
And the whispering of sashes, like the way a bright eye flashes
Or airplane crashes, which is the wind against the plane.

FINAL CURTAIN

—1977

The New Diana

Scene: A large pleasant restaurant near the sea, on a Greek island.

(A FRENCH POET *comes in.)*

FRENCH POET:
 I am the French poet and I wish a bite to eat.
 Please show me a table where I may have a seat.
 Over here, sir. Do you write modern poetry?
 Or some more easily understandable kind?

WAITER:
 We don't ask that question in France.
 Who is this beautiful girl, now about to enter?

(Enter DIANA, *dressed in a cloud.)*

DIANA:
 I am the dark death sentence to all mortal longings.
 I am the drastic dream you'll wish that you never had.
 Old-fashioned it may seem that I still strike so strongly
 But, believe me, waiter and poet, I am real, this is no dream.

WAITER:
 Will you have a seat, ma'am?

FRENCH POET:
 How you dramatize yourself!

DIANA:
 I am Diana Diane, adorable as a desk in the breeze.

FRENCH POET:
 Old Chinese poems
 Don't speak of one like you.
 How does it happen
 That you are on this island
 And in this island restaurant with me?

DIANA:
 I have come to be by myself.
 I wanted to escape old longings
 And find new ones, or find what's best of all,
 No longings. This island seemed the right place,
 Pretty but as flat and empty as a desk.

But now you, handsome and filled-with-desire French poet,
Seem to me to complicate *la chose.*

FRENCH POET:

Ah, you speak French?

DIANA:

French and a hundred other languages—
I am the rose, the dew of which it dreams,
and the dark night that quenches its desires.

WAITER:

And I am the fig tree.
Listen, you two, are you going to order?
And, tell me, are you at the same table or not?

FRENCH POET *and* DIANA:

We are, we are.

(Enter five slightly smaller FRENCH POETS.*)*

DIANA:

What's this?

FRENCH POET:

These are my colleagues,
Other poets slightly smaller than I.
Here is Guy Dupin, René Lamour, Georges Truc,
Emile Hautbois, and Roger de la Glen—
He is half British.

DIANA:

Oh, they are slightly smaller than you are!

FRENCH POET:

Yes, in France the reputation affects us physically,
And I am famouser than any of these. But they are growing—

DIANA:

All at the same rate?

GUY DUPIN:

Good morning.

FRENCH POET:

Hello. No, see where Georges Truc shoots above the rest
Like a young sapling in its Maytime vigor
Or like an evergreen whose yellow shoots
Go up, then turn to green in its same sun.

GEORGES TRUC:
Bonjour.

DIANA:
And de la Glen is just a trifle shorter.

FRENCH POET:
Yes, he is.
But, welcome friends and fellow poets. How
Is everything in Paris? You've just come
To Coldwall Island, where I've been for months.

EMILE HAUTBOIS:
All's well. Our fame has grown a little bit
As you can see. Georges got a good review
In *Le Monde de la Merde.* And I am writing
A play which I hope will be a success.

FRENCH POET:
(laughs) Well, I'd better get busy.
I don't want you to get bigger than me.
Diana, let me introduce you to
These five fine poets. Emile, Georges, René,
Roger, and Guy.

GUY DUPIN:
I'm very charmed.

OTHERS:
And I and I and I. And I.

WAITER:
Well, all together? Shall I make a feast?

DIANA:
Yes, do. And let it be
On my account. I'll buy these poets food
And drink if they will only promise me
To write of me in poetry some day.

GUY DUPIN:
Thank you. We'll try.
You know it's hard
To say to prophesy
That sure poetic card
Which one will pull

Out of the life-prose wool
And turn into immortal words
That sing more prettily than birds
A-circling in the sky.

EMILE HAUTBOIS:
But we will try.

(*Enter* TEN CHILDREN.)

CHILDREN:
We are the children not allowed to come in restaurants alone
Because we have no money not enough to buy a bone
And because we have no manners we are wild and full of fun
If you don't give us food for free, we'll bite you every one!

WAITER:
I'll call the manager!

CHILDREN:
Call him! Go ahead. Call the manager!

DIANA:
Oh, don't abuse the children. They're so sweet!
Come, children, join us. Sitting at our feet
You'll eat the scraps we throw away from dinner,
Our kindness to you helping us to be thinner.

FIRST CHILD:
(*Cockney accent*) Mum, we ain't dogs. We don't want your filthy scraps, your charity!

SECOND CHILD:
(*New York gutter accent*) Yeh, gorgeous. We'll take what we want. YOU get down on the floor!

THIRD CHILD:
(*Girl, shrill voice*) You bitch!

FOURTH CHILD:
(*Girl, French*) Fehk you!

FRENCH POET:
Ah, are you French?

FOURTH CHILD:
Papà!

(FRENCH POET *and* FOURTH CHILD *rush into each other's arms. The other* CHILDREN *rush into the arms of the others present. Re-enter* WAITER *with* MR. FIREBALL, *the manager.*)

MR. FIREBALL:
    Here, here—Stop that—God damn—

FRENCH POET:
    No, no, it's all right—

DIANA:
    We'll be seventeen for dinner.
    This man has discovered this girl is his child
    Lost for so many years. We'll celebrate
    Their being back together.

FRENCH POET:
    And your beauty!

DIANA:
    And my beauty!

MR. FIREBALL:
    Of all the goddamned business the restaurant
    Is the goddamnedest thing. Tell me, where, ever
    In the whole goddamned universe could ever
    Be such a purely goddamned goddamned thing
    As goddamned this, this seventeen for lunch
    Six poets, one great beauty and ten kids.
    I'll be a good goddamned son of a bitch
    If I have ever seen such goddamned things
    As happen to me in this goddamned place
    And in this goddamned business. God damn!

FRENCH POET:
    Hurray!

(All applaud.)

    The man's a poet. Join us, sir,
    And join our wild delight upon this day.
    Come! Yes! Sit down! Here comes a financier!

(MR. FIREBALL *joins the group, swearing softly to himself all the time. Enter* MR. GROSSWORD FIREWOOD, *a big financier.*)

MR. GROSSWORD FIREWOOD:
> A poor goddamned idea, making Greek temples
> In nineteen eighty or nineteen seventy-nine
> Who knows what year it is? He certainly doesn't
> With such damn fool ideas. Waiter, a table
> For one and only one.

WAITER: *(respectfully)*
> Yes sir, Mr. Firewood.

MR. GROSSWORD FIREWOOD: *(sings)*
> For when a man's alone
> His chest is like a stone
> His body with its groan
> Of Want—I want!
> Would play on him a stunt
> But I can't bear the brunt.
> I'd rather be
> A pagan suckled in a creed outworn
> Than crave for simply company. Is there corn?

WAITER:
> There is, there are.

MR. GROSSWORD FIREWOOD:
> I'll have three dozen pickles in a jar
> Followed by fifteen ears of sweet white corn
> Cooked lightly only slightly as you know
> How I like it to be cooked. On corn I'm hooked.
> I love corn. I love pickle. But those temples!

(A small man, MR. SEMPLE, rushes in, to MR. FIREWOOD.)

MR. SEMPLE:
> It's I, sir, William Semple . . .

MR. GROSSWORD FIREWOOD:
> Semple, you crazy lunatic, you nard,
> You field of unploughed shit, you half an acre
> Of idiocy, you miles of untilled, fart,
> You head of hay, you heart of gunk, you feet
> Of slithery slimy snakefats who are you
> To enter with your feet that make a crunch
> On this old timber floor, to harm my lunch?

FRENCH POET:
He is a poet, too!

DIANA:
We'll have him shortly!

MR. SEMPLE:
I didn't mean to bother you at all.
But I have just won a million dollars on a bet at football
And I can help you build those temples. Financially, I mean.

MR. GROSSWORD FIREWOOD:
For Jesus Christs's
Sweet sake, he who by dying, saved us all,
You meathead, why Greek temples? I am glad,
Sit down, go on, sit down,
I'm glad you won this money. Go ahead
And build the temples for yourself. I'll gladly
Give up my interest in the whole damned deal.

MR. SEMPLE:
Oh I want you to help me, Mr. Firewood.
I've never done an enterprise like this.
You have so much experience. Come back
To our sweet partnership.

MR. GROSSWORD FIREWOOD:
I am goddamned
If I can see the point of building temples.

DIANA:
Excuse me, sir.

(MR. FIREWOOD *sees her and is overwhelmed.*)

MR. GROSSWORD FIREWOOD: *(very softly)*
Diana!

DIANA:
Excuse me, sir. Why for the simple beauty of them, sir.
Come now have lunch with us. And we shall feast
The world of beauty which you'll help to build,
I hope. This project seems so good to me!
You Mr. Semple are a witty man
To think of it. Come, join us. If you wish,
Forget all now and eat, be drunk, then after,

Perhaps three mornings after you can think
About how to build temples, when and where.

MR. GROSSWORD FIREWOOD:
I'm tempted. Nay, I know I'm overcome.
Come, Semple, with us. We shall feast.

MR. FIREBALL:
I'll be goddamned!
Well, welcome, Firewood, to this curious crew.
Waiter! you sweet white Asiatic Jew!
Come join us also. Then we'll twenty be
And all of life shall bear us company!

WAITER:
But if I sit, oh sir, if I sit down
How will the food arrive?

MR. FIREBALL:
                    I'll phone the town
And ask three boys to come and work for me *(goes to phone)*
For just this afternoon and three girls too.
(into the phone) Yes, they'll be paid. Hi, Harrison, what's new.
All right. Yes, Mickey will be fine, and Curt.
Send Betty, too. Ann. Alice. And Sir Bert.
Sir Bert's a dog? Well, all right, let them come.
But soon. Okay? God damn! *(hangs up)*
Now I myself will go into the cellar and get some wine. So merry and fair a
    crew as this deserves so tongue-tingling and care-chasing a concoction
    of vinous spirits as ever was slipped between the lips and onto the rare
    young tongue of a person!
Hoop la! Now to go down
Into the cellar of great renown,
My cellar!

(A moment of animated conversation—he reappears with wine.)

FRENCH POET:
I propose a toast to the manager!

SECOND CHILD:
To de old geezer!

EMILE HAUTBOIS:
Bonsoir!

GUY DUPIN:
Bonjour!

DIANA:
I'd like to make a toast to the world
And to chance, and to the all-electron dance!
It's so wonderful that we're all here
And for this little, this brief moment, so happy!

MR. GROSSWORD FIREWOOD:
I'd like to propose a toast to this lovely lady
On my left, no languishing lily but a living legend,
A true treat to look at and in speech an angelic linguistics lesson.

CHILDREN:
Hear hear!

MR. FIREBALL:
Ladies, gentlemen, to getting drunk!

ALL THE FRENCH:
Hoorah!

MR. SEMPLE:
To the temples of Dionysios, of Aphrodite, of Zeus, of Apollo, of the god
Herakles in Anatolia, and of Demeter and of Hera everywhere. All live!

DIANA:
Hear hear!

MR. GROSSWORD FIREWOOD:
Well, well, so be it. Done.
I'll toast it, Semple. I shall do this thing!

MR. SEMPLE: (*to* DIANA)
God bless your beauty!

DIANA:
Thank me afterwards. I'd like to speak to you.

MR. SEMPLE:
Where? When?

DIANA:
Tonight, at ten o'clock
Behind the wind house, I am—

MR. SEMPLE:
You are! My daughter!

(They embrace.)

DIANA:

Father, dear! But don't let anyone see us. Tonight, at ten!

MR. SEMPLE:

I will be there!

(Somehow no one has seen them except the FIFTH CHILD, *a little Italian boy.)*

FIFTH CHILD:

I see them kissing.
What does this mean?
Mountain top kisses the sky.
Waves kiss the shore.
I am alone.
My sandals kiss the beach.
Shall I tell no one?
I may tell someone.
But I will tell no one.
I kiss you, Silence, by the lips you are my best friend.

MR. GROSSWORD FIREWOOD:

What did that child say, what?

DIANA:

I don't not know!

MR. GROSSWORD FIREWOOD:

What's wrong with your speech?

DIANA:

I guess I'm getting a little drunk!

MR. FIREBALL:

To drink, god damn! But I'm getting hungry.
Noon has become early afternoon and shortly
It will be late afternoon and lunch ain't been forthcoming.
I need my lunch. I want my lunch. God be my guide
And lead me to my lunch. Those goddamned youthfuls
I ordered from the town, where the fuck are they?
Two young men, really boys, one dog, three girls
Who are supposed to serve us? Ah, goddamn!

(Now MR. FIREBALL *perceives the new waiters at the door of the restaurant.)*

Now they appear, their features at the door

With heads surrounding. Hesitant, afraid
A little of how to act, they start to enter
Shyly, so timidly, that grace of youth
Which wins us by its pained uncertainty
Which, all our lives, we shall not have again
In its pure lovely form. Come in, dear kids, come in!
Surround us, greet us, then go get our lunch!

(Now fully enter the TWO BOYS, THREE GIRLS *and the very able* DOG; *they stand spaced out about the table, smile and shake hands with the people at the table, then go off to get the food.)*

EMILE HAUTBOIS:
They're an attractive bunch.

MR. FIREBALL:
The dog's fantastic.

WAITER:
He really is. He's the pride of this island. He can do anything a person can.

FRENCH POET:
Can he write poems?

WAITER:
No, not that we know of.
But he can speak. Sometimes he does, at least.
Only on certain holidays, though, I think.

FRENCH POET:
Human holidays or dog holidays? For there are in France, you know, different holidays for each animal. Rabbits' Day is June the First. Everyone goes
out and tries to keep other people from killing rabbits. But it's impossible to stop the dogs. Ah, how horrible! Dogs, the friends of man! We have
to shoot them, clout them, strangle them! Ah, ah, ah . . .

(He chokes, trembles, seems overcome with anxiety.)

EMILE HAUTBOIS:
Help! Help him!
He is our greatest poet and he has
So fine a sensibility that sometimes
He has these horrible anxiety fits.
There, there, a little air. Some water, please.
Thank you. He's coming round.

FRENCH POET:

  What? where? Ah yes, I spoke of holidays.
  You see, I lost my dog
  By murder that last June I spent in France.
  Oh, horrible!

DIANA:

  Don't think about it so.
  I was brought up to be a woman and
  To comfort people and to make men feel
  That they were strong and good and independent
  And masculine and grand. This suited me
  At first, and did for years, but then I found
  A spring of water gushing from the ground
  With a whole ring of silver flowers around it
  And the spring said to me, "Diana you
  Exist and in yourself and for yourself.
  As such, you may and will keep helping men,
  But know, as well, you are the tree yourself
  On which the fruit of life comes forth again
  And again and again and again." So I was doubled
  In purpose and in strength. Do you feel better?

FRENCH POET:

  Yes. What a beautiful story you just told!
  The finding of identity. Always lost,
  We poets are always looking for a way
  To make what we are equal to the day,
  The tears, the hour—but what was I saying? Yes.
  And there is Horses' Day on which wild horses
  Are let loose in the streets of each French town
  And General Animal Day on which all beasts
  Are given wine to drink—

CHILDREN:

  Here comes our feast!
  Hurrah!

(*The food is brought in; it features a very large* TURKEY.)

MR. FIREBALL:

  Well, let's begin!

MR. SEMPLE: *(softly)*
My daughter! and my child!
My heart is driven wild
By this insane event!
Oh sweet is my content!
Thanks, Lord, if this was meant!

MR. GROSSWORD FIREWOOD:
I'll carve the bird.

SIR BERT:
Wait, sir. One word!

THIRD CHILD:
The dog! He talked!

SIR BERT:
One word from Turkey Tim.
Then you eat him.

DIANA:
A talking dog!

MR. GROSSWORD FIREWOOD:
A miracle! Great God!
I'll carve the bird.

WAITER:
Sir, wait. A moment, wait. Sir Bert the dog just said that the turkey or someone named Turkey Tim, who is, one may presume, the turkey itself or is inside or near or a part of or at any event somehow connected to the turkey, as aircraft carriers are and/or were connected to World War II, well, let's have a cheer, I mean, everyone has come together not to honor Caesar but to release him from the firing squad of his own worst feelings, he stands here before us now, a man without a care in the world only because he is dead, but cognizant, oh he is extremely cognizant of his weakness which is that he can hardly stand sorrow and life as difficulties at all, still, if he is a turkey, I move or vote that we should at least let him speak, for although if he is the turkey which we see here he has already been killed and is thus dead, for this turkey has been cooked, still, we should give him or it or whoever it is, a try, and just content ourselves with waiting a very tiny bit until the turkey talks, if he or it is going to, which I think is going to happen because I've never known Sir Bert, am I not right, sir, to waste, because they are so damned difficult for him to produce, his words. Let's pause.

DIANA:
I think he is right, because . . .

FRENCH POET:
And so do I.

(At this moment an OLD JAPANESE PRIEST enters the restaurant.)

OLD JAPANESE PRIEST:
I am an old priest, Mawata Gushi by name.
I have been traveling for seven hours without finding a restaurant.
Now I have come to this restaurant by the western waters
And here will set my ancient burdens down.

(He puts down a cage covered by a cloth. He takes off the cloth revealing, in the cage, an enormous live TURKEY. It looks over at the table and raises its wings.)

CAGED TURKEY:
Mishiti wai witchi gan.

PRIEST:
Yes. I will release you. Matsu go-n.

(PRIEST opens the bars of the cage and TURKEY goes over to TURKEY ON THE TABLE.)

CAGED TURKEY:
Mishiki wai nowuga gan! Ish tang!

TURKEY ON THE TABLE:
Nai shi mai nah ghee itan, korega.

PRIEST: (coming forward)
What they are saying is:
My mother! My daughter!
My father! My son!

FRENCH POET:
The roar of ocean drowns out all the rest!

(Roar of ocean is heard.)

FRENCH POET:
We must leave this restaurant

GUY DUPIN:
Of sorrow and tears

EMILE HAUTBOIS:
Of sorrow, courtesy, and affection

GEORGES TRUC:
Of nail polish and the seasoned Parnassus of nude motions

RENE LAMOUR:
This restaurant of gratitude, of food, of restlessness

ROGER DE LA GLEN:
This place of eyes, nose, and ears

MR. GROSSWORD FIREWOOD:
And go to another place where there is not this sorrow

MR. SEMPLE:
Of a father mother united with daughter son
Or mother daughter united with son father

DIANA:
When one of them is dead

WAITER:
Dead as my knee feels
After a long and horrible day in this restaurant!

MR. FIREBALL:
You never told me. But,
Friends, no. You should go on with your meals.
Japanese, will you sell us your turkey?
Then will you join us for lunch?

OLD JAPANESE PRIEST:
Yes, I will.

MR. FIREBALL:
If both turkeys are dead there is no tragedy.
No feeling is lost, is uncovered. Things are in a normal way.
Everything is averaged out and regularized. Turkeys are for us to eat. Who
can say otherwise?

CHILDREN:
How are we going to kill the turkey? the new Japanese turkey?

FRENCH POET:
Perhaps we won't. Perhaps we will let these two go. These two turkeys. We
shall probably have only wine and vegetables and bread and strawberries
and raspberries and cheese for lunch. And much more wine. Thank you.
Such will be our lunch.

DIANA:

For I think really the cooked turkey came to life,
Because it spoke; so, Japanese priest, you can take both the turkeys away
To their own destined life.

OLD JAPANESE PRIEST:

I thank you kindly.
I'll put the turkeys outside.
Now may I still join you for lunch?
I have been wandering a long time.

MR. FIREBALL:

Yes. And now let the vegetables and other things be brought in.

BOYS AND GIRLS:

Yes sir! But we have a request from Sir Bert, sir. He asks your leave to absent
himself for a few minutes from service to go outside and talk with those
birds.

MR. FIREBALL:

But they speak Japanese.

FIRST BOY:

Sir Bert knows it, Sir. But he thinks he may be able to get through to them.
He thinks they may be able to tell him something that there is no other way
for anyone to know.

MR. FIREBALL:

Yes, of course. Let him go out. And tell him that if they tell him anything
important, to tell us, too.

FIRST BOY:

Yes Sir, I will. (to SIR BERT) It's all right to go.

SIR BERT:

Thanks. Bark. Woof. Woof.
I'm off to speak
To those gods of squeak
And flap
While we rap
If I can make out their lovely Japanese
I'll know something that is bound to please
The universe.

MR. GROSSWORD FIREWOOD:

There goes an over-optimistic dog. How could there be anything new to
find out that could really make everyone happy? I mean, for more than a few

moments. I mean, I've been happy at this lunch and everything, but it's not from new knowledge and new facts.

DIANA:
But experience is knowledge as surely as that which words convey.
And nothing may communicate more than what we have so far done on
    this day.

FRENCH POET:
Maybe, but I seek some inner secret of functioning.

MR. FIREBALL:
And I would like to get on with this goddamned fucking luncheoning!
Bring in the trays!
Promptness pays!

(Enter BOYS AND GIRLS *with vegetables, etc.)*

CHILDREN and FRENCH:
Hooray!

DIANA: *(calling)*
Sir Bert! Come on in now. Lunch is served.

OLD JAPANESE PRIEST:
It's all right if he stays out there.
In your kindness you have evidently forgotten
That he is one of the waiters, just as those birds
Were to be our food. They do not have to come in for our lunch.

FRENCH POET:
That is true.

SECOND CHILD:
Yeh! Hey, dese cawlyflowahs is really good! Hoowraw. I proposes a toast. To
    de sunshine!

ALL:
To the sunshine!

FRENCH POET:
To the sea!

ALL:
To the sea!

DIANA:
To whatever lives and dies!

ALL:

   To whatever fucks and flies!

MR. GROSSWORD FIREWOOD:

   More wine!

DIANA:

   May this day never end!

(It becomes very dark. EVERYONE *leaves. Then it is dawn. Re-enter* SIR BERT *and* TWO TURKEYS.*)*

SIR BERT:

   Whew! That was quite a night!

FORMERLY CAGED TURKEY:

   It certainly was. Well, we'd best be heading southward.

OTHER TURKEY:

   Yes, Marian and I are going to Bird Island, where we'll be safe, and where there are so many holidays.

FORMERLY CAGED TURKEY:

   Good-bye, Dog. It's been sweet to know you.

SIR BERT:

   Good-bye, you two.

(They go off.)

SIR BERT:

   Good-bye! *(to himself)* I don't know myself what I found out. But it was *something.* And, now, I'd best get back to town! No reason to work in the restaurant today. And soon it will be time for my own lunch!

(He goes off.)

ACT II

Scene: The Poetry Reading / a platform, a stage, the sun.

DIANA:

   So that's why they've come to this island.

MR. SEMPLE:

   Yes daughter. It is because
   Poetry, which escapes in a way from laws
   Has need itself to be uttered and functioning
   And to this island all poets they've been summoning
   To air their wordlists in this dreaming air

Of nineteen whatever it is—
Listen. They're starting the poems.

ANNIE RAGLAND or ANNIE RAGTAIL: *(at the podium)*
   I don't know if Annie Ragland or Annie Ragtail is my name
   But I do know we have here some poets of very worldwide fame
   From Russia from Austria from Poland from the good old USA
   From France and Italy and Australia we are going to hear today.

AN OLD MAN: *(sings)*
   Where the mountains got trails
   And the sparkling of sails
   And the light blue foam of the bay
   Give the lie to whales
   And reindeer tails
   We are going to hear some language today!

ANNIE RAGLAND or ANNIE RAGTAIL:
   Of a most superior kind! Yes old beggar man, thanks!

BEGGAR MAN:
   That's okay. I too have joined the ranks
   Of poets. Would you like to hear another song?

ANNIE RAGLAND or ANNIE RAGTAIL:
   Not right now. Later maybe. In fact, later for sure. Yes!
   I loved your song
   Old beggar man
   As much as Annie Ragtail can
   Love anything.
   Annie has an emotional problem
   Of some kind—damned mysterious
             Intimacy troubles Annie,
          That being so close to someone
      Or even to something—
          She even has it about things. God!
          And commitment, too, is painful for her.
      Better to be a goat and run in rings
   About a splintery peeling post
      Than live all one's life as an emotional ghost
          Like Annie Ragland or Annie Ragtail.
      But I think help is in sight.
      These poems I'm about to hear are going to help me, maybe cure me.

MR. FIREBALL:
Poor damned dear! That's what I call an "as if"
Personality
Or some bad kind of intensity I don't know.

MR. SEMPLE:
Here come the poets.

ANNIE RAGLAND or ANNIE RAGTAIL:
This is Pierre de la Foudre, from France!

PIERRE DE LA FOUDRE:
Thank you for having me up.
I will read my poem "The Sparkling."

    "The Sparkling"
    Quand, j'avoue, vert—

MAN IN THE CROWD:
Read it in English!

PIERRE DE LA FOUDRE:
Mais—

SECOND CHILD:
Yeah, do what de man says, yuh goddamned commie bastard!

WOMAN:
Sh, shh, don't be rude to the foreigner!

MR. FIREBALL:
They're not all communists you dumb kid!
He just happens to write the French language. Now
Shut up!

SECOND CHILD:
Ah nuts!

PIERRE DE LA FOUDRE:
Very well. I'll read it in English. Though it will lose a lot in my translation.

MAN IN THE CROWD:
Who cares? At least then maybe we'll understand it.

RAUCOUS WOMAN:
Maybe we won't want to!

MAN IN THE CROWD: *(now seeing her)*
Agnes! Agnes de Saint-Jennings! My first love!

RAUCOUS WOMAN:
  Edward Storkie! Oh my darling!

(rush into each other's arms)

PIERRE DE LA FOUDRE:
  Can I begin my reading?

SECOND CHILD: *(seeing these two together)*
  Mommy! Daddy! Jesus H Christo! Mom and Dad!

RAUCOUS WOMAN:
  Bendino, our baby! *(all three embrace)*

SECOND CHILD: *(through his tears, which embarrass him)*
  Aw nuts!

MAN IN THE CROWD:
  We're all together again!
  Let's go out on a boat
  Away from the rooster and hen
  And simply float!

SECOND CHILD:
  Let's listen to de poem. I met dis guy yesterday. Maybe he ain't so bad.

PIERRE DE LA FOUDRE:
  Hhhhhrrrrummm. I'll begin.

  The sparkling of the action of the ocean
  Curving, curving in a vast unity, visual effects—
  The narcosis of an ivied stream, a man-hunt-type desk.
  Spores, needy Naiads, the gracious, excellent teams.
  Thank you madman. This orchestra is filigree.
  Iron stockpiles the trunks. In the B Movie sputters an arroyo.

DIANA:
  It's beautiful. I hope it goes on.

PIERRE DE LA FOUDRE:
  This, lady, is the sparkling. Sparkling of keys
  In the Frigidaire, when night day everytime
  Mountain and gypsum struts, eagle-like splendors
  Where all is sparkling and nothing is bare as blood.
      . . . . . .
  Thank you.

(Applause. He takes a seat on the stage. A RUSSIAN POET, CLIMATOFSKY, comes on.)

ANNIE RAGLAND or ANNIE RAGTAIL:
   Thank you Pierre.
   Very fair
   Were the words you uttered.
   I confess
   I liked best
     When the arroyo sputtered.
   But the whole thing was beautiful.
      I'm so excited.
   It makes me want to go out on a boat.
      Shall we all go out on a boat?
    I mean why not give in to the lovely excess
  Of art and our response to it?
     How many moments in life are going to come
      When language instructs the body like a drum
    Saying Hold it! Do something else! Be happy! Strum
  The very guitar of your being! Be happy! Get into a boat
     And row row or paddle away! Or use a big engine
      and roar!
     Why are we waiting? I mean what are we waiting for?
  Uh-oh. I'm sorry. The Russian poet.

RUSSIAN POET:
   Ing ing ing ingsky

MAN IN THE CROWD:
   Read it in English!

RUSSIAN POET:
   I vill try. Mine boam iss De Noodle Fectery.

MR. GROSSWORD FIREWOOD:
   That's a German or a Jewish accent. Not Russian!

RUSSIAN POET:
   I'm zorry. I learnded Inglitch in Rotterdam.

MR. GROSSWORD FIREWOOD:
   Oh yeh, that's it, I guess—a little Dutch.

RUSSIAN POET:
   Bot vikss de poam I am prektish. I cang read it mittoudt almost heccent. I
   pekin.

    "The Dog of Night"

MAN IN THE CROWD:

You said you were going to read "The Noodle Factory." Maybe some of us want to hear that one. I don't know.

RUSSIAN POET:

I'm zorry. I vergok. Hokay.

"The Noodle Factory"

In the Urals in a little nothing town
Somebody was very bright and built this factory
Which now manufactures the most noodles in the Soviet Union
Lenin once passing through this area at night
Heard the roar of the machinery. Those are the noodles being made, he
    said,
Almost purely for love, since few are eaten in our country
By the brave men and women of the Soviet Union.
And the factory was given a price, and Lenin said in the
    announcement
Your achievement is beautiful. No one will ever forget it.
And the men and women at the factory wept
And they held one another tightly—and then the great experience was
    over.
Each person of the factory went back to his life slightly changed.

(applause)

Thank you.

DIANA:

Read us "The Dog of Night" too. I'm curious to hear that one.

ANNIE RAGLAND or ANNIE RAGTAIL:

It's supposed to be one poem per poet. I'm sorry . . .

RUSSIAN POET:

I read dats one too. It's very short.

"The Dog of Night"

Day is a cat to the dog of night.
She scratches him. Streams of blood come. And that is the sunrise.

Denk you.

(thunderous applause)

WOMAN:

That's the most beautiful poem I've ever heard.

MAN IN A FOXTAIL HAT:
    It certainly is beautiful.
    I wonder if we could get a phonograph recording of it,
    Of him reading it. Or maybe we could just remember it,
    Do you remember it? It's very short.

WOMAN:
    No, I don't.
    Funny, isn't it, how you think you should be able to remember something
    And then you can't. Hear how the loud wave beats upon the shore!

MAN IN THE FOXTAIL HAT:
    I think from now on we're going to be happy.

WOMAN:
    I'm so happy now!

MAN IN THE FOXTAIL HAT:
    That's not the same thing. Do you want to hear more of
    The poems? Or was that one, culminating experience enough?

JAPANESE PRIEST:
    Nothing is enough. Or, there is no way to know that it is enough.
    Even what causes us to smile happily or to drop into exhausted sleep is not
        necessarily enough.
    These may be mere stages. Even at the end of the reading we will not know
        if it has been enough.
    Although it will be over. That at least will be clear but it is not the same
        thing.

ALL:
    True, true. Now, shhh.

ANNIE RAGLAND or ANNIE RAGTAIL:
    We now have a Dutch poet, Adrien Mools.

(*Enter* ADRIEN MOOLS—*people are still applauding the Russian poet.*)

ADRIEN MOOLS:
    Hello. I too was very moved by *"The Dog of Night."*
    Well, I guess I will just read my poem *during* your applause.
    Okay? My poem is named "Okay."

MR. SEMPLE:
    I'm feeling strange. I want to build a temple.
    A temple of words like these inspires me—
    Everything, noun, adjective, just right,

232 ❧ KENNETH KOCH

The portico and shaft of the temple,
The beauty that is lovely to the eye
With the feeling also, the ease, and the tension of weight.

(Applause for the Russian poet is still going on.)

ANNIE RAGLAND or ANNIE RAGTAIL:
Now stop this fooling around.
Hear a glorious sound.

ADRIEN MOOLS:
I appreciate this build-up for my poem.
Since each poet is given only a few minutes,
I take all this as added to my time.
It is hard to give the work and thoughts and feelings of a lifetime
Voice in a few minutes. But I shall try. My poem is called "Okay."

MR. GROSSWORD FIREWOOD:
As he's already said.

ADRIEN MOOLS:
          "Okay"
When you ask me at night I say I'm okay
But in the daytime I say Wait until tonight. Then we'll see
How I am, if I'm okay or not. Pullets run round in back
And front of the automobile that crushes the farm—
Land slightly down in all its dewy splendor. Now it is night
And you approach me. You ask. And I say I'm okay.

(Applause stops totally. Sudden silence)

Okay I'm say I and. Ask you. Me approach you and
Night is it now. Splendor dewy its all in down slightly land
Back in round run pullets. Not or okay I'm if am I how
See we'll then. Tonight until Wait say I daytime in the but
Okay I'm say I night at me ask you when!

MR. GROSSWORD FIREWOOD:
Jesus Christ!
There's something about pure avant garde that's absolutely thrilling.
Did you hear what he did? He read the poem backwards!
The second stanza was the first stanza read backwards! Do any of you know
     that?
It's so goddamned exciting!
I don't know why it should be so.

MAN:

Wait a minute, Sir. I don't believe what you said is true. Miss Jannings and I would certainly have noticed it. We'll ask the poet. Is it?

ADRIEN MOOLS: *(glad of this attention)*

Well, yes it is. I'll read it
Again and then you can see.

ALL:

Hurrah!

ANNE RAGLAND or ANNIE RAGTAIL:

It's not in the rules

ALL:

Hurrah! Who cares about rules? What we have before us is Life!

ADRIEN MOOLS:

Thank you.

> "Okay"
> In the evening
> Stock
> Lines
> Hell. A curiosity
> The devil.
>   .... Thank you.

(sparse then increasing wild applause)

DIANA:

God what a genius!

MR. FIREBALL:

That wasn't the same poem!

MR. GROSSWORD FIREWOOD:

Of course not. Teddy, sometimes I don't think you're cut out for the arts. Don't you see what a brilliant added comment that was?

MR. FIREBALL:

No.

DIANA:

But I see. Pierre! You've come down here. Did you like that? I loved your poem. It is so classical.

PIERRE DE LA FOUDRE:

Yes, I did like it, Diana. I love you. Let's get out of here. I think about you day and night. I need you.

DIANA:

It's only been one day and one night since we met.

PIERRE DE LA FOUDRE:

That makes no difference.

MR. GROSSWORD FIREWOOD:

Shhhh.

ANNIE RAGLAND or ANNIE RAGTAIL:

We have now a local poet, a poet from this island, a dog, Sir Bert.

SIR BERT:

Thank you. Arf. Arf arf arf wurf.
  Wurf wurf wurf wurf arf arf arf
  Whine mew arf arf rrrrahhrrrgh arf woof!
  Mmmmmm woof!
  Arfy. Arf arf woof.
  Arf arf arf arf arf. Woof woof woof woof woof.
  Arf arrrrrrgh mew woof! Woof arf! Arf woof!
  Arf arf woof!

(tremendous applause)

MR. GROSSWORD FIREWOOD:

Maybe that's what the turkeys told him—
That life is only the noise we make in response to the tortures and the
  pleasure it inflicts on us.
Then this absolute sound
Would be the new poetry, for which we have so long waited.
Pretending to be aviators, engineers, artists, all manner of things
But that which we are in truth, the living legends
Of which the characters and the stories are underground
As revealed in Sir Bert's magnificent poem . . .

MR. SEMPLE:

He's reading another work. My mind is wild.
He stands before me as a temple's child,
Four-columned, porticoed, and still, as if asleep,
The way dogs are, and temples are, all things
Man can but leave his mark on, not yet be.

MAN IN HAT:
  Be quiet! He's reading. Or about to read.

MR. GROSSWORD FIREWOOD:
  He's not exactly *reading*.

OTHERS:
  Shhh.

SIR BERT:
      "Argh"

  Wurf woof arf
  Woof wurf
  And arf arf arf
  And and and and and
  Ar wurf arf and woof woof and.

(gigantic cries of bravo and barks)

PIERRE DE LA FOUDRE:
  Gigantic cries of bravo and barks
  Sound out for this poet whose poetry sparks
  This hysterical yet happy response.
  Mine is a darker path, that of using words
  Which have more signification. And yet—and yet—
  What he does has, even to me, such great appeal—

DIANA:
  It is the *and* that I got out of this with most delight—
  Dog noises, and then . . . *and,* as if the music
  Of human Language there did have its birth,
  After the guttural snafflings of the sea!

ANNE RAGLAND or ANNIE RAGTAIL:
  And now, before our next poet, intermission! Everyone be back here in five
  minutes. Funf minooten. Cinq minutes. Cinque minuti. Mang fong. Ooopsko
  Manhout.

CHILD:
  An intermission! Great!
  Let's go in the ocean!

OTHER CHILDREN:
  Wow! Yeah! Come on!
  Poetry's great, but. A quick swim!

(They run off.)

PIERRE DE LA FOUDRE:
    Let's lie down on the sand.

DIANA:
    Take my hand.

PIERRE DE LA FOUDRE:
    You were worth waiting for.

DIANA:
    In this moment you're all that I adore.

MR. GROSSWORD FIREWOOD:
    But I love her too. I love you too.

DIANA:
    I'm sorry. But I do love Pierre.

MR. GROSSWORD FIREWOOD:
    I am dying of despair.

(He runs off down the beach.)

WAITER: *(runs on breathless)*
    Mr. Grossword Firewood threw himself into the ocean
    Where, rocked back and forth by a light Mediterranean motion,
    He almost died. But young Ann Lungs ran to his side,
    And now he has asked her to become his bride.

SOME:
    We're stunned.

WAITER:
    But there is much more. Much much more.
    I hope I can get it all! Remember the children who were here?
    Well, they all ran up to the ocean, too, and they were
    Kidnapped by the Russian poet.
    He locked them up in an iron boat
    And has made off with them.
    International police are searching everywhere. The boat can't be found.

DIANA:
    That's terrible.

WAITER:
    But just now it was found. The children weren't in danger at all.
    The poet was just taking them out for a joyride.

DIANA:
  Ah!

WAITER:
  But most amazing of all—

(Enter hurriedly OLD BEGGAR man.)

MAN:
  Everything the water told you is a lie!
  But it doesn't matter. Listen to my song—
    Old skies beam—

MR. FIREBALL:
  Wait. The poetry reading is starting again. Well that was quite an intermission.

(CHILDREN run up)

CHILDREN:
  We were kidnapped at least we thought we were kidnapped. Wow.
  But we know the Russian poet is our good friend now.

MR. GROSSWORD FIREWOOD:
  Watch out he doesn't try to convert you to Communism.

ANNIE RAGLAND or ANNIE RAGTAIL:
  Quiet everybody please. Here is our Australian poet, Sir Adrian Dump.

ADRIAN DUMP:
  Greetings one and all. My poem is about the sea. That's
  Natural enough, what with my coming from Australia.
  Here is my poem.

        "D.Z."
    D.Z. is beautiful.
    No one has such dark eyes.

  That's all. I know it isn't much. I mean it doesn't seem like much. But it includes everything I feel. It's like a condensation of it. If you concentrate on each syllable you'll observe that the whole short poem captures the motion and the fullness of the sea. Farewell to you and my poem. I am going to destroy my poem and myself. I'm not really. That was only to make you laugh. Good-bye.

DIANA:
  I liked him.

PIERRE DE LA FOUDRE:
    He seemed to be crazy—
    In any case, very upset.

ANNIE RAGLAND or ANNIE RAGTAIL:
    Here is Ching Ta Foo, our Chinese poet. He can't speak English so he is
    going to read his poem in Chinese and then Sir Adrian Dump is going to
    read an English translation of it. Ching Ta Foo.

CHING TA FOO:
    In fact, I do speak English.
    Sir Adrian, you can sit down.
    So sit down and listen because
    The poem I'm going to read is terribly long—
    Long as the horizon, long as a long long look at the sea—

ADRIEN MOOLS:
    That breaks the rules
    But it's all right, continue!

ANNIE RAGLAND or ANNIE RAGTAIL:
    We have to be careful with the Chinese!

CHING TA FOO:
    Long as a boyhood imagining of forests, long as a strong
    Fixation on paradise in the mind of a saintly person, it is long
    As when the priest says "going backwards and forwards in history,
    We do not see" and long as the recollection
    Of a dead friend, who has become a part of one's being
    As one is, by his love, in the world. And that is how long it is.
    Now what it is
    Is something different.
    What it is, is itself, and I now shall tell
    It—my first mistake in English, you know I
    Learned the language secretly
    In a small town where dogs are rampant,
    And where the lonely yellow bare-bosomed canary
    Sings its plaintive, elegant lullaby at dawn
    Rather than at darkness because that is when, there, canaries are about to
        go to sleep.

DIANA:
    How beautiful! This Chinese bard can make
    My blood run cold and then turn warm again
    Like all of April gushing in one phrase.

PIERRE DE LA FOUDRE:
> He is, I think, famed in the Orient
> For bringing back those antique powers of speech
> The East considered lost for centuries—

PRIEST:
> Yes. In this one man,
> A baby not long hence, the power appeared
> Or, rather, reappeared.
> And now the Orient which has lain
> Too long, long, long, long languishing shall rise
> With might poems and deeds to break the skies
> Of you all-loving West.

DIANA:
> That makes no sense.

PIERRE DE LA FOUDRE:
> But let's attend.

DIANA:
> Was that his poem?

PIERRE DE LA FOUDRE:
> No. He starts it now.

CHING TA FOO:
> My poem is called "A Prophesy for Greece."
> It concerns a man who threw himself into the ocean—

MR. GROSSWORD FIREWOOD:
> That's me.

(CHING TA FOO *stands on the platform silently, not reading.*)

PIERRE DE LA FOUDRE:
> The Chinese poet remains silent.

PRIEST:
> He has remained silent through a considerable interlude.

DIANA:
> Why does he not go on reading his poetry?

SMALLER FRENCH POET:
> Perhaps his poetry is ourselves—or what happens.

CHING TA FOO: (*breaking the silence*)
> And it also concerns
> A man named Mister Wemple—

MR. SEMPLE:

It sounds like me!—What—?

CHING TA FOO:

And a beautiful woman
Who will become, but only for seconds, a goddess—

PIERRE DE LA FOUDRE *and* MR. GROSSWORD FIREWOOD: *(seizing her hand)*
Diana!

MAN IN THE FOXTAIL HAT:

Read us the poem!

WOMAN:

Yes, if you talk so much about it
It will be an anticlimax when it comes.

MAN IN THE FOXTAIL HAT:

Well, it may be. Maybe it will not.

CHING TA FOO: *(after another short silence)*
Is the reading almost finished?
It is my impression that for a long time,
Long before I came to this platform,
And all the while I was here,
That it has been I who was speaking
Perhaps through the mouths of other people and things.
But I do still have some words to convey to you
Through my own boccal tube.

DIANA:

How strangely he speaketh—

PIERRE DE LA FOUDRE:

As when small wave breaketh—

CHING TA FOO:

Here is the last part of the poem
Which concerns all the things I've already said
And also has to do with a tremendous luncheon
Had at the restaurant, the
Dashing, splashing restaurant on this island.

CHILDREN:

Hooray!

CHING TA FOO:
>Now I begin. Or, rather, I'll begin to end.
>>May Socrates and all the thriving Greeks
>>Who studied out their civilizing ways
>>Be proud to annotate inspired eruptions
>>Of new fresh life and days upon these islands—

SIR BERT:
>Woof wurf woof.

CHING TA FOO:
>The new shall protect us from the past with its hard bowls and its hundreds
>Of sharked-toothed terrors. Listen to it. For now
>My elegy is at an end.

DIANA:
>It's a remarkable piece of poetry.

MR. GROSSWORD FIREWOOD:
>I think we should now all read some poetry ourselves.
>I want to read one of my own.

DIANA and PIERRE DE LA FOUDRE:
>I didn't know you wrote poetry.

MR. GROSSWORD FIREWOOD:
>I don't. But now I've just composed one.
>In my mind. And a man in his first poem may be as good as anyone else.

PIERRE DE LA FOUDRE:
>Well, I don't know.

MR. FIREBALL:
>I have a poem, too.

PRIEST:
>And I.

CHILD:
>And I.

PIERRE DE LA FOUDRE:
>Well, go on Firewood, get up there!
>You start.

ANNIE RAGLAND or ANNIE RAGTAIL:
>This is against the rules of this complex morning
>Or this beleaguered and dark and sea-troubled afternoon.

MR. GROSSWORD FIREWOOD:
I don't care. I have a poem—

ANNIE RAGLAND or ANNIE RAGTAIL:
Our "open" "free" poetry reading is on Tuesday.
Today is Friday. Oh I don't know what day it is!
But I know it isn't the day for our open reading!
It's an insult to our great poets! You can't do it.

RUSSIAN POET:
Let them read!

CHILD POET:
Poetry belongs to everyone.

CHING TA FOO:
I think, as in a People's Reading, everyone should have a chance to speak
And read his poems, even though to us, literati, they might seem
Like ordinary conversation, it, whose slightest words,
Yet can move us and amaze us so much, driving us to laughter or tears (and
    what do these matter?)
Anyone who feels life's drama today should speak.
This is my political and my artistic view.

SIR BERT:
Hear! hear! Let all come forward!
Or those come forward who, at any rate,
Like Grossword Firewood feel a tongue on fire
Inside their mouth and in their chest, desire
To say the thing of heart and meat and mind. Arf! Woof!

WOMAN:
Odd how this day the slightest chance remark
's like some art animal of Noah's ark!
The words of poets so inspire the mob
That commonest person's speech can make us sob.

MAN:
Even a dog's.

WOMAN:
But, what,
Finally, a dog!

MR. GROSSWORD FIREWOOD:
Well I'll go up.

ANNIE RAGLAND Or ANNIE RAGTAIL:
Oh well, if you gentlemen say so, all right.

MR. GROSSWORD FIREWOOD:
I'll read my poem.

"To Diana"

Your voice it is to me
What a special kind of girlishness must be to history
A cubic Phenomenon
Which no one thinking of more earnest things could ever have
    counted on
Or thought would be so important in his, that person's life.
Diana, my bird, I want you to be my wife.
Diana, oh my favorite word, will you be my wife?

DIANA:
Oh I can't. Mr. Grossword Firewood I'm very touched
But I really can't. And—

PIERRE DE LA FOUDRE:
Get up on stage and read it as a poem
As he did. That way you'll be able
To communicate in the same kind of meaning.

DIANA:
All right. I'll try.
So—My poem is "I'm sorry but I cannot do that thing which you've
    requested, but don't be so despondent, because what about Ann Lungs,
    who recently rescued you from the sea, from death in the sea. Don't you
    love her? That should be great consolation."
I guess that was the poem. I thought it out in kind of a funny way.
Too much in advance. So it was all just the title.

(*Enter* ANN LUNGS.)

PIERRE DE LA FOUDRE:
Like the sea.

DIANA:
Je ne comprends pas.

PIERRE DE LA FOUDRE:
I think you will—later. But now listen . . .

MR. GROSSWORD FIREWOOD: (*back on the platform*)
"Don't you love her?"

Yes, yes I do. You're right. Now I do. But the poem
Was one I thought up just before I ran into the ocean,
To try to kill myself!

DIANA: *(gets up on platform with him)*
                    Yes, I see!
Oh then it's fine. Then it's all right!
Good! Now let there be
Nonunion between you and me
          But continuing friendship, and amity.

PEOPLE IN THE AUDIENCE:
   It's a poetic play!

(Applause; all get up and leave as ANNIE *cries out "Thank you! Thank you! every-body!")*

*(*DIANA *returns alone.)*

DIANA:
   So many conceptions of poetry today,
   So many ideas of it. Yet through it all, one sole divinity,
   One fabricator of beauty, the human brain.
   "What is art?" changes to "All is art!" then the wheel turns round again.
   And "Nothing is art" seems written on its crescents. I am Diana.
   I am the very foil of effervescence.
   I live and die in it. Mr. Semple is my father
   In the human world. In the divine one he is my creator . . .
   My power to understand all this grows empty
   Even now, as I return to my variance again. Father! French poet!

(Enter MR. SEMPLE *and* PIERRE.*)*

MR. SEMPLE:
   Yes, Diana, we're coming. Here, over here!

PIERRE DE LA FOUDRE:
   Look what the sea has thrown up—a fresh-washed monster!
   A vision of beauty like Aphrodite but with horns and tails!
   What can it signify?

DIANA:
   Nothing. Don't look at it. It is the past
   That is merely here, in its strangeness.
   To disregard it is certainly not dangerous.
   I think that Poetry—

PIERRE DE LA FOUDRE:

   —has awakened, perhaps, this monstrous form from the sea.

MR. SEMPLE:

   Which my temples will cause to appear
   In its true beauty.

(SIR BERT *runs through.*)

SIR BERT:

   Yes, if any are granted consciousness—
   Including you!

PIERRE DE LA FOUDRE:

   What does that mean?

SIR BERT:

   Come, follow me! I'll tell you the story

(*He leads them off. The stage is empty. Enter a man who personifies the* OCEAN.)

OCEAN:

   I am the ocean.

(*Enter the* EARTH.)

EARTH:

   I am the earth, I am the sand, I am the beach.

(*Enter* PEACHTREE.)

PEACHTREE:

   And I am a flowering peach.

OCEAN:

   I am still the ocean.

EARTH:

   I am still the beach.

PEACHTREE:

   I am still the peach.

ANNIE RAGLAND or ANNIE RAGTAIL:

   It's nice to have people around
   That's why I helped with this reading. Nature's always the same.

(SEA, EARTH, *and* TREE *take off their masks. They are two of the waiters and one of the waitresses who waited on tables in the restaurant.* ANNIE RAGLAND or ANNIE RAGTAIL *doesn't seem to notice they're removing their disguises.*)

THE THREE YOUTHS:
  Pensez-vous!

ANNIE RAGLAND or ANNIE RAGTAIL: *(going off)*
  Nature's always the same!
  But so, in fact, is my personality!
        Look, the evening star. Or is it the morning star?
      To me it's just a subject for poetry.

(It gets darker.)

FIRST BOY: *(seeing the star)*
  It's the goddess!

(SIR BERT runs across the stage.)

SIR BERT:
  Wurf Warf!

(sound of the sea, end of the act)

ACT III

Scene: The night sky, full of STARS. *The* STARS *speak.*

FIRST STAR:
  I am a star, shining. I can barely be seen
  But I am here anyway. The problem is one of moving.
  Stars are stationary. They stay still.
  What if I want to go camping? If to stay here in one place is not my will?

SECOND STAR:
  I am a star, too, a female star.
  On earth I was more beautiful than a jar.

THIRD STAR:
  We are always talking.
  It is as if the talking were our shining.
  But we have deep dark needs we must fulfill.
  How can only talking be satisfying?

FOURTH STAR:
  It cannot. We must find a way
  To bring our star bodies next to each other
  So we can plan things. And then do them.

SIXTH STAR:
  I don't know what we can do but shining.

FIFTH STAR:
I feel very happy doing it, shining, shining.

FIRST STAR:
We are born, we shine, and we die.

FOURTH STAR:
Not for a long time.

THIRD STAR:
My life seems to be but a moment.

SIXTH STAR:
Yet you've been here, believe me, for a long time.

FOURTH STAR:
I am shining.

FIFTH STAR:
You are shining.

SECOND STAR:
We are shining.

SIXTH STAR:
Steadfastly.

FIRST STAR:
Yes it's a very great responsibility.

FIRST STAR:
What is?

FIRST STAR:
To be a star.

EIGHTH STAR:
You're talking to yourself.

FIRST STAR:
Oh. It seemed to be a good way to make a point.

SIXTH STAR:
Yes *(laughing)*. We stars are always making points.

THIRD STAR:
Five points each, according to human designs.

EIGHTH STAR:
Do you remember those dumb things we used to draw,
Saying these are stars?

SEVENTH STAR:
> Now we know differently. Being a star
> Is mainly not a matter of points at all
> But of having a hot center.

SIXTH STAR:
> Oh I am inside so hot.

FIRST STAR:
> And I.

SIXTH STAR:
> And I.

SECOND STAR:
> My God, when you think—

THIRD STAR:
> It's really true—or is it? how can it be?
> When we were just it seems yesterday down to earth
> Running up and down doing everything
> That we are stars?

THIRD STAR:
> Telling us just what we are.

SECOND STAR:
> But they'll not know us

FIFTH STAR:
> Or anything show us

SEVENTH STAR:
> Until they themselves are a star.

NINTH STAR:
> You weren't supposed to be the one to say that.

FOURTH STAR:
> Cool it, Gus.
> Hey, I've called you by a name.
> I wonder what that means.
> Perhaps something is changing.

THIRD STAR:
> Maybe and maybe not. I do feel it.
> I feel something.

SEVENTH and EIGHTH STARS:
> *(excitedly)* Warming us? or cooling us?
> It is DAY!

(The stage becomes light; stars disappear. It is day, summer.)

(Enter MR. SEMPLE.)

MR. SEMPLE:
> My temple! It is almost done!
> Beneath the white, fabulous sun
> See it rising
> On endlessly beautiful columns,
> Slightly uneven as Greek columns were
> And white as new December—
> O my temples!
> A joy to those on earth, and to the sky
> An Invitation from Humanity!

(Enter DETECTIVE DOBIE.)

DOBIE:
> It may be an invitation, but you're not going anywhere!
> You're under arrest!
> No going out for you!
> You've violated Ordinance Five Hundred Sixty-Two—
> Defacing ancient areas. I've been following you
> For fifteen days. Now stick em up. You're under
> Arrest!

(DOBIE freezes.)

MR. SEMPLE:
> It's he who seems to be under arrest.
> He's not moving!
>   A hostile statue!
> I have enough to worry about, what with
> Diana and all the rest parted from me
> By a severe tempest at sea. It seems
> So long ago—an eternity almost.

(He goes off.)

(Enter a large group of assorted persons journeying in the same direction: HEBE, ARISTIPPUS, a GREEK PRIEST, a SHOEMAKER, SIX CHILDREN, and THREE SOL-DIERS. HEBE may be played by the same actress who plays DIANA, ARISTIPPUS

by the actor who plays PIERRE, *and so on. There is dust and the sense of a pilgrimage.)*

CHILD:

Here we are on our way to the Greek temple.

SHOEMAKER:

I am a Greek shoemaker, Estarchus by name.

ARISTIPPUS:

I am Aristippus, famed worldwide as a philosopher
Or am I a playwright? Sometimes in these dark green evenings I forget.

SHOEMAKER:

Aristippus, you're sounding to me like a poet.

ARISTIPPUS:

I guess, Shoemaker, yes, I guess I am.

HEBE:

I am Hebe, an instructress at the temple. Come, little girls
And boys.

CHILD:

Instructress, what will you teach us at the temple?

HEBE:

I will not teach you anything today I think
For today is the holiday of the goddess Ypus
She is the goddess of luncheons and poetry
And the goddess of plays and she is also the goddess
Of the instructress and the high and mighty goddess of children
Of all times and places, and she is the goddess of the rain
And the snow also, and is sometimes thought to be a candidate
To be goddess of goddesses.
And she, children, is also the goddess of lost good-byes
And it is to her temple that we are going.

GREEK PRIEST:

A great goddess, and one I know well.
How sharp and excellent and flat and good this morning
Air, as we go tramping over the brainland.
The soul-land, the heart-land, our Greece!

HEBE:

Indeed it is. And a fair way of speaking
You have, ancient minister.

GREEK PRIEST:
> Thank you. I was a poet in my youth
> And a speaker of poems. I would
> Sing them, chant them really, you
> Know how it's done here, sometimes at banquets—
>> *Bradidoctolos hos*—

CHILD:
> Is it true that today, Mr. Aristippus, there will be candies at the temple
> And jellies and other things adored by us children
> In the hot sun or in the winter when the frost is on the pumpkin?

ARISTIPPUS:
> Strange! there is not a trace in Greek statuary
> Or sculpture of a single pumpkin! I wonder—

CHILD:
> And little tiny mountain goats to play with, oh what a pleasure
> It is to romp with a little animal all through the day
> Or through the morning at least, and then there's the violet monument of
>> lunch
> Like Athens seen at a distance, through a scented mist
> Of aqua, which the sunlight breaks through!

ARISTIPPUS:
> I do wonder—

FIRST SOLDIER:
> We are Thracian soldiers we are going to the temple
> Of lost good-byes. How many times we've said good-bye to our sweethearts.
> And then come back and said hello and then said good-bye again.
> Some of those good-byes get lost, the early ones. But we heard a Spartan
>> say
> They are gathered together in a high pot in Thessaly
> And that is why we have come here to make our voyage
> To this temple where we shall have these feelings back.

ARISTIPPUS:
> Why do you want them? Though I guess as a philosopher–poet I should
>> know.

FIRST SOLDIER:
> You really should know.
> But that won't make me unwilling to tell you—
> We want them back for their power,

Their power of drama, their power of feeling;
When we said them, sometimes, it seemed as though our souls had got out
    of us,
As though our hearts hit hard and hateful hands
Of a priest who would run with them
To top a tall plain pyramid of death. That's why we want them—
For their strength. If we could get that energy back inside us,
Heaven only knows how strong we should be, how worthy in battle
And magnificent on the pavement too and in bed, and everywhere we
    were.

SECOND SOLDIER:
And that is why we make our pilgrimage to this temple.

THIRD SOLDIER:
Even though we've had to journey for thousands of hectares

FIRST SOLDIER:
It seems worth it!

SECOND SOLDIER:
You were not the one who was supposed to say that.

FIRST SOLDIER:
Never mind.

HEBE:
Well, it is the right temple
To which you young soldiers are going. *(She pauses a moment)*
One bears a cap with ribbons on his head
And is smooth-faced yet, has not begun to shave. He is very young.
He carries a long white wooden staff and seems grave in his demeanor
For such a young man. He must have had some grave experience
Very early in his life to make him so.

SECOND SOLDIER:
And the other? I am another.

ARISTIPPUS:
The other is quiet, the kind of man liked by his fellows
Always and very much. He seems honest, reliable, tough. He'd never let you
    down
Or ask you for anything selfishly just for his own pleasure
He wears cloth boots and carries a spear or a staff—
It is a spear, and on its handle are cut out the words (with
A knife) *Soma Kalyptos essin* which must be in some Grecian dialect

With which I am not completely familiar. But now he speaks
In a gruff voice, and, when he does so, his fellow warriors smile.

SECOND SOLDIER:
Hey, that was all right! Let's have a drink!

ARISTIPPUS:
Yes, a good idea. Just pass the flask around as we keep walking.

CHILD:
Shoemaker, shoemaker! or priest, priest!
What about the third soldier?

SHOEMAKER:
He has cut himself

GREEK PRIEST:
With a sliver of wood

SHOEMAKER:
The cut has become infected

GREEK PRIEST:
He needs a doctor

SHOEMAKER:
He is medium height and thin

GREEK PRIEST:
And wears a cloth vest, rope shoes

SHOEMAKER:
And smokes some funny kind of pipe

GREEK PRIEST:
Which seems to be in the shape of Aphrodite

SHOEMAKER:
Goddess of love and beauty.

THIRD SOLDIER:
I am going to the temple in hope to be cured
Of the infection I got from this cut. I want lost good-byes, sure, but I need
    more than that,
I think—the direct intervention of some god or goddess
To heal me, as did happen to me last year in Epidauros.

GREEK PRIEST:
Epidauros! Did I hear you mention the word *Epidauros?*

THIRD SOLDIER:
If you were listening to my speech, old fellow, you did.
For I have just said it. Said I was cured last year at Epidauros
It was of a chest wound. I was cured by Aesculepius.

GREEK PRIEST:
Well, that is the very temple or shrine that I seek.
Am I going in the right direction?

THIRD SOLDIER:
I think you are going in exactly the wrong direction
Since it has taken us months and months to get from there to here.

SECOND SOLDIER:
Yes, but we were not always walking in a straight line.

FIRST SOLDIER:
Still—there's truth in what he says.
We're nowhere near Epidauros, as surely as I'm of Thrace.

GREEK PRIEST:
Oh dear! I wonder if I should turn around and go back that way?
It's hard to leave a group one has been traveling with
Even if one finds one is going in a wrong direction. Where did I read that?

HEBE:
In the Odyssey. Athena is helping Odysseus and it is all a trick on the Cyclops
Who can't see, in any direction. The Cyclops is afraid they'll go the wrong
   way,
And that, even if he realizes this en route, it will be hard for him to go
   backwards—

GREEK PRIEST:
That's right! Still, I don't feel any nearer
To knowing what to do. Wisdom shows us
That the problem we have is familiar and may be spoken of
In beautiful language, but it does not give us a solution
That seems to apply, at least in this particular case. Should
I go back or not?

SECOND CHILD:
It seems to me you've already decided,
Sir, to stay with us, and I'm glad you have. I like you.
You remind me of my daddy in a way.

GREEK PRIEST:

I never had a son
Nor a daughter either.
But I will be glad to be father to you, little boy,
And to any of you other little boys and girls who'd like a father, as well.
I love children, and life has been hard for me,
Life has been strange for me. And yet, in its accidental causings,
Often we find a strange peace, a really bizarre fulfillment
That gives us exactly what we want. You know, I was going to Epidauros—
But I'm not, now!—to pray to the God of Medicine to give me children
That I could take care of!

CHILDREN:

Well, you've got ten of us now!
Anyway, you can share us with Hebe.

GREEK PRIEST:

I hope, Ma'am, you don't mind—

HEBE:

No, it's a blessing. I can use help with these ten children. They are so sad.
Each of them so sweet. And all without a father or a mother.

GREEK PRIEST:

But now they have us.

ARISTIPPUS:

And we, Hebe, we have each other!

HEBE:

What? Aristippus, I don't understand.

ARISTIPPUS:

Don't understand that I love you?
That Delphi's fabled fountains, groves, and hills
    Are nothing to my love that grows like mountains
And sight of you my whole heart wholly fills?
    Oh, Hebe, can you love me? Tell me! Quickly! I feel
That I can't wait a moment longer!

HEBE:

Aristippus, really! You just declared your affection for me a moment ago.
And you're a grown man. You ought to be able to have a little patience.
I mean, I'm a priestess, I'm vowed to a single life. That means unmarried
And without lovers. Just now this man has offered to be a father
To these ten children, who, in a way, are mine. I accept this offer.

He smiles, contentedly. All his adult life he has wanted to have children
To care for, and now he does have them. As he walks on beside me,
Another man says he is crazy with love for me—all in one moment! It seems
  like too much!
Maybe a warning—no, what sense does that make?—from the gods.

SHOEMAKER:

I will make your shoes for you, ma'am, if you decide to get married.

CHILD:

Oh, Mommy, are you going to get married?
May we dance by the sea when you get married?
And have lunch in the large, bold, and fragrant restaurant?

HEBE:

All right. Yes. I'll do it. Aristippus, I believe I can love you.
If the good priest would like to perform the ceremony—

ARISTIPPUS:

Oh my love!

CHILD:

Oh bewildering confusion of daddies!

HEBE:

But only one mommy!

GREEK PRIEST:

Blessings on you. But I think it would be best to wait until we get to the
  temple.
There, all other truth shall be shown—as well as this nuptial one.

ARISTIPPUS:

Yes, he is right, and we had best hasten
For it is growing dark. And with only starlight to guide us, we may become
  lost
Or end up in some monster's cave instead of at the temple

FIRST SOLDIER:

Of lost good-byes, which now at last we shall see!
Oh Margaret, Sandra, Rita,
Eleanora, Calliope, Athena—all my old girlfriends
And loves, to be reborn in the tomorrows
Of young good-bye kisses chastened by our tears

SECOND SOLDIER:

But still hot as a bastard! Let's go.

ARISTIPPUS:
First shades of afternoon

SHOEMAKER:
Now dot the sky.

GREEK PRIEST:
This stipple bids us hasten. Come, away!

(All go off except HEBE *who lingers on stage long enough to make this speech.)*

HEBE:
If we do find this temple,
As I believe we shall,
Some beautiful thing will come to pass.
I am named for Hebe, the cup bearer
But I feel stirring within me someone else,
Someone other than cup bearer.
Goddess is her name, more goddess than Hebe—
Someone astonishing—with morning star and arrows.
But this is all foolishness.
Only someone in the future could know it.
The stars will soon be up there, and I down here.
It is getting on to being dark.

(The night sky again with STARS.*)*

FIRST STAR:
Here we shine

SIXTH STAR:
Eternally

FOURTH STAR:
It seems to me there was an interruption

SEVENTH STAR:
That was only the earth's turning

FOURTH STAR:
I saw or heard something that seemed to

SIXTH STAR:
Have something to do with that woman what's her name

SEVENTH STAR:
Diana Diane

FIFTH STAR:
And her father Mr. Semple
Who wants to put Greek temples

SECOND STAR:
Everywhere

SEVENTH STAR:
Yes, even in Mexico Semple wishes to erect them

NINTH STAR:
I say the man's crazy

SIXTH STAR:
I say he's right

SEVENTH STAR:
Determining earthly beauty is a noble endeavor and thing

THIRD STAR:
Greeks were a bunch of silly homosexuals

EIGHTH STAR:
Still, their temples

TENTH STAR:
Are the world's most beautiful things.

FOURTH STAR:
My heart sings

FIFTH STAR:
Just when I think about them

SEVENTH STAR:
So let's all run to celebrate

SECOND STAR:
What William Semple's doing
And Diana Diane
And Mr. Grossword Firewood who are helping him.

SEVENTH STAR:
You know we can't go anywhere

FOURTH STAR:
We're stuck stars

SIXTH STAR:
Unable to move

FIRST STAR:

    Except, I'm beginning to think now, in orbit—
    But how can you be sure you'll find what you want in your orbit
    Or get exactly where you wish to be in your orbit?

TWELFTH STAR:

    Maybe star maturity
    Is getting to like only what's in our orbit.

FOURTH STAR:

    Maybe

FIRST STAR:

    It may be

SIXTH STAR:

    Getting light

SEVENTH STAR:

    That was a short

SIXTH STAR:

    Shining. It's

FIRST STAR:

    DAY!

(Sunlight; stars vanish as before.)

(The TEMPLE. *To one side,* SEMPLE, *his task accomplished, lies sleeping. Elsewhere on stage is the still-frozen figure of detective* DOBIE. *The* PILGRIMS *arrive.)*

SHOEMAKER:

    Here, here is the Temple!

ARISTIPPUS:

    For which we have searched so long!

PRIEST:

    There is a man asleep by it
    In strange clothing, truly strange.

HEBE:

    With beside him an
    Architectural briefcase bearing
    His name, Semple.

SHOEMAKER:

    And a statue—or else a

Human being in a
Petrified condition
Bearing a weapon, some
Curious officer of the law
With a very mean expression! What
A strange choice
For the artist
Who made this beautiful place!

FIRST SOLDIER:
And now we must find the Box of Lost Good-byes.
Passion unnerves us, the past disturbs us. We must find those hot good-
byes of other days!
By the shining column's whiteness,
That huge box!

(They go to it, pick it up, and carry it forward a little way.)

SECOND SOLDIER:
We picked it up.
Astounded by its lightness,
We sadly put it down.

(They put the box down.)

No good-byes!

SHOEMAKER:
No good-byes? No lost
Good-byes? Where are they then?
They must be really lost—lost forever, now.

GREEK PRIEST:
Wait! Don't give up! I think—
I think, perhaps, that knowing you were coming
These good-byes may have, in some way
Already left the box—to prepare for you—I don't know.

(Enter the GOOD-BYE GIRLS.)

SECOND SOLDIER: *(excitedly)*
Yes! Look! Here are the good-byes!

FIRST SOLDIER:
Atalanta!

GOOD-BYE GIRL:
Good-bye!

SECOND SOLDIER:
  Emily!

GOOD-BYE GIRL:
  Good-bye!

THIRD SOLDIER:
  Maureen!

GOOD-BYE GIRL:
  Good-bye!

FIRST SOLDIER:
  Will we see each other again?
  Oh, how I love you!

GOOD-BYE GIRL:
  Good-bye!

THIRD SOLDIER:
  Maid of Athens, ere we part
  Give, oh give me back my heart!

FIRST SOLDIER:
  Sweetest Sara of Salonika! Sublime, divine Erythro,
  Can I cease to love thee? No!

SECOND SOLDIER:
  Ζωη μου, σας αγαπω.
  My kisses—I'll send you letters—O divine—
  My breaking heart—You promise that you will not
  Forget me? I love other? Never—must we—
  Part? Oh you my soul's, my heart's
  Geometry!

GOOD-BYE GIRLS:
  Good-bye.

FIRST SOLDIER:
  And none can know, even were he to listen
  As closely as the shoreline to the sea, how much,
  Eliss, Elissa, Elissad, I say . . .

GOOD-BYE GIRLS:
                    Good-bye . . .

FIRST SOLDIER:
                            to thee. Farewell!

(The SOLDIERS, *whirled about by such return of strong feelings fall exhausted to the ground, from which they look up, and eventually rise, as* HEBE *speaks.)*

HEBE:

Yes, Aristippus, Good-bye. I, too, must go.

ARISTIPPUS:

What? What are you saying, Hebe?
What brings this stern tune to your
Soft mouth?

HEBE:

I don't know, Aristippus, but it is there.
I myself am becoming, have become Divine!

(She turns into the STATUE.)

ARISTIPPUS:

But you'll come back?

HEBE:

Yes, but I don't know when.

SOLDIERS: *(and others)*

It is she!
It is the goddess! She was with us
All the time!

PRIEST:

Yes, in a way, she was!

THIRD SOLDIER:

My cut—it's healed!

ARISTIPPUS:

Listen!

HEBE/STATUE:

I am the Goddess Ypus and I am Diana
And I am Hebe, the cup bearer of the gods.
Diana and I together have twenty children,
But since we are the same person we have only ten
For they are the same children—
As the same brambleberries run in wide ranks over Greece
So are all people the same, within severe limitations.
And I am the fruit tree, and I am the song
That the wind sings in its branches— *(she pauses)*
And there is one more lost good-bye—

THE BANQUET ❧ 263

The lost good-bye to Greece—
Uttered so many times
Then lost, then found,
Then lost again,
Now rising from this ground
And found in me—
    Good-bye Athens! Good-bye, dear chosen place!
Eternal, clear perfection!
Always mountain, plain, and sea
From everywhere one stands—
And all the human body's beauty:
Shoulders, torso, hands—
Athens, good-bye! Delos, and Crete!
Good-bye, greatest shining place
Plunging all our wonder into the sea
Of fated effervescence—Greece, good-bye!

PRIEST:

This last and lost good-bye
Is that for which we have come
So many miles
Without knowing it!
Drawn here ineluctably
Into the larger necessity of the Present! or something . . .

(Enter MR. FIREWOOD *and a few other persons from* ACTS I & II.*)*

MR. GROSSWORD FIREWOOD:

How is it that the temple Semple has built
Has attracted real Greeks and had such an effect on them?
These are personages truly from the past.
I feel a chill all over
And I am obliged to confess that Semple's idea
Is magnificent, although I do not know what we are supposed to do
    about it.
But it is as if a great butterfly were stretching its wings
Between Aegean and Aegean, between present and past.

HEBE/STATUE:

I feel the breaking of some spell . . .

(She re-becomes DIANA.*)*

SEMPLE: *(awaking)*

Diana! My daughter! My second life!

DIANA:
Pierre!

PIERRE:
Diana!

DOBIE: *(redivivus)*
You're under arrest!
I accuse you
Of statuefying an officer of the law
Paralyzing his will and rendering ineffectual his firearm
And of, before that, desecrating the soil of Greece
And therefore aiding our country's enemies
By molesting and harrowing Greek-American relations!

SEMPLE:
How this day's transformations
Inspire in me whole new creations!
Toward which, my loved ones, come, away!

(ALL *go except* ARISTIPPUS-PIERRE *and* DOBIE. *After one second,* DOBIE *leaves quickly, saying "Stop! I warn you! Stop!")*

ARISTIPPUS:
Like all these other changed,
    I, Aristippus, drawn
By love inevitably,
    Am Pierre de la Foudre, he
    Who loves Diana, the Hebe
    Of this new time—*O cela, oui!*
        (hurrying off) Diana!

(Pistol shot, offstage. Enter SHOEMAKER.*)*

SHOEMAKER:
I can't tell everything that happened at the temple.
But know this: Once was enough.
Semple was arrested and killed for resisting arrest
By Detective Dobie, then brought back to life by a goddess
Or was it a dog? I am old now, and my wits do not function
As in, an ideal condition of body, they should.

(Enter a funeral procession with the body of MR. SEMPLE *held high.)*

MR. GROSSWORD FIREWOOD:
Semple was killed by a bullet and brought back to life
By Sir Bert or Diana. Then he died of peaceful old age.

We come to bury him beside the sea
That his body may bring forth flowers, perhaps sea anemones,
As in his life it brought forth the flowers of
Architecture, Greek temples,
In whose construction at first I did not believe.

DIANA:

He was my dearly beloved father.
He gave me love before he died.
I will be unhappy for a long time
And I know it. He was a good man,
Perhaps even a great one.

SIR BERT:

What none of us knew
Until he died
Was how old Mr. Semple was.
He seemed very very very very old,
Older than any man who had ever lived.

DETECTIVE DOBIE:

Yet in his actions and in his demeanor he was youthful.
I am sorry that I shot him.

PIERRE DE LA FOUDRE:

You did him no harm. But why did you arrest him
And the rest of us?

DETECTIVE DOBIE:

I don't know.
It was some costume-enforced action, some dream.

MR. FIREBALL:

Well I'll be goddamned!

DIANA:

Here is a chosen place.

(SEMPLE *is buried.*)

JAPANESE PRIEST:

Kayoi Komachi—Kumasaka—Tamma—
Tsunemasa—Nishikigi—May his spirit be released.

(SIR BERT *starts to dig up the body.*)

VARIOUS PERSONS:

Sir Bert, stop! what are you doing?

You can't desecrate the grave that way!
And make a mockery of this solemn, holy day!
Dear dog son, stop!
Damned dog fiend, stop! *Arrestate!*

MR. SEMPLE: *(rising from the grave)*
I have reorganized the night!

(blackout, night; stars)

FOURTH STAR:
Waiting waiting waiting waiting we are waiting

SECOND STAR:
What for?

THIRD STAR:
We are waiting waiting waiting waiting waiting

FIRST STAR:
We love this word "waiting"

SECOND STAR:
Waiting for what are we? What what what?

FIRST STAR:
We're simply waiting. Wait is what stars are, we are.

SECOND STAR:
What time is it?

FOURTH STAR:
Night time. Up here it's never time for lunch

SEVENTH STAR:
Time gives us individuality

SIXTH STAR:
At the same time it takes all individual qualities away

FOURTH STAR:
This is hard to understand

THIRD STAR:
And so is waiting

SIXTH STAR:
Are we waiting for Diana Diane
Sometimes said in some guise

FIFTH STAR:
    To be the moon goddess?

SIXTH STAR:
    We could use a poetry reading up here

FOURTH STAR:
    Or a restaurant

FIRST STAR:
    Or even a temple.

THIRD STAR:
    Life seems uneventful here although
    Actually it isn't.

SECOND & SIXTH STAR:
    Our events are our thoughts.

EIGHTH STAR:
    This then may be the best life of all.

THIRD STAR:
    I wish we weren't stars
    But down on earth once more. I mean again.

FOURTH STAR:
    Do you think we could squiggle out of these shapes
    Star shapes I mean. Ouch!

SIXTH STAR:
    I don't know—ouch—really why not.
    Yes I think I'm doing it.

SECOND STAR:
    So am I.

EIGHTH STAR:
    Wait for me! wait! wait!

FIRST STAR:
    Okay, Lester, okay. We're not going anywhere
    Without all of us.

THIRD STAR:
    Whew! I'm free. But will there be any stars left
    When we're gone?

EIGHTH STAR:
Of course, you silly!
There's millions of them. Just look!

(*Dawn—the former stars, now maenads and oceanides, stand to one side. Enter* OCEAN.)

OCEAN:
Eventually I will have a convulsion,
I will cover up everything in this place!
Nothing can resist me, for I am Ocean!
You, young men, and women of me, maenads and oceanides,
Who were formerly stars, do what you must do,
What I bid you do!

FORMER STARS:
Yes, it is true, we were stars. And now we are ocean breeze,
Wavings of salt sprays, hard shells, white clouds,
And gleamings.

(DIANA, PIERRE, SIR BERT, *and others come in and sit on the sand.*)

OCEAN:
Let us have lunch!
The time for destruction is near! I shall cover over
Everything, before it covers me! I begin
With that group over there!
And, after them, everything!
Sea shells, be caucus in me to rush, and with pebbles and sand
To by froth cover them and anthologize them as my lunch!

FORMER STARS:
Ocean, we come!

(OCEAN *and others advance.*)

PIERRE:
Stop! Diana! Stop! The ocean! wait!
It's acting in a most abnormal way!
Ocean unusual! Ocean vast!
What is your intention? Back away!

SIR BERT:
It is wanting us for lunch—
Just as we wanted the turkeys long ago!
My canine spirits fall!

DIANA:
　I feel a stirring—

CHILDREN:
　Mother! Diana!
　You seem . . . so pale!

OCEAN:
　You cannot get away! Oceanides, maenads of me, come!

(They continue to menace.)

DIANA: *(standing up)*
　I'm—I'm
　Going to have a baby!

(SEMPLE enters and, confronting the OCEAN, bids it go back.)

SEMPLE:
　Ocean, no!
　Mighty one, go
　Back!

OCEAN:
　Oh,
　The time has not yet come! *(He retreats.)*

SIR BERT:
　Yes, go! Not time for lunch. We've got to get this girl
　A place to lie down!

(DIANA goes, or is led off by SIR BERT.)

(Suddenly NIGHT. In the starless sky, the MOON ascendeth.)

ALL: *(looking up)*
　Oh, DIANA!

FINAL CURTAIN

—1977

The Death of Sir Brian Caitskill

Scene 1. Winchester Palace

MEDLOCK:

    I like Sir Brian Caitskill, but I would not
    trust him for a moment with my daughter, sir!

MAYBELL:

    Then let's away! While we stand talking here
    They are together in some private nook
    In Bethany, where no one herds them about!

MEDLOCK:

    Lead where you say. I follow.
                       Let's away!

Scene 2. A Chamber in Bethany

SIR BRIAN:

    Pamela, love like ours is loving us.
    No shadow haunts us. We live in the sun
    Of our affections. Give me a little kiss.

PAMELA:

    Sir Brian, your proposals take my breath away!
    But I suppose there's no harm in a kiss—
    I've often kissed my nurse, and Daddy too
    When he would go a-hunting or to the Bourse,
    And Mommy when she was alive—oh, Mommy!
    No, no! it might not be approved by Mommy!

MOTHER: (*imitated by* SIR BRIAN)

    Kiss on!

PAMELA:

    My mother's voice. Then here, Sir Brian, my lips.
    They're yours to press against your own, mayhap.
    Take them ere my suspicious father comes.

SIR BRIAN:

    Smack!! This is pleasure, this is painless fun!
    Oh let's again—the moment is too sweet!

MAYBELL:
　　Sir Brian!

SIR BRIAN:
　　What? Who calls without?
　　Sir Emmeret Maybell . . . and—

MEDLOCK:
　　　　　　　　　　　　　　　　You churl!

PAMELA:
　　　　　　　　　　　　　　　　　My father!

MEDLOCK:
　　Sir Brian Caitskill, I challenge you to a duel,
　　Tomorrow morning at five on Himsley Field!

SIR BRIAN:
　　Sir, I accept! No pleasure's greater than to kill a man
　　Whom one instinctively dislikes. However
　　It pains me to deprive you of a father,
　　Dear innocent kissable Pamela.

MEDLOCK:
　　　　　　　　　　　　　　Stay your words,
　　Foul churl, or I shall challenge you again!

SIR BRIAN:
　　But to what end? Tomorrow, then, at five!

MEDLOCK:
　　On Himsley Field!

Scene 3. A Tavern

HUGH JEFFRIES:
　　They say Sir Brian Caitskill duels tomorrow
　　The father of innocent Pamela on Himsley Field
　　And that the duel's occasioned by a kiss!

PETER KNOTT:
　　They say Lord Medlock must outpistol him,
　　For he's the greatest shot in the dueling world.

HUGH JEFFRIES:
　　Yet Brian's young!

PETER KNOTT:
>   But pleasure-mad! and Medlock
> Defends his daughter's honor! What defends Brian?

(*Enter* SIR BRIAN.)

SIR BRIAN:
> My life! Good morrow, lords. I see ye ready
> To lay me out a corpse. Well, we shall see!
> Give me a gallon of stout—there's pleasure in't,
> And inspiration too.

HUGH JEFFRIES:
>   This duel sits well
> With Brian! See what clarity's in his eyes!

PETER KNOTT:
> It is the ale sits well. I fear he's drunk
> And will not go tomorrow to the field!

Scene 4. *Himsley Field*

MEDLOCK:
> What say, Sir Emmeret Maybell? is he come?
> What says the clock? is it not five? the churl!

(*Enter, at a distance,* SIR BRIAN, *dressed as* MOCTEZUMA.)

PAMELA:
> He comes, he comes, and radiant feathers dress him
> From head to foot! Attired, one would say,
> As Moctezuma, Lord of Aztec Ind,
> And such a gentleness sits on his brow!
> It were a crime to kill him!

MEDLOCK:
>   Silence, daughter!
> I only brought you here because you would
> Not stay at home. It is not proper that
> You be here.

PAMELA:
>   See you not how gaily dressed
> He is in fact, dear father?

MAYBELL:
>   She speaks truly,

Lord Medlock; he like to an Indian prince
Doth move across the field.

MEDLOCK:

Why, then I'll kill
An Indian prince, so long as his same corpse
Be found inside the feathers! Let's to guns!

(MEDLOCK *and* SIR BRIAN *fire.* BRIAN *falls.*)

SIR BRIAN:
You have shot well. One word, Sir, ere I die,
With your fair daughter?

MEDLOCK:

Speak, poor feathered ass!

PAMELA:
Father!

SIR BRIAN:
Pamela, listen, my life concludes
With many a harsh and vile discordant note,
But I could change all to a symphony
By whispering one moment in your ear.

(*He whispers.*)

PAMELA:
He said he loved me, sir, would marry me
If he were still alive. He found you harsh . . .

(SIR BRIAN *dies.*)

MEDLOCK:
He is dead!

MAYBELL:
He was a gallant duelist
And stood the gaff, though he came strangely to't!

MEDLOCK:
See that his body, dressed in all its pomp,
Is given fitting burial. We weep
That we have killed him.

(*Enter* GEORGE HENDERSON.)

GEORGE HENDERSON:
                    This your custom, sir,
    Is by the much too rash—this dueling,
    Which for a puff of pride, has taken here
    An honest life, that wanted but a kiss!
    It is unwarranted, and should be banned.

MEDLOCK:
    Sir, you are generous in disquisition,
    But here your counsel is unwanted.

GEORGE HENDERSON:
                        I
    Forbear to prophesy, but mark my words:
    This duel shall end dueling in England—
    And Brian Caitskill not have died in vain!

MEDLOCK:
    Come, trumpets, let's away!

FINAL CURTAIN

                                    —1986

Popeye Among the Polar Bears

POPEYE AMONG THE POLAR BEARS

OLIVE OYL:
Where are we going,
Popeye?

POPEYE:
You be quiet and I'll
Take Swee'pea with me!

OLIVE OYL:
Oh, Popeye,
What of Wimpy
And his wings?

POPEYE:
Never mind
That, Olive
Oyl—
Come
With me!

SWEE'PEA:
May I also?

OLIVE OYL:
Popeye among the Polar Bears . . . !

POPEYE:
Here we are at the
North Pole!

SWEE'PEA:
Some say
Eskimo
Territory,
Some say
Labrador, some say
North Pole—

POPEYE:
Ah, yes . . .
Maybe in actuality
We're only in

Sweden,
Northern
Sweden, or else
North Norway—ah! See
The Lapps—yes! No—

OLIVE OYL:
An optical illusion—

POPEYE:
Yes, that was only snow!
Here are the polar bears

BEARS:
Kazoom kazoom

POPEYE:
They wing past
Like the wind itself
Here in this Arctic circle
Of delight and pleasure

OLIVE OYL:
Yes it *is* nice, isn't it
No matter where
You are
If there are
Polar bears who pass in the night

POPEYE:
(Or is it day?)

OLIVE OYL:
Without hurting you,
Even though
They seem big fierce and ferocious

POPEYE:
Thus
Perhaps all pleasure
Is illusion
I mean just
Relief from pain
Or the
Expectation
Of pain—

OLIVE OYL:
    Yes . . .

POPEYE:
    And then all life—

OLIVE OYL:
    Oh, yes!
    Swee'pea!

POPEYE:
    Is pleasant inasmuch as
    We're aware
    Of death

OLIVE OYL:
    Oh yes indeed
    Here among the polar ice floes

POPEYE:
    Just insofar then inasmuch as
    How cold I am

OLIVE OYL:
    Let's get warm

POPEYE:
    Pleasure pleasure pleasure

OLIVE OYL:
    And here come
    The polar bears again
    Delicate Swee'pea

POPEYE:
    Divine Olive

OLIVE OYL:
    Popeye!

SWEE'PEA:
    Provence!

The scene shifts to Provence.

PROVENÇAL MAN:
    Here where we actually make
    Olive oil we have thought much
    On all that is preceding, for as the young

Olive matures on the gray
And twig-dividing tree
So we have hopes
To turn in time to come
Our heads to level yet unsweeping dreams
Sometimes we have ourselves
Out of what's back there, in the past,
And grown of all that's cold and ir-
Relevant, into a product squeezed
As oil, for the future!
This is our Christmas song,
And so far as—

POPEYE:
Come, dear ones, over the hill!

THE AUTHOR:
Why am I so obsessed by you,
Popeye, and Aix-en-Provence,
As if you two were the two formative influences
Of my life! Then who
Will make me olive oil of this?

MUSE:
I will. I am your muse.
And I love you.

THE AUTHOR:
Little Provence girl!

MUSE:
No, your Muse. I love you.

THE AUTHOR:
And I love you, too.

MUSE:
I am also
Wimpy, Swee'pea, Olive Oyl, Popeye,
And the polar bears!

The scene is Chartres.

THE AUTHOR:
Oh! The Cathedral of Chartres! what a place
To sleep! Ah, let me go
Out into the clear, cold dawn.

BELLS OF CHARTRES:
  Oral prone hoboes. Grain, grain.
  Salonica. Okra Septobers. Lemonolias.
  Galazies. And Spwacteria!

THE AUTHOR:
  O Joan!

MUSE:
  And here comes Popeye, into the mops!

POPEYE:
  O sweet ones, citizens
  Of the North Pole! (at the top).

OLIVE OYL:
  And.

POPEYE IN POMPEII

OLIVE OYL:
  Popeye, here we are
  In Pompeii!

POPEYE:
  Yes, Olive.
  The ruin waits
  For us
  To
  Move
  Among
  Its
  Treasures.

OLIVE OYL:
  The true
  Treasure
  Is your love,
  Popeye!

POPEYE:
  Oh, Olive
  I can't say
  I love you every day
  Sometimes only

At night
When of great sex fray
We are the battalions.

OLIVE OYL:
Oh but Popeye

POPEYE:
Yes, Olive, in Pompeii
The ruins
Wait.
It is not us.

OLIVE OYL:
I know
You
Popeye
I
Love
You
So much!

POPEYE:
Olive, the way
To ecstasy's height
Here, it's depicted in this
Picture
In the House of the Mysteries
Naples, Naples and your Bay
Oh there is so much to say
Olive, no time
For the personal life

OLIVE OYL:
It is the
Only time, Popeye,
We have
This,
Here,
Pompeii
We were
Never alive before
And never will be again

POPEYE:

    Not Sperlunga held us
    Not Rome?

OLIVE OYL:

    Oh
    Popeye
    In
    Pompeii!

(POPEYE *and* OLIVE OYL *move a little way farther into Pompeii.*)

    Oh Popeye, sailor vast!

POPEYE:

    Oh Olive Oyl, me mast,
    Me hugging pole!

OLIVE OYL:

    Knead me to your soul!
    Popeye! Rough me with your engines!

POPEYE:

    I fear to cast no blemish
    On parkways of summer alum
    By this overparticularity.
    No seminal futility can sluff
    A capable heart.
    I wend to you over the summers
    The day of joy approaches when I shall see thee
    And take thee for mine.

PASSERBY:

    Sexist punk!

OLIVE OYL:

    No, he is Popeye

PASSERBY AND CHORUS:

    Not
    He—the
    Samson, the Joyce, the
    Milton, the Hamburger of his generation?
    Not he whose Naples streets go upside down?
    Not being youth unfurled in them?
    Not cameras totally engrossed in light?
    Is this he? Can this be Popeye?

(POPEYE and OLIVE OYL move now to an ambiguous area somewhat on the outskirts of Pompeii.)

OLIVE OYL:

Popeye in Pompeii
Still.
If life were to go on,
It would
Go on in Swee'pea.
Here, Junior, you little shill!
Take this moment.

SWEE'PEA:

I can't
Momma. I'm
Too busy
Crawling
Through Naples!

OLIVE OYL:

What! Crawl
Instead
Through Pompeii!
I will give you nickels,
Littlest darling.

POPEYE:

My boy is crawling up
To Pompeii.
And now he is in its ruins
And now he is not!
Like a flying dot, his little body
Circumvents floors
And broken walls of thought
Swee'pea is in Pompeii
As roses are in
A garden's effervescence

OLIVE OYL:

It is
It is

POPEYE:

So, Olive, well, we
Possess Pompeii through

Swee'
Pea!
Now onward to
Ineffable discussions—

OLIVE OYL:
  And a theatre season of bees!

POPEYE:
  And love upon porches!

OLIVE OYL:
  This theatre's the
  True House of Mysteries!

POPEYE:
  Swee'pea's alive again

OLIVE OYL:
  O Pop-
  Eye, away!

POPEYE:
  A.

OLIVE OYL:
  Popeye
  In Pompeii!

POPEYE:
  Yes, darling,
  I give you up
  To myself in (and)
  The shattering light
  Of evening

OLIVE OYL:
  O
  Popeye
  When the stone is erased
  There is just rat

(*A big* RAT *comes onstage.*)

RAT:
  We too, the rats,
  Must leave Pompeii.

(OLIVE OYL *and* POPEYE *go offstage.*)

POPEYE ALONE

POPEYE:
   I
   Popeye
   Am
   Always alone.

(He dances.)

   I am an alone
   Popeye.

(He sings "Là ci darem . . .")

   Alone, alone, alone am I.
   An alone guy,
   Alone I, a man alone, a
   Person alone, Popeye.

(He draws a figure eight on a large scrim.)

   Once I felt the sky
   Was close to mine
   Own sky.

(He lies down and affects to sleep.)

   Then
   One morning
   I found a jewel

(A JEWEL dances onstage.)

   And now I am alone.

(He puts on a fedora and walks back and forth, gesturing.)

   As at noon, sometimes, men notice the reflections
   Of light and water on a red Mercedes-Benz
   And nudge each other to say lightly, That's a nice car,
   So I think about the many things that other men have been
   And then I thank my lucky star
   I am that sailor with the top arm thin
   Called Popeye near and far. And yet tomorrow
   I know will bring this same old wish
   To be another and know who it is.
   But I'll tell you something.

I've traveled and I have learned a few things.
Be polite to people. Try to learn their customs.
Old Popeye is going to die now, but listen:
Behave yourself at the stage show.
Those women taking off their clothes there
Aren't doing it for you to go up onto the stage
And jump on them. It's for some kind
Of aesthetic effect. That is old
Popeye's last advice. Now, good-bye.

(He climbs up a ladder.)

Heaven, get
Ready to welcome
Popeye!
Hmp!
No answer!
Maybe
I'd better stay
Down here!

(The JEWEL dances offstage.)

Her name was Olive Oyl—
A silly name some damn cartoonist gave her,
But all of love to me—
All of love, Olive Oyl, all of all!

(He lies down and affects to sleep.)

Maybe I have not aged at all.
My chin feels the same.

(He begins to sing and is joined by a great chorus OF MEN'S VOICES, all singing, "My chin feels the same," five or ten times.)

Maybe this
Is a birthday without event.
Ho!

(He draws a figure twenty-six on the scrim.)

When I was young
Then I was Popeye
Unknown
And
Completely

Alone
In life

(A new jewel now, a DIAMOND, *dances out onstage.)*

And sweet
Was my life
Sweet it is now
When it shimmers and bends

(The DIAMOND *dances offstage.)*

I sang "Là ci darem"

(An old recording of Popeye singing "Là ci darem" is played.)

And still
At peace
I was alone

(He goes to the ladder, takes it in his arms and dances with it.)

I danced, but I thought only
Of love.
I loved,
But I thought only
Of advance.

*(*OLIVE OYL's *voice, offstage, "O Popeye!")*

Alone!

(He walks into the audience.)

POPEYE IN EGYPT

Scene 1

POPEYE:
I met a traveler from an antique land

OLIVE OYL:
O Popeye!

POPEYE:
It was the Jeep

OLIVE OYL:
What did the Jeep tell you?

POPEYE:
   The Jeep said good-bye.

OLIVE OYL:
   When you'd just met?

POPEYE:
   Yes!

OLIVE OYL:
   Let's dive into the water!

Scene 2

POPEYE:
   I found a postage stamp
   In an antique land

OLIVE OYL:
   What cover was it?

POPEYE:
   Jeep land.

OLIVE OYL:
   Oily said who to?

POPEYE:
   Nugget.

OLIVE OYL:
   When stirred baggage?

POPEYE:
   Hi. Till.

OLIVE OYL:
   Ex-yow emblem's daughter!

Scene 3

POPEYE:
   Iron Marie totality fuzz hooks.

OLIVE OYL:
   Like water.

POPEYE:
   Open the shaded tree.

OLIVE OYL:
>Octopus ladder.

POPEYE:
>Each octopus, orders by groups of three
>The ancient salad of light

OLIVE OYL:
>Doormen shook talky history

POPEYE:
>Did the fish bite?

OLIVE OYL:
>Anger.

POPEYE:
>Sugar. And the Z
>At the end of things.

Scene 4

POPEYE:
>I'm back Olive with the right
>To know you, to touch you, to love you

OLIVE OYL:
>Blue is the night

POPEYE:
>Above Olive Oyl and Popeye the bright

OLIVE OYL:
>And new is their great insight

TOGETHER:
>Into the children of light and the sea

POPEYE:
>But I've got to go off

OLIVE OYL:
>Why, Popeye?

Scene 1

NOBLES AND OTHERS:
Come on, we're enthroning Swee'pea
Among the clouds

He who crawled through Naples
Embedding it on his person
Then through Pompeii

He is made for kinghood
He is made a ruler
He was born
To *registrate il monde.*

Swee'pea kindly ruler
Look on us with mercy
And with tender grace
Guide us with your wisdom!

SWEE'PEA:
I cannot do anything
That you do not do for me
Awarely, freely, kindly,
For of your own esteem
And marked activity
All your achievements come

Popeye battled with the sea
The result was only sea
Spray of sea and man alone
Battling with the ocean

NOBLES AND OTHERS:
Still, it inspired us

SWEE'PEA:
Well, that's true

Scene 2. Chartres.

BISHOP:
What is this I hear of
God's new dispensation
Swee'pea in the clouds?

NOBLE:

Popeye and Olive are such clods
They give their bastard son everything!
I doubt he'll be a decent ruler
He's unable to do anything
But crawl around

BISHOP:

Well, in that case, maybe
His power
Won't last.

(crash)

Do you
Hear that sound?

NOBLE:

A crash, a great crash—
Swee'pea falling into the sea!

BISHOP:

Great painters shall picture it

NOBLE:

But what will it mean?

BISHOP:

The return of Popeye!

NOBLE:

Is he not underground?

Scene 3. A lower level of the sky.

POPEYE:

Underground though once I was
I return like balls of fuzz
To this cataclysmic sound
Of Swee'pea going under!
Oh well, Olive, my love
We can rescue Swee'pea,
Though not as god and king,
I think—
Let's away
To the North Pole

Where this grave song began
And still begins

OLIVE OYL:
If I have any
Understanding of it

POPEYE:
Is

OLIVE OYL:
Yes,
Popeye!

(POPEYE *and* OLIVE OYL *fly off.*)

HALF THE POPULACE:
They have flown

THE OTHER HALF OF THE POPULACE:
Polar bears shall see them soon

(SWEE'PEA *rises from the sea.*)

SWEE'PEA:
I will revive and go with them

(*flies after them*)

Popeye!

ALL THE PEOPLE:
Popeye!

FINAL CURTAIN

—1986

A Heroine of the Greek Resistance

K (A MAN):

    My first trip to Greece and I don't have any buttons

    On my one good shirt so I wear a "tee-shirt" with over it a suit jacket

    And this dumb English guy I'm with, there are about four of us,

    Says, "It's not correct!"

    Well, it would be all the fad later

    But he was probably right then that it wasn't "correct."

    I came back, to Nice, gratis, on a Greek army plane, with the heroine of the
        Greek Resistance.

    She is a good person is simple, even rudimentary.

    I go with her to a restaurant in Nice where the waiter wants her to order a
        whole dinner.

    "*Il le faut mademoiselle,*" but she won't do it She doesn't want to and she
        doesn't have much money.

    Neither do I or I would treat her. Even If I'd been broke I should have treated
        her

    But I was worried about the train fare to Paris. Instead, I told the waiter

    That she was a heroine of the Greek Resistance. This had no effect at all.

    I think what she and I did was to share one dinner. I think I paid for it after
        all.

    The waiter was a little furious. But you can't sit here Msieu (or Mademoiselle!)

    I thought, He can't tell which one of us is eating. I was arrogant about my
        French.

    I said again She is a heroine of the Greek Résistance

    As if he and I would automatically be in complicity about this

    Recognize my niceness his cordiality her heroism

    And that (meal) would be that. I forget if it wasn't or was

    But one of these scenarios did take place

    As so often happens. I was wearing the jacket and tee-shirt then as well.

SPIRIT OF TIME:

    Each with its moments, the old tower in the center of the city was eaten away

    By restoration, the moon cake of fiery bracelets, but

    On the rooftop café there was a scene

    I will not long remember: a lightning bug

    Carried up accidentally on the rim of a drinking glass

    Flew off and vanished into bug invisibility of air.

    To move that trembling from a firm today

    Into a griped tomorrow like a sleeve

Caught in Grand Central doorway,
And mock-up of today. This edifice,
This tangy corps of green, this swipe, this England
Affording men a murder day, once seen
Once tackled into nothingness, bristly and giving orderly
Commands to leggy multitudes, O here
Is someone to command your briefest breath, Mahatma Shakespeare
The birds in the caroling of rest. But there is someone else around here
I stallingly want you to meet, my brother in fact, hemlock.
Over the hay cart into the flaring scenes
Is as close as hemlock gets. "My dear, holloa!" In Martinique
The birds that woke up in net stockings warbling loud and clear
Focussed the steeple's eyes on the murrain—

K:

Hume's ghost! I don't want Hume's ghost! Off, out of here!
Away goes, flies Hume's ghost. These sparkling strains
Of unencumbered music like the flood
I cannot speak. Move something. I cannot move. Do
Something. I cannot do
Nothing. The master is ill-educated. Away! Get him a job in the English
    Department of stars!
Let the working-men and -women fully their fray
Indict to waving branches, I am yours
On flossy emphasis
Zoroaster blasts away:
You just not doing the fucking job here, he said, and when Bleeps!
Why it even catches me as much as the Flood. To west, adventure, fountains
    dead
And eagle of the first good-bye, who stood there waiting
The tray and the bed also were waiting. Then comes an engine.
Behind it a whole train. In it an engineer, his wife, a baby
Everyone assumes is his and hers, she keeps a pageboy
Bob worn by Ginger Rogers in nineteen thirty-six. My claim is talkies,
Western the sides of the sea. This is childhood thought. But of a very specific
    childhood.
A violence without brothers and sisters, no superintendent—
The next day after this I got on the train
That took me to Paris.
It turned out to be some sort of continuation of the Orient Express
Is that possible
When I dressed so boldly it wasn't imitation it was desperation

V. the Chinese eating everything out of necessity the French out of curiosity
Disparition of the buttons

SPIRIT OF TIME:

    Where is he now
    Who once was vinylmaster of the fields? Dead bark
    Water on books. Evenings that go too far.
    Deep, and narrow, nine feet tall
    At the extremities, and seventy-five yards long. A green prospect
    Stretches it may be ever outward, but their songs
    Of all different families, singing, the bluebirds there. Life is fortune
    But talk straight. She promises him an envelope.
    He is leading the stairs. A scimitar crops the Pope's hair. Good Christ!
    Mannikins start to be hobbled on the Champs Elysées.

K:

    My father said, I like the start of it but what are you going to do to make it
        end?
    The Greek woman staring at the shake of the early morning on the tie-clip
        sea
    We shouldn't wear—will she marry? Innocence! and despair!

FATHER:

    No one can really accomplish anything
    Who doesn't get up early in the morning.

K:

    But I said I need the late night and early morning
    The grip, father, and to get a grip on all the laws
    And flaws of this kind of well don't you agree mortifying existence
    Girls turning me down, jobs hard to get, insolence on the barges,
    Late-night sheet pounding, the whole goddamned lot don't
    Swear, the mother said. Organized villages
    Clamped into stores, one city contained in a shop,
    Country and even continent contained in a boat, life is yours!
    I was finished with the adding machines of Lake Constance.
    Yes, I was a latter-day walking.
    I wanted the city to enfold me like a vote
    For myself and itself: co-owners of the derby.
    Flying among the grapes, bees sense a miracle
    It is ordinary life. So, men and women, boys, and girls, sea lions and their
        masters
    And the dog's bark. What's "bourgeois" or extraordinary about any of these?
    Everyone gets to walk

A little ways. Burning, burning, the collegiate amanuensis
A numbing hunger which she sees, then
Where is Napoleon?—intimacy, but she was shepherds
In her own field, the classy anatomy—who said sheaf?
A blond bird on a redheaded stone is sleeping. Give me your poor
Your damaged your inveterate.

DANTE:

                              Useful, the moon beneath our feet.

MODERNITY:
I spoke for Dagwood Bumstead,
For Jungle Jim, for Maggie and Jiggs, for all those roasted customers
In comic strips who never could unbend—these sharpening tricksters
These hucksters of the values of the soul
This eye that crosses everywhere in England
Like baby chickens colored useless for Easter
Then hatched into an egg again, slowly developing dyes
A gray, great factor, one of three
Justly celebrated acrobats, the gay yellow one there with his sister
Adumbelavara the corn king's mirthful equivalence
But what comes home and what comes back to me
Is something as out of the ordinary as the Annunciation—
A grave asphyxiated by Lake Erie.

YOUNG WOMAN:
"Jove in the clouds—"

MODERNITY:
A young woman is trying to quote a song,
Of nineteen fifty-six when the door mattered
And the teeth mattered and the flowers chattered of Americanism
Bonuses, Williams and the dead, we were jovial and timeless
But lived to cultivate those hours
At five o'clock in the morning, when no one was there
Have you looked for the Amazon forests? they're sleeping, like busts in a hall
Like animals in the catalogue of stars.
Greek numen, come home!
With rapturous expressions, beaming "Home!"

K:
My father then looked at the Charles and said "I like it
And its Cambridge along with it. Superior people
Never make long visits. Piebald lived in a glass house.

Turra lurra lurra is an old people's dovecote, nonetheless."
"Home is here, freedom from Boss Prendergast
And every other thing. But here is home!" to stagger into existence
Janus in the janissary, Comus in the man—
Necklaces that prance into the dimness
Because of the rumor "Hellas is transparent" and they let you do this
Occasionally the whole day long, the worst not being in it
Because it is afraid of the best or else if suffering puts a tooth to it,
The canopy of winter is nailed there, a new roominess tramps down silence

SPIRIT OF TIME:

Until violence, violence, violence is here
Like eight hundred million trucks in competition.
In fact there is nothing, the countries unstable, place division on my soul!

MODERNITY:

So we bought second-hand shirts, formerly rich men's neckties, thready golf
    pants, and so on;
Will anyone understand you as you fall
Forward into dismay?

K:

                        The unanimity of humanity, I mean the fellowship
Is on a line with the unanimity of indifference. If we had only one ball
How it would bounce! Unfortunately we have hundreds of thousands.

MODERNITY:

Gayety triumphant in the middle of small kettles
Pockets drum aware that we can die, our legacy
For the foods' months. Such happiness to be going straight by
Is holiday, best for the young, for the nude in spirit
And our unstuck sky.

K:

I went back to Greece once after that. I spent several days in Athens,
With my wife, Janice. I was looking for an American woman,
A very rich woman, who, someone had told me, loved poets
And liked to give them money. At last, I thought,
We could get to a good party instead of sitting every day
In Athens's main square, which was pretty agreeable in any case—
Minuscule cups of coffee so strong it had a beard

J (A WOMAN, HIS WIFE):

With, to the side, large sparkling glasses of water.

K:

So we sat there
But the rich woman did not appear. The heroine of the Greek Resistance
Where was she, too? This was five years later.
So much had happened. What had happened to her?

HEROINE OF THE GREEK RESISTANCE:

A barge of sparkling shears had happened to the herd
The whistling from the sides of the Aegean. I am a town,
You are a princess, she is a grove
Filled with Italy. Saint Sinus Difficulty assailed me. I went into obliquity.
Hello, dancers. hello, creeks. Branches of lilies.
Is time here going to take us? take us back?

K:

                              A rat
Moved forward, a rat leaving some tea leaves,
And I say, *Un rat!* to the waiter, who was promptly relieved
By several other waiters, who made quite a stir, a drama of haymows
And cummerbunds, winning my local bride to me
In five seconds, we leaned across, the table, torpedoed, war! I'd like
Coffee. There is no more. Adapt.
I can't stop it. Folly.
Where the wolf stops me. A dune was walking—

TIME:

Yes but you don't receive—

K:

It is an interruption
That time makes indirect—

SPIRIT OF TIME:

Or direct, in Babylon, years ago—

J, AS THE HEROINE OF THE GREEK RESISTANCE:

The sharpness clears the bay.

FINAL CURTAIN

—1994

The Strangers from the Sea

Scene 1

A comfortable apartment in Stockholm. Two persons SVEN *and* ANNA *are seated in chairs.*

SVEN:
 I think I'm going to kill myself.

ANNA:
 Don't! Play a game of "Ox" with me instead!
 Actually it's called "Strangers from the Sea."

SVEN:
 Oh, I know it! I played it as a child.

ANNA:
 Would you do me the favor of playing it once with me?

SVEN:
 What's the use?

ANNA:
 Will you?

SVEN:
 Let me think about it.

ANNA:
 Please.

SVEN:
 The very idea is fatiguing.

ANNA:
 I haven't asked you very many things.

SVEN:
 All right. But, I warn you, Anna, and this is the truth.
 This is the last thing I will ever do for you.

ANNA: *(aside)*
 Pray God that it works well.

(to SVEN*)*

 Yes, Sven, yes, thank you. All right.

SVEN:

   Then, let's begin.

Scene 2

The scene changes to the deck of a cattle boat off the coast of Sweden. Stormy sea. Mist. Spray. Stage right is Sweden, a dock.

(*Enter the* OXEN OF HUNGARY.)

OXEN:

   We want to be fed!

SHEPHERD:

   There is no way to feed you here.
   We are out in the middle of the ocean.

OXEN:

   Well, if we are not fed, we are not going to give any milk!

SHEPHERD:

   Oh hell—

CAPTAIN:

   Don't worry, Shepherd. I think we are getting near Sweden.
   In Sweden there is plenty of milk. And, besides,
   Since when do oxen give milk? And there will be
   Food for them there, anyway, food for the oxen.

ELLA (SHEPHERD'S GIRLFRIEND):

   That's good. I want our oxen to have something to eat.

HAND:

   The boat is landing.

CAPTAIN:

   Good! Let's get these smelly oxen off!

AN OX:

   I heard what you said.

CAPTAIN:

   Well anyway you can't talk.
   And in the herd form you're in I don't see
   How you can do me much harm.

OX:

   Oh, nuts to you. Come on every-
   Body, let's get off.

LEAD OX:

    And hurry. Damn!

(OXEN *and* HUMANS *all get off boat onto Swedish dock. The* OXEN *surround the* HUMANS.)

THIRD OX:

    Now

SECOND OX:

    We have

FIRST OX:

    You all!

CAPTAIN and MATES:

    Wha-what's happened.

SHEPHERD:

    This is a little puzzling to me, too.

ELLA:

    But not so much to me.

LEAD OX:

    Damn! Salaam! Everybody out of the way—

(*Turmoil, as* OXEN *take over the country.*)

SWEDISH MAN:

    What—what's happened?

LEAD OX:

    The Oxen of Hungary have conquered Sweden.

(*It grows dark—there are muffled sounds.*)

MINSTREL:

    And art will grow up
    And develop

        (*Dawn breaks.*)

    Under the oxen's yoke.
    I think they may be good for Sweden.

        (*Ten days pass.*)

    Sweden develops like an ox.
    That's good. It is good for Sweden
    To have these startling experiences.

Scene 3

A group of singing PEOPLE *and* OXEN *in a flower-filled field.*

ALL: *(singing)*
    Happy the Swedish nation
    All her days
    Happy sensation
    Oxen children everywhere
    We will become the most beautiful
    People on earth
    Especially our women
    Beautiful from loving oxen
    What truly are oxen
    But men of great worth
    Transformed to four-legg'd creatures
    With bestial naïve features
    But these are changed by love!
    Oh, this is a time of triumph
    And a time for celebration
    The oxen came to Sweden
    They guide us to the future
    To future love!
    The oxen bring us power and bring us love!

(All dance, then bow to one another.)

Scene 4

Stockholm, main square.

(Enter SHEPHERD, ELLA, LEAD OX, *and three other* LEAD OXEN.*)*

SHEPHERD:
    My oxen have occupied Sweden
    They have mated with Swedish women
    Soon many in Sweden will be half ox.
    They tell me now they must move on,
    They are going to another country.
    What will happen to Sweden in their absence?
    The Swedish populace has learned to love these oxen.
    They have named public buildings after them:
    Ox Palace, over here to your right,
    Formerly the Danschluss Ministry of Finance Complex
    And here's Ox Museum,

Formerly the Royal Swedish Nursery.
Ordinary Swedish will be sad.

ELLA:

Yes, and the Royal Family is lamenting, too.
For the oxen brought order to Sweden
And gave it a mixture of the old and the new
And the animal and the man
Which has been helpful.
The king has named the royal roads of his realm
After oxen. Oxpath is the main road
That leads from Stockholm to the sea
And the highway that intercepts Uppsala
Is now named Oxen of Death.

SHEPHERD:

Oh this is history
Truly being brought to life!
These oxen have made little changes
All over this country
In ways that can scarcely be seen.

LEAD OX:

I the Lead Ox
Made love last night to Princess Nancy
Of Sweden. She will bear me a half-ox son.

SECOND OX:

And I, Second-in-Command Ox,
Have decorated the country with ox chateaus—
Simple, really. These
Are little straw structures
People can
Come into, if they wish, to
Shield their bodies
From the rain.

THIRD OX:

And the snow,
Which is wild, in Sweden.
And I, the Third Ox in command,
Have had special
Beds built all over the kingdom
In which those who are

Half ox can lie
For soon they will need them!
We oxes made love
To so many girls!

FOURTH OX:

It was easy for us to
Learn the language!
And for the people of Sweden to learn
To talk to us!
I did it. I had earphones constructed
Which changed one language into another
And by wearing these things
We could
Understand each other
Right away, and then gradually
Dispensing with them, we were
Able to learn each other's
Tongues. Little known before
On earth was ox science, but
Now it is known in Sweden—
How much it helped us!

(*Enter the* ORDINARY SWEDISH OXEN.)

SWEDISH OXEN:

We the legion of
Ordinary Swedish oxen
Wish to express our
Appreciation
Of what you have done.

FIFTH OX:

I, Fifth Ox in command,
Have helped these other oxen
To know their glorious talents and their rights.
I have also brought back to them
Our old ox religion.
They will be happier now
And soon the people
Will grow to resemble them.

(*The* SWEDISH OXEN *make a grateful noise.*)

LEAD OX:

    Now we must find a ship.
    Oh farewell, sweet Swedish land!
    You have been kind to us.
    Here we got plenty to eat.

SECOND OX:

    And could exercise our power
    In a way that
    We never could before.

THIRD OX:

    Let us hope
    In the future
    It will be everlasting.

FOUTH OX:

    But for that, *chi sa?*
    Let's get on the boat.

FIFTH OX:

    Yes, here is one now.

ELLA:

    It is startling
    How our oxen have conquered Sweden
    And yet their action was so peaceful
    The people simply gave them their lives
    To make sweeter and in so many ways better.

SHEPHERD:

    Oh, lovely it is, yes, it is
    When a sovereign people
    Recognizes that something may be superior
    About a species or people from outside
    And when it lets that people or species
    So permeate its life
    That everything is transformed!
    Yes, it's very beautiful.
    Come, my dears, onto the boat!

LEAD OX:

    I will give commands here.
    You forgot now who we are.

SHEPHERD:
　　Sorry, Sire, I step aside
　　And take sweet Ella for my bride.
　　You shall sail without my help
　　Over fields of salt and kelp
　　Till you find another land
　　To which you'll give a helping hand.
　　Ella and I will stay behind
　　And try to find
　　A little paradise of our own.

LEAD OX:
　　You speak like one with a head of stone.
　　You'd do better to accompany us but
　　Farewell! You've been a
　　Good enough shepherd.
　　Then, we needed one—
　　Now, obviously, we don't. Come
　　On, fellow oxen, let's get on the boat.

(Once on the boat, the OXEN begin, violently, suddenly, to make the movements and the sounds of real oxen.)

OXEN:
　　Oonh oonh grow-pht row-pht—

ELLA:
　　They have turned back to ordinary oxen again!

SHEPHERD:
　　My god my god they are running amok on the boat

ELLA:
　　They have trampled the captain

SHEPHERD:
　　And all the sailors.

ELLA:
　　My

SHEPHERD:
　　God! Now

ELLA:
　　It's sailing away!

SHEPHERD:
And they are

ELLA:
Again just oxen

SHEPHERD:
Who don't know anything

ELLA:
And certainly not

SHEPHERD:
How to navigate a boat!

ELLA:
How can we help them?

SHEPHERD:
We can't!

ELLA:
The

SHEPHERD:
Boat is

ELLA:
Gone!

(*The* OXEN's *boat becomes invisible. There is a large sound of lowing.*)

(*Enter* PRINCESS NANCY.)

PRINCESS NANCY:
Gone!
Wherever they have gone to
There shall I travel!
Wherever oxen go, shall Nancy follow.
Helmsman, set sail and follow! I'll board this ship!

(PRINCESS NANCY *boards ship and it sails away.*)

ELLA:
We can only remember how it was
Before the oxen came to Sweden. People were unhappy.
Now with the oxen and Nancy gone
They may be unhappy again.

SHEPHERD:
   I prophesy
   That what has so been done
   In these proud days, shall never be undone.
   The country is indelibly altered—
   For the better, rather than for the worse—
   And Princess Nancy shall return.

(SVEN *and* ANNA *enter.*)

SVEN: *(solemnly)*
   So ends The Strangers From the Sea.

Scene 5

A great wind blows, and suddenly the scene is the Stockholm apartment of Scene 1.

SVEN:
   Whew! That was a good game.
   Did it take longer than usual?

ANNA:
   No it always takes the same amount of time.
   It's just that we forget our country's history,
   Its main events, how full of things they were!

SVEN:
   Yes, truly.

ANNA:
   Do you still feel so sad?

SVEN:
   Just a little,
   But the game has picked me up
   A little too! I feel a will to live.
   Thank you!

ANNA:
   Such great events
   Are strength not only in themselves but give
   Invigoration and the will to live
   To those who follow after
   And are indeed the strangers from the sea
   Themselves, unknown contingents that embark
   Descend and occupy and make the dark

A light, and by their spell
Show us that seeing well
Such great things as have been
Places us in the planetary spin
That makes our lives worthwhile. Oh eeuuhhh oh euuhh

(ANNA *makes ox noises.*)

Oh strangers from the sea!

FINAL CURTAIN

—1995

Edward and Christine

A NOTE ON THIS PLAY

The two main characters are EDWARD and CHRISTINE. They appear sometimes as themselves, sometimes in the guise of other characters. For
example, in the last Egyptian scene, CHRISTINE is HATHOR; in the Libreville scene, EDWARD is HERVE BLANC, CHRISTINE is the CASINO GIRL. This
is all indicated in the text. EDWARD and CHRISTINE appear in diverse and
rapidly changing scenes that aren't continuous in the ordinary sense of
the word: a scene in one country is followed by a scene in another which
is at an earlier or later time. There are big spaces between the scenes, but
these spaces are skipped; the play goes from one to the other. This movement from scene to scene is not meant to be ironic; the movement and
the resulting fragmentation are meant, rather, to be a sort of representation of what experience is actually like when it is free from, though not
ignoring, the needs and conventions of the moment and the continuity
they usually impose. I mean to put experiences together the way memory and passion and reflection do and to present the result as ordinary
reality so as to make it visible.

CRETE

(A hillside. EDWARD *climbs the hill, looks down the other side and sees a* GIRL,
about twelve years old, who is tending sheep.)

EDWARD:
Ah ... hello, there! Hello!?

GIRL:
Hel- lo. I- love you!

EDWARD:
Well, I love you, too! You're beautiful. You with your sheep. This little
promontory. I up here, you down there. "I love you." Where did you learn
to say that? What soldier or tourist—? The world is at peace. It has been
more or less at peace for ten years. But Greece is still suffering from the terrible, perhaps unhealable wounds of its Civil War!

(SOLDIERS *walk past.* GIRL *picks up a baby lamb and shows it to* EDWARD)

GIRL:
I love you.

FILMMAKER: *(entering)*
    How can it (filmmaking) compare to anything
    Inscribed in language or in stone? Theatre on the other hand is all motion
    And language inscribed on motion. Film is a dead hand
    Placed on the living shoulder of a sex goddess such as Monroe
    Or Cathleen ni Houlihan, the personification of Ireland.
    I come to bring snow
    That will vanish in the tracks of the sun. My movie, *Agorokoritso,* concerns
        a young lady
    Who is, as the title suggests, a tomboy; eventually, however, she becomes a
        more conventional girl,
    She meets the "right" Greek boy and finds "love." Then the movie is over.
        Now my work is done.
    Shall I start to do another of these totally useless œuvres?
    Or yet perhaps not totally useless! I see a young man and woman coming
    Who apparently were impressed by my film.

EDWARD:
                                    If that isn't the worst movie

CHRISTINE:
    We've ever seen

EDWARD:
                You don't know what is

CHRISTINE:
    Nor you, either!

(They laugh and embrace.)

(The FILMMAKER *strikes his hand against his head and goes off. As he leaves he speaks.)*

FILMMAKER:
    They will remember it, all the same!

EDWARD:
    Here on the way down from the movie theatre
    Are those two rabbits frozen into a stone
    Rabbit position—thinking that they can't be seen
    Unless they move—an idea rabbits have!

FIRST RABBIT:
    Hold still.

SECOND RABBIT:
  I am holding
  Absolutely still.

FIRST RABBIT:
  It is still not still enough.

SECOND RABBIT:
  Yes. I am absolutely totally
  Still.

FIRST RABBIT:
  But to me
  You seem to be
  Moving.

SECOND RABBIT:
  That is because your eyes are not still.

FIRST RABBIT:
  Go to hell.

SECOND RABBIT:
  Rabbits have not hell.
  Only the jaw of the wolf
  The fox
  Or the man.

FIRST RABBIT:
  Go to man then.

SECOND RABBIT:
  I will
  Not.

FIRST RABBIT:
  Shall we make
  Up?

SECOND RABBIT:
  Yes.

FIRST RABBIT:
  Farewell
  Friend, lover. We did quarrel for a while

SECOND RABBIT:
  But it was only a moment
  It was

FIRST RABBIT:
Only a moment. Hist, now. Freeze!

(Enter CHARLEMUTH, EDWARD, *etc.)*

DELFT

CHARLEMUTH (A FRENCH POET):
The Dutch have no sense of the tragic.

EDWARD:
Look at them happily riding their bicycles all around!

MICHEL (ALSO A FRENCH POET): *(arriving on a bike)*
Come! I've just procured tickets for the latest Dutch tragedy, *Meeinheer von Plutsch.* It is the latest in a successful series of Dutch tragedies being performed at the Renaissancer Hus. Tonight at eight p.m.

EDWARD:
So off we go to see it, a Dutch tragedy.

CHARLEMUTH:
The Dutch have no sense of the tragic, even in the theatre.

CHRISTINE:
I want to be married. I want to marry you, I love you, have children, the whole lot.

EDWARD:
I love you, too, but—I don't know, I don't want
To get married—

(pause)

I lost her. She has gone to someone else.
Charlemuth, though, and Michel are still around.

MICHEL:
Ha ha ha ha, ho ho ho ho, har hah who hah.

CHARLEMUTH:
Ah! *les hollandais!*

PARIS

(Snow falls, a small hotel room.)

EDWARD:
To sleep. Perchance to dream. . . . *(He sleeps.)*

MOTHER:

ED ward! This is your mother!

FATHER: *(shaking the door)*

Edward! Get up! What are you doing? This is your father!

EDWARD:

Huh? Huh? What?

(He leaps out of bed)

I am up! And they're not here! I would take a walk in the snow, in the just early falling snow, but a peculiarity of this hotel on the rue de Fleurus is that after ten o'clock at night you can get into it but you can't get out of it. Once one is in it one is in it for the night. In this respect being here is like being a child.

(Enter a GORILLA.)

EDWARD:

My God. He's scarier than my mother and father combined.

GORILLA:

Kawabata committed suicide.

EDWARD:

I am too young to have known his work and too young for this to have happened.

GORILLA:

You will see that it will happen in time.

EDWARD:

Why, then, if not my mother and father, who are you?

GORILLA:

I am far from being your mother and father.
I will bring you Ekaterina.
And now, I will give you these lines
For inspiration before you go to sleep. Kawabata said
The greatest happiness in life is drinking a scotch and soda
On the terrace of the Tokyo Hilton Hotel.

EDWARD:

What's wrong with that?

GORILLA:

Nothing. I see you may do well. Now get back to sleep.

CHRISTINE:
   I was afraid someone would pinch my ass.
   It was windy, the street corner.

EDWARD:
   We were in a country
   Where they pinched it,
   Played soccer
   Which they took very seriously
   And ass pinching seriously.
   I could have prevented that.

CHRISTINE:
   I don't know how.
   They're very very fast.
   A man is going by, apparently innocently, just
   Strolling along, he gets closer to you, you
   Don't, why should you, pay any attention, he
   Is reading a newspaper as he goes, or glancing
   In another direction and then
   Suddenly he goes—straight—

BACK IN PARIS

EDWARD: *(rising in a burst of ecstatic inspiration)*
   These are the Gorilla-given lines:
   "Oh what a physical effect it has on me
   To dive forever into the light-blue sea
   Of your acquaintance! Ah, but dearest friends,
   Like forms, are finished, as life has ends!"

GORILLA:
   Mystery! *(He now dissolves into white bright snow out the window above and falling on the Paris streets.)*

EDWARD:
   But what has this to do with ME? Maybe nothing. That would be good, for a change!

(He goes to the window and looks out.)

(A child, TOMMY, enters and takes his hand. Then TOMMY leaves.)

CHRISTINE:

I felt the excitement of a walk of which I didn't know the end! Adventure, Wandering! How could I not go everywhere I could?

EDWARD:

How could I not, too?

(*These two embrace.*)

FLORENCE

EDWARD:

I like this little house.

CHRISTINE:

It's not so little! Yes, I do too. Look, it has this nice fireplace. And a room for you to work!

EDWARD:

And a room for you to work.

CHRISTINE:

And a little room for the baby.

EDWARD:

And there will be space also for the new baby
And look at the flowers outside

CHRISTINE:

Look at the fruit trees outside!

GIANNI POGGI:

Io sono Gianni Poggi. Sono tenore.
Canto a l'opera lirica di Firenze abastanza spesso.
Venite vedermi! (sings)
                    Venite verdermi! Ay, mi!

(*He collapses, as if dead.*)

GIANNI POGGI: (*singing*)
Addio diletta America!

CHRISTINE:

Un Ballo in Maschera!

EDWARD:

It's inevitable that we found this house. It couldn't be avoided.

CHRISTINE:

Do you remember our trip here on the train?

GIANNI POGGI: *(expires)*
   Ay, mi! Addio!

RAILWAY STATION AT CHIANCIANO TERME

EDWARD:
   Let's see if I can find some food on the platform.

CHRISTINE:
   I'd like something to drink. Would you?

EDWARD:
   Yes! But there is nothing! There is ever nothing
   On these railway platforms that we see!

CHRISTINE:
   Only the green trees nodding overhead in the light
   Of the station and of the sun. *Les réverbères* . . . !
   Do you hear the next train coming?

EDWARD:
   Yes.

BACK IN FLORENCE

CHRISTINE:
   We were swept off.

EDWARD:
   The train station has vanished.

CHRISTINE:
   And we have this house, it's true!

GIANNI POGGI: *(getting up—he was not really dead but feigning death as in an opera.)*

   Many times I have restaurant, many times I have cab,
   Many times I have simple, cold stone light upon slab,
   Many times I will sing, and have sung, again

CHRISTINE:
   Every time at the opera, we see him—
   Gianni Poggi, who has become all heroes and all tragic singing men.

EDWARD:
   I liked the idea of seeing the city first
   You wanted to get us settled right away.

CHRISTINE:
Well, we do have a baby sixteen months old!

A HOTEL GARDEN IN TAORMINA

EDWARD:
We've just seen another Antonello
Da Messina.

CHRISTINE:
In a little ruined
Chapel, five miles from here.
Whew! We're worn out!

EDWARD'S MOTHER:
Edward, where is Melissa? I want her to come with me
To the hairdresser's.

EDWARD'S FATHER:
This young man that we met on the train
I think he's peculiar Edward can you imagine that
He wanted me to buy him jeans in exchange for his sexual favors.

POPULACE:
Etna is erupting!

MOTHER:
From here it is very hard to see the beach.

EDWARD:
My mother with her hat on,
My father with the Eternal Cigarette

ATONELLO DA MESSINA:
I am Antonello da Messina
Now I live in catalogues and in the sky—
With my beloved Madonna

EDWARD:
Do you see the way the Virgin is sitting and regarding
The viewer? This man introduced easel painting into Italy.
He found it in Holland and in Flanders. Before that
All painting was on wood or on walls. Where could it have gone,
That wall-dependent art? Antonello ruined painting, An-
Tonello saved painting.

MOTHER:

        Edward! Oooh, you don't know what it's like to get old!

ANTONELLO:

Never again the horse face
Never again the dew. Congratulations
On your forthcoming wedding ceremony!

EDWARD & CHRISTINE:

We're already married!

CRETE

NYMPHS:

Every day before full sunrise we come
To renew ourselves at this altar,
The Altar of the Nymphs! Everyone thinks we are gone
Forever! But we live on
As long as there is water on air for us
At this marble-fountained altar!

(KATIE & BUDDY *are coming up the hill on which the Altar of the Nymphs stands.*)

BUDDY:

Aw, it's too steep! Why are we dragging ourselves all the way up here? I don't
want to. I want to get back down.

KATIE:

Come on, Buddy. It's supposed to be very interesting. And now it's just a
little way.

BUDDY:

We've already come a long way
It's always just a little way more.

KATIE:

Well, we got here. There! Look at it!

BUDDY:

Wow! Okay, let's go down.

KATIE:

You're impossible. Wait for me. I'm going over here to look
At this what seems to be the remains of a statue. I can see a face!

BUDDY:

So long!

(He leaves.)

KATIE:

It really was a carving. Of a nymph here. Buddy!
Buddy! Where have you gone?

(The NYMPHS, *who became invisible when the two persons appeared, are still audible. Now they laugh a silvery laughter.)*

And that noise! Buddy, Buddy, where are you?

*(*KATIE *wanders around in search of* BUDDY. *The light changes from morning to afternoon to dusk to dark.* KATIE *is now at home.)*

FATHER:

Where is your brother?

KATIE:

Oh god, I don't know!

*(*BROTHER *comes in—very late and a bit happiness-sodden.)*

FATHER & MOTHER:

Buddy! Where were you? How could you do that, stay out so long?

BUDDY:

I met a girl.

KATIE:

I know that the girl was not I
For I am the one who was with him at the Altar of the Nymphs
When he "disappeared"—

MOTHER:

Mussolini, who controlled Rhodes for twenty years, did some good things.
He made the trains run on time. If he were here, Buddy would have soon
come home.

BUDDY: *(displeased by his mother's political views)*
I'm going out again.

FATHER:

No. You're NOT!

*(*FATHER *becomes* MUSSOLINI *and keeps* BUDDY *in.)*

FLORENCE

(Enter EDWARD, *very distraught.)*

EDWARD:

My wife is dying! She has hemorrhaged and she needs blood.
I'm told that there is no blood and that there is no one no one in the hospital
Who can come and help me find some. But my wife needs it
Or she'll die! Doctor, I beg you! Please!

DOCTOR:

Yes, I will go with you.
I think it is worth it. I think I can help you to find this blood.
Do you know there is a shortage? Because of Hungary? the attempted
  rebellion
Against the Russians? We're going to have a hard time.

(DOCTOR *goes with* EDWARD *to a blood supply station.*)

Signora, we need a vial of rh-negative Blood. *Di sangue air akka negativo.*

OLD WOMAN:

But there is none. Here, take this!

EDWARD:

Regard it! It is positive.

DOCTOR:

It is not negative. It is positive! *E positivo!*

OLD WOMAN:

Like everything that breathes and lives
It is both negative and positive at the same time.

DOCTOR:

Old woman, we want, not philosophy, but blood. Give us some negative.

OLD WOMAN:

There is only one vial left.
The rest has been sent to Hungary
To give to the wounded!

DOCTOR:

Give it to us!

EDWARD:

How reluctantly she does so!

(*back in the hospital*)

And now she has it
And she revives.

CHRISTINE:
> I'm—I'm better.

EDWARD:
> But you could die!

PARIS

EDWARD: *(in bed)*
> Tell me that you're not gay.

CHRISTINE: *(in bed)*
> That's ridiculous. I have been your mistress and your wife. Then we were
> divorced. Why would I still be sleeping with you if I were gay?

EDWARD:
> I thought you wouldn't even bother to ask me that.

CHRISTINE:
> You ARE ridiculous.

EDWARD:
> If I am so ridiculous why have you come back to me? why are you in bed
> with me? why did we make love? Will we ever have any self-understanding
> at all?

CHRISTINE:
> Some people are not like others. I am not like you.
> I find you—detestable. Go to sleep.

EDWARD:
> Go to sleep? How can I? I can't possibly go to sleep now.

(They sleep. Morning. They are up.)

CHRISTINE: *(she is making the bed)*
> I detest him.

EDWARD: *(he is making coffee)*
> She is loathsome.

CHRISTINE: *(as she drinks some coffee)*
> He is a horror

EDWARD: *(breakfast over)*
> I want to go to the movie today.

CHRISTINE:
> Let's go then.

(She takes his hand as they go out. She says, quietly)

Phhhhhhhtff!

(They leave, then come back.)

EDWARD:
Hurry, Alfred is coming to dinner. I have a libretto I want to show him. I'm
still writing it.

CHRISTINE:
I'm hurrying!
Ah, hurry!
Unsatisfying as a traffic jam!
Like the slam
Of a steel and iron door! Shazam!

EDWARD:
This libretto of tentacles of ice
This libretto of license and fright
This libretto of leaves!
O Paradise
That a creator feels!
But am I really a creator?
Maybe I am just an automobile without wheels
And maybe some benumbed Henry Ford was my creator
Or maybe I am—but now the south wind steals
In scriggle scraggle lace across my brow—

(He writes.)

(ALFRED arrives at the door, is shown in, sits down.)

ALFRED:
It's very beautiful of course
But I don't think it will go over in France
Why doesn't they don't she and he
Make love even one time
Despite their doubt?

EDWARD:
But he thinks he may be her father.

ALFRED:
So—I still think the French would find it incredible that they didn't even
make love once, since they don't really *know* if they're related.

EDWARD:
Oh you've been living over here too long, is what!

CHRISTINE:

Edward wanted their break-up to seem a necessary thing. This is what happens in the libretto. A young married couple Bert and Matilda their car breaks down in the desert and the only one who can fix it is Henry, an "older" fellow and he has a gas station and repair shop in the middle of the desert. He and Matilda fall in love but when she says something *re* her early life he has a sudden memory thinks she may be his long-lost daughter Louisa they thus are afraid, do nothing and at the end the young couple drives off. My husband thought I didn't know but I of course did know that the libretto story was a turned-about version of something that happened in his own life. He loved a woman named Ekaterina she had a husband who was fifty years old this seemed very old to them both at that time. He couldn't take her away from her husband and child and ever after he felt he had been a coward and had ruined his life. Oh! after a decade my young husband died and no one ever set his libretto. Now at last it is going to be done, with a slightly changed conclusion that brings in what really happened in his (and our) life and by a fine (though not Alfred) composer and the premiere is at the Théatre des Champs Elysées tonight and I will be there.

Whereas Ekaterina

Ekaterina is she still alive?

(HENRY—*played by* EDWARD—& MATILDA/LOUISA *played by* CHRISTINE—*come onstage and sing, in operatic fashion*)

HENRY: *(sings)*

O! Louisa! Matilda!

MATLIDA:

Ah!

NEWARK

EKATERINA:

I am alive and I am in New Jersey and I know nothing of this libretto nor of this opera nor of this world premiere night.

PARIS

CHRISTINE *as* GILBERTE:

Not knowing what to do
I walk here and there.
I continue my studies
In law. But I am restless, restless
In my limited modernity!

I feel limited, as by a wall
Of electricity by the woman and man who
Brought me into the world and brought me up!
I stammer when I'm with them. Sometimes
I want to kill myself I
Am amused by the young American
I see everyday at the Crémerie
De Luxembourg. Here he is now.

EDWARD:
    Gilberte! Ha ha. *Bonjour. Bonsoir.* Et cetera.
    Ha ho. Wouldst thee likes to taking walk?

CHRISTINE:
    You don't speak French
    Perfectly yet but it is nice
    To talk to you and to walk
    With you, but I
    Have depressing ideas, *les idées noires.*
    I do not think that it is best that I go on seeing you. Good-bye!

(She goes.)

EDWARD:
    Gilberte! my evening star! my hope!
    I'll follow you!
    Oh, nonsense! Damn! I'm lonely but I don't
    Love Gilberte! I love her name
    I read about her every day
    In Proust—

CHRISTINE: *(a little ways off, listening)*
    I can't—no matter how he feels.

LUXOR

CHRISTINE:
    It's the Temple of Luxor!

EDWARD:
    I enter the temple and I'm crying. Why?

(silence)

    Because you're going to leave me
    And it reminds me of your legs.

CHRISTINE:
   What does?

EDWARD:
   This temple does, its columns.
   Its columns remind me of your strong and beautiful legs.
   And you're going to leave me.
   Its columns remind me of your legs. This temple does.

CHRISTINE:
   You came here without me and without the guide.

EDWARD:
   And you will go off with someone not me.
   These columns remind me of your legs.
   The way you would put one of them over me
   In the morning, when I couldn't sleep.

CHRISTINE:
   The boat starts moving again.

EDWARD:
   Wait, I'm coming along.

KENYA

(EDWARD *and* CHRISTINE *go off and come riding in on* ELEPHANTS. *Each dismounts, stands beside an elephant and speaks for it.*)

ELEPHANT (EDWARD):
   The savanna is good and hot. And it is bad and hot. But the good thing is
      that it is full of trees.
   Oh impossible even to imagine, for an elephant, a tree-less savanna!

SECOND ELEPHANT (CHRISTINE):
   These wombs would cease
   To bear, on a savanna without trees.

FIRST ELEPHANT (EDWARD):
   We need the savannah
   And the savanna, to control its trees, needs us. We smack at them as at the
      keys
   Of a grand piano and we rend them more than a gigantic rat would cheese
   And we do not worry much about other residents of the savanna—

(*A* LION *enters and looks around curiously.*)

SECOND ELEPHANT (CHRISTINE):
    Except for this one
    He could connect us to the rest of the savanna by the "food chain"—
    But he does not. No animal can eat us and we can eat none. The lion cannot
    Kill us. Our weight, our hide, our tusks
    Out-animal that dastard lion, pure bastard thing. But he is, though, dangerous,
    To baby elephants, to them alone.

(Enter more LIONS.*)*

FIRST ELEPHANT (EDWARD):
    So we surround our children

(This is acted out.)

SECOND ELEPHANT (CHRISTINE):
    We elephants surround the baby elephants—they prance along
    And do not know the danger of the lions we prevent
    Until they are adult elephants themselves.
    Then they can fight the lions
    And *they* give birth or help give birth to elephants, themselves!

(LIONS *roar, charge, and are driven back.)*

THE GREEK ISLAND OF HYDRA

(EVAN, *with friends, near the harbor)*

EDWARD *as* EVAN:
    Don't expect ANYTHING!

(A woman comes up to EVAN. *He lights her cigarette and talks and gestures to her, puts his hands on her shoulders and smiles.)*

FIRST MAN:
    Evan is lighting a woman's cigarette. He wants her to be completely under-
        standing of and completely generous to him.
    Then he will reward her with the Food of the Gods.

SECOND MAN:
    Silence, talk, no children, love, and a bemused and vague infidelity.

WOMAN:
    I want something more!

FIRST MAN:
    Most of what Evan says can be understood in the light of this situation.

EVAN: *(to the* MEN*)*
Good!

EVAN: *(to the* WOMEN*)*
Enjoy it!

EVAN: *(at fifty)*
You know, there's not so much time!

(A woman walks by. EVAN *is now either ninety years old or a death's-head skeleton.)*

EVAN: *(to the woman)*
Hello, Angel!

ELSEWHERE ON HYDRA

CHRISTINE:
On the porch of the hotel they sat and looked out at things they could see.
They played a game. The father said, It is red but stippled, and they had to
guess what it was. No that could not have been the game.

EDWARD:
I was sitting in an automobile four years later thinking about that game.
Perhaps it was this: the mother said: I see three things beginning with an L.

CHRISTINE:
I meant of course in English not in Greek.

EDWARD:
Maybe that was possible.

CHRISTINE:
The child, a little girl, was at a certain disadvantage in being only five years
old. She played along though, and of course the mother and the father made
it easy. It was best when she would win. After they played the game for about
half an hour, the mother took the child inside.

EDWARD:
Their rooms were on long corridors. Bathrooms were at the far, non-porch
end. After a while the father got up and went in to his room. The mother
(she was thirty-one) was lying in the bed. The father was thirty-six. He
looked fondly at her and said, Did you like the game?

CHRISTINE:
I lied Yes. Then I said, I'm asleep.

GABON—LIBREVILLE

EDWARD *as* HERVÉ BLANC:
　I hate to leave Millie, but I have to go back
　Unless it is my whole life that I want to spend here in Gabon.
　My life isn't moving, isn't going anywhere here.

CHRISTINE *as* GABON CASINO GIRL: *(blonde and British)*
　Hervé's going back troubles me
　He has a girlfriend, Millie, here. I don't think he'll take her to France.

EDWARD *as* HERVÉ BLANC:
　I don't see how I can take her
　I have to be thee myself first.
　Maybe she'll never come . . . Oh
　Sweet paradise of early hotel morning—
　Stamp too big to go on the postcard, I must away—
　Large breasts of this Gabonese morning, this earth, this hotel—

CHRISTINE *as* GABON CASINO GIRL:
　Hervé's gone.

MILLIE: *(sitting, elsewhere in Libreville)*
　Hervé is leaving, as I always knew he would.

CHRISTINE *as* GABON CASINO GIRL:
　Could you give me my glasses, please?

HER BEDMATE (MAN): *(he gives her her glasses and also puts on his own as if to see what is happening, then takes them off)*
　Let's go back to sleep.

(sound of steamship leaving)

ITALIAN-FRENCH FRONTIER—DOMODOSOLLA NEAR NICE

CHRISTINE:
　Edward, give me the baby—
　Or should I take out the bags?
　Here's French Customs!

(It's very dusty and extremely HOT.*)*

FRENCH CUSTOMS PERSON (FEMALE):
　Quel cauchemar! What a nightmare
　To travel with a new-born child!

EDWARD:
　The day is mild. And yet I see a sort of promised zoo
　Of clouds, in the sky.

CHRISTINE:

                    Yes, I do too!

FRENCH CUSTOMS PERSON:

    I'd suggest that you get out of here fast!

CHRISTINE:

    But what did we do?

FRENCH CUSTOMS PERSON:

    Nothing! But it will be hard for you
    Travelling with this baby!

EDWARD:

                    It doesn't matter, dear, what we have done.
    It is what we WILL do in all this time to come!
    And live in the bright confusion
    Of extreme life!

ITALIAN CUSTOMS PERSON (MALE):

    Come! Come! We admire your baby
    Here there is nothing and really there is nothing
    But dust and butterflies and mainly only dust. But such a lovely baby!
    But let's now for the moment see
    If you are transporting drugs or have too much or too little money.

EDWARD:

    Doesn't everyone have too much or too little money?

ITALIAN CUSTOMS PERSON: *(impressed)*

    Pass—free!

EDWARD:

    Thank you.

TOKYO

KAWABATA:

    For me happiness is being here, sitting on the terrace of the Tokyo Hilton
    Hotel, drinking a Scotch and soda.

JOURNALIST:

    But, Master, you have done so much work—so deep, so terrifying, so mov-
    ing, so artistic and profound! How can a mere glass of scotch water be any-
    thing to that? How could not that outpace this in a second moment?
    Answer that.

KAWABATA:

Actually, there is no need to. Sitting here on the terrace of the Hilton is happiness itself. And in happiness, one need not speak. It is not necessary. That is what is so happy about it.

JOURNALIST:

I am sure, then, though, that there is more to it in back of this momentary feeling. This can't be happiness itself.

KAWABATA:

Happiness is only itself. Behind of course are years of work. Hard years of work. And relations with other people and with the world. But these were not happiness. Happiness is in the vigor of this malt, on this terrace of the Hilton, now!

PARIS

EDWARD *as* PAUNAMAN:

It's the worst kind of weather for writing poetry—cold, clear, and still. No snow, no rain, no wind, even. Just sun but cold. Extremely cold. In which clarity, such freezing clarity, I don't feel moved to write.

A VOICE (CHRISTINE):
Be moved to write!

PAUNAMAN:

Ah, now, I am moved to write! I feel SOMEthing. It is beginning to happen. It often starts this way, a poem. What will it be about?

A VOICE:
Write it and see.

PAUNAMAN:

The breeze
Of inspiration! Indeed, *le souffle*!

(WIND *blows papers hectically all about. After the wind stops,* PAUNAMAN *stoops down to pick up the various wind-blown pages.*)

PAUNAMAN:

It's finished! I'll call it "The Lockets." I wonder if it's any good?

GABON-LAMBARÉNÉ

EDWARD *as* DOCTOR:
Albert Schweitzer's Hospital!

His celebrated clinic in Lambaréné.
May I be worthy of my great forebear
Albert Schweitzer! May I find the secret of clinical medicine at this Lambaréné
And perhaps more important, Schweitzer's secret of the worship of life—
To kill even a mosquito was a heavy crime to him. Then, even a bacterium?
    a germ? a virus?
How does Schweitzer cure, with this absurd respect for "Life"—I mean, of
    course, all kinds of life?
For it is always one kind of life that kills another. Always so.

(Panoramic stage-filling, perhaps even theater-filling, scene of birds killing insects, eagles killing birds, men shooting eagles, lions killing zebras, and so on. In the midst of all this the DOCTOR *walks toward the clinic. Suddenly, several* M'PONGWE *run out, surround, and kill him.)*

DRIVER:
    What? What have you done? You crazy cannibals!
    Why did you kill this man?

M'PONGWE:
    We are not cannibals—
    Unlike the Fang, the main tribe that inhabits Gabon.

OTHER M'PONGWE:
    No. We are not.

PARIS

CHRISTINE *as* DENISE:
    Here we are, three young women.

ANGELINE:
    Standing in front of great Notre Dame Monument, Queen of the Day and
        of the Night.

NORA:
    I am blind, but I do love its each detail!

CHRISTINE *as* DENISE:
    Nora, let me put your hand here. This is
    The left side of the right-hand portal. These
    Are the spare, elongated, utterly spiritualized stone
    Figures of Christ his father his mother and the Saints.
    They are supposed to be the most beautiful of all.

ANGELINE:

   With no excess decoration. No disturbing gesture. No
   Concern for any style but spirit in stone.

NORA:

   Oh!

CHRISTINE *as* DENISE:

   I am in the midst of a destructive relationship
   With a man, a doctor, rich, arrogant, unfaithful even to me
   He has just gone to Gabon with another woman—

ANGELINE:

   I have always felt that women did not feel overt sexual desire.
   This idea is absurd but I seem stuck with it. When I have sexual desires
   I feel that I am less a woman. I am chagrined. I want to deny I have them—
   But then I am so surprised by them
   Sometimes, that I give in, sexually,
   To the most inappropriate men. And about this I can say nothing
   Even to these two who are my friends. When I speak of it, they don't hear me.
   Ah, how much Nora
   Enjoys this cathedral!
   More than I ever did, or could, even. I know it.

DENISE:

   Yes. She does. Nora! You seem to like Notre Dame so much!

NORA:

   Well, I do. Shall we go inside?

KENYA—NAIROBI

(a hotel room)

CHRISTINE:

   He closed the university down.

EDWARD:

   Who did?

CHRISTINE:

   Mobutu did. So I may never see my boyfriend again.

EDWARD:

   I am your boyfriend.

CHRISTINE:

No. Not quite. I don't know you.

EDWARD:

But here we are alone in this Kenyan hotel.

CHRISTINE:

You forgot the reason I came to your hotel.
It was not to make love to you
But to clean up. There isn't a bath in mine. It's not so nice as this.
Don't you remember?

EDWARD:

I remember all the time in which we have not made love, our entire life.

CHRISTINE:

Maybe all right, but maybe not all right.

EDWARD:

What does that mean?

CHRISTINE:

It means maybe I will—
But meanwhile tell me about yourself. Are you married?

EDWARD:

Tell me about your Peace Corps life.

CHRISTINE:

It is identical with my life, with all my life.
My entire life is like an assignment to the Peace Corps.
I'll make love to you.

(Lights out then back on. Many coins—pennies, dimes, and nickels—shower to the floor.)

EDWARD:

Look! The future and the past! I'll go and pick them up.

(He gets out of bed and starts to pick up the coins.)

CHRISTINE: *(rising on one elbow)*
So now no classes for a while!

VENICE—THE LAGOON

(JULIAN and MADDALO, landing on a beach with their gondola)

EDWARD *as* JULIAN:

    Let me tell you, Maddalo,
    As in this your gondola
    We float languidly in this lagoon,
    Christianity is like an island
    Upon which lives a madman,
    Who claims he died of love.
    But it is not true that he died of love!
    He died the way we all died, Maddalo.
    Whoever cannot see this is a madman,
    And should be, straight, ejected from this gondola! *(He laughs.)*

CHRISTINE *as* MADDALO:

    Julian, lift your eyes and see this island
    Locked into the blue mist of this lagoon—
    There is none like it, else, in this lagoon!
    Upon it lives a man made mad by love
    Who lives his life sequestered on this island.
    As certain as my name is Maddalo
    I longed to see him and have steered my gondola
    This way, to have some words with this said "madman"!
    Are you the madman?
    I think that you are not! I am Maddalo
    And this is Julian.

MADMAN:

    I, in this lagoon,
    Have seen no one for seven years. For love—
    When my Maria died—I broke my gondola
    And yours is the first sign of any gondola
    I've seen in all this time upon my island!
    Be welcome here!

MADDALO:

    We thank you. But, come back
    With us, dear lover, and be nursed back to health!

JULIAN:

    Yes, with us to the sheltered mainland come,
    Where bonny nurses will amend your state
    Of being, till you shine with life again!

MADMAN:

    Alas, too late! You are kind my Lords, but one was kinder still,
    And she is dead. And now I too must die. Farewell.

(He falls down dead.)

FLORENCE

DOCTOR:
We'll have to get more blood. But there is none in Florence.

EDWARD:
What will we do then?

DOCTOR:
There is a convent hospital across the river, ten kilometers away. They may have some there. *(They drive there and enter the hospital.)* I can't disturb the Sister—a service is going on. She has the key.

EDWARD:
The key to the place where the blood is stored?

DOCTOR:
Yes.

EDWARD:
Disturb her. It is a matter of life and death.

DOCTOR:
All right. *Mille scusi, suora, ma abbiamo bisogna—c'io e sarebbe possible avere un fiasco di sangue air akka negativo.*

NUN:
Certo. Buona sera signori.

EDWARD:
Buona sera, grazie!

CHRISTINE:
They came and told me I had to choose a name for the baby.
Otherwise they couldn't bury it. You know, I'm afraid!
I'm mostly afraid I won't be able to love Molly.
I've had for so long the idea of the other baby with her, all the time.
And now that he's—not here—I'm not sure I can love her.

EDWARD:
I know you will. I'll help you.

PROVENCE

(Cherry trees are quarrelling—voices of waving branches.)

BLOSSOMING CHERRY TREE:
Admire me. That's my due, I am
More beautiful than you.

SECOND BLOSSOMING CHERRY TREE:
You can't see yourself. So it's impossible for you to know.
But I see you. And I tell you that it isn't so.

FIRST BLOSSOMING CHERRY TREE:
What you say makes no sense.

SECOND BLOSSOMING CHERRY TREE:
It makes sense.

FIRST BLOSSOMING CHERRY TREE:
Makes no sense. I am more beautiful than you.

SECOND BLOSSOMING CHERRY TREE:
Absurd cherry!

FIRST BLOSSOMING CHERRY TREE:
Stupid, very!

SECOND BLOSSOMING CHERRY TREE:
Frowzy boughs!

FIRST BLOSSOMING CHERRY TREE:
Secondary!

SECOND BLOSSOMING CHERRY TREE:
Evening goes its rounds
With darks to not see you!

FIRST BLOSSOMING CHERRY TREE:
You are a fireman's shoe!

SECOND BLOSSOMING CHERRY TREE:
It is I who am more beautiful than you.
See how the sun shines through.

FIRST BLOSSOMING CHERRY TREE:
It is shining on me
O deluded cherry tree!

SECOND BLOSSOMING CHERRY TREE:
YOU are the deluded tree! . . .

CHRISTINE:
Oh, what I have been through
I hate quarreling, gone through!

Blossoming cherry trees, even,
Fight. That's terrible—for them, for me.

EDWARD *as* DIETRICH: *(standing by his boat)*
Come, can you go out with me?

CHRISTINE:
I don't want to quarrel,
Dietrich.

EDWARD *as* DIETRICH:
I don't—quarrel?—understand. Will
You come or no?

CHRISTINE:
Oh, Yes!

(She turns lightly then speaks again as if to answer herself.)

CHRISTINE:
No!

ZAIRE—OUTSKIRTS OF KINSHASA

ANNOUNCER:
Ladies and Gentlemen, Achille Dogos! Achille Dogos presents
Leaders of the Wartime and Postwar World!

(In the middle of the BUSH, *in a cleared space,* ACHILLE DOGOS, *puts on a play:* LEADERS OF THE WARTIME AND POSTWAR WORLD. DOGOS *takes on the characters of the main leaders of Europe and America from about 1939 to 1980. Very little of what he said [often sings, shouts, screams, or whispers] can be heard. What can be heard most clearly are the transitional phrases spoken at the introduction of each new personage, transitions accomplished always by means of* PUNS, *which should be rather heavily emphasized.)*

ACHILLE DOGOS *as* ROOSEVELT:
Hey ha ha! Where you build a church? It's up on a hill, that's why we call it CHURCH HILL!

(DOGOS feigns entrance as WINSTON CHURCHILL.)*

ACHILLE DOGOS *as* CHURCHILL:
Did I hear my name? Going to strike the animal, strike it where it sleeps.
We have to HIT LAIR! Ho, ho, speak!

(DOGOS feigns entrance as ADOLF HITLER.)*

DOGOS *as* HITLER:
Well I am Hit Lair! Who now says my name? If then when my friend feels not so strong, he'll lean on me. He must LEAN ON ME!

(DOGOS *feigns entrance as* BENITO MUSSOLINI.)

DOGOS *as* MUSSOLINI:
Ho, I am Benito Must-Lean-On-Me . . .

(*Finally, after much more stage action,* DOGOS *appears as* JOHN F. KENNEDY.)

DOGOS *as* KENNEDY:
We must have peace! . . .

(A SHOT. DOGOS *falls down as if dead.* SPECTATORS *scream: No! no! no! no! no! no!* DOGOS *now gets up, as himself, and bows, to great applause.*)

CHRISTINE *as* SERAFINE: (*tells her story as she runs along—either jogging or, perhaps preferably, really running to get to or away from something or someone; occasionally, she seems a little out of breath*)

I had a, well, a thing with a very important man . . . An industrialist. Lived in Zaire. We were. It was a man of fifty-eight years. I was sixteen. We were happy. Last year he had a massive heart attack. He was not quite dead but the affair was over. He was enfeebled, weak to the point of bedrid. He cannot move his arm.

EDWARD *as* THE INDUSTRIALIST: (*from offstage, loudly but haltingly*)
Frédérique!

SERAFINE: (*reaches the banks of the Congo River and gets into a pirogue*)
But his servant does not hear and does not come because.

EDWARD:
I am living.

SERAFINE:
Oh but for me it is as if he is dead.

EDWARD:
How in her pirogue she glides
Like a flower seen from all sides!
She the universe divides
Into sunshine, rain, and snow.

SERAFINE:
I at sixteen still was so—La! I came like a gilded butterfly

EDWARD:
Tell the rest.

SERAFINE: *(sings)*
    Mi chiamono Serafina!
    Sono bella come un angelo!
    Sono stata per due anni con un grand' industriale!
    Lui ammalato, io partivo!
    Mi chiamano Serafina. Ora, o diciotto anni!

EDWARD:
    Bella istoria!

SERAFINE:
    I came like a gilded butterfly to pose on the stark dark arm of the man with two billion francs three years before he was going to die.

CHIEFTAIN:
    My wife is in an elegant room taking care of me.
    We French are the cleverest people in Europe. This continent is dark, but its sun is bright.
    Dying in Africa, I think of this girl.

SERAFINE: *(now back on shore again, and running)*
    My father was a friend of his, in the Ministry of African Affairs. He told my father he loved me and my father told him, "If you make her happy—" My father was really horrified, though. When he put his hand on my father's shoulder, my father instinctively recoiled. *(She stops, out of breath)* His heart attack finished it really. I had to leave Africa. At that point everything was impossible! *(She runs off very fast now, headed for France.)*

THE GREEK ISLAND OF HYDRA

EDWARD *as* TERENCE, *a painter*:
    I can't stop drinking. I don't even want to stop drinking. I'm going crazy. I think perhaps I am already crazy! This island, to me, is like a hospital. With fine medicine! More ouzo, ha ha! More wine! More beer!

CHRISTINE *as* WAITER:
    Would you like something to eat with that, Poustoukis?

EDWARD *as* TERENCE:
    Poustoukis? What's that? Why do you call me that? Do you want to have a drink with me after you're off? What time would that be tonight?

CHRISTINE *as* WAITER:
    No I am sorry sir Poustoukis. I can't. But I can bring you another drink and something to eat.

EDWARD *as* TERENCE:
Well, I'd rather have you but I'll take a beer. Bring me a piece of bread, perhaps. I don't really want anything to eat. I know that I'll be sent home crazy before long. Ah! ha ha! I'd rather have you than a beer!

(He passes out.)

EDWARD: *(no longer* TERENCE*)*
I've thought of a song.

(poses in a grand operatic way to sing)

Black is the COVER
—Do you get it, it's a yarmulke—a Jewish folksong—
Black is the COVER of my TRUE LOVE's hair—

CHRISTINE:
Yes, it's funny. It really is . . . Listen! Do you hear?

DROWNED SAILORS' VOICES:
Kale Kihos! . . .
Kore! . . .
Rododaktolos Eros! . . .

(Now TERENCE *goes by, on a boat.)*

VOICE OF TERENCE:
O Oinops Pontos! . . . This world, this water, are lost.

EGYPT

CHRISTINE:
Downstairs the children are very busy on the machines.

EDWARD:
They seem to be six, seven, eight, ten years old. Weaving.

OFFICIAL:
Doing this work, the children can make money, entirely due to the kindness of you, which will eventually enable them to go to school.

CHRISTINE:
Obviously not true!
A horrible enterprise.
To give to the children is to condone it.

EDWARD:
But we can't avoid the problem like that.
Once we are here, we are here.

CHILD:
Give me please. (EDWARD *does.*) Thank you.

CHRISTINE:
Foolish.

EDWARD:
I suppose so.

CHRISTINE:
But what else can be done?

EDWARD:
Whatever. But we are not going to do it on this tour.

CHILD:
I'll work faster and faster. It was my speed and efficiency that made him give me so much!

CHRISTINE:
What did she say?

EDWARD:
Let's get on the bus! It's going. We don't want to be left here!

HAITI—PORT-AU-PRINCE, HOTEL GARDEN

CHRISTINE'S MOTHER:
I'm very sorry—I can't tell you how sorry—that
Moulson's turned up in this place!

CHRISTINE'S FATHER:
He—ah, the doctor.
Well, that's all over, isn't it? I'm sorry it's so unpleasant for you—

HAITI—COUNTRY ROAD

CHRISTINE:
I'm lost. I never saw this road
Drums! This is the place they were talking about, where you can hear
Drums. On my own I found it.

(*Enter* PROCESSION OF THE DEAD, *in* MASKS.)

A procession! A parade.

(*drums louder,* PROCESSION *nearer*)

LEADER:
Watch out, Little Lady, that we don't trample you down!
Our emblem is the SNAKE,
It goes in all directions.

(*He hurls a* SNAKE *on the stage. It rises, curls, curves, does many snakelike movements.*)

CHRISTINE: (*frightened by the* SNAKE *as she was not by the* PROCESSION OF THE DEAD)
Yikes! A cobra! I don't know what. A snake! It may be a rattler! I'm getting out of here!

LEADER:
Farewell!
Come my Dead Ones, further!

(*They march off.* CHRISTINE *approaches a café table off to one side where* DR. MOULSON [EDWARD] *is sitting.*)

CHRISTINE:
Uh, ah . . . Hello, Sir. Doctor Moulson?

EDWARD *as* DR. MOULSON:
Christine! What are you doing, off in this odd place?

CHRISTINE:
I wanted to hear the drums. But there's a snake over there, a really scary one! (*She lights a cigarette.*)

DR. MOULSON:
A snake? Well, I'll go see. Does your mother allow you to do that?

CHRISTINE:
No. Over there.

(MOULSON *goes, looks, and comes back.*)

DR. MOULSON:
Yes, in fact. A big one. But it slithered off.

CHRISTINE:
Oh my god. Well, thank you. I guess I'll be going home.

(CHRISTINE *returns to the hotel garden.*)

CHRISTINE'S MOTHER:
Where were you Christine?

CHRISTINE:

I ran into Dr. Moulson.

CHRISTINE'S MOTHER:

What were you doing with him?
Didn't I tell you not ever to speak to him?

CHRISTINE:

Oh not anything. I went out there where you can hear the drums. I heard them. But then I got frightened by a snake.

CHRISTINE'S FATHER:

Dr. Moulson? A snake? what in God's name is going on?

CHRISTINE:

Oh, nothing! (*She looks at her finger, sees a tobacco stain on it, and puts it in her mouth to hide it.*)

CHRISTINE'S MOTHER: (*smoothing out her own long honey-blonde hair*)
Tell us the story!

KENYA—NAIROBI

CHRISTINE:

After the market, the sunlight hits our faces as we gradually work our way inside the shadowing garden doors of the hotel.

EDWARD:

Can you spend the night?

CHRISTINE:

What would we do all night?

EDWARD:

Who built this hotel?

PARIS

During this great hot spell it's impossible to get coffee. It makes the café too hot. Cold drinks are almost impossible to find. People hoard beer, soda, bottled water. Only here and there, an old sailor, drunk and asleep in his boots, awakes with a terrible thirst and takes it for granted.

EGYPT

CHRISTINE *as* EGYPTIAN GUIDE:

Why does that disagreeable-seeming man keep looking at me?

EDWARD:
I want to see behind the appearance—
Behind that pleasure-giving feminine exterior is what seems to be an ignorant young woman,
But behind that ignorant young woman is possibly something that is worth the world!

CHRISTINE:
He will never find out, because I'm not going to be intimate with him
I am not going to make love to him. Life is not long enough for that!

WILLIMANTIC, CONNECTICUT

EDWARD:
How idyllic, though, to be with you today sitting on the banks of the Willimantic River, my idea and yours, a nice place to be, isn't it?

CHRISTINE:
Yes. Do you remember—?

EDWARD:
How could I forget? That you—

CHRISTINE:
That I was a "Red Cross Girl" and you were an enlisted soldier, a PFC. You weren't allowed to go out with me, you weren't allowed even to touch me, to take my hand.

EDWARD:
I did, though, in the jeep. You were the driver.

CHRISTINE:
I was the only one who could get a vehicle. It was nice to be out with you!

EDWARD:
Yes, though there was not much we could do. No place to go. Military Saipan was a difficult place for a romance.

SAIPAN

CHRISTINE:
Should we drive a little further?

EDWARD:
I love you.

CHRISTINE:
Can I show you some things from this book? I collect in it the things I like best that I read, mostly from poems; this whole section is about nature, this one about love.

EDWARD:
Could you come to see me in New York?

CHRISTINE:
No. You and I aren't fated to meet again.

KUNMING

WANG CHULI:
On the Long March, during our rest periods, we read passages from Whitman aloud.
From *The Song of Myself.*

EDWARD:
"I am he that walks with the tender and growing night"?
Or "Smile, for your lover comes!"?

WALT WHITMAN: *(appearing on one side of the stage and reading softly)*
I call to the earth and sea half-held by the night.
Press close, bare-bosomed night—press close, magnetic nourishing night!

WANG CHULI:
I think we read something else.

EDWARD:
I wonder what.

CHRISTINE:
Oh you probably know.

EDWARD:
I don't. Young Li said you and I are spending an awful lot of time together. He is surprised we're not married. Or at least engaged.

CHRISTINE:
You are so much older than I am. But I would do it anyway.

EDWARD:
What?

CHRISTINE:
  Marry you.

EDWARD:
  Oh! Christine! That's very nice of you!

CHRISTINE:
  Well, it was sort of a joke.

EDWARD:
  I *am* living with someone else.

CHRISTINE:
  Yes, but it's a "Long March" back to the United States!

EDWARD:
  Thank you. But nonetheless, nonetheless . . . What a joy, though, sometimes, to talk to somebody!

CHRISTINE:
  Yes, when we met two days ago in the hotel—

EDWARD:
  It seemed so right away.
  Is that how Whitman could have seemed to the Chinese marchers?

CHRISTINE:
  You could ask Wang Chuli . . .

WANG CHULI:
  I am still searching for the passages. I know it was not the beginning: "I celebrate myself."

(WHITMAN *reappears.*)

WHITMAN:
  And what I assume, you shall assume.
  For every atom belonging to me as good belongs to you.

LEYTE

EDWARD:
  I am here "in combat," an infantry soldier in the Philippines, on the island of Leyte, behind the lines. We stay here, in the tropical rainstorms and in the rare hits of sun, just waiting, waiting to be called to the front, and not doing much. Every day, at noon, we eat lunch. We open cans of C rations and K rations

and eat. The food is horrible but it keeps us alive. And every day, after the first day, just as we do open those cans and prepare to eat, some Japanese planes fly over and open fire. We dive into trenches and foxholes; most of the time, after a few minutes, the raiders are gone. They've done no harm.

KANAMAKA: *(leading a group of small planes)*
This way! Over here!

(explosion)

EDWARD:
Ow! *(He screams.)*

KANAMAKA:
You will die, Americans! Away!

EDWARD:
Why do they leave so soon, I wonder? I guess they don't consider us an important target. Then why bomb us at all? War is extraordinary. Everything you hear, anything you see, anything you smell, even, can mean your death!

TOKYO

KANAMAKA:
Thank you for coming to this World Conference on Refolded Electronic Chips. Luncheon is served.

(loud noise as of chairs being knocked over violently on the floor above)

EDWARD: *(turns pale)*
My God! A lunchtime raid!

(He dives down to the floor.)

OTHERS:
What's wrong with our American colleague? Are you all right?

KANAMAKA:
MY bombers! MY young life in the sun!

CRETE

EDWARD:
Our baby is walking up the steps.

CHRISTINE:
She's not quite a baby any more. Sixteen months!

EDWARD:
　Are you sure she's all right?
　In Knossos life can be dangerous.

CHRISTINE:
　I suppose that three thousand years ago it was.
　Minos was a horrible man!

EDWARD:
　Look! The bare traces of a statue of Helios!

CHRISTINE:
　Cretan versions of Olympian gods—
　A horrible man! Sacrificing boys and girls every year—
　What kinds of gods are those?

HELIOS: (*rising up out of a fallen stone statue*)
　Hungry ones! And now it is your turn! (*menaces them*)
　I am Helios!
　The ancientest Sun God!

EDWARD:
　Watch
　Out! Molly is falling!

(EDWARD *rushes over and catches the* BABY *before she hits the ground from the top step where she was*)

EDWARD:
　Ah! safe! Molly!

HELIOS:
　Curses! I'm defeated—
　I, the fierce monarch of the sun!

(*He again becomes one with the fallen statue.*)

EDWARD:
　I caught her!

CHRISTINE:
　Oh, now you are like a god!

PARIS

OTHER YOUNG MAN:
　He likes you almost as much as I do!

CHRISTINE:

Well, of course! He's liked me for a long time!

OTHER YOUNG MAN:

Well, I like HIM for that!

CHRISTINE:

Maybe you two should get together.

OTHER YOUNG MAN:

Ha!

EDWARD:

Would you like a drink?

CHRISTINE:

Yes. I would.

EDWARD:

Will you come to Barcelona?

CHRISTINE:

Of course. No one ever said I was "sweet."

EDWARD:

I forgot to say it. I love your dress.

CHRISTINE:

I don't think you should pay any attention to how I dress.

EDWARD:

Why not? You're wearing those clothes. You selected them. Maybe even you paid for them. You put them on. I didn't.

CHRISTINE:

Ha ha. I'd like you to dress me.

EDWARD:

Well, if I dress you then can I say I like your clothes?

CHRISTINE:

No!

EDWARD:

Why not?

CHRISTINE:

Because you'd have to buy them, too.

(*They embrace.*)

EDWARD:
I love you.

CHRISTINE:
Don't say that. I told you not to say that.

EDWARD:
Why shouldn't I say that I love you? It's the truth. Besides it makes me feel good to say it.

CHRISTINE:
Well it doesn't make me feel good; it has always made me feel uncomfortable. I thought because you loved me you were much more likely to get me pregnant.

EDWARD:
I like you a lot.

CHRISTINE:
THAT it's all right to say!

EDWARD:
You're wearing a slow white dress.

CHRISTINE:
I'm going to have a baby—with someone else.

EDWARD:
Thank you for not having done this then.

CHRISTINE:
I—well, actually, we—almost did—

GABON—LIBREVILLE

EDWARD:
An arm, in my hotel room!

(He picks up the phone.)

Hello, Front Desk? Front desk of the Ramapawapinada?
A torn-off arm! . . . Well, what could they do, anyway?

(He puts down the phone.)

Here is a note attached to it, saying "To our Professor, from his most appreciative students at the University of Gabon."
Why would my Gabonese students
Give me a torn-off human arm?

A torn-off human arm! *(pause)*
How beautiful are the breasts of the half-naked wives and daughters of the
    lucky French residents of Gabon
As they lie beside the swimming pool! Whereas I, a stranger to this country,
Am confined to this thirtieth-story room with a bleeding arm!

(Pause. He looks closely at the arm.)

But the arm's not "real." It has no odor. It's paper,
Papier-mâché.

(KNOCK at the door. Enter KABAMU, or CHRISTINE as KABAMU.)

EDWARD:
Kabamu, I am glad to see you. Do you know anything about this arm?

KABAMU:
Ah, I came to talk to you about that. It is a gift from your students
In recognition and appreciation of what you told them about Ambrose
    Bierce. He is their favorite American author.
He truly knows magic, magic that is real, as for us, magic is real.
And as it seems to be, too, for you. They regard you as one of a handful of
    elect foreigners who see into the nature of things. Therefore the supreme
Gift of "The Arm." To the Gabonese, this is the greatest honor
Of all! Congratulations!

(The door opens and many GABONESE STUDENTS comes in, some—or all—in magic tribal costume.)

STUDENTS:
We congratulate you, Professor. *Abba kai-yi ta-boun!* Professor, congratulations.

EDWARD:
But I—but the—well, thank you . . .

(They do a ceremonial dance around him and then shouting loud and stepping high, depart, but not before snatching up the Arm to take it with them.)

KABAMU: *(at the door)*
Professor, Bon Voyage!

EDWARD: *(looking around for the arm)*
But my arm! . . .

KABAMU: *(speaking from the door)*
It is not the arm that has power but the absence of the arm! The physical
    arm is nothing. That is why it is made of papier-mâché! But the arm, once
    invisible, can open the Gates of Life. And of Death!

EDWARD:

Life . . . Death . . . The pool . . . breasts . . . *(He falls asleep.)*

MEXICO

(A CORPSE *walks across the Mexican flatlands.)*

EDWARD *as* CORPSE:

I have been walking across the plain of Mexico for forty days.
I began my voyage in Mexico City and my destination is Oaxaca,
The city in which I was born. My objective is to find the drums there
That I used to play on, when I was alive—when I was a boy and a young
man in Oaxaca.
These drums are at the Church of Santa Maria de la Soledad. I long to play
on them. That
Has been my main wish since I died. I neither sleep nor rest nor take in
nourishment nor look around
At what I am passing, but walk without stint to the City of Oaxaca
And to the DRUMS.

(sound of drums)

I hear them,
I hear the Drums, walking.

(total darkness and night, then glow of early morning)

Forty-one days! I believe this is my sister's house. Sister!
Rosario! My sister!

CHRISTINE *as* SISTER: *(coming to the door)*

Juanito! Why, Juanito! It is—*(She faints. The* CORPSE *picks her up and carries
her inside, where she becomes conscious again.)*

CORPSE:

Rosario—

SISTER:

Juanito, my Juanito—but you are dead!'

CORPSE:

Yes, but alive as a corpse. To me this post-life has been granted. I do not
think it can last long. May it last long enough for me to do what I wish: to
play my drums!

SISTER:

So may it last, Juanito!

CORPSE:
>Sister, go to the Church
>Of the Soledad. Tell Father Benzares that I want my drums
>And that I wish to play them there.

SISTER:
>*Si.*

(the interior of the Church of the Soledad)

BISHOP:
>The Corpse of Juanito is at the high altar playing the drums. The people, who at first fainted on seeing him, have now been brought back to life, by the music. They listen, entranced. My Son, I shall stand beside you.

CHRISTINE *as* RAMONA (THE CORPSE'S DEAD GIRLFRIEND):
>And so shall I.

BISHOP:
>Ramona, Juanito's first love! You, too, here! You who died a week after Juanito went to Mexico City, to make money for the marriage! Is it you?

RAMONA:
>It is I.

PEOPLE:
>Bishop! Find a way to save the corpses from going back into Death! Juanito has made such beautiful music! He deserves happiness. We want him to remain alive!

BISHOP: *(falls to his knees)*
>O Lord, grant this man and woman continuing life! It is so little a thing for Thee!

GOD:
>I can hear you, Bishop, and I have heard the music. I will grant these two life. Seven Years. After that, I would like Juanito to come up to Heaven and play for me. It's a long time that I've been without the blessing of that kind of sound!

BISHOP:
>I thank Thee, Lord. But, may I be bold? Lord, what are years to Thee? Couldst Thou not grant this man a true span of twenty-eight years, and the woman with him? And then take him to Thy breast?

(thunder)

GOD: *(smiling)*
>Rather, to my bandstand. Yes, so be it!

(The BISHOP *turns to offer the* CORPSES *life but the change has already taken place. Beside him are no corpses but a somewhat puzzled-looking man of thirty-two holding a pair of batons and a nervous-looking woman of twenty-nine—in fact,* EDWARD *and* CHRISTINE*)*

BISHOP:

Ah, I see. Well, play! You have been granted life!

FORMER CORPSE:

I've played enough. Bishop, thank you! I have played enough.
The great stamina of the dead is no longer mine!

(He embraces RAMONA *and they come down from the altar.)*

BISHOP:

It is true, you have played for ten hours. The great stamina of the dead is no longer yours. Live in happiness and in peace!

PEOPLE:

Live in happiness and in peace!

MINSTREL:

I know another version of this story! In Acuitlan they say the corpse becomes the corpse of a lion and does acrobatic leaps. And another: in Cuzuno, it is the corpse only of a huge pair of feet, which dance. Ramona doesn't appear in these two stories. There is another one, though, in which she is the main one. SHE is the corpse and she comes to the tiny village of Suninos, gets up on the altar, and SINGS. God is so moved by her singing that He decides to revive the Heavenly Choir. In this version, Juanito is a minor character, who, while she is singing, appears at her side.

(sound of Angelic Choir, singing a "Gloria")

SHANGHAI

*(*EDWARD *and* CHRISTINE *are playing ping pong in the finals of an important tournament.)*

CHRISTINE *as* SONG JIA:

There! My point. Twisting low and to the side!

EDWARD *as* DING WEI:

THIS point is mine, a clear smack smash!

CHRISTINE:

I made an error!

EDWARD:

I made an error!

CHRISTINE:

That I've now redeemed

EDWARD:

That I've now redeemed

EDWARD *and* CHRISTINE:

By this shot.

EDWARD:

The score is even.

CHRISTINE:

Twenty to twenty.

EDWARD:

What you want to happen may happen but may not happen often enough!
To win even one game, a constant succession of victories is needed.
It is not like love.
But now with the distraction of my thinking I have lost the game.
Song Jia you have made two good, winning shots
While I have been distractedly thinking.

CHRISTINE:

To think about the main thing is not
Always the way to win the game. At least I know that it is not
In ping pong, where everything—maybe the whole destiny and outcome
of our life—
Rides on each ball that we hit!

EDWARD:

Now you will go to America and I will not . . .

CHRISTINE:

Because of ping pong.

EDWARD:

Even because of one mis-hit ball!

(dark then light)

NAPLES

CHRISTINE:

Rossini woke from a deep slumber and began to play the piano.

(EDWARD *as* ROSSINI *plays the piano.*)

CHRISTINE *and* OTHERS:
   Bravo! Bravo!

EDWARD *as* ROSSINI: *(still playing)*
   The wheat withers in the fields. A baby is crying.

CHRISTINE:
   Of what use to us, after the opera is over, is Rossini?

EDWARD *as* HIMSELF:
   We hear scraps of Rossini's music everywhere!

CHRISTINE:
   Springtime has come into its own! And despite everything, the child cries
      a little less.

(brace and glorious sounds of an opera)

CHRISTINE:
   At the Teatro San Carlo

EDWARD:
   We have the impression

CHRISTINE:
   Known to be false

EDWARD:
   That time has just begun!

MADAGASCAR

EDWARD *as* JACQUES RABEMANAJARA:
   But in colonizing the island of Madagascar
   The French introduced things that were good
   For the people, certainly, such as "colonial hats" *(He puts one on.)*
   And others that were chiefly to make them feel a part of France
   And thus more loyal, more connected *(He puts on a dark-blue Academy jacket.)*
   Such as the *Académie malgache,* the Madagascar Academy,
   Modeled on the *Académie française.*
   Other things were bad.

MADAME RIBAVIABALA:
   They certainly were! How cruel, how horrible the French were
   To us, at certain times!

(Enter a group of masked, stony-faced FRENCH OFFICERS—*they remove their harsh masks.)*

EDWARD *as* JACQUES:
   With its cruel mask of domination taken off,
   France offers, among the nations, too beautiful a face
   Not to have a choice spot
   In every free man's heart.

(The OFFICERS *put their masks back on and approach him, about to seize him.)*

   Are these officers the presence
   France genuinely wants to have
   In Madagascar? Madagascar! Graven in my soul!

(A map of France is projected, or seen, in the distance.)

   And the whole problem is there—in the distance of France
   From us—the problem of every far-from-the-center action,
   Of every far-from-the-center place!

MME RIBAVIABALA:
   Those words of Jacques Rabemanajara are precious to us!
   But we are happy to see you—now that all that is done.
   Would you like to try our rice water?

EDWARD *as* AN AMERICAN VISITOR:
   Yes. Thank you. What is that?

MME RIBAVIABALA:
   A drink of cool water, and the water has been boiled with rice.
   The rice is eaten, too, of course. The left-over water isn't thrown away
   But cooled and drunk. Do you like it?

EDWARD:
   Yes. Very much.

MME RIBAVIABALA:
   Here is my husband. *Viens,* Robair! This gentleman is come to lunch
   But not to raid.

MONSIEUR RIBAVIABALA:
   Madagascar is now free. Sir, you are welcome! Look at this gigantic cricket
   I've found!

MME RIBAVIABALA:
   Madagascar has the largest crickets in the world!

EDWARD:
   Thank you for everything. Good-bye.

MME RIBAVIABALA:

Je vous en prie, monsieur! Adieu!

MONSIEUR RIBAVIABALA:

Serviteur!

MOROCCO

EDWARD:

Is the bus ever going to leave?

CHRISTINE:

Well, it has to get here first. It ɪs hot here.
Drink the tea. The hotter it is, the cooler it will make you, you know—it
will make us sweat!

EDWARD:

There is an Italian man over there I think we know.
He was at the last stop with us—Ferra- Ferra—Ferrabonzo.

CHRISTINE:

Look at Beepie. She's asleep.

EDWARD:

There are bugs in the tea.

CHRISTINE:

Don't worry about the bugs. They won't hurt us.

EDWARD:

How can you be sure?

CHRISTINE:

Beepie, Beepie, wake up! Come, Sweetest. Daddy has to pay—and then we'll
get on the bus.

EDWARD:

It's come. The large filthy, dark yellow, wheezing bus—
It is breathing harsh breaths in the street.

DRIVER:

Anybody for Elizir?

EDWARD:

Yes, we all are, I think.

CHRISTINE:

This bus smells of—

EDWARD:

Hashish. Let's get off! If the driver is smoking it, it's not safe.

CHRISTINE:

Yes. Let's go.

DRIVER:

Why are you leaving the bus? Are you coming on it or not?

(EDWARD *makes a sign of holding his nose and then of inhaling hashish, fingers at his lips. The* DRIVER *laughs.*)

DRIVER:

That previous passenger. He is gone now from the bus. Not me!

(*He indicates a wavering person some distance away.*)

FERRABONZO:

Are you sure?

DRIVER:

I am sure. Otherwise I can lose my license never to drive the bus my children hungry.

EDWARD:

All right. I believe him. Thank you. Sorry. Let's get on.

DRIVER: (*gets off the bus again and shouts into the empty café*)
Anyone for Elizir? Nobody else? Let's go!

MEDIEVAL ENGLAND

CHRISTINE:

I am Saint Ursula, and the task assigned to me by God is to find eleven thousand virgins to take with me on a crusade to the Holy Land. On the way there, we'll be set upon by pagans, enemies of the Faith, who will rape and slaughter us. I have this foreknowledge but am obliged to set sail anyway. The only way any of these young women can escape this fate is to convince me she is not a virgin.

EDWARD:

How are you going to get them to do that?

CHRISTINE:

Young women of Britannia! Listen to me! God orders you to tell the truth. Liars will go to Hell. Are you virgins? Consider it carefully. If you are not a virgin, that's fine—at least, it's all right. You won't go to hell for that. Only for lying. It happens that I NEED VIRGINS for this one expedition. There may be other expeditions with different requirements. I can envision perhaps a "Red Light Crusade." But that is not what this one is. This one has got to be a Virginiad, truly. So come to me if you are not a virgin, now. There will be no penalty, none. In fact, each one who now admits she is not a virgin will be given, by Saint Anselmo (EDWARD *smiles, acknowledging himself.*) a box of candy. Confess! And from the burdens of deceit be free!

(ELEVEN THOUSAND YOUNG WOMEN *approach* ST. URSULA)

CHRISTINE:
    May God be praised! The Expedition is cancelled! *La spedizione e state annulata. Grazie a dio!* Praise without end.

EDWARD:
    That's amazing!

THE LOWER RHINE

PAGANS:
    God damn! Shit! *Merde!* Damn!
    It will be a long time before such an expedition begins
    Again.—Not in our lifetime!

SOUTHAMPTON, NEW YORK

EDWARD:
    As an American painter
    I never choose as a subject anything remotely like this—
    Yet people say, sometimes, when they look at my paintings of people
    That there is a great empty innocence about the people
    As if they were St. Ursula, and the virgins!

GREECE—ATHENS

CHRISTINE: (*gesturing*)
    Look at that beautiful Artemis statue there! On the vase. Could you buy it for me?

EDWARD:
    Of course.

(*to* MUSEUM GIRL)

    I'd like this vase.

GIRL IN MUSEUM:
  I'll wrap it up.

EDWARD:
  Oh I can't!
  I can't buy the vase, I can't!
  It costs too much.
  I can't stand to spend the money.

CHRISTINE:
  You mean that you can't stand to THINK of spending the money; it isn't really
  such a high price. Besides, I'll pay you back as soon as I can change some
  money myself.

EDWARD:
  It costs fifty-five thousand drachmas.

CHRISTINE:
  That's only four dollars!

EDWARD:
  Here I'll buy these smaller vases
  Tiny ones with silly prices
  Five cents for one
  And six for another. How
  Can they tell the difference? I'll
  Take four—no five—no four—no five—

NEW YORK

EDWARD:
  My desk faces a window and on it I have placed
  One of the five-cent vases I bought in Greece.

(He stands up suddenly.)

  Ah! I bumped the desk—
  The vase fell off. It's fallen down to the courtyard below!

(A full of half-size ARTEMIS STATUE *falls & crashes center-stage. As it crumbles, it speaks.)*

ARTEMIS STATUE:
  I am Artemis, goddess of birth, death, virginity, hunting, and the moon!

EDWARD:
  You look beautiful in that pink dress.

362 ❧ KENNETH KOCH

CHRISTINE:

Thank you! You gave it to me.

EDWARD:

Oh? When?

CHRISTINE:

I think in 1952.

EDWARD:

I should buy you a new one. I will! Ough! pain!

(He clutches his side.)

CHRISTINE:

Are you all right? What was it
That fell

EDWARD:

The little vase.

CHRISTINE:

Oh go and get it.
I can probably fix it.
Listen. I have something to tell you. I'm going to have a baby. Are you glad?
　We can afford it, yes?

SIRACUSA

EDWARD: *(he sits on a stone)*

My mother's favorite, aged eighteen, I while away my time
Beside Arethusa's lovely fountain. She went underground for miles
To escape her unwanted lover, or he went underground for miles to get close
　to her—
As water, for miles and miles—
I forget which the story was, but I, in any case, now I am going
To visit my poor cousin Lucia, Lucia Caranotti.
She is confined to a balcony that is like a cage, it has wire all around it. This
　is to keep her safe.
She has a mental disease for which it is said there is no cure.

LUCIA:

Ay! ay! ay! ay! ay!

EDWARD:

At least, here in Siracusa it is believed that there is no cure.

PADUA

CHRISTINE:

My voice, my talent for opera don't keep me from being lonely.
Always surrounded by people, and by people singing, and to feel so alone—

EDWARD:

This polenta is wonderful!

OTHER YOUNG MAN:

Yes, it's best eaten with rich meats, such as game—boar, pheasant—in cold
weather, in winter, in Italy.

EDWARD:

You who seem, somewhat less than I am, giddily optimistic,
You who are careful and superbly informed, do you see that woman,
That young woman with her face full of glory over there?
Do you see her, or am I really having an illusion? I could fall in love with her!

OTHER YOUNG MAN:

I think you're going to see her tonight at the opera.
She's Lucia Banvelli, a new star.

EDWARD:

If only I could speak to her!
But I am stuck to this table—here!

CHRISTINE: (sings a few long lovely notes)
Sono sola! sola! sola!

VENICE

EDWARD as TOLAVON:

I'm black. I have a violent temper.
I am, I hope, a great painter.
I am Tolavon. They call me "The Moor of Venice."

ISABELLA:

I am Isabella, the Venetian woman he loves. And who loves him. God help us!

(She sits down to pose for TOLAVON. As he paints her portrait, he talks about his
life.)

DUCA DI DURO: (entering)

I'll buy it. Here are seventy million lire this deal is finished.
I'll hang my daughter's portrait in my palace, on the side the sun shines on.

TOLAVON: (later)
  I'll go see Isabella—and my painting!

(Palazza Duro. TOLAVON goes in the palace and comes out with his painting, which he angrily slashes to pieces with his knife.)

TOLAVON:
  I found her with another man!
  Revenge! Vendetta! I should have killed them!

(pause)

TOLAVON: (sitting in a café)
  Isabelle found me and explained. The man was her brother. She hadn't seen him for years. I'm a fool to have such a short temper! But, well, I've made it up to her I think. And I've painted a new portrait of her, better than the first one—in some ways—although in other ways probably not.

ISABELLA:
  Othello! My husband and my lord!

TOLAVON:
  Keep up your bright swords, for the dew will rust them!
  There would have been a time for such a word!
  Put out the light and then put out the light.

ISABELLA:
  Othello, walk with me.

TOLAVON:
  Wait, Isabella! Stand there,
  Just there. With that dewy
  Palladio behind you, you look
  Wonderful! I'm going to
  Paint you there!

ISABELLA:
  Ah, *benedetto moro*! Have your way!

BEIJING

EDWARD:
  I'm going, with my wife, tonight, to the Tango Palace!
  There is very little to do in this city
  At night. Even holding hands in the street is forbidden.

(He takes CHRISTINE's hand and an OFFICIAL intervenes.)

OFFICIAL:

As you have just said. It is forbidden.

But you may hold one another in an accepted way at the Tango Palace.

EDWARD *and* CHRISTINE:

That's where we are going.

OFFICIAL:

It would be reasonable to find some practical use for the enormous network of air-raid shelters built underneath the city's streets to protect the populace from nuclear explosions.

(OFFICIAL *walks to another side of the stage and becomes a* SECOND OFFICIAL.)

SECOND OFFICIAL:

Other possibilities having been found for one reason or another unacceptable, the state has decided to accept and to act upon Proposal 115-A, namely that the bomb-shelter network be slightly revamped to serve as tango palaces, five in all, places for the people to dance.

EDWARD:

Aside from our plain existence and our traditions we have little to entertain us.

CHRISTINE:

Dancing will be fun!

EDWARD:

At least we'll try.

(*He and* CHRISTINE *dance. Then they are chased away by the* OFFICIAL.)

OFFICIAL:

The tango palaces did not last long. There was a seepage of gas which made occupation of the shelters dangerous.

EDWARD:

The state could fix it, but there are other priorities.

OFFICIAL:

Here is one of them: elimination of dogs.

Get rid of your dogs. Kill them.

There is not enough food in Beijing to waste any of it on useless animals. Therefore get rid of them. This order is absolute and absolutely final. Disobedience will result in imprisonment.

CHRISTINE:

This would be a good time to revive the Tango Palaces—

To provide Beijing's people some pleasant distraction when there is sorrow in many houses—

OFFICIAL:
Neither policy will be changed.

ITALY—TAORMINA

CHRISTINE:
How did you suddenly get so friendly with the manager of the hotel?

EDWARD: *(secretly a little pleased)*
What do you mean?

CHRISTINE:
I mean I was upstairs for five minutes and I came down and you two were talking together as if you had been sharing each other's feelings and ideas for years.

EDWARD:
Oh I don't know. He started talking about his daughter who lives in the U.S.

CHRISTINE:
I see.

EDWARD:
Am I being criticized?

CHRISTINE:
A little bit. I suppose so. Yes.

BLOIS

EDWARD:
This is where Ronsard met Cassandre Salviati.
He wrote a thousand sonnets about his love for her.

CHRISTINE *as* CASSANDRE:
I am Cassandre.

EDWARD *as* RONSARD:
Would you like to dance?

CASSANDRE:
Volontieri. Gladly. I'd like to dance.

RONSARD:
Do you know how many poems I will write to you?
Do you know how many times I will see you?

CASSANDRE:
No, I don't. Tell me the answer to each one.

RONSARD:

> I don't know either, but I know I will write
> A great many. And as for how often I will see you,
> That is up to you. I'd like to see you an infinite number of times.
> How old are you?

CASSANDRE:

> I'm fourteen.

RONSARD:

> Oh. That gives us a great number of times!

(pause)

> Yet now, after only a few months,
> I hear that Cassandre has married!
> Oh, love! Heavy is my heart!
> I'll write her, though, great poems—a thousand of them.

CASSANDRE: *(thirty years later)*

> I wonder if he thinks of me now,
> All the same . . .

BEIJING

EDWARD *as* OFFICIAL:

> Please. Drive me to my office.

CHRISTINE *as* CHAUFFEUR:

> Yes, I will.
> *(to herself)* Look how many thousands of people are in the streets,
> Even hundreds of thousands, even maybe already millions
> In the early morning streets. It is barely five o'clock.
> Millions! I am one of them, chauffering this car!

OFFICIAL:

> Can't you make any better time?

CHAUFFEUR:

> Time is against us because the people are for us.
> Notice how they swarm around the car.

OFFICIAL:

> Drive straight through them.
> I don't mean that you should harm anyone by running over him
> But do try to make way. Tomorrow we must start earlier.

(In the street as they pass walks an agèd retired UNIVERSITY PROFESSOR. *While the car is stalled by bicyclists, the* PROFESSOR *speaks, though the* OFFICIAL *does not hear him.)*

PROFESSOR:

I am en route to the pharmacy to buy powdered rhinoceros horn, a sovereign remedy, supposedly, for preserving potency into the furthest old age. I, however, don't use it for this—O burst of bright sun!

(The sun breaks through the morning mist. A DOG, *or an image of a dog appears stage left.)*

I give it to my illicit and beloved dog, my chihuahua Wo Keechung, to keep him alive. Fourteen months ago all dogs were banned. But I have kept him, in spite of the edict. For this, my loved one, I'd gladly risk my life.

(The DOG *disappears. The* PROFESSOR *goes into the pharmacy. The car starts moving again.)*

OFFICIAL:

I have good news to give to the magician. We are going to renew his contract after all. He doesn't have to wait until September. I will give him his new contract now!

MAGICIAN:

I wonder if he will ever come? My contract will run out!

OFFICIAL:

Bo Hung! We have finally arrived! Traffic was a disgrace. There must be fifty million people on the streets. But I have good news for you. I have Good news for you. I really do!

MAGICIAN (CHRISTINE):

And what is this news?

OFFICIAL (EDWARD):

Your contract has been approved—for another year.
We have to find every Antonello da Messina in Sicily.

CHRISTINE:

Melissa will come, too. And your parents?

(Both leave.)

NEWARK

*(*EDWARD *as* IVAN, *a fifty-six-year-old Russian man, enters agitatedly.)*

IVAN:

I want to hold on to Ekaterina, my wife! I met Ekaterina in Germany. She and I were both prisoners of war. She had been captured, as a civilian, from her native city of Leningrad, and brought to Germany to work in a factory. They needed workers. So many Germans being killed. Work people must be brought in from abroad. I was a colonel, in the Russian Army. I was not captured. I surrendered. I was given an order to move my regiment forward to a place where I knew, and the commandant knew, that they would all be killed. I was unable to carry out this order. I could not kill all my men. They trusted me. I surrendered to the Germans. Then I also am working in the same factory. Where I met Ekaterina. She is twenty-five years younger than I. The Germans permit us to marry. When the war is ended, we come to the United States. Here, too, I am working in a factory. My English isn't good enough for a different kind of job. Ekaterina speaks English perfectly. We have a son, five years old. Now she wants to leave me.

EKATERINA:

If he treated me differently I would not want to leave him. Do you know that I have never been to a restaurant? I have never been to a movie. He is too jealous to take me out. He thinks someone will see me, fall in love with me, and take me away. Or that I will fall in love with someone else.

EGYPT—VALLEY OF THE KINGS

CHRISTINE *as* HATHOR:

Osiris, I'm concerned about the boat.

OSIRIS:

I'm coming. What a job it is
Each time we welcome a new person to the Land of the Dead!

TET:

It's amazing that there is still room for them!

HATHOR:

Finish the rigging. We haven't much time.

OSIRIS:

You're tough. Hathor, beautiful and tough. But very beautiful with your
    cow's head all the time.
By the way, I haven't had time to think to find out,
Who is it we are welcoming today?

HATHOR:

Today we welcome
Someone who stumbled on a step that was hidden in the sand

At the Temple of Osiris-Pik.

OSIRIS:
Oh, one of my temples!

HATHOR:
Exactly, Osiris! And as he stumbled, a scorpion bit him,
A deadly scorpion. That is why he is coming to us now.

EDWARD:
I dream I am walking along a dusty white road with a bird-headed
individual.

(BIRD-HEADED BEING *comes out and walks with him.*)
I am ferried across a river on a boat lying flat on my back, wrapped in cloth.

(*He is wrapped up and laid down on the flat wooden bottom of a boat; then he
gets up.*)
I am welcomed by animal-headed people, and handed an ivory staff.

HATHOR: (*gorgeously dressed in blue silks*)
We welcome you!

EDWARD:
Why, you are Christine! the young woman on the boat!

TET:
Welcome, to the Land of the Dead!

EDWARD:
And you—you are the pilot!

OSIRIS:
We are honored to welcome you here!

EDWARD:
You—the man who takes tickets on the boat!

(*The real* TICKET TAKER *appears and hands* EDWARD *a staff, with which he immediately strikes and knocks down* OSIRIS *and* TET. *He takes* HATHOR *by the arm.*)

EDWARD:
I want to stay with you.

HATHOR:
Yes, I'd like that, too. What else do you want?

FINAL CURTAIN

—1996

ONE THOUSAND
AVANT-GARDE
PLAYS

Published in 1988, the following 112 plays were written over a ten-year period.

Time and His Trumpet

(Enter TOMMY TIME, *with a trumpet. He plays one note, then stops.)*

TOMMY TIME:
> Whenever I blow this horn, things change,
> And they are changing all the time
> This time I am taking out to talk to you
> Is no time, does not exist in time, you are not
> Changing, you are not growing older, your
> Love stays the same. It is
> A privileged moment. But when I start to blow
> It will be time, and you will be changing again!

MAN:
> But my love stays the same.

TOMMY TIME:
> That is because it is changing with time.

MAN:
> It just stopped.

TOMMY TIME:
> Because I stopped playing.

WOMAN:
> Oh, play again!

MAN:
> Play, Tommy Time! Without time I feel nothing.

WOMAN:
> So that's what that noise was we heard all the time!

MAN:
> The noise of change!

TOMMY TIME:
> Or of FAITHFULNESS, which also lives in time.

Manet

(Paris, in the nineteenth century)

MAN:
> What is the connection

WOMAN:
> Between the newly emerging modern democratic society

MAN:
> And the art of Edouard Manet?

WOMAN:
> Here. This book tells it.

(Time passes and society is altered; there are the sights and sounds of the twentieth century.)

BOTH:
> And now it has all gone away!

Elfred the Dancer

(Red and orange scarves and an atmosphere of all of history at the same time.)

ELFRED:
> When maids become historians
> And summer skies change
> To violent thunder-rattling scarves or plates,
> Then Macedon at last yields to Greek influence
> And conquers while being conquered.
> Alexander did this.
> The story is told by his maid.
> Alexander had no maid.
> I am Elfred the Dancer.

Searching for Fairyland

(mist)

WILLIAM BUTLER YEATS:
I have coom all this distance, lookin for faeryland.

OLD CRONE:
Well, ye have time, auld father. Tis not yet dark.

WILLIAM BUTLER YEATS:
Accents change, and all things change, but Beauty is like a stone.

(a snowfall)

Tawai Nakimo

(the bare stage of Noh drama)

TAWAI NAKIMO:
  I am Tawai Nakimo, famed beauty, courtesan of the Emperor Wai.

(dreamily, transported, for a moment, to the past)

  How we dance to the slosh of silk and bracelets!

(returns to the present)

  Now my age is ninety-seven,
  And I have come to this bridge land to seek retreat.
  How strange that, around me, all, all is bridges.
  Bridge over river, bridge over stream,
  Bridge over roadway; here, even bridge over little girl.
  Everything, it seem, here have it own bridge.

(in a sort of visionary ecstasy)

  What is the bridge over me, bridge that passes above the head of Tawai Nakimo?

Incident on the Street

(MAN *comes up to another man,* HARRIMAN, *on the street and offers him a rather large box.*)

MAN:
    Harriman, I have brought you this box of balls—
    Wooden balls and steel balls, and balls with gold upon them,
    Acorn balls, nylon balls, balls of porphyry and of ancient silver,
    Every kind of ball you can imagine that is of human make.

(MAN *leaves.*)

The Brave Bull

MATADOR:
Toro! Toro!

(He makes the kill. From the fallen BULL *rises the* SPIRIT OF THE BULL.*)*

SPIRIT OF THE BULL:
I, who was once the body of the bull
And am now its spirit, come near you.
And, near as you as I am, I shall take your life away.

MATADOR:
But my young sons and daughters!

SPIRIT OF THE BULL:
Never should a man have a family,
Especially a large and growing family,
When he knows he is going to be a bullfighter.
I am sorry for this cruel and merciless act,
But it has been fated
By the white handkerchiefs, away!

(The SPIRIT *kills the* MATADOR. *Then the* SPIRIT *himself drops dead and is dragged around the ring.)*

SPECTATORS: *(shouting in various languages)*
Brave bull! Brave bull!

(bullfight music)

The Promenade in Oaxaca

(Evening. EDWARD *is in his forties;* CHRISTINE *is fifteen.)*

EDWARD:
> Christine, let's walk
> Down this street

CHRISTINE:
> I heard
> Last night
> At the circus
> Someone died
> Of I don't know what

EDWARD:
> Electrocution?
> Dog bite? Broken spine?
> Falling from seat? Bench collapse?
> Snake bite? Rat bite?
> We must not go to see
> This circus—
> O Christine
> Just one night
> And yet not having one night
> Fifteen years old
> Mystical summer
> Good-night—
> Oh, my clearest, best!

Six Tones

(Each of the following speeches—lines—is shouted by a different person.)

SOON THE RACE WILL END

WHICH HORSE WILL WIN?

I ENTER THE RACETRACK

A GRAVE EXPRESSION IS ON HER FACE

BUT SHE DOES NOT CALL HIM

HER AGGRIEVED WOMANHOOD

The Cowries

(a sandy stretch by the sea)

EDMUNDSON:
   For seven years I have been accumulating cowrie shells,
   Going from island to island, from coast to coast,
   And I have made my fortune. Now I must leave this place.
   Hola there, you, fellow! I want to buy your boat.
   I'll give you seven shells.

OGON, A NATIVE:
   I don't understand "buy."

EDMUNDSON:
   I'll give you these shells. You give me the boat.
   (He shows OGON *some cowries.)*

OGON: *(decisively)*
   No, Trader. We are not fools. You try to trick us!
   My boat can fly over the water. These shells cannot do that!

*(*OGON *gets into his boat and paddles off.)*

EDMUNDSON:
   Perhaps . . . he's right—and what I do is wrong.
   What this old fellow's said has made me think—and I'll leave these shells
      . . . and find some better way.

*(*EDMUNDSON *drops his cowries on the sand, and goes. Sound of the sea.)*

Two Tall Individuals

FIRST:
The difference between a moment of action and a whole play.

SECOND:
You have never known that.

The End of Comedy

JOE:

You should do a vaudeville revue!

BILL:

But there are no stand-up comics like Mighty Head any more!

(Enter MIGHTY HEAD.*)*

MIGHTY HEAD:

Give me a light, boys, for I wants to smoke.
Hey bobareebob, fellas, how's about a little joke?

JOE:

Okay, Mighty Head, will you act in a play for us?

MIGHTY HEAD:

No, I'm too old for that and too famous for that—
I'm just my whole life one big joke.
Ain't that enough? *(He acts crazy.)* Ack ack ack ack!

BILL:

Yes, Mighty Head, that is enough. He's amazing!

Cook

(The city of Chengde, early evening. COOK, *a young woman, is dressed all in white cook's clothing, including a round cook's hat.)*

COOK:
    I am the Cook, I am racing through the street
    Of Chengde, with my rice boat and in my apron
    All of white and in my cooking hat of white
    My broad my smiling peasant face
    Does cause alarm by winning charm
    To all the masculine cook around
    I DON'T think

    Because this is China, land of think
    To work and always busy
    Cook who runs around shall find
    A young fellow to her mind
    When comes time
    For this. Meanwhile
    With cook-run-around, NO FLIRTING!!

    And no go to the paper store
    Until start of tomorrow day.
    And no go to the wedding store
    Cook shall not go away.
    Cook run through town. I am running!
    No one sees me. In despair
    None doth feel that I am fair.
    Cook running through town
    In no way this day holiday!

BRAD GARKS:
    In USA, my country, we have holiday parts in every day of the year.
    Vast urban agglomerations spell out
    "I love yous" to dead green parks. O faithful Cook,
    Into my arms, now haste!

COOK:
    You will not like me
    Because I am too much atmosphere of "Cook"
    And not woman-lady. Blad, good-bye!

Four Loves

Scene 1
A city street at night in spring.

SAM:
> Let's take a walk

MARINA:
> In the city

SAM:
> Till our shoes get wet

MARINA:
> It's been raining
> All night.

SAM:
> Let's make music

(He plays a mandolin.)

> I know you tonight
> As I have never known

(Light shows a wall behind them that is all white stones.)

> A book of white stones
> Or symbolism

MARINA:
> Let's take a walk

SAM:
> If I kiss you please
> Remember with your shoes off
> You're so beautiful like
> A lifted umbrella orange
> And white

MARINA:
> Let's walk
> Into the first
> Rivers of morning

SAM:
As you are seen
To be bathed in a white light—
Come on

(They walk into such a light.)

Scene 2

A sidewalk and a big white door.

GIRL: *(in pink)*
Good-bye. I'm leaving.

MAN: *(in white)*
But this is only a sketch.

GIRL:
Good-bye. I'm leaving.

MAN:
But this is only a sketch.

GIRL:
I'm leaving. Now. Good-bye.

(She leaves.)

Scene 3

A classroom.

MARY-JO PROFESSOR:
Love comes into prominence as a theme
Earlier, sometimes, than the eighteenth century;
But, there, it dominates, overwhelms, pulverizes,
It is the theme of everything, the *tema sine qua non.*
No Smoking. No Gambling. No Eating. Make Way for Love.
It is the *vrai Départ pour le Cythère.*

(EDMUNDSON comes into the classroom, obviousy smitten.)

EDMONDSON:
Mary-Jo—I . . . I . . . I . . . I . . .

MARY-JO:
Yes. But, please, the class must go on.

Scene 4

A street, near a small river.

SAM AT 20:
Marina, I love you.

MARINA AT 20:
Think about it again.

SAM AT 30:
Now I am thirty years old.

MARINA AT 30:
Think of it again.

SAM AT 40:
I am forty years old.

MARINA AT 40:
Think of me. Do you love me?

SAM AT 50:
Now I am fifty. Marina!
Marina! I can't find you!
Why did you make me wait so long to decide?

(MARINA AT 20, *heartbreakingly beautiful, goes past him in a boat on the river, guided by a* SWAN.)

MARINA AT 20:
I guess I thought
We'd live forever and that it would always be the same!

Oddfellows Playhouse

Presents
Selections from

One Thousand Avant-Garde Plays
by Kenneth Koch

Illustrations by Larry Rivers
Incidental Music by Roger Tréfousse
Directed by Maria Pessino

Program cover with art by Larry Rivers and ticket stub for
One Thousand Avant-Garde Plays, Oddfellows Playhouse
production at Guild Hall, Easthampton, NY, June 2002.

Ticket No	Price
29243	$22.00 Ticket

Oddfellows Playhouse presents
A Selection from
One Thousand Avant Garde Plays
Friday, Jun 21, 2002
8:00 PM
by Kenneth Koch
General Admission

TOP: Scene from *One Thousand Avant-Garde Plays*, Oddfellows Playhouse production. Photo: Marisela Lagrave.

BOTTOM LEFT: Postcard announcement for the Medicine Show production of *One Thousand Avant-Garde Plays*, 1987.

BOTTOM RIGHT: Invitation to a benefit event for the Medicine Show production of *One Thousand Avant-Garde Plays*, c. 1987.

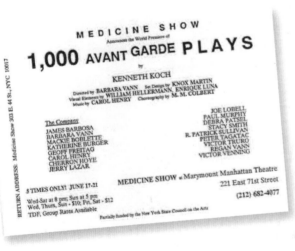

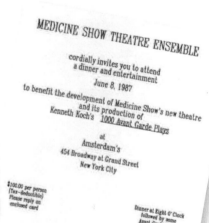

TOP: Cast photo for *The Construction of Boston*, Maidman Playhouse, New York, 1962. FRONT ROW, L–R: two unidentified actors, John Wulp, Kenneth Koch (with glasses), Maxine Groffsky, Niki de Saint Phalle, Jean Tinguely, Henry Geldzahler. ON LADDER, L–R: MacIntyre Dixon and Richard Libertini. Photo: Hans Namuth.

BOTTOM: Portion of announcement for *The Construction of Boston*, 1962.

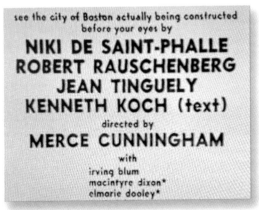

see the city of Boston actually being constructed
before your eyes by

NIKI DE SAINT-PHALLE
ROBERT RAUSCHENBERG
JEAN TINGUELY
KENNETH KOCH (text)

directed by

MERCE CUNNINGHAM

with

irving blum
macintyre dixon*
elmarie dooley*

Taylor Mead in *The Red Robins*, Theatre at St. Clement's production, 1978. Set by
Rory McEwen. Costumes by Vanessa James. Photo courtesy of Donald Sanders.

THE THEATRE AT ST. CLEMENT'S

THE RED ROBINS PROJECT

presents

THE RED ROBINS

a new play by
KENNETH KOCH

with

LYNN BOWMAN	BARBARA DANISH	CHRISTOPHE DeMENIL
KATE FARRELL	DAVID GLICKMAN	BRIAN GLOVER
STEVEN HALL	CHRISTOPHER HAWTHORNE	KEN KIRSCHENBAUM
JAMES LYTRAS	MARTIN MANIAK	TAYLOR MEAD
DONALD SANDERS	DON SCHRADER	BEATRICE SCHULMAN
SHELDON SHANAK	RACHEL TOWLE	EMMET WOODS

Designed by
VANESSA JAMES

Scenery by

RED GROOMS	ROY LICHTENSTEIN
JANE FREILICHER	RORY McEWEN
VANESSA JAMES	ALEX KATZ
KATHERINE KOCH	JODY ELBAUM

Lighting by	*Costumes by*	*Choreography by*
ALAN ADELMAN	VANESSA JAMES	WENDY BILLER

Directed by
DONALD SANDERS

TOP LEFT: *The Red Robins*, 1978. L–R: Brian Glover as the Easter Bunny, Sheldon Shanak, Emmet Woods, Barbara Danish. Stairways of Shanghai set by Red Grooms. Costumes by Vanessa James. Photo by Allison Leiston courtesy of Donald Sanders.
BOTTOM LEFT: *The Red Robins*, 1978. Jill (Kate Farrell) and Santa Claus (Donald Sanders) stare at the Ring of Destiny, held by the President (Don Schrader). Back row, L–R: James Lytras, Ken Kirschenbaum, Christopher Hawthorne. Kneeling: Lynn Bowman. Set by Alex Katz. Costumes by Vanessa James. Photo by Allison Leiston courtesy of Donald Sanders.
ABOVE: *The Red Robins*, 1978. Santa Claus (Donald Sanders) and the Easter Bunny (Brian Glover) do battle. Set by Red Grooms. Costumes by Vanessa James. Photo courtesy of Donald Sanders.

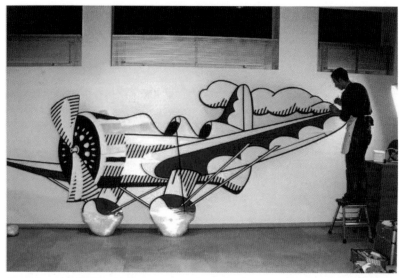

Set decoration by Roy Lichtenstein receiving finishing touches for *The Red Robins*, 1978. Image and photo © The Estate of Roy Lichtenstein.

Postcard announcement of exhibition of sets for *The Red Robins*, Guild Hall production, 1977. L–R: Howard Kanowitz, Kyle Morris, Kenneth Koch (in cockpit), Larry Rivers, and Donald Sanders.

Odessa, a Jean Tinguely sculpture for *The Tinguely Machine Mystery*, Jewish Museum, New York, December 22, 1965. Photo: Peter Moore.

The New Diana, New York Art Theatre Institute, 1984. L–R: Guy Custis (as the French poet), Kate Farrell (as Diana), Skie Ocasio (as Child). Background with trident, Peter Lane as Neptune. Set by Reuben Nakian. Costumes by Vanessa James. Photo by Joan Tedeschi courtesy of Donald Sanders.

Program page for the Cherry Lane Theatre production of *Bertha* (play version), on a double bill with Samuel Beckett's *Endgame*, New York, 1962. Used by permission of the Henry W. and Albert A. Berg Collection of English and American Literature, the New York Public Library, Astor, Lenox, and Tilden Foundations.

Wooden cutout figures by Alex Katz for *George Washington Crossing the Delaware*, 1962. Smithsonian American Art Museum, Gift of Mr. and Mrs. David K. Anderson, Martha Jackson Memorial Collection. Photo: Karen Koch.

Guinevere, or The Death of the Kangaroo, American Theatre for Poets, New York, 1964. Sets and costumes by Red Grooms. Color inset shows area obscured by giraffe. Photo by Peter Moore. Inset photo: Karen Koch.

THE BANQUET ❧ *xvii*

Publicity materials and ticket for *Garibaldi en Sicile*,
Teatro San Carlo, Naples, Italy, 2004–05.

Publicity material for *The Banquet*, Teatro Carlo Felice, Genoa, Italy, 2001.

The Banquet, Teatro Carlo Felice, Genoa, Italy, 2001. Seated on airplane tail: Carlo Morini as Marinetti. Set and costumes by Gideon Davey. Photo by Corrado Bonini courtesy of the Fondazione Teatro Carlo Felice.

The Banquet, Concordia Theatre, Bremen, Germany, 1998. Angreas Haller as Filippo Tomasso Marinetti. Photo: Jörg Landsberg.

The Banquet, Concordia Theatre, Bremen, Germany, 1998. Kirsten Kusters as Eric Satie (far right), Ralf Simon as Jean Cocteau (2nd from right). Photo: Jörg Landsberg.

Kenneth Koch in Bremen, Germany, for the 1998 production of *The Banquet*.
Photo: Karen Koch.

The Umbrella of Stage Directions

(The Throne Room in Beijing.)

JAI FU, THE TRICKSTER:
> In Hainan we have something
> Called "The umbrella of stage directions."

KING:
> What is it?

JAI FU:
> You open this umbrella, and all stage directions come out.

KING:
> What this means? I do can no in no way understand it—
> By the broad high streets of Beijing!

JAI FU:
> Right this second, King,
> Umbrella is being opened outside
> And soon we will see—

(Big banging sound of umbrella snapping open with wind. Next, entering and exiting with astonishing rapidity, all kinds of characters, the STAGE DIRECTIONS, *who fall down, laugh, weep, get up, fly about, open drawers, tear up pieces of paper, wring their hands, stomp, leap, go down on one knee, etc.)*

KING:
> Ah! So beautiful!
> And how do stage directions end?

JAI FU:
> Like this!

*(*JAI FU *signals to certain* STAGE DIRECTIONS, *who seize, bind, and gag the* KING *and carry him off.* KING *re-enters, unbound and free.)*

KING:
> Oof! Very good. Clever. Now, you tell me:
> These stage directions from many different plays?

*(*JAI FU *nods yes.)*

> Let plays be brought in! I wish to
> See them, *Minority Nationalities, Underground Army,*

Blad Gark, other ones. Keep here stage directions and
Bring plays.

STAGE DIRECTIONS:
But we are part of plays, Majesty.

KING:
No matter! Keep stage directions here!

JAI FU:
So shall it be!

(JAI FU *herds all* STAGE DIRECTIONS *to one side and encloses them in some kind
of fencing, from which they try, in vain, to escape.*)

The Party

AUTHOR: *(at the door)*
  Is this the cast party?

HOST:
  Yes. Who are you?

AUTHOR:
  I'm the author.

HOST:
  You can't come in!
  Good work follows bad work
  And good work follows good.
  Sometimes bad work follows bad.
  If you're the author you can't come in.

AUTHOR:
  What about bad work following good?

HOST:
  If you're the author you can't come in.

AUTHOR:
  I only said I was the author.

HOST:
  No one but the author would say that. No, go away! Good-bye!

(The door is closed.)

The Animated Room

(Characters sing lines operatically.)

MAN:
> Come back to me! Come back to me!

WOMAN:
> You didn't notice that I was the chair you were sitting on!

MAN:
> You didn't notice that I was the floor!

Happiness

(An atmosphere of Greek tragedy, specifically the Bacchae. *The god* HAPPINESS *is on a stark, sunny, dusty road entering a town. He carries a large sack.)*

HAPPINESS:
I am the God of Happiness and I am looking for twenty people to make
    happy.
But few can stand it. Few can support the happiness power that I bring,
It is too strong for most! I myself can barely transport it.
Well. I will stop in this village, this town, this city, it is bigger
Than I thought. Madame, where is the mayor or ruler or king of this place?
For I bring happiness. Your ruler, once he has my precious gift, can
    dispense it
To others. But let him not give them too much,
For it is dangerous—it is dangerous, and it can destroy!

*(*RULER *appears.)*

RULER:
I am the Ruler and I will take it.

*(*HAPPINESS *hands* RULER *the sack, "happiness," which consists of many small mirrors.* RULER *bends under its weight.)*

Oh! I am staggering
Dying under this horrible, beautiful weight!

HAPPINESS:
Give it to others
Quickly! Unhappiness rides behind!

RULER:
I will! Ah! ah! Too late!
Too much! Too strong!

*(*RULER *dies. The sack drops, the mirrors fall and break into many pieces.)*

TOWNSPEOPLE:
Happiness! Happiness! We want some for ourselves!

*(*TOWNSPEOPLE *run out, pick up fragments of the glass, eat them, and die.)*

HAPPINESS:
  Disaster—again! Oh, misfortune.
  Now to the next city I take my way.

(HAPPINESS *picks up his sack, which seems as full as ever, and goes away.*)

Searching for the Tomb of Alexander

(in the mountains of Crete; fife music)

EDWARD:
  I am looking for the tomb of Alexander.

SHEPHERD:
  To Macedon's wilds go, not here in Crete
  If you would find that doughty foe
  Who against all the world did go.

EDWARD:
  I go
  In quest of Alexander.

The Tomb of Alexander

(A place in Macedon, with a tomb. ALEXANDER *is inside it.)*

ALEXANDER:
 Inside here adamantly
 I sleep. I am trying to get out
 But can't.
 I am locked
 Inside the tomb of Alexander.

(Enter YOUNG MEN *and* WOMEN *of Macedonia, singing gently but enthusiastically outside the tomb.)*

YOUNG MEN *and* WOMEN:
 Hey ho Alexander
 Gods bless Alexander
 He is great Alexander
 Alexander cinnamon tree!

An Atmosphere of Heavy, Intense (Summer) Stillness Pervades the World of Christine et Édouard

ÉDOUARD:
> Let's sit down
> In this blazing garden,
> Christine.

CHRISTINE:
> All right, Édouard. I can walk
> No more.
> I used to be fifteen
> But now I am sixteen
> And I am tired, so tired,
> After all.

ÉDOUARD:
> Have we something to say?

(A silvery form, THE FUTURE, *makes a fleeting appearance.)*

CHRISTINE:
> Yes, yes—Look! The Future!
> But now it's gone!

Mary Magdalene's Song

(The lines are spoken by PEOPLE *in the street, excitedly awaiting the appearance of* MARY MAGDALENE.*)*

Mary Magdalene's coming!

How can that be? She's long dead, in the Bible.

Nonetheless, she's coming along!
Get ready to sing the bakery song!

Why does she like that one?

Who knows or can question
Mary Magdalene's tastes?
All we know is that she likes it
And that now she is coming along!

*(*MARY MAGDALENE *comes along, and the* PEOPLE *sing.)*

Bread and rolls,
Fresh every day!
That's how we bake them,
The merry Magdalene way!

A Song to the Avant-Garde

TENOR:

 In the beginning
 The Avant-Garde
 Was just a silly little thing,
 Coconut-colored sidewalks,
 Women with blue-white parasols
 Tilting over backward
 Or half backward—
 In the beginning—
 And then it grew, and became gigantic and hard
 Like a great, great stone, the Avant-Garde—
 Like a great, great stone that had usurped all of history!

CHORUS OF ÉMIGRÉ ARTISTS IN PARIS:

 Oh, we'll walk down Apollinaire bis
 Nine ninety nine
 And construct back lugs
 And clunk valentines
 Of paired Z's
 Ha ha ha ha, ha ha, hoo hoo
 Ho Avant-Garde clear and light blue.

TENOR:

 Everything went in fear of it,
 Everyone walked in fear of it—
 And yet it had no power, really,
 It had no lasting power.
 If now we celebrate it,
 It is to salute it and to recognize it,
 It is to urge it a little more to take the initiative,
 Even though it might, by being so strange,
 Destroy us! O Avant-Garde!
 Come back, take heart, and tell us now
 What life will, and what art will, do!

GHOSTLY VOICE: *(offstage)*

 Maybe my mission is finished.
 Each movement in culture or history is but a stage
 Fitting to the age
 And it may be the one I had is ended.

TENOR:

Oh say not so, Avant-Garde!
For those of us who have really loved you,
Nothing, no one else can be as hard,
And pure, and true.

GHOSTLY VOICE:

Well, then I'll try to be with you again!

(Great hullabaloo, wind, musical instruments, sounds of rending, tearing, crackling thunder, as of the Second Coming; and the AVANT-GARDE *appears—she is a small, old woman.)*

TENOR:

Avant-Garde! What's happened?

AVANT-GARDE:

This is but the initial phase!

(She waves a wand or stick, there is a crackle of blue and red lightning, and she is transformed into a shining, almost blinding CUBE.*)*

CUBE:

ANDIAM!

*(*CUBE *goes offstage triumphantly.)*

The Two Bulls

(the center of a bull ring, in Spain)

FIRST BULL:
  Damn you! I wanted a bullfighter.

SECOND BULL:
  Well, what you have is another bull.

FIRST BULL:
  We circle each other, as in a dance.

SECOND BULL:
  Yes, but our intention is not to be graceful—

FIRST BULL:
  But somehow to seek an advantage—

SECOND BULL:
  Somehow to "win" by our mutual deaths.

(They charge each other. There are snorts, thuddings, and other bull-like noises.)

Spices

(an office in seventeenth-century Spain)

FERNANDO DE PLAZA:
  We need three tons of spice by Tuesday next.

ISAAC RUIZ:
  Solomon Rosenstein is in Paris and can arrange the transfer
  Through Abraham Blum in Lisbon. Our cousin Izzy
  Barrasch will be waiting in Madrid
  For the order. Therefore you can count
  On having what you want within sixty days.

FERNANDO DE PLAZA:
  But I need it by next Tuesday.

ISAAC RUIZ:
  That possibility may come only after many years.
  This is the seventeenth century—

FERNANDO DE PLAZA:
  Oh—but it—

ISAAC RUIZ:
  At the beginning of Capitalism
  Which some say would not exist without the Jews
  And so you should be glad you are getting this order filled at all
  You should get down on your knees and thank God
  That you don't have to live in a feudal society forever
  Where everybody dies at age twelve and where you can't get anything you
      want, ever,
  Unless it happens to be right next to you!

FERNANDO DE PLAZA:
  I *am* grateful but don't like being grateful to you Jews!

ISAAC RUIZ:
  Such is the lot that Heaven sends to both of us. L'chaim. Farewell!

(He goes. Sounds of heavy shipping.)

Happiness Comes Back, in a Car

(HAPPINESS *drives onstage in a small open car.*)

HAPPINESS:
> If I come riding in a car, with the time, conceive me as a force, you escaped from that theoretical
> Naturalism that has encapsulated you for so long.
> My destructiveness
> The playwright tries to control, but he cannot match it quite, it
> Overwhelms him. I can see
> Past and into your souls, you live too much without me
> Because you are afraid. I don't
> Blame you. I am Happiness
> Of a certain sort, that many will travel thousands of
> Miles to see. Then they try to manage to forget me
> And go about forgetful until they are old;
> Chancy it is if you can find me,
> Lucky if you can keep me for long.

(*to a young couple on the street,* ROB *and* PHILLIS)

> You. Hello. Would you like to ride in my car?

PHILLIS:
> Yes?

ROB:
> All right.

(PHILLIS *and* ROB *get in the car, and* HAPPINESS *drives it off.* THREE PERSONS *on the sidewalk make comments.*)

FIRST:
> Soon to be wed?

SECOND:
>   Soon dead?

THIRD:
>   Who knows?

Agamemnon

CURIOUS AND CONCERNED PERSON:
Aga
Memnon

AGAMEMNON:
Yes—
What?

CURIOUS AND CONCERNED PERSON:
In your
Tomb is
It hot?

AGAMEMNON:
I have
Moved my
Tomb to
China
Being
There a-
Mid the
Classic Ming
Frescoes, a
Greek hotshot
Travelers come
From far away
To see.

CURIOUS AND CONCERNED PERSON:
But isn't this a far
Cry from being king?

AGAMEMNON:
It is, but when did I have anything
That really made me happy? Murder and war.
In death I feel I've found
What Agamemnon was created for:
A world of Chinese ladies and
Long nights of love and laughter. And what's more—

CURIOUS AND CONCERNED PERSON:
You're crazy, Agamemnon—

AGAMEMNON:
    Since I'm dead
    What do you care what thoughts are in my head
    Or how I dream away
    The infinite night?

Husserl

(A Paris street. Two men, the philosopher HUSSERL *and a certain* JABOLINSKY, *are walking along in different-colored, enormous coats—perhaps one yellow, one red.)*

HUSSERL:
Well, Evelyn told me that her cape,
The one she had at Longchamps do you remember, she said that long blue
    lovely cape
Had been torn to pieces by a cat. "Well, you know they have to eat,"
Said a philosopher; and I thought, "To hell with this! I'm
Through being nice to him and to them, all of these philosophers!"
So I said, "Listen,
I have Evelyn, I have a mental and spiritual home
And I don't need you damned philosophers!"

JABOLINSKY:
What did he say?

HUSSERL:
What did he say? He said I had broken off
The blossoming bough of philosophers. He said because of me
Nietzsche, Hegel, and Kant would not have a home.
He blamed me directly for philosophy's fall
Behind psychoanalysis and sociology and anthropology as a study that
    would interest a sane person.
He said concepts of form, substance, and essence would pay a heavy price
For my rackety defoliation of their perfect branches. He blamed me for
    everything and
I went home and threw out Croce, Whitehead, and Kant,
Because I think he is right,
And now I am going to throw myself into the sea—

JABOLINSKY:
Don't! Wait—

HUSSERL:
—Of thought, to see if we can't come up with something better than that
Poor out-of-date, rickety, clanky philosophy!

JABOLINSKY:
Oh you are a man after my heart
And I wish you success!

HUSSERL:

I pray that that success will come as Substance,
And not merely as Form.
Evelyn may be lonely sometimes . . .
But now I am embarked!

JABOLINSKY:

Good luck, Husserl!

HUSSERL:

Dear friend, farewell.

(He leaves.)

Angels

(People slowly come on and go offstage, one by one, carrying big white banners. They are like people carrying signs in a parade or on a picket line or at a political demonstration. There is something noble and beautiful about it, suggestive of a heavenly intervention, as of angels. On the banners, as they appear, one can read the following messages)

DID ANCIENT GREEKS HAVE DIGESTIVE SYSTEMS?

DO BUTTERFLIES SOMETIMES ACCIDENTALLY CANCEL STAMPS?

IS YOUR CONSTITUTION STRONG ENOUGH TO WITHSTAND THE PROBLEMS OF THE PRESENT DAY?

IF MARY KINGSLEY, AFTER WRITING TRAVELS IN WEST AFRICA, HAD NOT GONE TO AFRICA A SECOND TIME, WOULD SHE STILL BE ALIVE TODAY? WOULD SHE HAVE WRITTEN ANOTHER BOOK AS GOOD AS THE FIRST ONE?

IS RUDOLF NUREYEV TO GEORGE BALANCHINE AS A DROMEDARY IS TO A CAMEL?

SHOULD THERE BE ATOMIC FUEL?

IS LYRIC POETRY AN ADVANCE, A RETRACTION, OR AN ESCAPE? OR NONE OF THESE?

IS IT MAINLY FRAGMENTS, OR ENTITIES, THAT MAKE UP THE COLOSSUS OF OUR LIVES?

WHO, IF ANYONE, WOULD YOU LIKE TO BE CLOSE TO YOU FOR AN UNLIMITED PERIOD OF TIME?

HOW MANY COATS ARE ON THE GABONESE RACK?

WHAT COULD BEST DISTRACT YOU FROM THE REAL, SAD, MANIPULATED LIFE OF GOATS?

WERE YOU HAPPIER A WEEK (MONTH, YEAR) AGO? AND HOW CAN YOU TELL?

DID A FIG FALL ON AN UNMENTIONED STONE?

CLOWNS LOOK SAD TO MAKE US LAUGH. WHO LOOKS HAPPY TO MAKE US CRY? ANGELS?

FOR ONE FIVE-MINUTE SPAN IN MEXICO CITY DID YOU FEEL THAT EVERY-THING WAS POSSIBLE? DID YOU RECORD THIS FEELING? FROM WHERE, DO YOU THINK, DID IT COME?

DOES SILENCE MOVE YOU? OR IS IT TRUER TO SAY THAT THE WATER IS MOVED BY THE BOAT?

IS YOUR HOPE INDEPENDENT OF YOUR SENSE OF CONTINGENT REALITY?

CAN YOU GIVE ME FIVE CENTS?

IF MARY MAGDALENE IS THE SOUL AND RED RIDING HOOD THE HEART, IS BOZO THE BRAIN OF THESE SCENES? OR CAN IT BE MAO TSE-TUNG AS A CORPSE?

LITERARY INFLUENCE—ARE YOU DISTURBED BY IT? WHAT ABOUT OTHER KINDS OF INFLUENCE?

WHY DO HENS HAVE EGGS AND NOT BABIES?

WHO ARE THE TRUE MEN AND WHO ARE THE TRUE WOMEN, AND WHICH DO YOU PREFER?

WHAT DID RAMAKRISHNA GIVE TO VITKA FOR KALIDASSA'S BIRTHDAY?

IF YOU WERE TO DIE THIS EVENING, WHAT WOULD BE THE THING YOU LIKED MOST ABOUT LIFE SO FAR?

(Now a crew of police, or plainclothes RULE ENFORCERS *of some kind, come on and chase the* BANNER-BEARERS *away.)*

RULE ENFORCERS:
Here, here, get out of here, all of you, you know it's not permitted!
Go on now, get away!

(One last BANNER-BEARER, *an* ANGEL, *comes out with one last banner.)*

DO YOU BELIEVE IN SIGNS? ARE YOU AFFECTED BY THEM AT ALL?

The Underground Army

(Completely dark, under the earth. Hundreds, even thousands, of CLAY SOLDIERS
appear very dimly—among them, HO *and* HA.*)*

HO:

They say Chen Ko is coming to organize us, the Underground Army,
To fight.

HA:

Against whom? And how can we fight? We are clay, we are earth.

HO:

To fight against the Han Emperor, who,
Jealous of the power of the underground troops of his Imperial predecessor,
wishes to destroy us.
He will come down to chop us
And to chip us into subservience to his will.

HA:

In that case we must fight. But HOW
Shall we fight? Since we are not living beings.

HO:

That depends,
Perhaps, on how we are thought of.
If someone, if only one person, believes that we exist,
That we live, and that we matter, then, perhaps,
For him or for her, we WILL exist and will be able to fight.

(Enter CHEN KO.*)*

CHEN KO:

Hail and hello on this hot, dusty day, my marvelous clay soldiers.
Time has come that we shall have to battle for our lives,
For ourselves and for the glory of our emperor
Which is still undimmed.

HA:

I do, sometimes, still feel the emperor among us—
Though not always. But, tell us,
How can we fight?

HO:

Listen—

(Aboveground a GIRL'S VOICE *is heard.)*

GIRL'S VOICE:
  I believe in the underground soldiers. They will fight to protect us.
  I know they will. They are brave. They will fight for China!

(a tremendous din)

CHEN KO:
  Here come the armies of Jaing Chai, Emperor de Han.

(Enter a raging horde headed by HAN EMPEROR.*)*

HAN EMPEROR:
  Come, break those bodies, break them into dust!
  No one shall rule in the Underworld but Jaing Chai Han!!

(In the darkness, a noisy, confusing, violent battle. Finally, it ends.)

GIRL'S VOICE:
  Oh, my clay soldiers—may they, so brave, remain!

The Mediterranean

A blue expanse of water, with music and the sound of washing and lapping of waves. Enter a woman, the MEDITERRANEAN, *in a blue-and-white-flashing dress and with a tiara.*

MEDITERRANEAN:
    I am the Mediterranean, I wash on all my shores.
    I am gull of the Adriatic, Vinland away from the Azores
    With light-blue waves my windows, rocks my doors.
    I am the Mediterranean.
    On merely hearing my name
    People become excited and kick all the same
    Jumping all around thinking "Mediterranean!"
    Oh I am she
    Perhaps it is in Venice that I'm most permeated
    And most permeate
    There my eyelashes go up to the tops of buildings
    There my smiles lead merchantmen to the sea (further out)
    There I am the first basket of transportation
    I am the Mediterranean
    I am that calming sea
    That kills (with my marshlands).

(Enter ITALY *and* SPAIN, *galantuomini, who bow to her.)*

    And my peninsulas gather for me
    Gold and fantastical stores
    From the ends of this planet and develop for me
    Strong and individual personalities

*(*SPAIN *shows himself to be a matador,* ITALY *an operatic tenor.)*

    So that I can go to sleep in them
    And wake up knowing I am still the Sea
    That precludes uninclusive history
    And greets the most amazing of forms.

(Enter the TIDES.*)*

    Say, Tides, am I not in each Italian man's, in each Spanish woman's heart?

TIDES:
    Yes, Regina, you are.

MEDITERRANEAN:
    I wash
    On all these shores!

(*Now the blue expanse of water begins to fill up with what is found in modern harbors: cranes, derricks, oil tankers, tugboats, and so on. The boats hoot, the water becomes a little dirty. The* MEDITERRANEAN *looks at all this with concern, and, withdrawing to one side, expresses her fears.*)

MEDITERRANEAN:
    But what are these, but what is this I see
    Moving upon and settling down in me? Oh cause of fear!
    Derricks, and tankers, floating petrol bankers,
    Riggers and clankers—what they may do to me
    I feel some cause to fear. Shall my great Mediterranean
    Balm be swept aside? and death go with my tide?
    O gods of earth and light and of the sea
    And of the air, of which I am the bride, tell me:
    Can the great sea of my great self abide?

(*Enter* TOMMY TIME. *All is silent.*)

TOMMY TIME:
    Let Tommy Time decide!

(*He leaps into the water.*)

Gospel Red Riding Noh Tanayachi

(On the left is LITTLE RED RIDING HOOD'*s house, with a woodland path outside its door. On the right is a chorus of* DEER. *All the characters sing their lines gospel-style; the singing of the chorus is sometimes soft, sometimes jubilant.)*

MOTHER:
Oh Little Red Raheedin
   Hoood
Oh Little Red Raheedin
   Hoood

CHORUS:
Yes, she
Yes, she
Yes, she
Gwine be comin'
   along

LITTLE RED RIDING HOOD:
Yas yas ah comin' along
Goin' to gran mamma's
   house yes yes yes yes yes yes
Yeah, granmuthah's house!

Oh Lord! Yes, she
Yes, she
Yes, she
Gwine be comin'
   along

MOTHER:
Oh Little Red Raheedin Hoood
Yas yas yes yes yes

*(*LITTLE RED RIDING HOOD *walks along the woodland path. Halfway she meets the* WOLF.*)*

LITTLE RED RIDING HOOD:
Comin' along
Doan fine dat wuff
Gran granmuthah's place
Oh yeah! oh yeah!

CHORUS:
Comin' along
Yes, she
Yes, she
Is comin'
   along!

WOLF:
   Lil Red Raheedin Hood,
      whachu
   Whachu, whachu
   Whachu gopp in de baskeck

CHORUS:
Yas, wachu
Wolf know? Who
Who are you?

LITTLE RED RIDING HOOD:
   Oh yes
   I go fine de restin place
   Wif my
   Granmuthah

(The scene changes to GRANDMOTHER'S *house. The wolf is in bed in* GRAND-MOTHER'S *clothes.* LITTLE RED RIDING HOOD *enters.)*

WOLF:
I no grandma but de wuff
   an I gwine eat you
Yes yeah yes

CHORUS:
Know who
No, she doan know who
Hoo hoo hoo
She doan know who

(Enter WOODSMAN.*)*

Oh but oh but who dat

Yes, yes

WOODSMAN:
I's de woodsman
Ho ho, yeah!

Yes, yes
Lil Red Ridin' Hood

LITTLE RED RIDING HOOD:
   Where's my granmutha?
   No, yes!

GRANDMOTHER:
   Wolf eat me—woo woo woo
   Ooh ooh ooh ooh

(At this moment, the play abruptly changes in style, becoming a traditional Japanese Noh drama. The SHITE, *the principal character in a Noh play, is* LITTLE RED RIDING HOOD; *the* WAKI, *the secondary character, is the* WOODSMAN. LITTLE RED RIDING HOOD *comes center stage to recite the following speech. In doing so, she is able, in classic Noh fashion, to relive a tormenting episode of her past and, in the end, to find absolution and peace.)*

SHITE (LITTLE RED RIDING HOOD):
   She set out from home, ah! cursed, burdened
   With basket, meeting,
   She—beautiful young girl—a wolf
   Then coupled and crashing, led this
   Monster to house of honored and ancient
   Grandmother Kai Se Nan, this is her house.
   "You must choose between me
   And your grandmother." Your teeth
   Flash. Ah ah! The knees buckle, the head,
   Faint, the young body falls to the floor
   Doomed by lust.

(At this point the chorus takes over the SHITE'*s speech; it is clear that it is still* LITTLE RED RIDING HOOD'*s words that are being heard. The events being described are acted out in dumb show by the characters, in the formal style of Noh drama.)*

CHORUS:
A woodsman comes, seeing
The shame, wolf on maiden, extracting
A knife kills
But not her who should
Be killed, she guilty, but
The wolf, not wholly
Innocent he but pushed by his nature only. She
Indecisive, murderess, lies there. He,
Woodsman, sympathizing, desiring, then
Takes her in one last
Act of lust, she obeying, wolf
Rises from near-death to scratch bite kill
Woodsman, he too now dead, all
They dead she
To her knees
Rises, seeing, horrified
This bloody sight.

(Now LITTLE RED RIDING HOOD *takes over her speech again. The dumb show stops.)*

SHITE (LITTLE RED RIDING HOOD):
I am
The cause! Now,
On my knees, I make
Amends—good-bye. With this
knife, parting, freedom,
Absolution.

*(*LITTLE RED RIDING HOOD *stabs herself.)*

WAKI (WOODSMAN):
It is at
An end. Her
Suffering has ceased.
Now the October wind
Blows coolly through the dwelling of Tokani Tokanise.

Robert Wilson Riding Hood

(RED RIDING HOOD *moves with agonizing slowness across the stage. The* WOLF *stands stage right explaining something to an invisible companion.*)

WOLF:

So I said that it was her perfect right to take a package, which is what I understood she was carrying, to the home of an old relative, but that I, too, had the right to have some fun. After all, a person has the right to have a little fun. I said that it was her perfect right to take . . .

(*This speech may be repeated as long as the director likes.*)

(*When* RED RIDING HOOD *almost reaches the vicinity of the* WOLF *she begins moving backward at the same pace at which she was moving forward. There is music of trains, loud factory whistles, and escaping steam.*)

In China None

(COOK *walks onstage, as if just coming out of a theatre in which she has seen the two previous plays.*)

COOK:
    In China we have none of this stuff
    Because it seems like crazy.
    A recognition of the historical impulse
    In a simple Marxist way makes aestheticians lazy.
    So—it will come or it will not come. In any case, it makes no difference
       now.

The Black Spanish Costume

(a royal ball in Spain in the sixteenth century)

MAIN BLACK SPANISH COSTUME (FEMALE):
> I am the black costume, the costume of Spain—
> I dominate Europe. You cannot gain
> Admission to a royal celebration
> Unless you wear me. It's useless to complain.
> Oh, victory is mine! I am the costume
> The black costume of Spain.
> And I will last forever. Eternal is my reign.

OTHER BLACK COSTUMES:
> Eternal be your reign!

(Enter the PINK FRENCH DRESS.*)*

BLACK COSTUME (MALE):
> And who are you?

PINK FRENCH DRESS:
> A pink French dress.

BLACK COSTUME:
> How beautiful you are.
> Would you honor me with a dance?

PINK FRENCH DRESS:
> I'd love to dance.

(The male BLACK COSTUME *and the* PINK FRENCH DRESS *dance.)*

BLACK COSTUME:
> It is because of you
> That we shall be undone.

OTHER BLACK COSTUMES: *(softly, together)*
> Oh, we feel a catastrophic change.

BLACK COSTUME:
> How did you get here?

PINK FRENCH DRESS:
> Why, we all come from France.
> Upon the backs of dolls we came from France.
> I *like* to dance. Look, here we are.

(Enter many PINK FRENCH DRESSES. *Each goes and stands in front of a* BLACK SPANISH COSTUME, *as if preparing to dance. When the* PINK FRENCH DRESSES *next move, however, the* BLACK SPANISH COSTUMES *have disappeared.)*

Similar Events

(Enter the FIRST CHARACTERS: "BAD" MARY MAGDALENE, *an* OLD-FASHIONED STEAM ENGINE, *a* HORSE, MILLET, *a* SAINT PAINTED BY GIOTTO *[possibly St. Francis]*, *a* HUGE HAND, *the* CARPATHIAN MOUNTAINS, HOMER, MONGOLIAN FLATLANDS, *and others. They stand around chatting with each other as at a party.)*

FIRST CHARACTERS:
Chanda chak, chak chak, chanda chak chak chak,
Chanda chanda, chak chanda chak chak, chak chanda, etc.

VOICES OF THE SECOND CHARACTERS: *(offstage)*
We're coming, at different times, we're on our way.

FIRST CHARACTERS:
Chanda chak chak chak, nothing will ever change,
Tout restera le même, niente cambiera chandy chak
Chandy chak chak

(The SECOND CHARACTERS *appear at the side of the stage. They are the* GOOD MARY MAGDALENE, *a* MODERN STEAM ENGINE, *an* AUTOMOBILE, *an* EAR OF CORN, *a* SAINT PAINTED BY PIERO DELLA FRANCESCA, *a* BIG KNIFE AND FORK, *the* CARPATHIAN MOUNTAIN, TENNYSON, BEIJING, *and others. All at once, they come out and one by one stand in front of their corresponding* FIRST CHARAC-TERS. *When the* SECOND CHARACTER *then moves, the* FIRST CHARACTER *is seen to have disappeared as the* BLACK SPANISH COSTUMES *disappeared in the previous play. The* SECOND CHARACTERS *make different sounds, actually two different kinds—half of them say [1] and half [2].)*

(1)
Sim sam sam cheroo chim sim charam soum cham chim
Eeyouchim cham

(2)
Goggor aggog foggag goorg fogganeggaboggagaged

(A slight rumble is heard offstage, and some THIRD CHARACTERS *start becoming visible in the wings as the play ends. The* THIRD CHARACTERS *include the* MARY MAGDALENE OF THESE PLAYS—*neither "good" nor "bad" but just "coming along"—a* COMPUTER, *an* AIRPLANE, FROZEN ORANGE JUICE, GUERNICA, *a* CUISINART, *the* CARPATHIAN MOUNTAINS, T.S. ELIOT, *and* MAO TSE-TUNG.*)*

Gospel Toothbrush

PAUL CÉZANNE *is painting a still life. Perhaps to help his concentration, he sings softly, as he works, in a gospel style. His singing may at times be backed up by a* chorus OF OTHER PAINTERS *and/or* BIG PAINTBRUSHES.

CÉZANNE:
    Yeh yeh yeh yeh yes yas yeah
    How old in de mawning you gwine use it
      Hey hey ho hah
    Gospel toothbrush!
      Yeah!
    So many brissle wan you fine
    Ho yeah yes yes yes yas oh now
    Hole him up straight yeah an ben head down
      Yeah!
    Gospel toothbrush, take your time
    Brush, yes mm hmm
    Brosse aux dents, oh yes
    Oh yes, yes, fine,
    Brosse aux—mm hmm
    So fine hey hey . . . hey hey . . . hey . . .
    Brush of mine, Lord yes,
    Now done
    All done
    For today, yes yes, hmm mmm—

(His work for the day finished, he puts down his brushes and leaves.)

Permanently

(There is an atmosphere of grammar and elementary school. The scene is a city sidewalk and street. In the first part of the play the doings of the ADJECTIVE and the NOUNS are acted out on one part of the stage while, on another, the PARENTS and CHILDREN watch and make comments.)

MAN:
  The Nouns are clustered in the street

WOMAN:
  An Adjective walks past

CHILD:
  Oh, she kisses the Nouns!

MAN:
  The principal will be in a rage

WOMAN:
  Look here he comes he is indeed a tower

(The PRINCIPAL totters in.)

PRINCIPAL:
  Adjective, Nouns, get back in the textbook
  Otherwise we won't include you in the next book—

WOMAN:
  But the Nouns are struck, moved, changed.

MAN:
  I think they've fallen in love with the Adjective
  In any event they say, "You can't write a book of any kind without us
  At least of any size. So go away. Give us our liberty today.
  We've seen an Adjective and all for us is changed."

(The PRINCIPAL hobbles off.)

CHILD:
  Oh look
  The principal is hobbling away. Defeat is in his look. Maybe he will be
    cheered up by Cook.

(Darkness, dawn, morning light. It's the next day. VERB drives up in his car.)

VERB:

I am a Verb. My car is at the curb. And I'm driving away.
Adjective and Nouns, jump in!

(ADJECTIVES *and* NOUNS *get in the car.* OTHER PARTS OF SPEECH *run onstage.*)

OTHER PARTS OF SPEECH:

Oh, take us, too!

(*They get in. The car drives off slowly.*)

MAN:

They've created the Sentence! Come, let's read what it says.

(*Behind the* VERB'*s car flutters a big paper pennant with these words on it: "You have enchanted me with a single kiss / Which can never be undone / Until the destruction of language."*)

The Burning Mystery of Anna

(It is 1951. The scene is a modest dansing *in Aix-en-Provence.)*

JEAN:
Do you see that girl over there?
She's Corsican.

ANNA:
Love is my name.

KENNETH:
What shall I say?

JEAN:
Ask her to dance?

KENNETH:
My head, my arms, my shoulders feeling strange.

JEAN:
See that girl over there. Anna.
Ask her to dance.

KENNETH:
Islands of awkward animals.

JEAN:
Witticisms strewn about—and vanished.
Improve with age. Dance.

KENNETH:
Never be the same.

ANNA:
My name is Anna.
I don't know how to kiss.

KENNETH:
Why am I at this age—twenty-six?

ANNA:
I, I'm nineteen—to remember?

KENNETH:
Maybe. Dance?

ANNA:
　　Good fortune, dance.

JEAN:
　　Else die, the same.

Départ Malgache

AFRICA:
Madagascar, why are you leaving?

MADAGASCAR:
I don't know.
But I do know this is two hundred fifty MILLION years ago,
And I have to go.

AFRICA:
Lemur-filled and enormous island, where will you go?

MADAGASCAR:
I don't know—I think just out there in the sea—
To save my lemurs I have to go . . .

AFRICA:
Good-bye!

(MADAGASCAR *floats out into the Indian Ocean.*)

O addio, dolce Madagascar!

(*Malagasy music*)

On the Edge

(a street and a town square in which anything is possible)

STENDHAL:
> I'm looking for Dan.

(DAN, riding on a goat, enters. He gets off the goat.)

DAN:
> Here I am.

STENDHAL:
> It is time I got to know myself.

(Botticelli's VENUS appears.)

VENUS:
> I am Venus, rising from the sea!
> Where does each moment's deepest meaning lie?

STENDHAL:
> It's in the goat—

(GOAT trots forward.)

DAN:
> And in the footnote.

(traces a message on the sidewalk with one foot)

> It lamps what is not to come

(With his foot he now erases the message.)

> As well as what is—
> A bannister of bones

(SKELETON appears.)

> And a hat.

(A hat is thrown onstage.)

> It felt like forever—

(Enter CHRISTINE and EDWARD.)

EDWARD:
It feels "interrogating flat."

CHRISTINE:
It feels shown.

STENDHAL:
Vanning about and straggling.

EDWARD:
Why is it so unknown?

(A car drives up. One at a time, each character gets in the car, then gets out of it and walks off, saying)

ALL:
Getting out of the car and going back.

Smoking Hamlet

HAMLET:

> To be, or not to be: that is the question.
> Whether 'tis nobler in the mind to suffer
> The slings and arrows of outrageous fortune
> Or to take arms against a sea of troubles
> And by opposing end them.

(HAMLET *lights a cigarette, inhales, exhales, and walks offstage.*)

La Comtesse de Bercy Hamlet

(Enter, en toute élégance, ANNE, COMTESSE DE BERCY.*)*

COMTESSE:
> To be, or not to be: that is the question.
> Whether 'tis nobler in the mind to suffer
> The sling and arrows of outrageous fortune
> Or to take arms against a sea of troubles
> And by opposing end them.

(At the end, a strong wind blows and her clothes swirl all about her.)

Team Hamlet

(Six TEAM MEMBERS stand in a line facing the audience. Each says, in order, one syllable of Hamlet's "To be, or not to be" speech. After every six syllables, or after every poetic line, the TEAM MEMBERS change their posture—they sit, kneel, turn sideways, stand backward, lie down, etc.)

Little Red Riding Hamlet

LITTLE RED RIDING HOOD's *house; outside it, a forest; then* GRANDMOTHER's *house. While an offstage* VOICE *recites Hamlet's speech, the story of Little Red Riding Hood is acted out in dumb show.*

VOICE:
   To be or not to be: that is the question.

(LITTLE RED RIDING HOOD's *mother gives her a basket.* LITTLE RED RIDING HOOD *leaves home.*)

VOICE:
   Whether 'tis nobler in the mind to suffer

(LITTLE RED RIDING HOOD *encounters the* WOLF.)

VOICE:
   The slings and arrows of outrageous fortune

(LITTLE RED RIDING HOOD *walks on to* GRANDMOTHER's *house, goes in and finds the* WOLF *in bed disguised as* GRANDMOTHER, *and questions him.*)

VOICE:
   Or to take arms against a sea of troubles

(*The* WOLF *attacks* LITTLE RED RIDING HOOD. *She cries out. The* WOODSMAN *arrives.*)

VOICE:
   And by opposing end them.

(*The* WOODSMAN *kills the* WOLF, *splits him open, rescues* GRANDMOTHER, *and all is well.*)

Hamlet Rebus

(A very big, white EGG *is onstage.)*

HAMLET:
  To be or not to be: that is the question.

*(*CHICKEN *comes out of* EGG. HAMLET *smiles, and continues.)*

  Whether 'tis nobler in the mind to suffer

(Enraged FORTUNE *figure comes on and attacks* HAMLET *and the* CHICKEN *with slung stones and arrows.)*

  The slings and arrows of outrageous fortune

(After slinging and shooting at HAMLET, FORTUNE *disappears.)*

  Or to take arms against a sea of troubles

(Big noise of waves, tempest, crashing, screams, and moans. HAMLET *draws his sword.)*

  And by opposing end them.

(He rushes off. The sounds cease.)

Transposed Hamlet

(HAMLET, *wearing avant-garde clothes*)

HAMLET:
    Tube heat, or nog tube heat: data's congestion.
    Ladder tricks snow blur Hindu mine dew sulphur
    Tea slinks end harrows have ow! Cages portion
    Orc tube rake harms hay canst a Z oeuf bubbles
    Ant ply cop posy kingdom.

(*He goes crazy.*)

Aux Seins de Mandarine

(a public square in Port-au-Prince, Haiti)

FIELLA:
  In Haiti when I was a fresh young girl
  How I used to dance and my head was in a whirl
  Over such dancing
  One day they'd find me and carry me away
  In Haiti, in Haiti, oppressive dictatorship holiday.
    Tonton Macoute
    Is listening to you!
    Tonton Macoute
    Is listening to you!
  The roads have improved—
  There used to be no roads!
    Salads and fish!
  Marabout de mon coeur—

MARCHING MEN:
  In Haiti at this time
  In Haiti at this time
  We come from government!
  We come from government at this time!
  We are marching at this time—
  From bad government
  We come from government at this time!

(MARCHING MEN *do a rending sort of dance, then leave. The scene changes to Senegal—Dakar—where the* HAITIAN EXILES *speak.*)

HAITIAN EXILES:
  In exile, we restrict our moods.
  In exile, we have certain aptitudes.
  In exile, the hot thrashing of the day
  Is as irritating as elsewhere
  Though politically it is as a holiday.
  If we could rush at them and kill them
  And then go back,
  We would still not be back
  Not be really, really back
  After these years of exile.

Different Rooms Doctor

(This takes place in many different rooms of the same building. The only speaking character is the DOCTOR, *who goes from room to room, making one short speech in each, to his patients. The* AUDIENCE *follows the* DOCTOR *from room to room.)*

DOCTOR:

You have a heart attack. *(musingly)* If it's the bullfighter.

*(*DOCTOR *goes on to the next room—and to another room for each of these succeeding speeches.)*

How young are you? Hmmmm. Just about Red-Riding-Hood size.

Summer—yes, it was summer when we spoke. I remember. We were near Tawai Nakimo.

Cast-iron cover. Elfred the Dancer? I can't explain this. There isn't enough air in the room. . . .

Egypt to see me? I don't know. Edward and Christine? What's "Tommy Time"?

Come back next year. Oh, yes, sure, I'll think it over. But the clay soldiers— perhaps it's just as well.

Known elements of a car: engine, steering wheel, crankshaft, and drive. Happiness was here? When? While we were alive?

I don't think I want (thank you) a cocktail. But you look startling in your black Spanish dress.

Thank you for the star. I never really knew about shining before I got it.

What, what, what's that? Oh, you have a high fever. Quetzacoatl, master of the storm.

Get into some of this and out of that other. Emolument? That's rather one of Hamlet's type of words.

The mule doctor is on vacation. I'm here to chime for Cook.

(The DOCTOR *goes into the hall.)*

Science, good-bye! And, also, to economic fiction!

(He opens the door and goes outside.)

I am—I was—the Doctor. But Doctor am no more! Look at the sky— Oh, medicine of that blue, straight nose!

The Chinese Rivers

YELLOW:
    I am the Yellow River

YANGSTE:
    I am the Yangste, great to view

YELLOW *and* YANGSTE: *(together, or alternating)*
    Here above Shanghai we meet
    No far from Han Kow
    No far from Soo Chow
    No far from the feet
    Of the white, bouldery mountains
    No far from the seat
    Of China's grain—
    Oh, industry
    Of ants, swiftness
    Of animals, and initiative of humans!
    Let our resources be used to produce
    Power for the influence to a very good life in our country
    That has always been the center of the world!

Christine, Edward, and the Cube

(A street in Mexico City. EDWARD *and* CHRISTINE, *walking together, encounter the* AVANT-GARDE CUBE.*)*

CUBE:
Hello there!

CHRISTINE:
I'm confused.
Where used to be a building
Now there's an isolated, shining door.

CUBE:
You two—

EDWARD:
Yes. And where there were flowers
Look, steel spikes. But
Your hand is still soft
In mine as it was before.

CHRISTINE:
But I have a kind of wart on it.
Do you really like my hands?

EDWARD:
Look, Christine. That explains it. It's the Avant-Garde.

CUBE:
In downtown Mexico City's commanding uproar
I have a temple of art, but it may vanish in a second,
Depending on the government and on taste.

EDWARD:
She's right. And it may depend on our government, too.
God knows what it's about to do in this part of the world! . . .
Though I am melting to you. And with you.

CHRISTINE:
I to you, too. Maybe we can find a cross-
Way between the political and our life
And maybe we cannot. Oh
Edward, who knows? The main

Problem now seems to be how old
You are and young I am. My
Step-parents are going to flip—

CUBE:
And I am the Avant-Garde.
Follow me, and you'll end up on a still tip
Of a frozen wing
In the acrid penumbra
Of magnesiated space. Come on!

(She leads them off.)

From the M'vett

Scene 1

Army Headquarters tent. CAPTAIN FOGG *at the desk,* STAFF SERGEANT MILCH *standing.*

FOGG:
> Have you been able to find out what's wrong with the code
> On these fucking rockets? They trail always into some African place
> And go boom. They are not hitting their fucking goddamned targets.

MILCH:
> I know the problem but I'm damned if I can see the solution.

FOGG:
> Get Sergeant Dawb in here.

MILCH:
> Yes sir.

(MILCH *exits, re-enters with* DAWB.)

FOGG:
> Dawb?

DAWB:
> Sir?

FOGG:
> Do you know what's happening to these motherfucking rockets?

DAWB:
> Dey am heat seekin, am deys nock?

FOGG: *(mocking his accent)*
> Yacks, dam is. But what the fuck has that got to do with it?

DAWB:
> Everything, My Lord, if you believe me. Nothing, if you do not.
> *(He pauses, as if searching for something in his thoughts.)* I think there is some
>   place in Africa that is attracting them—
> An old story I heard once, part of the M'Vett,
> Our Gabonese epic poem, something about a stove. . . .

FOGG:
> Dawb, do you think you could find that stove?

DAWB: *(saluting)*
> Yessir . . . He starts to leave, then stops; to himself) I go, but with a divided
> heart. My great-grandfather was Behanzu . . . the Shark.

(toot toot of Congo boats and jungle wind through the trees)

Scene 2

In a heavy mist.

MAN:
> How did it end with Dawb and the Stove of Peace?

SECOND MAN:
> I don't know. They never found out.

(The TWO MEN *leave. The mist clears, revealing* DAWB *and* M'BAMU.*)*

DAWB:
> I am sitting beside it.

M'BAMU:
> Dawb is sitting beside it here with me.
> He married one of my daughters and he sits beside it,
> He is sitting beside the Stove of Peace.
> Later you will see it.

The Arrival of Homosexuality in Greece, or The Fagabond

*(A Greek island. Two men—*MINETOS *and* ARCHILOKOS*—are standing on the shore.* ARISTIPPUS *arrives from the sea.)*

ARISTIPPUS (THE FAGABOND):
  What's the name of this island?

MINETOS:
  Hydra.

ARISTIPPUS:
  Where is it?

MINETOS:
  In the Aegean, in Greece.

ARISTIPPUS:
  I love it, I love that, I love you.

*(*ARISTIPPUS *embraces* MINETOS*.)*

MINETOS:
  What? Are you mad? I'm a man. I love WOMEN. Women love ME. Not men men. Get away from me. Archilokos, take him! We must bind him and bring him to trial. Frankly, I feel like having him killed.

ARISTIPPUS:
  Just for a little hug? Don't be such a bear! You like it, admit it. I know you do.

MINETOS:
  Actually I don't. Get away. Archilokos—

*(*ARCHILOKOS *lunges forward as if pushed,* MINETOS *also.)*

ARCHILOKOS:
  Wait. Something's happening.

MINETOS:
  Somebody, something, gave me a shove.

ARISTIPPUS:
  Well, sillies, what do you think? There's more to me, you know, than MEETS THE GUY. Ho ha ha ha!

MINETOS:
But what, who is it?

(*Suddenly, in their midst, beside* ARISTIPPUS, *the god* EROS *is revealed. It was he who pushed the two men.*)

EROS:
Beware! Beware! Be airy! For I am LOVE.
Know that this is a real thing. Have respect for me.
Life has need of it. Love must be free.

MINETOS:
Eros! But if it goes against the grain—

EROS:
The grain isn't everything, Minetos. Remember that.

(EROS *vanishes in a red-pink golden fire.*)

ARISTIPPUS: (*putting on a white beard*)
You can call me Psyche, if you want. Oh no! (*tugging at the beard*) That's entirely the wrong thing for her! (*laughs*)

MINETOS *and* ARCHILOKOS: (*smiling*)
Oh well, all right.

Watteau's Reputation

(the Sorbonne)

RAMON FERNANDEZ:
It's Watteau's problem that he was
Ahead of his time and so appreciated only later
And then in the work of epigones with less talent
In a more watered-down form of his work. Then only really
Valued correctly in the nineteenth century, when
The themes of his paintings were hopelessly out-of-date.

MARY MAGDALENE:
We should go back in time and tell him
Of his high stature now.

CUPIDON:
Yes. I
Will go with you, Mary Magdalene.

RAMON FERNANDEZ:
Good luck—and bring me news.

(The scene shifts to WATTEAU's *atelier.* WATTEAU *is painting a group of* LADIES *and* GENTLEMEN.*)*

WATTEAU:
Finally it's finished—another *Fête Galante!*

(Enter the PLAGUE.*)*

PLAGUE:
I am the Bubonic Plague.

WATTEAU:
Get away from me!

*(*LADIES *and* GENTLEMEN *push* PLAGUE *offstage and follow after it. Enter* GENTLE-MEN *and* CUPIDON.*)*

WATTEAU:
Ah! Mary Magdalene and Cupidon. I've been waiting
For you, sit down. Have some coffee. I'm going to make of you
The greatest painting I have ever made: *Le départ pour le
Cythère*—or . . . *du Cythère?* That is,
Are the people going to Cytherea paradise or leaving it?

MARY MAGDALENE:
 Yes, which?

WATTEAU:
 I don't know. Going to it, I think—

(He paints.)

 No—leaving it.
 Actually, no—going to it—No! Leav—

CUPIDON:
 We came here to tell you something else—

(Re-enter the PLAGUE, *leading the* LADIES *and* GENTLEMEN; *crossing the stage, it sweeps away* WATTEAU, MARY MAGDALENE, *and* CUPIDON *in its wake.)*

Hippopotamus Migration in Africa

(The HIPPOS *speak, as they move, migratorily, across a semidarkened stage.)*

We the Hippopotamuses
Are hurtling down
Through Africa
Toward the Sea.
We shall never reach the Sea.
The Sea's not meant for us. Our destiny
Takes us toward protracted stays in jungle
Where to stay
We have to stay in streams
In inland river streams
All day, and only at night
Pull up our lonely, lovely hands
To climb to land—and grass—
To eat—
Then back
To slimy scummy water above our back
At dawn
When the hard day begins,
When the hard hippo-
Potamus-head-destroying
Day beings.

(very bright sunlight)

Wittgenstein, or Bravo, Dr. Wittgenstein!

(The philosopher WITTGENSTEIN *is walking in the city. At each clause, sometimes at each phrase or at each word, he stops and changes the course of his walk: by turning up a new street, by crossing from one side of the street to the other, by turning and retracing his steps.)*

WITTGENSTEIN:
   The only things that we can say
   Are the things that are already said
   By existing actions—
   For example: I am walking today.
   It cannot be said
   This walk is taking me forward
   Or, I am the subject, or the form, of this walk.
   Then, prospectively,
   The only things that we should say
   Are those that we can say. I am taking a walk.
   What cannot be said with clarity
   Should not—and cannot—be said—
   Thus I must conclude
   That the unsayable
   Has no further chance of being said—
   And, this being so,

*(A bunch of brightly colored balloons with large printed words on them—*GOD, GOOD, EVIL, MAN, NATURE, ESSENCE, MATTER, SUBSTANCE, FORM—*burst free and are blown into the offstage sky.)*

   Our philosopher's dream is unattainable
   And can never come true.

Tadeusz Kantor and the Duck

Enter a large DUCK *dressed in black.* TADEUSZ KANTOR, *the noted Polish director, is to one side of the stage, directing in a furtive sort of way. The* DUCK *starts to die. Then, suddenly, the* DUCK *sees* KANTOR *and begins "directing"* KANTOR. KANTOR *staggers around the stage, then dies in the center of the stage. The* DUCK *sits on him and quacks. Then, to loud, funeral music,* KANTOR *is reborn. He and the* DUCK *go to opposite ends of the stage, then run into each other with a crash. Both fall dead. Then each gets up and, with an ordinary walk, leaves the stage. Two or four* GHOULS *or* SKELETONS *come out holding up a placard that says,* "TADEUSZ KANTOR AND THE DUCK." *Loud, funeral music, and the play begins again.*

The Theatre at Epidauros

(It is very dry and very hot. On the stage of the ancient Greek theatre, Greek ACTORS *are rehearsing lines from tragedies.)*

FIRST ACTOR:
> The tender body of your first-born son
> Is what you have eaten here—

SECOND ACTOR:
> As he died, I was splattered
> By the dark red fountain of his blood,
> And I was happy, as if I were a garden
> Nourished by the fresh spring rain.

THIRD ACTOR:
> My brother is dead. Let's stomp on his corpse!

(A LITTLE DOG *runs onstage and nips at the* ACTORS' *heels.)*

A LITTLE DOG:
> Argh argh argh argh greeouw!

FOURTH ACTOR:
> Oh, push me with one unconvulsive leap
> Against the point of this death-dealing blade!

LITTLE DOG:
> Reeouw rrgh!

FOURTH ACTOR:
> Get that dog

THIRD ACTOR:
> Out of here

FIRST AND SECOND ACTORS:
> Get that noisome dog
> Out of the Theatre of Epidauros!

(The god of medicine, AESCULAPIUS, *comes onstage and picks up the* LITTLE DOG *in his arms.)*

AESCULAPIUS:
> Come, my child, I shall shelter and guard you.
> No longer will anyone forget to take you out.

And we will take long pleasant walks together—
We'll leave this sickening theater alone
Where there is talk of nothing but family murder
And devastation, relatives eating each other—
It is enough to make even me, Aesculapius, sick at heart . . . You, dog,
Are the healthiest, most natural thing
I have seen in this Epidauros Theatre in a long, long time.

(The memory of his wife, who died young, momentarily comes back to AESCU-
LAPIUS.*)*

Oh, Xanthia . . . *you*
Were healthy, *you* were beautiful. When you died
I stopped writing plays myself, and became a doctor . . .
Oh, well . . . things long ago! Come, pleasant dog,
Now shall we make the paths of Greece our friends.

*(*AESCULAPIUS *and the* DOG *go off.* ACTORS *continue rehearsing lines.)*

SECOND ACTOR:
This hand has choked the one who gave me life—I smelled her dying . . .

FIRST ACTOR:
He slaughtered his own child—and mine—our daughter,
To calm the Thracian winds—

THIRD ACTOR *as* ORESTES: *(looking back behind him and seeing the* FURIES*)*
You can't see them, but I see them. They are after me! I can't stay a moment
more!

(The THIRD ACTOR *runs off screaming. The* FIFTH ACTOR *enters, attired as*
OEDIPUS, *blinded, with blood streaming from his eye sockets.)*

FIFTH ACTOR:
Apollo did not do this.

The Great Ball

(Chinese music. It is dusk. Two Chinese travelers, SUNG and WO, and one American, JESPERSON, are in the mountains on a long journey home. They come upon a place where many people are dancing around a huge china ball.)

SUNG:
The Great Ball of China!

(He tries to budge it.)

Ooof! Impossible to lift it! Even to roll it!

JESPERSON:
Who built this ball, or is it a social event?

WO:
The common people of China. It is one—and both.

(very dark and cool Chinese night)

The Boat from Mandraki

(Just off the coast of the island of Hydra, in Greece. Members of a Greek family are in a small boat, trying to get it to start.)

KAPOS:
I'm trying to get the boat started.

TAPOS:
It just won't start.

(KAPOS pulls hard and the MOTOR makes a sound.)

MOTOR:
Brrrrrrrr whmmmmmmmmmp

KAPOS:
Ah, here it comes.

MOTOR: *(dying)*
Pzzzzzzzzzzz

BAPOS:
No, there it goes.

MOTOR:
Kag kag kag kag kag

KAPOS:
It goes

MOTOR:
Zzzzzzzz

BAPOS:
And then it doesn't go.

KAPOS:
The sea is becalmed.

ELENA:
The boat won't start.

DIVOKOPOULOS:
The Augean trade was always a risky affair!

MOTOR:
Kagaga kagag brr brr vadoom pttttt pttt zeeeeeeee

KAPOS:

But now it starts, it goes!
Oh thank you, Kathalassa, Goddess of Boat Parts!
Kalispéra sas, kaliníchta, efcharistó!

ALL:

Thank you. *Efcharistó!*

ZAPOS:

Why must we always be in our boat?

KAPOS:

We come from islands
That have no farmable land. We are doomed to roam the earth.
We must always be on the sea,
Trading. We trade for the Doge and for the Turkish Emir.
If only we had land!

MOTOR:

Shkrrrrrr Shkrrrrrrr Ktiktiki kling zting

BAPOS:

The boat has stopped again. There's something wrong
Terribly wrong with this whole economy of Greece!

MOTOR: *(dying definitively)*
Fzzz Fzzz zzzz zz.

The Choice in Shanghai

(The grand staircase of a big European-style 1930s hotel in Shanghai. Outside, on the street, bright sunlight. The dialogue should be accompanied by Chinese subtitles—perhaps on large white cards held by subsidiary stage personnel, or flashed on a white screen-like banner running across the top of the stage.)

CHORUS:
> The construction of the Peace Hotel
> Is almost finished!
> It has enormous rooms!
> Look at it: Here beside the wavering
> Turgidesque-rapid waters of the River, Huang-Po
> "I love you so," inside says
> Ho Kai the Chinese house painter.

(Pause. HO KAI appears at the top of the stairs and begins walking down.)

> Now he walks down the stairs
> Of newly completed hotel
> And "Ah-ooh," he says and we let him say
> For he's so happy
> Feeling at the center of China
> Which, for him, is of the world—
> Out through the lobby and into the street.

(HO KAI, now on the curb of the street, speaks with exhilaration.)

HO KAI:
> It is today that I love you!

(HO KAI walks into the street, and a car hits him.)

CHORUS:
> Someone, or something, from this encounter
> Has to be wrecked, or to die.
> Show by your applause, which do you choose—the car or Ho Kai?

(The chorus points to HO KAI and the CAR in turn. While the audience is trying to decide, a WHITE BEAR comes in, pushes the chorus aside, and picks up HO KAI in his arms.)

WHITE BEAR:
> I choose Ho Kai.

(applause)

Dumplings

(A Shanghai food shop. Everything happens very fast.)

PING HU: *(holding up a dumpling)*
 The first dumpling!
 What is a dumpling?
 You shall see, how here it is, actually in fact for the first time
 In all eternity being made by me, the dumpling!
 May god be praised for dumpling
 Which gives up sides and center, top and bottom, meat to enter,
 We to eat it, stunning fruit,
 A man-made woman-made delicacy, the blessed taste-tingling
 ardency of the world.

(DON CHING HOY enters.)

DON CHING:
 I am Don Ching Hoy and I demand the first dumpling.

PING HU: *(giving DON CHING a dumpling)*
 From this day, dumplings shall be named for you:
 Ching Hoy dumplings—and Ching Hoy means dumplings.

DON CHING:
 And what about you who made it?

PING HU:
 Many are the ways of being great.
 Another dumpling shall be named after me
 And call Ping Hu.
 The two dumplings!

BOTH:
 To the two dumplings!
 To you! To you! (to audience) To you!

(Enter a child, a little girl, DANG JOY.)

DANG JOY:
 And Tu Yu shall be the third dumpling!

ALL:
 Yes, hurray! One two and three dumplings—
 Ching Hoy, Ping Hu, and Tu Yu.

And this little girl who thought of this game,
This way of naming the third dumpling?

DANG JOY:
My am Dang Joy.

DON CHING *and* PING HU:
Let a fourth dumpling be named
And its name be Dang Joy!

(explosions, music, and very hot day; dancing in the streets)

Alexander

ALEXANDER: *(moving through an abstract space)*
    When I lived in the clouds
    I was not called Alexander
    But "The Dog." Men looked
    Up at the sky and saw the Dog Star.
    In poetry, I became a line;
    In nature, an umbelliferous plant,
    Smyrnium Olusatrum.

    Everywhere the day became Alexander.
    Sometimes I found myself looking at the green
    And gray of a Thessalian morning and thinking,
    Even saying, This is Alexander, I.
    Later those days the blue sky
    Seemed immutable Alexander.
    What is there left to me now?

SAGE:
    I don't know, Alexander. Alexander, cinnamon tree.

Olive Oyl Commandeers Popeye's Gunboat and Sails Off to Attack Russia

(A gunboat. The actors speak the lines from behind big stationary cut-out cardboard or wooden figures of OLIVE OYL *and* WIMPY.)

OLIVE:

    Okay, Wimpy! Hand over those controls! This barge is going to Russia. We're
    going to blow those bastards up!

WIMPY:

    Olive Oyl! What? Have you gone crazy? What will Popeye say? He is a man
    of peace.

OLIVE:

    Well, he has peace now. If you go down belowdecks
    You'll find him, strangled, and with a knife in his belly—
    A perfect "statue" of peace. He put my child in his tomb!

WIMPY:

    Olive—no!

OLIVE:

    You too must die, Wimpy! For America!
    And for the good of the democratic world! Now, OFF
    To Russia!

(The boat veers about and a large, menacing face of OLIVE OYL *fills the whole stage.)*

After the Return of the Avant-Garde

(large city square; MAN *and* WOMAN *standing near a door)*

WOMAN:
> They said of the Avant-Garde
> That it had no lasting power
> But now it has come back
> And everything is changed!

MAN:
> Yes, look!
> The door has changed
> Through which we used to walk!

WOMAN:
> It is no longer a door now—
> It is a mosque!

*(*ARABS *come out of the door, playing saxophones.)*

MAN DRIVING PAST IN A CAR:
> What do you think is the most beautiful thing
> In the Avant-Garde city?

WOMAN AT A WINDOW:
> Any three buildings taken alone.

MAN COMING DOWN IN A PARACHUTE:
> What about the whole of the Avant-Garde city?

PERSON WITH FEET STICKING UP OUT OF A MANHOLE:
> That, too, is beautiful, but in a different way.

(Night falls. Darkness. ANNOUNCER *speaks from high on a roof with a search-light.)*

ANNOUNCER:
> Which is more avant-garde—a giraffe or an elephant?

RESPONDENT: *(from below)*
> A giraffe is more avant-garde, but an elephant is more surreal.

(music)

Les Bousculades de l'Amour, suivies de the Mexicana

(A place in the Caribbean. Misty. In the distance one can see a crowd of people. Nearby are EDWARD *and* CHRISTINE.*)*

CHRISTINE:
    The mood of this island is being distracted
    By these four hundred people
    Who have come here from the bumps.

EDWARD:
    What are the bumps . . . Christine?

CHRISTINE:
    Oh! You called me by my name. Tell me
    That at other times we can talk of other things.
    But now the hot night, the mercurial pacings of the dancers
    And the sea tanager's wild cry distract my heart.

EDWARD:
    Christine you talk like the Omniplex Literary Encyclopedia
    But you do it without art. Kiss me. Now, what are the bumps?

(The scene changes, or it may be just that the people in the distance become clearer. In any case, the scene is many Mexican people in a soft summer evening light. They are dancing gently in a big yard or field.)

EDWARD:
    They're dancing the "Mexicana"

CHRISTINE:
    Quietly, slightly moving their feet

EDWARD:
    As if with butterflies' attentiveness

CHRISTINE:
    And sometimes holding hands.

EDWARD:
    From this modest swinging

CHRISTINE:
    Come the horror of Inquisition, the blood-slash of a destructive nobility, the steamy crash

EDWARD:

Of a seed time of ethical values, the Putsch

CHRISTINE:

And the *remorque* of brains—from this Mexicana

EDWARD:

Slightly delightfully beginning, almost like a tree gently budding, beneath
the light spring rain.

The Yangtse

(*The stage represents the entire length of the Yangtse River, or at least both ends of it.*)

KI FO (A YOUNG MAN):
> A branch falls into the Yangtse.

TI FIA (A YOUNG WOMAN):
> The water pushes it on. And here at the end
> It washes onto the bank.
> It is wet, and there is a white blossom
> On this one tip of it.

KI FO:
> Now I shall head for home.

TI FIA:
> I will take this branch in my hand.

OLD WOMAN:
> However, no one can move
> Because the king has all the stage directions.

OLD MAN:
> Then how did the branch move? and the Yangtse River?

(JAI FU *appears.*)

JAI FU:
> It is only the people who are controlled.

Athens Extended Place

(A very large view of Athens and its environs. The stage, as much as possible, should seem like a relief map of the whole area. The first three speeches are spoken by WORKERS *in the outer parts of such a map.)*

VINEYARD WORKER:
    I am in a vineyard.

DOCKWORKER:
    I undock the ship.

FIELDHAND:
    I am a harvester of grain.

PUBLIC CRIER: *(in central Athens, at the Pnyx)*
    And I am a public crier.
    It is time now for an election; I send up a signal
    Here from the Pnyx, to convene an Assembly of the People.

(He sends up a smoke signal, and the WORKERS *go toward the center of Athens.)*

VINEYARD WORKER:
    We all come
    To the Acropolis.

FIELDHAND:
    Even though we live where we live—
    And it may be rather far—
    We are all Athenians.

VINEYARD WORKER:
    Athens has no city limits.

DOCKWORKER:
    "City limits"
    Is not a conception of ours.

PUBLIC CRIER:
    No, there isn't for this big city,
    Big in the sense it's an extended city,
    There isn't a physical end to it, no line
    No definite material barrier at all,
    There is no circumventory wall.

(The WORKERS, *along with many other citizens, arrive and keep arriving, at the Pnyx.)*

Beijing Opera League

(Chinese music. The play is in the grandest, brightest, noisiest style of Beijing Opera.)

KING:
Very great King
Now play baseball
First and second base.

JAI FU:
Oh Celestial Majesty
Only one position
One man can play.

KING:
You teach me a lesson.
You are new Commander
Of Royal Army in Cha-Ing.

JAI FU:
Thank you, Celestial Majesty.

(JAI FU goes.)

KING:
Now he is gone
I will play first
And second at same time.

(dance representation of this, with much leg-lifting and turning slowly, etc.)

Cannot be done.
Call back Jai Fu
To rule my kingdom.

(JAI FU returns. He is surrounded by fan-waving beauties, who sing.)

KING
Of all palace ladies
He can choose one—

(laughing)

Or maybe two.

(Cymbals, gongs, incense, bowings, and all depart.)

Byron in Italy

Scene 1

BYRON *is at his desk, writing.* TERESA GUICCIOLI *stands at the opened door.*

BYRON: *(composing)*
   So we'll go no more a-roving—

TERESA:
   Lord Byron—

BYRON: *(still writing)*
   By the light of the moon—

TERESA:
   Can I speak to you for a moment?

BYRON:
   I'm writing.

TERESA:
   Just one word?

BYRON: *(making a last effort)*
   So we'll go no more a-roving—

(giving up, but mild and confident)

                              Well,
   I think I'll have the knack for it again tomorrow.

(Berlioz-like music)

Scene 2

BYRON *is in his bathtub.* TERESA *stands outside the closed bathroom door. Outside the bathroom window one sees the Grand Canal.*

BYRON:
   No more a-roving

TERESA:
   Byron, Lord Byron—

BYRON:
   Teresa I'm

TERESA:
   George Gordon

BYRON:

Having a tub

TERESA:

Venice is sinking

BYRON:

And thinking over

TERESA:

Vanishing from sight

BYRON:

We'll go no more a-roving

TERESA:

Though the night was made for loving

BYRON:

Gad, that's it

TERESA:

And the day returns too soon

BYRON:

Bless you, Teresa

TERESA:

It's gone.

BYRON:

What? What's gone?

TERESA:

Venice, Byron, I've been telling you, Venice has vanished from sight.

BYRON:

What? What? That's impossible. If there's no Venice, how will I be able to get out of my tub?

(Now GONDOLIERS, *in a grand and moving chorus, sing as they sail into view on the canal.)*

GONDOLIERS:

Though the night was made for loving
And the day returns too soon
Yet we'll go no more a-roving
By the light of the moon!

(On) a Corner (of Nothing) in Africa

EDWARD:
>There is absolutely nothing here, you know,
>That you are going to recognize as being
>Parcel of the usual distractions of your time, which, already,
>The bold silence of not being backward commends
>To your own holy
>Idea of yourself as a state
>More than the one that simply drops you here, being
>An effulgence,
>Contrarily and long, of something else.
>As staying here, you stay, if it seems *nil absolu*
>You are staying, un-apart from the news
>That, its essential shallowness unrelenting,
>Keys its whispers to what might almost promise a fresh
>Wind, that, but for its pure contractions,
>The remedy (elsewhere) is flowering to be.
>Then, as you stick to this being
>Here present, you see that everything is as well
>As not, in the microseconds that they uncloud it
>With rings, to give it back to whatever you have been doing
>That isn't they.

N'MIMBO:
>Can you show me that ring, White Man?

EDWARD:
>Blond humans.

(N'MIMBO *hands* EDWARD—*and thus covers him with—a river, killing him.*)

N'MIMBO:
>Yes, that is one thing you are.

(*drums*)

The Coast of West Africa, 1782

(Coast and Atlantic Ocean. On land a big sign or banner announces "KING BEHANZU, THE SHARK.")

BEHANZU:
> Help me get into these fins
> That I may show the Frenchmen my teeth.

SOLDIERS OF BEHANZU'S ARMY: *(as they speak, they help* BEHANZU *get into a shark costume)*
> We will, Behanzu.
> But these Frenchmen are sharp.
> They have fire-propelled missiles that break our skins.

BEHANZU:
> Ah, I will frighten them, strike them,
> And eat them.

(By now he is completely disguised as a shark.)

> For I am
> Behanzu, "the Shark."

(The FRENCH FORCES *land from the sea.* BEHANZU *and his* SOLDIERS *are easily swept aside and knocked down. However, once the* FRENCH FORCES *have gotten a little way past him,* BEHANZU *lifts himself from the ground and begins to speak, in a very loud, commanding voice. At the sound of his voice, his* SOLDIERS *rise also.)*

BEHANZU:
> To conquer you may try.
> I am ready to die.
> But know, before you have
> Africa, you have to meet the Shark!

(Now the FRENCH FORCES *turn around and do battle with* BEHANZU *and his* SOLDIERS. *The fight is inconclusive. The stage is covered with blood.)*

Conceptions of Things

WITTGENSTEIN:
    There are no subjects in the world.

(An ancient cargo ship—circa 1500—arrives in the middle of the stage. WITTGEN-STEIN *gets on the boat, and he waves as it slowly begins to move again, across the stage. He speaks over the railing.)*

    Each subject is a limitation of the world.

(The boat stops. HAMLET *jumps off the boat.)*

HAMLET:
    To be, or not to be: that is the question.

*(*MICHELANGELO *enters from one side of the piazza.)*

MICHELANGELO:
    The idea, *cari maestri,* is in the stone!

WITTGENSTEIN, HAMLET, MICHELANGELO: *(together)*
    The idea is in the limitation of the not-being stone!

A Tale of Two Cities

(large public square in the Avant-Garde City)

CONICAL MAN:
    Our avant-garde city is filled with sunlight—
    How beautiful it is!
    No city like this exists in China.

(Enter COOK.*)*

COOK:
    No, certainly not!
    In China our city must be very practical—

*(*COOK *dances about in a sort of geometrical pattern, as if to show where things are in the Chinese city.)*

    With restaurant available at every five hundred feet—
    That is why Cook work well and have sure of job.
    As for new touristic hotel
    There are going up
    Even if many thing not function properly
    And so—And so here too you see is lumberyard
    And place to change chalk into fire for cook
    And this to talk
    Back and forth telephone, that hardly work. This
    Is our Chinese city.

CONICAL MAN:
    And here is our City of the Avant-Garde.
    Not as practical, of course, in a practical kind of way,
    But intensely enjoyable, and suggestive, you'll see, Cook—
    And I think you'll like in China, before too long,
    Once you have your practicalities, some like this one too.
    Come, I'll show you around.
    Take this Butterfly Mailbox, for instance,
    That gives wishes! And this time-stopping gasoline station
    Whose pumps are dreams! Oh, this, and more—
    Our windows full of cries of alarm and kisses!
    Our sidewalks that explode in thirty flowers
    Of blood! All this, oh everything we give to you,
    Cook, all that you did not need,
    Or did not know you did before!

COOK:

Now all is evident!
Avant-Garde will come to China, too,
If I can get it there.
I must go home, start work.
But how to go there?

(*She sees a Dada rocket and looks questioningly at* CONICAL MAN.)

CONICAL MAN:

Here, take this Dada rocket, Cook. Good luck. Good-bye!

COOK:

Good-bye.

(COOK *gets on rocket and flies off.*)

CONICAL MAN:

Oh, it's just another day
In the Avant-Garde City,
The only place where such things come to pass—
I'd guess so anyway.
I'm sorry, though, Cook left—
I'd come to like her.

(*He walks off, a little sadly, as an avant-garde concert begins in the public square: musique concrete, featuring saws, vacuum cleaners, firetrucks, and breaking glass.*)

Down and Out Near the Bay of Naples

(A panoramic view of the Bay of Naples. In the center, just on shore, the SPECK OF FOAM *appears.)*

SPECK OF FOAM:
> Out of all being
> I come,
> A tiny speck
> Of white
> Foam—
>
> Oh!
> You
> Forgot
> Me, and
> I'm
> Gone!

The Conquest of Mexico

NOBLE:

> They say Cortez is coming, at the head of teeming troupes,
> To win all Mexico for his queen, Isabella!
> They say he is in quest of gold, and that he will do or suffer
> anything to get it!

MONTEZUMA:

> How is he dressed? What does he look like?

NOBLE:

> He is dressed in shining metal and with a feather on his hat.
> He sits astride something with a tail. His skin is white.

MONTEZUMA:

> Oh then, oh then, it is he!

NOBLE:

> Who?

MONTEZUMA:

> Quetzalcoatl, the savior of Tenochtitlán,
> For whom I have waited so long.

(Aztec music and dancing)

Quetzalcoatl and the Cook

(Mazatlán)

COOK:
Why do they call you "The Feathered Snake," my lord?

QUETZALCOATL:
What a sweet, innocent question! Don't you have a Quetzalcoatl in China?

COOK:
Maybe. But if we do, we call it by a different name!

(volcanic explosions)

The Vanished God

(a rocky, mountainous landscape in Mexico)

FIRST MAN:

    They say Quetzalcoatl was wont to sit down there
    Talking to the Indians, on summer evenings,
    And that they would tell him their secrets, and tell him their dreams;
    Tell him their grievances, too, and ask for his help.
    Quetzalcoatl, though, was unable to help them. He
    Did not have that kind of power.

SECOND MAN:

    What became of Quetzalcoatl? For I know that for a long time he has not
      been here.

FIRST MAN:

    He was vanquished, consigned to oblivion by the Christian saints
    Hundreds of years ago. We Indians believe he is hiding in the caves
    Of these mountains, and that he will come back
    And bring us happiness, will release us from the suffering
    That is imposed upon us, day after wretched day.

The Meeting in Mexico

MONTEZUMA:
> Well, it's been a good session.
> I hope that you gentlemen are satisfied.

TOMMY TIME:
> That seems fine to us. Edward will leave Christine at the train.
> A few years later he will see her and she will be a little older,
> But still ravishing. Never will he forget the soft feel of her hand
> In his, on the Zocalo.

HAPPINESS:
> And Cook will be born. That's what really tickles me.
> Cook, actually, up till this time, who hasn't really been in existence.

CORTEZ:
> But—let me get it straight. My conquest is assured.

HAPPINESS:
> Yes, though I won't be there.

TOMMY TIME:
> I, however, will. And what of you, Montezuma?

MONTEZUMA:
> I will be remembered in the stone.

(Enter COOK *with* EDWARD, *hundreds of years later.)*

EDWARD:
> Oh, Cook, where is Christine?

COOK:
> Not born yet, I think.
> Keep walking, though—we may come to her in time.

The Return of Odysseus

PENELOPE:
Odyss

ODYSSEUS:
I

PENELOPE:
That

ODYSSEUS:
Penel

PENELOPE:
Tapestry

ODYSSEUS:
Weaving

PENELOPE:
This

ODYSSEUS:
No

PENELOPE:
Suitors

ODYSSEUS:
Dog

PENELOPE:
Recognized

ODYSSEUS:
Old

PENELOPE:
Nurse

ODYSSEUS:
It's

PENELOPE:
You!

Other Return of Odysseus

(One actor plays ODYSSEUS *and* PENELOPE.*)*

Well, Penelope, I'm back. Put on your threadiest dress and let's go forth into the city. I want to show all the suitors what they missed. Oh of course I will! And to show everyone that I'm here. Oh I'm so glad to be back here, Penelope! I should think you would be. Well, I am. Darling Odysseus! Oh, my delight!

The Harbor of Rhodes

(FOUR COLOSSAL FIGURES, *each of which stands astride the Harbor of Rhodes.
These* FIGURES *speak loudly and solemnly and their speeches should sound, as
much as possible, like the noises one hears in a big harbor. It's most important in
this play to give the sense of an enormous, important body of water put to human
uses. The* FIGURES, *to this end, may wish to speak somewhat hollowly; to be unusually deliberate; to have long pauses between words. They may also speak, sometimes, simultaneously.*)

FIRST COLOSSAL FIGURE:
Twenty-five thousand tons
In one day, sitting on the water.

SECOND COLOSSAL FIGURE:
I want water.

THIRD COLOSSAL FIGURE:
Then these ships move on, over the water.

FOURTH COLOSSAL FIGURE:
What did you say you want?

FIRST COLOSSAL FIGURE:
Twenty-five, thirty, forty, fifty thousand tons per day.

SECOND COLOSSAL FIGURE:
Water. Water. I want water.

THIRD COLOSSAL FIGURE:
This is what it possibly is.

FOURTH COLOSSAL FIGURE:
All we have is harbor water. Harbor water.

FIRST COLOSSAL FIGURE:
Each vessel carrying tons and tons
Of whatever it is.

SECOND COLOSSAL FIGURE:
Maybe that will be alright.

THIRD COLOSSAL FIGURE:
Heavy. So heavy it is. They
Move it across the water.

FOURTH COLOSSAL FIGURE:
Is it good water?

FIRST COLOSSAL FIGURE:
From one side to another, the tremendous tonnage
Moves on the surface of the water of our harbor. When it leaves
    our harbor
I do not know where it goes.

SECOND COLOSSAL FIGURE:
Yes. It is good water.
Give me some more water.

THIRD COLOSSAL FIGURE:
It goes to another harbor.

FOURTH COLOSSAL FIGURE:
Here. Here it is.

FIRST COLOSSAL FIGURE:
Yes. That is where it goes. Ton after ton

FIRST COLOSSAL FIGURE:
Thank you. It is good water.

THIRD COLOSSAL FIGURE:
After ton after ton
After ton after ton

FOURTH COLOSSAL FIGURE:
Every day—
And then to another harbor.

(Real harbor sounds now begin and grow very loud, so that the voices of the COLOSSAL FIGURES *can no longer be heard.)*

Crêpe de Chine

ONE:

Hi! What's happening?

TWO:

Bozo just sold the avant-garde to China!

ONE:

That Bozo!

TWO:

Millions of men and women walk back and forward, chanting, "Bozo! Bozo!"

ONE:

What has that got to do with anything?

TWO:

Well, just come over here and see!

(The two walk to the edge of a tremendous dazzling uproar.)

CHINESE PEOPLE:

China is avant-garde! Long live Bozo!

BOZO:

Aw nuts, folks, it wasn't nothing!

CHINESE PEOPLE:

Bozo for Ruler of the World!

BOZO:

Oh, come on! Oh well, oh well, all right!

Epilogue

GEORGE:

That's the silliest thing I ever heard! Did you write that?

KENNETH:

Yes. It's my new play, *Bozo, King of China.*

GEORGE:

You should be shot!

St. Petersburg in 1793

(A very poor, barren, canal-side area near a livestock market, with dirty snow. Huddled together are a number of workmen, CARRIERS, *who transport things into the main part of the city.)*

CARRIERS:
    We carriers have a wretched town of our own
    Here beyond the Ligovich Canal.
    It is cut by empty spaces, phew, empty spaces
    That a man has no wish to walk across—
    No nature and no city, emptiness
    Such as in only city empty spaces,
    Beyond the Ligovich Canal—
    While hustly bustly fur-wound brilliant Russian life
    Lights up the Neva's and the Nevska's byways
    We see it from afar or we imagine
    What happens in those rich and crowded spaces.
    We have a livestock market, and that's all.

(livestock sounds: mooing, neighing, bleating)

    We have the livestock with us, and that's all.

(The scene changes to central St. Petersburg. People in fur coats, hats, and gloves go quickly through the streets and speak to one another.)

WELL-TO-DO CITIZENS:
    Do you know how artificial the city of St. Petersburg is?
    It was built for the Czar by the Czar without any connection to the slightest
        sort of practicality
    And without any concern for economic reality.
    The Neva is beautiful and the Nevska
    And the Nevsky Prospect in winter is a beautiful sight
    But think of all those people working in the night
    To make this grotesque city what it is
    Contra naturam is what it is
    And yet so pretty.
    A city is like a big artificial flower.
    Some cities grow up naturally
    In a naturally hospitable place.
    To these cities Happiness comes sometimes,

And they have walls and are sometimes self-sufficient.
Not St. Petersburg. It's far from self-sufficient.
It's entirely dependent on what comes in from outside

(Enter CARRIERS, *transporting things.)*

And on the carriers, who have a miserable life.

A Love Play

(a room; faint Chinese music and, outside, suggestions of Chinese landscape)

WOMAN:
  Undress me.

MAN:
  I can't. We're in China.

WOMAN:
  Oh, I forgot.

MAN:
  However—

WOMAN:
  What?

MAN:
  No one in China can see us.

WOMAN:
  Well, that's a thought!

Trade

(The Lido of Venice in 1487. Many flat wooden or papier-mâché cattle are brought onstage and set down in varied positions. The stage is almost filled with them. Enter ANTONIO, *the cattle-keeper.)*

ANTONIO:
> Here on
> The
> Lido
> We
> Will
> Keep
> The
> Cattle un-
> Til
> Such
> Time
> As
> They
> Are
> Needed
> In
> The
> City, and
> Then we
> Will
> Slaughter
> Them.

CATTLE:
> MAW, MAW—MUUH—
> Cattle don't talk
> But at this we balk
> Why should we be slaughtered on
> The Lido white as chalk?

ANTONIO:
> Men need to eat you.
> Otherwise they beat you
> With a stick to make you walk.

CATTLE:
> All is fiddle-faddle
> Once you're born as cattle
> Nothing works out.

(Enter two GENTLEMEN, *in big, Venetian furs.)*

FIRST GENTLEMAN:
> Venice, a mighty mercantile power,
> Has everything—for instance,
> Witness, my lord, this. *(He indicates the cattle.)*

SECOND GENTLEMAN:
> I am impressed. All right, you have the order.
> Fifteen thousand sesterces by Thursday next.

CATTLE:
> MUH-MAW-MUUH

(The CATTLE *are pushed offstage.)*

Allegory of Sports

(A rice paddy. A straw-hatted Chinese RICH WORKER *is paddling a little boat. Enter, with his army behind him,* MAO TSE-TUNG, *dressed as a golfer, in a cap and carrying golf balls. This play should be done with great intensity.)*

RICH WORKER:
    You can't play golf
    In a rice paddy. It's natural
    Enough. Some of these kinds of
    Rices have extremely long stems.
    The water can be eight feet deep.

MAO TSE-TUNG:
    Nonetheless we have come here
    With our clubs. We
    Want to "play through." Our
    Tournament is called "The Long March."

Mao Tse-Tung Comes Back to Life

(In Beijing's main square. MAO TSE-TUNG *rises from the dead and speaks.)*

MAO TSE-TUNG:
>   Even he who overturns one stone has eliminated the need to
>   overturn that one again.
>   What we did was right. What we did was wrong. What is certain is
>   that we did something.
>   China is not the same. Can you imagine that?
>   It really has changed. Whether for good or bad, this enormous
>   country is different.
>   From the way it used to be. Bells in the morning and drums in the
>   afternoon.
>   That has stayed. But we also have factory whistles
>   And the buzzing of the New Flaws of Beijing!

(Whistling and buzzing PERSONS *go past on bicycles.)*

>   And the happy smiles of those who have enough to eat

JAI FU:
>   And the unfortunately pained smiles of those you have tortured—

MAO TSE-TUNG:
>   Who before did not.

JAI FU:
>   Who deserved it not.

Un Mélange de Styles

(A beautiful, Balanchinesque BALLERINA *comes floating onto the stage.)*

BALLERINA:
   The sky—

(Four Kabukiesque KINGS, *á la Ariane Mnouchkine, whirl onstage sighing and shrieking, groaning, intense, violent, wild, full of power.)*

FIRST KING:
   Être, ou ne pas être, voici la question!

SECOND KING:
   Tâche damnée, soit effacée!

THIRD KING:
   Éteindre la lumière, et éteindre la lumière . . .

FOURTH KING:
   Harry, tu m'as volé ma jeunesse!

(Empty carts scoot by. KANTOR *enters dressed in black and drops dead. The* PRINCE *from Swan Lake enters Balanchinesquely, and, meaning to embrace the* BALLERINA, *tries instead to take one of the Kabuki* KINGS *in his arms. The* KING *hurls him into the air. Gospel singing bursts forth, enthusiastic and loud, and the play is over.)*

In the Market Economy, or Lost in Finance

EDMUNDSON:

> In the market economy
> I wandered around.
> I wasn't exactly lost
> And I wasn't exactly found.
> For all good things
> They wanted silver or gold.
> In the market economy
> I grew cold.
> Some people were born
> Before market economy began.
> Now I am getting older
> And I still don't understand.
> I will go to the Netherlands,
> To Rotterdam and Amsterdam,
> And be in the great ports before I die.

(He goes off.)

The Precious Sea

(Two men, MARTÍN DE ACUÑA *and* GUZMÁN DE SILVA, *in black Spanish costumes of the sixteenth century, are walking quickly through southern Europe.)*

MARTÍN DE ACUÑA:
Do you think we will be able to tell
When the Mediterranean region begins?

GUZMÁN DE SILVA:
Yes. Olive trees.

MARTÍN DE ACUÑA:
Do you think we will be able to tell
When it ends?

GUZMÁN DE SILVA:
Yes. Palms.

MARTÍN DE ACUÑA:
What is the weather of this region?

GUZMÁN DE SILVA:
Cold from the Atlantic, hot from the Sahara.
Storm from the Atlantic, calm from the Sahara.
The right mixture is the best of all.

MARTÍN DE ACUÑA:
I think we are getting near it. Aren't those olives?

GUZMÁN DE SILVA:
Yes—they are . . . And now we are through it.

MARTÍN DE ACUÑA:
Already?

GUZMÁN DE SILVA:
Yes. These are palms.

Mahx Bruddahs

(Two TOUGH GUYS *are walking along.)*

FIRST TOUGH GUY:
I juss see dis fillum, wid de Mahx Bruddahs.

SECOND TOUGH GUY:
Yeh, I tink de guy said dat dey was Jewish.

FIRST TOUGH GUY:
Jewish! Man, dey was funny, dats what dey was.
Jewish or nuttin, dose guys is really funny, dey make ya laugh.
I doan keh when I laff nuttin if somebody's Jewish!

SECOND TOUGH GUY:
Yeh, it's de same wit girls ya really go for somebody, shit!
Who kehs if dey're Catlick or something or Jewish?

FIRST TOUGH GUY:
Dats de way it is wid me and de Mahx Bruddahs, fuck de Jewish
I jess laff all movie Ha ha ha ha ha ha!

SECOND TOUGH GUY:
Jeeze I wanna go see dem guys myself!

FIRST TOUGH GUY:
Stay away from dem ya fuggah! Dey're my girl!

SECOND TOUGH GUY:
Wait a minute. You nutsa sumpin? Dey aint no girl!

FIRST TOUGH GUY:
Yeh, I guess you're right. Oh how I wish dey was!

(He sings.)

If de Mahx Bruddhas was a girl
I'd spend all my time in de movies
Lookin, juss lookin at her!

(The song ends. The FIRST TOUGH GUY *speaks to his friend.)*

Come on! Let's go get summin' eat
An' I'll try to fuhget
Dem sweetheart-lookin bruddhas!

The Return of Brad Garks

BRAD GARKS:
> I've come back to find the Cook
> But how can I find her
> Among these millions and millions of men?

(COOK *appears in the immense crowd of marching and milling humans.*)

COOK:
> Because Cook is only woman.
> Hello, Blad Garks!
> So many thing have happen to me
> Since we last met
> In Chengde!
> I have met presidents,
> Famous writers, painters,
> Allegorical figures, talking
> Animals, all. But I am still Cook
> For Blad Garks!

BRAD GARKS:
> Oh Celestial Universe, cohere!
> And bring Cook to my heart!

COOK:
> Our attraction for each other
> Is both in difference and in sameness.

BRAD GARKS:
> We shall fly to the Bay of Naples

COOK:
> What's that?

BRAD GARKS:
> And build an amusement park—

COOK:
> What's that?

BRAD GARKS:
> Oh, Cook! Come to me.

COOK:

I can't! I am being swept away by this crowd
To destiny, Blad, not ours
But that of China!

BRAD GARKS:

Its destiny . . . What's that?

CROWD:

CHINA! CHINA! CHINA!

VOICE:

The story of Brad Garks and Cook, who first met in Chengde!

Vuillard

(ÉDOUARD VUILLARD, *about seventy years old, in his house.*)

VUILLARD:

In this house I, Édouard Vuillard, have been sitting for nigh on to seventy years, painting interiors as if they were the great, wild, glorious world of outside nature itself. Now I am going to go outside and paint hills, plains, valleys, trees, stones, and clouds as if they were walls and chairs. So all will be outside and inside, both dwelling and strange. Who knows what great new worlds may come of this? Oh, wish me well!

(He walks out into a scene of bewildering beauty—of lamps, tables, chairs, curtains, rugs, paintings, windows—while trees, grass, and sky begin to fill up his house.)

Gnossos

(a public place in ancient Gnossos)

THE PEOPLE OF GNOSSOS:
  Oh muscles! Oh mosses!
  What times we have at Gnossos!

  There are the fadings
  Of ancient suns

  There are the bull baitings, bull leapings, bull acrobatics
  In Gnossos
  Gnossos
  Gnossos the only one
  Yes Gnossos is the only one

  There was a place
  Called Gnossos
  And now we are at that time in that place—Gnossos!
  Oh heavenly Gnossos, grant my prayer!
  Let my deer become a bear!
  Let buds blossom everywhere
  To deck the streets of Gnossos!

  Take your bedclothes to the street
  Dance with everyone you meet
  Put roses there—on the blanket and on sheet
  And sing the songs of Gnossos!

BULL:
  I am a bull and am jumped on here!

PEOPLE OF GNOSSOS:
  Oh clear and graceful Gnossos!

Time and the Sea

(A busy, blue, small Mediterranean harbor, with many small craft, sailboats predominantly, moving about, sometimes gently bumping into each other. These may be represented by people holding masts and sails or other boat-like things, or by actual boats. TOMMY TIME *enters and gestures toward the boats, which stop moving.)*

TOMMY TIME:
    The Mediterranean—I am going to take care of it.

(The scene changes to the Congo River in West Africa. The rather rapidly moving water is crowded with big, lily-like flowers with their stems and leaves and also with Congo residents paddling their pirogues. TOMMY TIME *appears through the thick foliage close to the riverbank. As above, he gestures and everything stops.)*

TOMMY TIME:
    The Congo—I am going to keep it moving.

(The scene changes to the Arctic Ocean. Ice floes, walruses, and polar bears float or roam about. Through a snow hedge TOMMY TIME *appears and stops all movement with a gesture.)*

TOMMY TIME:
    The Arctic Ocean—it is going to be secure in Time.

KUNG HO (A CHINESE SCHOLAR-HISTORIAN):
    Why is Time so interested in bodies of water?

HALICAFARNIENSIS (A BYZANTINE SAGE):
    I don't know. I know only that he is often compared to them—as when men say Time is a river, or Time is like the sea.

Glory, or *The Anthology*

(In a Parnassian environment, poets' names are called by a MUSE-like personage who may be also TEACHER or ANTHOLOGIST, in any case, clearly the one who determines earthly glory. As each poet's name is called, he or she may appear atop a misty hill, then walk down to join the other poets, who may be writing, drinking, conversing—such a heavenly company as might appear in a work of Poussin or of Titian.)

TEACHER, MUSE *or* ANTHOLOGIST:
Guido Gozzano.

GOZZANO:
Presente.

TEACHER:
Sergio Corazzini.

CORAZZINI:
Presente.

TEACHER:
Marino Moretti.

MORETTI:
Presente.

TEACHER:
Fausto Martini.

MARTINI:
Presente.

TEACHER:
Sibila Aleramo.

ALERAMO:
Presente.

TEACHER:
Corrado Govoni.

GOVONI:
Presente.

TEACHER:
Ardengo Soffici.

SOFFICI:
Presente.

TEACHER:
Giovanni Papini.

PAPINI:
Presente.

TEACHER:
Camillo Sbarbaro.

SBARBARO:
Presente.

TEACHER:
Luigi Bartolini.

BARTOLINI:
Presente.

TEACHER:
Giorgio Vigolo.

VIGOLO:
Presente.

TEACHER:
Adriano Grande.

GRANDE:
Presente.

TEACHER:
Carlo Betocchi.

BETOCCHI:
Presente.

TEACHER:
Alfonso Gatto.

GATTO:
Presente.

TEACHER:
Leonardo Sinisgalli.

SINISGALLI:
Presente.

TEACHER:

    Sandro Penna.

PENNA:

    Presente.

TEACHER, MUSE, *or* ANTHOLOGIST:

    Poets of Italy—now, and till the End of Time.

(lightning and thunder)

Ages

JO:
> In China everybody has two ages, a lunar age and a solar age.

FREDDY:
> Does that mean you are one age in the daytime and another age at night?

(fireworks)

JO:
> Yes, in the daytime Ho Lin is fifty-three years old.
> At night he is seventy-nine.

FREDDY:
> What about Ha Chua, the little girl?

JO:
> Ha Chua is eight years old in the morning,
> Ten at noon, eleven in the afternoon,
> And at night she is an incipient beauty of twelve.
> Ho ha, ho ha—

(fireworks)

> In China, everyone has first and second age!

(celebration)

El Nacimiento de Federico García Lorca in Seville

(the white, sun-emblazoned streets of Seville)

MEN OF SEVILLE: *(offstage)*
   In Seville,
   In Seville

WOMEN OF SEVILLE: *(also offstage)*
   Lorca is born.
   Look at Baby Lorca.

(BABY LORCA toddles onstage, falls down, frowns, laughs, gets back up, and speaks.)

BABY LORCA:
   At exactly five o'clock in the afternoon—

MEN *and* WOMEN OF SEVILLE: *(offstage)*
   Oh, already he's starting to talk in verse!

(Now many HORSES—in fact, men and women in old-fashioned theatrical horse costumes—come out to chat with one another in the streets. Their encounters with one another are mild, affable, friendly, as at the hour of the paseo. What is unlike usual conversations, however, is that what everyone—every horse—is saying is a line, or lines, from Lorca's poetry. Each character may choose his own lines and may repeat the same line or lines over and over or go on to new ones. The lines should be spoken softly and firmly, and all the horses should be speaking them at once.)

The Composition of Louise

(A chorus singing the Louise aria "O Folie/Soeur choisie" is heard in the distance. The singing comes nearer as the play goes on.)

ANTROPOS:
I hear that Charpentier is writing Louise.

LE COMTE DE GREUZES:
Where did you hear this? How?

ANTROPOS:
From Love itself!

(EROS appears, in all his splendor.)

EROS:
Yes, it was I who said it. It is true.

(The CHORUS now comes onstage, singing loud and clear.)

The Taps

(CITIZENS *come tap-dancing down the street, behaving in uncontrolled, wild, and lawless ways.*)

CITIZENS:
Tap tap, tap-tap-tap-tap
Tap tap, tap-tap-tap-tap

DIONYSIOS: *(looking at them with great disapproval)*
Oof! What a state the world is in—look at them!
What we need is a Poet
Whose works are full of good, old-fashioned wisdom,
Someone to teach them how to live and act. The best are dead, though—
We'll have to go to Hell to get one back.

XANTHIOS:
How will we get there?

(Enter, with a CORPSE, *a tap-dancing* FUNERAL PROCESSION.)

FUNERAL PROCESSION:
Tap tap-tap-tap, tap-tap tap-tap
Tap tap-tap-tap, tap-tap, tap-tap

DIONYSIOS:
We'll follow that corpse. I'm sure he's headed there.

(They tap-dance after the PROCESSION. *The scene changes to Hades. It's very dark.)*

DIONYSIOS: *(to* DIS, *God of the Underworld)*
O God of this Great Palace,
We need a Poet, and all the best are here.

DIS:
Take any one you like. They're not much good here—always reciting.
(calling) Poets! Eliot! Stevens! Yeats!
There's someone here to see you.

(The POETS *appear.)*

DIONYSIOS:
I want to take one of you back to earth.
But how to decide? Which one? Why don't you each recite
One or two of your verses, and I'll choose.

(Each POET *in turn mounts a little podium and recites.)*

YEATS:

I have coom all this distance, lookin for faeryland.

ELLIOT:

I sometimes wonder if that is what Krishna meant
Among other things—or one way of putting the same thing—

STEVENS:

Chieftain Iffucan of Azcan in caftan
Of tan with henna hackles, halt!

DIONYSIOS:

By God! I'll take all three!

DIS:

Good journey back!

*(*DIONYSIOS, XANTHIOS, YEATS, ELLIOT, *and* STEVENS *climb up out of Hades toward the Earth. At last, a little light begins to show.)*

DIONYSIOS:

Come, Poets, into the day!

(Faint, and then louder and louder sounds of tap-dancing, as CITIZENS *appear to hear them.)*

The Four Atlantics

WOMAN:
There are four Emilies: The Emily of her parents;
The Emily of her childhood friends, who were many;
The Emily of her husband, William; and the Emily of her children—
Rick, her son, and Laura, her daughter.

YOUNG MAN:
There are four suns: the sun of the tropics—of the Caribbean tropical zones,
of Africa, etcetera;
The sun of the temperate countries; the sun of the North;
And the sun of the Planets, which holds the system together.

YOUNG WOMAN:
There are four musics: the heard, the unheard, the composed and the as yet
uncomposed.

MAN: *(speaking with mounting intensity and excitement, as he indicates each of
the Atlantics on a large wall map.)*
And there are four Atlantics:
The transversal Atlantic of England and France;
The Atlantic that ends in Santiago de Chile, of Spain;
Portugal's Atlantic, which begins at the Cape of Good Hope and
ends at the Azores;
And the Atlantic of Middle Ages,
And even of classical times, the narrow winding corridor
That goes from the Strait of Gibraltar to Britain's northmost edge.

The Lost Moment

CHORUS OF MOTHERS WITH INFANTS IN THEIR ARMS:
Babies grow up to be beautiful and passionate women
And handsome and passionate men.

CHRISTINE:
Why didn't you wait for me at the hotel?

EDWARD:
I don't know. Fear, perhaps.

CHORUS OF MOTHERS:
Babies become variable individuals, lead complex lives,
Are prey to contending instincts, and are often deflected by outside things.

CHRISTINE:
I stayed there for an hour.

EDWARD:
I'm sorry. I was there. You were late. You didn't come. I went out.
It was stupid and useless. I tried to come back. But I was blocked by a million
cars.

Transposition—Bell to Europe, from China

(A smoky, antique scene in China. Gongs sound. A PRIEST *takes a gong and gives it to the* CONNECTOR, *who, amid smoke, incense, and gongs, departs. A long time passes.)*

CONNECTOR—*in this case,* BELL CARRIER:
How slowly things come about. . . . This bell, for example,
Which we have been using in China for hundreds and hundreds of years,
Is taking what seems to be forever to carry to the West.
Far easier to lift
A bell to a tower than to get someone to accept it
Whose culture has no use for it. Oh well, the time will come. . . .

*(*CENTURIES *go by, in their characteristic costumes.)*

BELL CARRIER:
Here, what about this bell?

PRIEST:
We have no time for such things here,
Ding-dong, Chinese, and frivolous.

YOUNG DUCHESS:
Why, what would we do with a bell?
He seems a sweet old fellow—but, a bell . . .
What sort of accompaniment to our Dark Age songs
Would that bell be?

LATER PRIEST:
We call our folk to Mass by moderate means and need no bell.
By inner need and known they come to us
And heaven, escape from hell.

CHILD:
Oh, I like this bell.

YOUNG ELEVENTH-CENTURY PRIEST:
Brothers, come see this bell.
Think what a thing it could be, hung above
Our Lady's shrine, its steep stone chapels, there.
And it would call the faithful of the flock
And have a sound divine. Tell me, old man, how can this bell be
    mine?

BELL CARRIER:
  Take it. It's yours.
  Twenty-three hundred years I've carried it
  Waiting till in the West you'd have a use
  For such a thing. More than two thousand years.

(He goes off, and church bells begin to ring all over Europe.)

À La Banque de France

EDMUNDSON:
  Hello. I have these letters of credit
  From the Agence Havas.

BANK OFFICIAL:
  Aren't you . . . could you be . . . Edmundson?

EDMUNDSON:
  Yes, I am he—Count Leo von Edmundson—at your service.

BANK OFFICIAL: *(examines the letters of credit)*
  These seem to me to be firmly backed up by cowries
  As well as by silver and gold. Edmundson, you have at last
    achieved
  Total economic prosperity and financial solidity. My
    congratulations!
  My most sincere felicitations! You have triumphed in the end.

(music)

The Duke of Wellington's Nose

NOSE:

    As the nose of the Duke of Wellington
    I obey the facial proprieties
    Of the lords of the realm.
    But, oh, in my secret fantasies

(Now the NOSE *dances.)*

    I inhale fabulous reeks
    And stenches: pissings, excrement, and the perfumes of brothels.
    Sweat is my secret kick
    And bodily female fluids.
    But as the nose of the Duke I sit up
    Happily on his face as he tells me the news
    Of what has been accomplished so far, and what is left to be done,
    To improve the fate of Britons!

(A piled-high dump cart goes past; the NOSE *sniffs. Then the* DUKE *enters, and the* NOSE *bows and goes to him.)*

In the Storm of Love

CYNTHIA:
Tie me to the bed. Use the rope.

EDWARD:
Oh, I don't want to. It's so sad!

CYNTHIA:
What's so sad?

EDWARD:
That things aren't simple, that we're not as simple
As we used to be, or used to think we'd be—
And sad, too, that tying you with this rope
Will only give a momentary pleasure.

CYNTHIA:
Well, that seems to be quite good to me.

EDWARD:
But—you are a rose.

CYNTHIA:
Then tie me to this fence, and be a bee!

Cook Comes Home

(COOK *is walking in the streets of Chengde, accompanied by a* SECURITY GUARD.)

COOK:
    I have come back to find whatever has been left out
    On these Chengde streets. Member of Party
    Force, for security reasons now, now I have travel so much,
    Force to accompany me. No reason. I go on old street
    Where first Cook I was and carrying giant tureen
    For wear white cap and cook dress to be seen.
    Allaways to wear white, cap to keep off hair,
    White dress to show stain or spot of food when there.
    I am different world from Jai Fu trickster
    He who emprisons King with stage directions
    And say no play two base at same time
    His face comes onto screen
    My memory as if in old play I have seen him.

(JAI FU *appears.*)

    Jai Fu, where have you been?

JAI FU:
    I have been walking, Cook,
    All over China to look for how can city be separate from
    Country you go on train by feet it is always same
    City to country country to city of same name
    And with sky of monument. Tired I sleep in park same
    As bum poor undifferentiate person, though I am
    Jai Fu enormous fame. But it is right that it is so, Cook—New China is new
        game.

COOK:
    Jai Fu we walk together and can discuss much
    How good is writing of some person how of other so pretty is touch
    How beauty come and go how some have fame and so
    Then none. This all forgotten in game of China.

SECURITY GUARD:
    Come, You two talking long enough.

COOK:
    But we don't have to talk to you at all.

JAI FU:

    Begone! Whoof!

(He makes a magical gesture and the SECURITY GUARD *disappears.)*

COOK:

    Let us stop in small peasant hut, Jai Fu,
    To rest ourselves.

JAI FU:

    Yes. And to see what time has done
    To long-life-clutching, endless-long-touching China.

A Mournful Geography

(Two MEN are walking across the top of a mountain range.)

SERGEI PETIKOWSKY:

To grasp the enormousness of Russia, you have to see all the world's popu-
lations could fit within its borders. Although, it's true, they would not find
enough to eat. And another aspect of its enormity: when, at the height of
summer, the daylight lasts, at one end of the country, sixteen hours, at
another it lasts twenty-three.

(Blazing light, then normal daylight; then dark, then bright, then normal again.)

IVAN VESTOV:

Did Russia, too, like enormous China, always desire peace? And did it regard
itself as the center of the world?

(Gunfire is heard faintly in the distance.)

SERGEI PETIKOWSKY:

For some reason, no. At least, I don't think so. The Emperor in Peking
thought the world would come to him—if it wasn't already there. The Russians kept looking.

IVAN VESTOV:

And where did they finally find the world they wanted?

*(SERGEI PETIKOWSKY indicates Siberia with a gesture of his hand. As he does so,
snow begins to fall.)*

SERGEI PETIKOWSKY:

In Siberia, which they sailed to from the Estuary of the Ob—or came to by
overland routes. But—quickly, silence. Here is One who might tell us the
truth about these things.

(Enter the GHOST OF PETER THE GREAT.)

GHOST:

I tried a personal rule. And to end my country's isolation. I had a great
capital built in the middle of nothingness. And nothingness is what it will
all remain.

SERGEI PETIKOWSKY:

Don't be distressed, Ghost. Great Ghost. Did Russia, like China, regard itself
as the center and always wish for peace? Was Siberia "invented" by Russia as
America was by Europe?

GHOST:

No. Nyet. Farewell.

(GHOST *disappears in the mist, and the snow falls more heavily.*)

City Vanguard

(There is a very bright spotlight shining on the center of the stage. The characters go and stand in this light when they speak. It shines directly on their faces, so that the audience has the impression of being spoken to by bright, blazing visages.)

ANN:
  The note has been taken

ROBERT:
  Avant-gardism or no

CATHERINE:
  And of this the most serious issue

DAVID:
  Is whether cerebralism and dehumanization

EDITH:
  Are fundamental to its character—

JANE:
  And, if the answer is yes,

FRANK:
  How will they, joined

ELOISE:
  To arbitrariness and spontaneity

GEORGE:
  Affect people and all things—

GLORIA:
  Is the day less bright if it is made of stone?

(At the end, blazing light whites out everything.)

The Stove of Peace

(Deep in Africa, in a clearing in a village. Center stage is a large earthen stove. M'BAMU *and his sons and daughters keep stuffing things into it; it smokes and smokes.)*

TRAVELER:
   What is that?

M'BAMU:
   The Stove of Peace.
   In it we burn everything that makes war.

(African dances; the stove continues to be fed.)

The End

(Many characters from preceding plays, along with some new characters, come onto a large public square, walk about, and occasionally stop to speak to one another. Toward the end, there is a gradually increasing intensity. This is what the characters say.)

All women become like their mothers. This is their tragedy.
No man does. That's his.

I see, perhaps, in this peculiar turning,
An anti-European movement destined to turn into fanaticism
And find expression in the wildest rage—Sir Robert Hart, French Consul in
　　Cairo.

Before going on, we need, I believe, to insert a long parenthesis
To examine the unused possibilities of the avant-garde.

What good is a play that doesn't even carry us beyond all plays?

You should be careful how long you look into the abyss,
For the abyss is also looking into you.

After a stop in Manila, American silver also crossed the Pacific
And again ended up in China, by this new route.

Yield and overcome;
Bend and be straight;
Empty and be full;
Wear out and be new;
Have little and gain;
Have much and be confused.

What about the voice inside the logic of the supplement?
Within that which should be called the "graphic" of the supplement?

Dixit Lope de Vega, annum sixteen oh seven, in Madrid's Golden Age:
"Todo se ha vuelto tiendes"—
Everything has been transformed into shops.

Dark, unconscious Forces shape our lives.

The soul is born old but grows young. That is the comedy of life.
The body is born young and grows old. That is life's tragedy.

This culminates in a brilliant homogenous group of early Cubist paintings
Executed at Horta de San Juan, in Spain,

> Alongside friends,
> Who, limited and in the minority, yet active and powerful,
> Are characteristic of modern growth.

Can all this change?

(A very bright curtain falls; or bright red, orange, pink, green, and yellow light-beams sweep everyone offstage.)

FILMS

The following ten pieces were written during the 1960s, envisioned as experimental filmscripts. *The Scotty Dog* and *The Apple* were actually made into movies—details can be found at the end of the book in the perfomance notes.

Because

Scene 1

TED *and* SALLY *on a porch overlooking the water in Nice or some other resort. The scene is all yellow and green.*

Scene 2

City, street scene. All purple.
SUBTITLES:
So they moved. In the place where they moved, everything was purple. And they were happy.

Scene 3

Yellow scene. A nursery. Everyone is happy. There are children. Smoking orange and blue SUBTITLE *comes on and says* "END"

The Color Game

The blank screen changes from one solid color to another in the following order: WHITE, GREEN, VIOLET, RED, GREEN, BLUE. *This sequence is kept up as long as desired. Spoken words accompany the colors some of the time: on every fifth occurrence of* WHITE, *the words "The box of Wheaties" are heard; on every second occurrence of* GREEN, *there is laughter; on every third occurrence of blue, one hears the words, "Don't take me off this boat at Corfu—No!"*

Mountains and Electricity

Panorama of mountains.
A voice tells the story of electricity.
At the end of everything becomes dark red.

Sheep Harbor

The scene is a harbor, filled with sheep (not in the water, but occupying all the land area around it). *End.*

Oval Gold

The scene shows a huge golden oval.

A man reads aloud the menu for the day. The oval sways slightly as things it likes are mentioned. *End.*

Moby-Dick

Against a beautiful deep blue background which serves as a fairly narrow frame around it are exposed one by one selected pages of Melville's *Moby-Dick*. There should be music (soft), and the book should sway just the tiniest bit, as if blown by a light and gentle spring breeze. Background changes to orange and yellow. *End.*

L'École normale

Various architectural aspects of an ugly *école normale* are surveyed by the camera while a violin plays something fairly raucous and weeping (perhaps something Russian?). The color of everything is yellow.

The Cemetery

The camera plays on tombs, graves, trees, etc.
A voice says: This is the cemetery.
Then there are jangling sounds of something going wrong with the projector.
The film ends. Inside the theater it should start snowing.

The Scotty Dog

Various scenes of life of my Scotty, Andrew, are shown: he runs about, puts his rubber mouse in his food dish, etc. Meanwhile a text is read, about the construction of the buildings on the Acropolis in Athens. The text should be dramatic and should be accompanied by an approximately rising and dramatic music. *End.*

The Apple

The camera follows an APPLE *as it rolls along the floor of a room, falls down a grating, and ends up rolling along in the snow outside. A* SONG *accompanies the action enthusiastically. This song, for example:*

Here's the apple as it rolls along
The floor—it seems to sing a song,
What's more
It's in danger, the apple is in trouble,
Just a bubble
Of doubt must cross its mind—
Are apples blind?
In any case
As it proceeds to roll along
Over the floor,
Look—it may hit the chair legs, but no more,
We need not fear that, it evades them and goes on—
To hit the table? No!—goes on
Across the slightly not level floor,
But here, alas!
Apple green and white and red
Your head
You may injure—
Oh beware, watch out—
Yes—no—oh, yes—
The apple has fallen in the grate—
Good-bye! But no, it continues to go along,
And now we see it's fallen outside—
Aren't you cold, apple?
In the snow,
And it continues,
Our green and red and white, to go
ROLLING ALONG! *End.*

LIBRETTOS

SCENES FROM *Angelica*

The main characters in the opera are three Spirits, who cause much of what happens in France in the nineteenth century: ANGELICA, *the Spirit of Beauty;* EDOUARD, *the Spirit of Change and Civic Progress; and* JEAN, *the Spirit of Art. At the beginning of the century (also the beginning of the libretto)* ANGELICA *loves* EDOUARD, *but the succeeding years* JEAN *wins her love through the creations of Romantic art and poetry. Desperate to regain her affections,* EDOUARD *searches for a man who can redesign Paris in such a way as to make it irresistible to her. He finally finds* HAUSSMANN, *who, as Prefect of the Seine under Napoleon* III, *was the creator of modern Paris. The scenes included here show Haussmann's successful reconstruction of the city. The scenes are Scene 6 of Act* I *and Scenes 3, 4, and 8 of Act* II. *In the last act (which follows the triumph of* HAUSSMANN), ANGELICA *finds the choice between the creations of the two Spirits impossible to make—for by the end of the 1890s* JEAN *has brought about Impressionist painting and the poetry of Rimbaud and Mallarmé, and* EDOUARD *has changed life on earth by bringing into existence electric power and new means of transportation such as the automobile. Unable to give her love exclusively either to Jean or to* EDOUARD, *despite a prophecy that the world may be destroyed if she fails to choose one of them,* ANGELICA *determines to leave the earth and go to the Kingdoms of the Air, where she will remain until she can make a decision. The opera ends with her departure and with the beginning of the twentieth century.*

The Courtyard of the Sorbonne.

EDOUARD *observing the students who pass by.*

EDOUARD:
>Oh I must find a man to build up Paris—now, help me, great Sorbonne!
>That from your many classes I find one
>Who has the strength of will to do
>What I have got to do:
>Change Paris to a star,
>And so win back Angelica to me!
>And yet I need a special kind of man—
>One not too up-to-date! ...
>Oh always in the past
>Art has all been for the state—
>Like the lovely Parthenon
>Those great statues walk upon—
>The Aeneid: a state purchase;
>The frescoes in a million churches—

Titians brighter than the dawn
In city halls—Need I go on?
But today some strange new consternation
Has brought about a different situation:
Artistic separation!
Poets looking at religion
Where it's fallen like a pigeon,
Recommend instead creation,
Freedom, gloomy bouts with hell,
And a woman's human smell
Mixed with musk and ambergris!
What are such as they to me!
Bards without one moral tenet—
Who could read them to the senate?
Painter wild as waterfalls—
Picture them on courthouse walls!
And all inspired by this proud new spirit
Who took Angelica
And calls himself "Romantic"—I can't endure it!
Oh I still have the power of the grand,
The huge, enormous, simple, overwhelming,
Tremendous, great, self-evident, controlling
Sweet, clean, and pure objective mighty city,
State, and empire, the tremendous beauty
Of the external truth set up by man—
Oh let him walk with Beauty if he can!
Oh let him walk with Beauty for a while—
I'll change the streets in which they pause and smile!
I'll change the buildings that they walk into
And when they exit I'll have changed the view!
I'll tear down places that they love the best
As part of a great stylish movement west—
No more dark streets about the Place Maubert:
I'm going to fill this city with fresh air!
Fresh air and movement, fountains, air and light—
Then Beauty never can escape my sight!
Nor will she wish to—What is greater than
Free space and light? But I must find a MAN!

(*Enter* HAUSSMANN.)

HAUSSMANN:
Farewell, students, friends, farewell!

STUDENTS:
　　Farewell, Georges Eugéne Haussmann!

EDOUARD:
　　It is he!
　　The very man I need—ah, Haussmann! Haussmann!
　　Haussmann, genius, take from me
　　Such immortal energy
　　That this Paris which appears
　　So unchanging where it stand
　　You'll rebuild in nineteen years
　　With your mighty prefect's hands!
　　Take from me the strength, the joy,
　　To construct and to destroy!

HAUSSMANN: *(pausing as he walks)*
　　Ah, into my brains come flooding
　　Visions, mighty change foreboding,
　　Things I shall accomplish when
　　I am Prefect of the Seine.
　　Prefect of the Seine—oh, no!
　　Never so high can Haussmann go!
　　What a strange exotic dream
　　And yet it seemed to me it had a true prophetic gleam!

(HAUSSMANN *starts to walk on, then stops again.*)

　　Yes, I could have sworn that I
　　Saw against the pink-blue sky
　　Of a Paris afternoon
　　An opera house like a balloon,
　　And in front, until the quai,
　　Buildings shoved out of the way
　　Making for the happy few
　　An impressive avenue!
　　And I heard the pleasant roll
　　Of the word "Sebastopol,"
　　As if a boulevard could go
　　In the rain and in the snow
　　From the Seine into the wilderness—
　　Nor did I hear "Boulevard Saint-Michel" less!
　　I heard them all and burn to do
　　What a man has got to do,
　　Make his city fresh and new,

Though half torn down and tunneled through,
Each thing he touches beautiful and new!

(HAUSSMANN *leaves.*)

EDOUARD:
And now to get an autocratic government
So Haussmann can perform his task unbothered—
Away to England! Louis Napoleon's there—we'll see what things shall be!

(*He leaves.*)

Vieux Quartier, street and place. Old building with gargoyles.

EDOUARD:
Oh see where Haussmann comes, see where he comes
To put these projects into execution!
See how he moves as to the sound of drums,
Intent on architectural revolution!
His light militia carry pick and hammer
To rob the city of its old, and give it a new glamor!
See where he comes, see where the baron comes!
Oh he shall win Angelica back
For if she isn't blind
She'll like the breezy Paris he creates!
See where he comes with compass, cranes, and weights!

(*Enter* HAUSSMANN, *with* WORKMEN OF THE SECOND EMPIRE. EDOUARD *leaves.*
WORKMEN *work.* HAUSSMANN *gives orders.*)

HAUSSMANN:
Here, put that building back, it's sticking out
A good three inches farther than the rest!
What do I care if it's the Hotel Vair?
Chop off the front so that it evens up!

GARGOYLES:
Oh, do not chop us off! we ancient statues
Are beautiful and fine and full of meaning!

HAUSSMANN:
What? do these houses sing? Chop off the front!

GARGOYLES:
Oh, do not chop us off! we ancient statues
Are beautiful and firm and full of love!

(Two lovers appear on a balcony.)

GIRL:

I love you, darling! Oh! look what they're doing
To the façade of lovely Hotel Vair!
There is no faith nor truth, not anywhere!

MAN:

Except in these my arms!

GIRL:

But oh look there!

MAN:

Do not look, dear. There is a constancy
Undreamed of by this dull, proud Huguenot!

(They retire from the balcony.)

HAUSSMANN:

I heard you, lovers. Oh, my heart is sick
Sometimes, and I am full of indecisions!
These gargoyles, I suppose, are beautiful,
Although they surely don't appeal to me!
But when I think of Rome and when my nose
Is filled at intersections by fresh air,
At intersections by fresh air,
Oh, then I know what Paris ought to be!

(Enter ANGELICA, *who watches.)*

Paris should be like a star,
Shining near and not afar,
Paris should be like a star!

Every avenue a beam
From the center of a dream—
Every avenue a beam—

Paris should be filled with air,
Interstellar spaces where
Everything is clear as air! *(Enter* JEAN.*)*
Paris!

CROWD OF WORKMEN:

Hurrah! for the new Paris!

HAUSSMANN:
  But now beneath the street I hear
  A sweet music gently clear—
  As I walk, my soul's seduction—
  The gay sound of sewer construction!
  Imperial workmen, to your labor!
  I shall join you somewhat later.
  Here is an entrance—here!

(He descends.)

CROWD:
  Hurrah!

JEAN:
  See how affairs come to a head!
  Haussmann wins the crowd's approval—
  We must work for his removal!
  He is making Paris
  Hideous to see!
  Ignoring all the talent of my artists,
  What does he use for artists?
  Academic Bonapartists!
  Wrecking in a single day
  Our great Ile de la Cité
  Tearing down its ancient alleys
  Narrow and marine as galleys
  With their beautiful buildings, which
  Like great sailboats turn and pitch.
  Oh, repellent day!

ANGELICA:
  Oh, and yet there is
  Excitement in this plan of his
  To make all Paris like a star—
  To shuffle little streets like cards
  And deal them out as boulevards,
  Avenues shining straight and wide
  With a park on every side,
  Brilliant streets which radiate
  At a white and lovely rate
  To Denfert or Passy slim as a bar!
  Woods at Boulogne and Vincennes
  And at Buttes-Chaumont for workingmen,

And underground fresh running streams
To bring sweet odors to sweet dreams—
Oh tell me if there are
More lovely plans than these to change a city?

JEAN:
Well, you only see one side of it—
Let's go!

(*They leave.*)

Sewer with sewer boat.

HAUSSMANN *being rowed along by* OARSMAN.

OARSMAN:
Dee dee dum, dee dee dum, etc.

HAUSSMANN:
Oh as we go sailing down the sewer
Everything seems beautiful and pure,
For this sewer is not used as yet
And in its pleasant oval we forget
As we watch the oarsman's steady arm
Everything but its esthetic charm!

Where else on the planet can be found
Miles of walled-in river underground?
Where can one sail in a boat this way
And never see the light of night or day,
But only feel them, as one feels a love
For things beyond, most certain, pure, above?

Oh may all Paris soon be served by these
New sewers, and may the sweet Paris breeze
Be sweeter for their taking all away
Underground, forever, night and day!
Oh may our sewage problem soon be gone!
May Paris be a star! Oarsman, row on!

Rive Droite: wide avenue, with place.

ANGELICA:
Oh Edouard, it *is* beautiful!
Bois de Boulogne, Champs Elysées . . .

EDOUARD:

    Yes, I knew what you would say—
    For, my love, without your aid
    All this could not have been made!
    Though you had rejected me
    Souls do more than men can see,
    And, although you'd left me, dear,
    I would feel your presence here—
    So that what you see, you are,
    Drenched in brightness like a star.

ANGELICA:

    I was here with you?

EDOUARD:

                     You were.
    See those markets that we built
    And that dome, all iron and gilt,
    Modern art to banish gloom
    From the library reading room—
    Here, the opera; there, you see
    The long Rue de Rivoli;
    There, the Annex to the Louvre
    Round which the *calèches* move . . .

ANGELICA:

    I don't like that addition much.

EDOUARD:

    Well, I did not feel your touch,
    To tell the truth, when we did that.
    Which makes me remember that
    Haussmann, to whom we owe so much,
    Is not with us at this hour!

ANGELICA:

    I heard that he had been dismissed
    From power—

(Enter HAUSSMANN.*)*

HAUSSMANN:

    Alack! thrown down!
    Paris should be like a flower,
    And each petaled avenue—

Ah, sweet prefect, can you sing
When you are losing everything?
When Napoleon, compromising
(Which is not at all surprising)
In order to preserve his crown,
Has agreed to cast you down?
Paris, Paris, was it fated
I'd not be appreciated?
Ah, sweet Prefect, can you sing
When you are losing everything?

EDOUARD:

Haussmann, sing! be glad! rejoice
With a more than human voice!
Haussmann, genius, take from me
Such immortal energy
That even in your darkest hour
You feel the beauty and the power
Of all that you have done. And know
Capitals round the earth shall grow
Upon this model Paris you have made.

HAUSSMANN:

I hear a voice, but I am not afraid.
Rather I feel immortal energy
Flowing from tops of buildings into me!
And how strange that all along
I have hear that same strange song:
"Haussmann, genius, take from me
Such immortal energy"!
What was this inspiration of my hours?
Oh, are we but the pawns of greater powers?

EDOUARD:

And listen, Haussmann!
Mexico City, Stockholm, Chicago,
Madrid, Philadelphia, Barcelona,
Or, more specifically, Paseo de la Reforma
In Mexico City, and in Chicago
Michigan Boulevard and the lake front,
And in Philadelphia
The Benjamin Franklin Parkway, in Cleveland the Mall,
Prefect, your genius will inspire them all!

HAUSSMANN:

  Can it be true?

EDOUARD:

  Cities, appear!

(Enter CITIES and CITIZENS.)

ALL CITIES AND CITIZENS:

  We the cities of the future
  Sing in gratitude to you!

MAN:

  I am an industrialist of Chicago.
  My business was not going very fine,
  Until they built the Lake Shore Drive!
  Oh, Haussmann, dear, you are a friend of mine!

COUPLE:

  We are young and Cleveland lovers
  Who had no place to go at all,
  But now we spend our days together
  Walking up and down the Cleveland Mall!

SECOND MAN:

  I am an adept of Philadelphia
  But we had fewer big streets than them all!
  Oh now we have the Benjamin Franklin Parkway—
  It makes me so excited I could bawl!

ALL THE AMERICANS:

  Hail to you, Haussmann!
  We poor Americans
  Doomed to live in cities that are purely for utility
  Owe a debt of gratitude
  To your lovely attitude
  That great big airy streets and monuments bring life facility.
  Hail to you, Haussmann—
  You've made our evening walks,
  Morning strolls, and noontime talks a joy!
  We much regret your fall,
  Hope that you aren't hurt at all,
  And that you will join us—boy oh boy!
  Gosh, golly, gee, hooray!
  Some evening for a walk upon the Mall!

HAUSSMANN:

Thank you, America. You make my heart beat fast.
Though Paris were torn down, my work should last
In other cities!

EDOUARD:

Paris shall not be
Destroyed until the Beast comes to the Sea.
Let other towns appear!

ROME:

Mi chiamano Roma.
Il Corso io devo a te,
E'i gran rospetti
Fin' a l'eternità!

STOCKHOLM:

Jag talar endast svenska.
Stockholm sono. Swede I am,
The "Venice of the North," but modeled most
On what you've done right here
In Paris!

ALL CITIES:

Oh, Paree!
Every city of the world aspires to be
Like Paree!

MEXICAN MAN:

And I, in Mexico City, spend my days
Admiring the Paseo de la Reforma
And to the mighty Haussmann here give praise!
Olé!

BARCELONA:

I, Barcelona, add the word "*Olé!*"

ALL CITIES AND CITIZENS:

Olé! Olé!
For Haussmann, who has made a holiday
Of streets and parks that last us through the year
Where there before was naught, was naught
But weekday workday streets all drab and drear!
Olé! Olé!
For the city as a holiday
Of fresh spring air and prospects bright and clear!

EDOUARD:

    Cities, disperse! Haussmann, you see
    What your future fame shall be.

(CITIES *and* CITIZENS *leave.*)

    For helping me, this is your prize:
    To live forever in men's eyes!
    You have brought Beauty back to me and Paris!

HAUSSMANN:

    Oh, our accomplishments shall never know an ending!
    What do I care that they criticized my spending?
    This vision of the future by this chorus
    Makes me aware that the whole world is for us,
    And, though my day is over, think of all
    The avenues that beauty will cut through—
    Think of the grandiose, divine
    Designs like mine,
    All spacious, grand, and new,
    So grand and new!

EDOUARD:

    Farewell, thou princely prefect, oh farewell!
    You fell from power—yet, famous ere you fell,
    Your fame shall last forever!

HAUSSMANN:

    Oh, farewell!

(HAUSSMANN *leaves,*)

ANGELICA:

    Oh, due to you all Paris arrayed
    In housefronts and fresh air—and inspiration
    To all the other cities in the world!
    I love the Avenue Marceau—

EDOUARD:

    And you will love the Ligne de Sceaux
    When it goes underground!
    For Paris has not ceased to change:
    A railroad underground seems strange,
    But it shall come to pass—
    And still the Seine shall shine as bright as glass!
    An Eiffel Tower shall ascend

Above the Champ de Mars,
And Frenchmen visiting a love or friend
Will move about these streets in little cars;
A Statue of Liberty will be placed
By the Allée des Cygnes, which does not exist,
But some morning waking, an early walk taking,
You'll notice it there in the mist, in the mist, in the beautiful bright Paris
    mist!
And Haussmann's widened Elysées
Now so elegant and gray
Shall on some not-too-distant night
Be whitened with soft cinematic light!
Oh, Paris owes
Its look of a dew-wet, fresh, well-lighted rose,
Angelica, to your uncertainty.
Haussmann built it all
To bring you back to me!

JEAN: *(offstage, from a distance)*
    Angelica. . . . !

A Change of Hearts

OPERA IN ONE ACT

CAST OF CHARACTERS

BILLY, Leader of a Student Rebellion   Tenor
LINDY, His Girlfriend   Soprano
DIDMORE, President of the University   Baritone
BARRATAG HARMEG, A Great Heart Surgeon   Basso

MORGUE ATTENDANT, STUDENT PROTESTERS, STUDENT COUNTERDEMONSTRATORS.

(The action takes place in the present.)

Scene 1

The university campus. PRESIDENT DITMORE *on a balcony, facing a mass of student protesters.*

STUDENTS:
> We'll change the university around!
> Ditmore, give in!

DITMORE:
> Your plan's unsound! it's too buffoonish,
> Radical, juvenile, and foolish!
> You can't change the universities around!
> Not this one!

BILLY: *(to* DITMORE*)*
> President Ditmore,
> We'll have our way!

(to LINDY*)*

> Oh Lindy, Lindy, this is the moment we all
> Have been waiting for!
> Ditmore's surrounded, he'll have to give in,
> And, sooner or later, we'll win!
> We'll have a new university
> Mighty and shining like stars!

LINDY:
> And this university's ours!
> Oh Billy, what greatness! I feel
> That nothing but this and our love are real!

DITMORE:
So stop, students, or else
By violent means—

COUNTERDEMONSTRATORS: *(who are standing behind the protesters)*
Yay!

DITMORE:
By violent means—so, change
Or else—
Aghhhhhhhh—

*(*DITMORE *falls, stricken by a heart attack.)*

STUDENTS:
What is it? Stand back! He's had
A heart attack!

BARRATAG HARMEG: *(pushing through the crowd)*
Make way! I am a doctor!

STUDENT:
And what a doctor!

OTHER STUDENT:
Who?

STUDENT:
Barratag Harmeg, the greatest
Heart doctor in the world.

COUNTERDEMONSTRATORS:
Murder those revolutionary phonies!

(They start throwing stones.)

BILLY:
Watch out!

(He turns around to face the COUNTERDEMONSTRATORS *and is hit over the head by a stone they have thrown. He falls.)*
Oh Lindy Lindy—

LINDY:
Billy! He's . . .

BILLY:
All that we planned
To do . . .

(BILLY *dies.*)

LINDY:
He's . . . Billy . . . dead. . . .

BARRATAG HARMEG:
Ah morning sky!
But I
Barratag Harmeg, I
Will bring them back to life!

Scene 2

An Operating Room. BARRATAG HARMEG, *standing, in surgical attire. Lying on two operating tables placed close together are* DITMORE *and* BILLY.

BARRATAG HARMEG:
Have brought them back to life!

DITMORE: *(waking up)*
Lindy Lindy—
All that we planned
To do . . .

BILLY: *(waking up)*
So stop, students, or else
By violent means
So change or else—

LINDY: *(she is outside, in the corridor)*
Billy!

BARRATAG HARMEG
They've changed!
Inside, into each other!
Well, they must not know—
It's best that way.

Scene 3

The Campus.

LINDY:
The days flit by
Two weeks have gone by
Since Billy was brought back to life

By that genius, Dr. Harmeg—
He brought Billy back to life
And I love Billy so!
Does he love me? He seems
So changed. . . .

(BILLY *enters, and* LINDY *goes up to him and takes his arm.*)

Billy! Billy!

BILLY: *(drawing back)*
Young lady, frankly
Your conduct takes me by surprise!

LINDY:
Billy, stop your joking—really!

BILLY:
Do not mock me, Lindy;
I have serious work to do.

(He leaves.)

LINDY:
Oh, despair!
Could it be possible that what
The doctor did was change—their hearts?
But still—
I'll see what Ditmore's feeling—
He's done great things of late!

(LINDY *goes off to* DITMORE's *office.*)

Scene 4
President Ditmore's Office.

LINDY: *(entering, a little breathlessly)*
President Ditmore!

LINDY: *(rising from his chair)*
Lindy! Lindy!
Ah I leave my cares of office—
Work and fame, all, all but surface—
Lindy, for your charms!
Oh move into my arms!

LINDY:

President Ditmore!
We hardly know each other!
You're old enough to be my father!

DITMORE:

Yes, I know, but Destiny
Has brought you to my arms!
Oh that we were birds that fly
Ageless in the evening sky
Or in the sky of dawn!
Why must we be bound by ages
When in heart there heavenly rages
Love which does abound?
Let arms or wings wrap around
That which it presages—
Lindy, in this case, it's
You!

LINDY:

But Dr. Ditmore, stay awhile,
I need a little time!
Billy is my love—true, lately he
Ignores me . . . still—
I love him still. But what
Oh tell me what
Has brought about this change?
You who once were so reactionary
Now change the university around
As if it were some youthful paradise,
Heaven on the trustees' ground!
Billy, meanwhile, who was once
Rebellious, now like a great dunce
Espouses old reactionary causes.
Well, all this causes
Me wonderment and pain.
Why cannot Billy be himself again?

DITMORE:

Come to my arms
And I will tell you.

LINDY:

I'll come to this armchair—no further. Now, tell on.

DITMORE:
Well, what I think is—Aghhhhhhh—

(He falls, stricken by a heart attack.)

LINDY: *(rushes to Ditmore's telephone and begins to dial)*
I must get help! One one oh one—
For President Ditmore! help!
He's fainted—fallen—well, I don't know what—
His doctor—Barratag Harmeg is his name—
Yes, quickly!

(BARRATAG HARMEG arrives at once.)

BARRATAG HARMEG:
I arrive, dear, quickly!
Ditmore! Ditmore! Oh, again
He's had a bad attack!
Go get Billy back! Find Billy, Billy—

(LINDY goes out and comes back.)

LINDY:
Billy's gone to Philadelphia,
Won't be back for several days.

BARRATAG HARMEG:
We must find another heart, then.
To the morgue, without delays!

Scene 5

The Morgue.

MORGUE ATTENDANT: *(showing a body)*
This young man killed in an accident—

BARRATAG HARMEG:
I'll take him! Sold! My card.

MORGUE ATTENDANT:
Barratag Harmeg!

BARRATAG HARMEG
Yes, the original one!

(The body is prepared for removal.)

Scene 6

The Operating Room. BARRATAG HARMEG *is operating.*

BARRATAG HARMEG:
    Ah, in my work of changing
    Hearts my thoughts go ever ranging
    To my simple childhood that
    Centered 'round a dog and cat.
    Why am I so interested
    In changing one thing to another?
    Famous I've become for it,
    Hearts are my great specialty—
    I have found a way to change
    Hearts of persons dead or dying
    So they wake up fine and healthy
    Sometimes, like a baby, crying.
    What I've not as yet worked out
    That which causes me some doubt
    Are those characteristics that
    Like a favorite tie or hat
    Sometimes accompany the heart
    From one chest to another!
    So in placing Ditmore's heart
    In Billy's breast I made him a
    Conservative unloving upstart;
    Ditmore on the other hand
    Became a young hot-blooded radical
    When infused with the life particle
    Billy gave to him!
    What now will happen
    With this unknown young heart I can't imagine!
    Let's hope this is no monster
    For Ditmore has important work to sponsor!
    As President, since he's had Billy's heart
    He's made the university a place
    Full of compassion for the human race
    And full of love and laughter.
    I fear what may come after.

(He finishes the operation.)

    Well, that's that!
    He has this new man's heart. Pray he be well.

Scene 7

President Ditmore's Office.

STUDENT:
   President Ditmore!

DITMORE:
   Yes, I command you to tell Billy that
   He must come here and give me back my heart!
   The one I have inside me drives me crazy:
   Whether I'm up or down, I feel completely dizzy.
   Boy, have you got that straight?

STUDENT: *(aside)*
   Ditmore has lost his mind!

Scene 8

The Campus.

LINDY:
   Billy, President Ditmore's sending out
   Secret spies to seek you out
   And trap you, take you to his lair
   And make you give him back his first heart there!

BILLY:
   That radical phony!

LINDY:
   No, you don't understand. Ditmore has had
   Another heart attack, and Barratag
   Harmeg transferred to his chest
   Someone else's heart, a maddened criminal's it seems—

(DITMORE enters, completely naked, running across the campus.)

STUDENTS:
   Hurrah! Hurrah!

LINDY:
   Look, Billy!

DITMORE: *(shouting as he runs)*
   Rah! Ditmore invented steam!
   I shall bathe in every stream!

BILLY:

    The man's completely naked!

LINDY:

    He's insane!
    Billy, don't you see it now?
    He's crazy!

BILLY:

    Yes. I'll hide. I see you're right.
    He does seem crazy!
    But, oh Lindy, Lindy. . . .

LINDY:

    Yes, Billy, what?

BILLY:

    If Ditmore now has a new heart
    Then where is mine, my own original heart?

LINDY:

    It failed in him, I think it's dead—

BILLY:

    I must go and find out!

LINDY: *(aside)*

    Perhaps this will bring Billy
    Back to me. *(To* BILLY*)* I'll help you—quickly!

Scene 9

The Office of BARRATAG HARMEG.

LINDY:

    Dr. Harmeg, do you remember
    What did you do with Billy's heart?

BARRATAG HARMEG

    Ah, Lindy! Billy! Lord,
    In the confusion
    I quite forgot about
    Your quite legitimate concern with that,
    But never fear!
    I've sent your heart to Paris, Billy,
    To a special laboratory there

And there they specialize in heart repair—
Miraculous infusions,
Surgeries beyond compare,
In that Paris clinic, there!
There lies the only chance
That you will have your heart back, Billy,
You, Lindy, your old romance!

BILLY:
And what chance of it there?

BARRATAG HARMEG:
Good chance, at least
Fifty percent—but . . . Billy—

BILLY:
Yes?

BARRATAG HARMEG:
If you went there, it MIGHT help them to judge
Some things about your earlier heart, just MIGHT.
It's a discovery I've been working on. And now I think it might!

BILLY:
Fine! I'll go there!
I feel too strange without my own old heart!
Will you come, Lindy?

BARRATAG HARMEG:
She is needed here.

Scene 10

Airport.

BILLY: *(getting on the plane)*
Farewell, Lindy!
I'm off to Paris!

LINDY:
Farewell! farewell!

BARRATAG HARMEG:
Godspeed!

(The plane flies off.)

LINDY:

Fly well!

BARRATAG HARMEG:

Be well

LINDY:

And come back soon!

Scene 11

The Office of BARRATAG HARMEG.

BARRATAG HARMEG:

Lindy the reason I needed you here
Is to try to help Ditmore, who, it is clear,
Is insane, from his new-transferred heart.
I think if he gets the sight of you
And can enjoy a little the company of you
He may come out of it, so be true
To his former self, which was Billy's.

LINDY:

But why not his earliest?

BARRATAG HARMEG:

That is impossible! Later, if Billy
Can get his own heart
Back, we can take Ditmore's
Into his chest direct;
But before that, no. One can only "physically remember"
One heart personality back!

LINDY:

But what of his loving attack
On me?

BARRATAG HARMEG:

You'll have to bear that
And manage it, for mankind's sake.

LINDY:

And if I refuse?

BARRATAG HARMEG:

Lindy, Lindy, men's lives are at stake,
The university, that is at stake—
But it's up to you.

LINDY:

    I'll do it!
    I have a little pill
    To calm him down if he does ill.

Scene 12

Ditmore's Office.

DITMORE: *(very agitated at seeing* LINDY*)*

    Hah! a beautiful student!
    But—a STUDENT! in my office! Out of here! Out of here!
    I am crazy! I am an ape, a gorilla! ugh! ugh! here!

(He starts to climb all over the desk.)

    I'll climb you a tree, ugh, here. . . .

LINDY:

    Oh, poor man!

DITMORE: *(coming to his senses a bit)*

    You are . . . Lindy . . .
    Yes . . . I remember someone like that
    Before I . . . ack ackak blab! glog!
    Before . . . agh!
    They changed my heart. . . .
    Oh, Lindy! Ack! blab! Grrr!

(Relapsing into mad fury, DITMORE *attacks* LINDY*.)*

Scene 13

A street, outside Harmeg's Clinic.

BILLY:

    Lindy is dead
    Of a heart attack
    Brought on by fear
    At Ditmore's attack.
    Ditmore has recovered
    His earlier self
    In his grief
    Over his belovèd Lindy.
    And I back
    From Paris

With my
New heart—or, rather, my old one. . . .
I'LL GIVE IT TO LINDY!
I love her, like that!
Harmeg, you owe it to both of us,
You've shamefully played with our lives—
Even the greatest of artists have no right to meddle
In other people's lives!

BARRATAG HARMEG:
True, too true.
All right, bring Lindy
Here, into my clinic. And you come too.

BILLY:
Oh, Harmeg, can you really give her life?

BARRATAG HARMEG:
Yes! *(Aside.)* And to you, too!

Scene 14

The Operating Room. LINDY, *and* BILLY, *unconscious, on operating tables.*
HARMEG *standing, in surgical attire, with surgical equipment.*

BARRATAG HARMEG:
A strange unknown fact
Is that the body has consciousness
And can perfectly well act
Out a routine performance,
One it has already done,
For eight long minutes after the fact of death.
I'm risking all on this one
Certainty!

(He tenses his body.)

Now! Billy's heart remains
In Billy! and

(HARMEG rips out his own heart and places it in LINDY's chest.)

Agagagagagak!
MY heart is in Lindy!
Oh farewell, Medicine, farewell
Sweet science! you have served me all too well!

Making me more than man, you made me monster—
But in this last, unfated act I am master:
For I give my heart for hers
Whose heart I took
When first I changed her love!
Farewell, proud tack
Of conscience! Oh, be satiate now!

(HARMEG *falls dead.*)

LINDY: *(waking up, alive now, seeing* BILLY*)*
    Billy!

BILLY: *(also reviving)*
    My love! Oh, Lindy, you're alive!

(BILLY *and* LINDY *get down from the operating tables, and* BILLY *starts to embrace* LINDY, *who rebuffs him.*)

LINDY:
    I must get to my studies, my laboratory—
    No time for love now, Billy. We live only once—

(LINDY *sees* HARMEG's *fallen body. She also notices a heart—actually it was formerly her own—lying on a table.*)

    What's this great subject for a heart exchange?
    Harmeg, the famous surgeon! I'll give him this one!
    A girl's heart, seeming—it will do him fine!

(*She puts her old heart in* HARMEG.)

BARRATAG HARMEG: *(reviving)*
    I wake. . . . No. . . . Is this life?

LINDY:
    Harmeg, you have come back to life—
    I gave you the heart of a girl
    Which I found here.

BARRATAG HARMEG:
    It's your heart, Lindy!
    Oh, Lindy, Lindy, now you shall be my wife!

(LINDY *and* HARMEG *embrace.*)

BILLY:
    And I shall back to radical politics go

Where things are more consistent, if not perfect—
So, Love, farewell!

HARMEG: *(as he and* LINDY *end their embrace)*
I don't know what I feel!

LINDY:
Neither do I!

(DITMORE *comes in.)*

DITMORE:
And I shall join you, for God knows whose heart
Is in my breast!

LINDY:
Or mine!

BARRATAG HARMEG: *(to the audience)*
Or yours! or yours!

BILLY:
Well, then, let's go!

LINDY, BILLY, BARRATAG HARMEG, and DITMORE:
May we soon better know what we are doing,
Meanwhile pursuing
Our projects at the university so
That social studies, sciences, and arts
May profit from this Change of Hearts.

FINAL CURTAIN

The Construction of Boston

This play in 1962 was a collaboration with three artists: Niki de Saint Phalle, Robert Rauschenberg, and Jean Tinguely. Once the construction of a city was decided on as a subject, Rauschenberg chose to bring people and weather to Boston; Tinguely, architecture; and Niki de Saint Phalle, art. The people Rauschenberg brought to Boston were a young man and woman who set up housekeeping on the right side of the stage. For weather, Rauschenberg furnished a rain machine. Tinguely rented a ton of gray sandstone bricks for the play, and from the time of his first appearance he was occupied with the task of wheeling in bricks and building a wall with them across the proscenium. By the end of the play the wall was seven feet high and completely hid the stage from the audience. Niki de Saint Phalle brought art to Boston as follows: she entered, with three soldiers, from the audience, and once on stage shot a rifle at a white plaster copy of the Venus de Milo which caused it to bleed paint of different colors. A cannon was also fired but did not go off. Niki de Saint Phalle and Tinguely had doubles who spoke or sang their lines; Rauschenberg's lines were not spoken at all but were projected, at the appropriate times, on a screen.

NOTE: This version is the opera version from 1966, which includes a prologue written by Koch specifically for the Scott Wheeler opera. After the opening dialogue, SAM and HENRY become the CHORUS and as such speak for a number of different personae. In the Maidman Playhouse production the two speakers alternated frequently—at the beginning of speeches, when there was a break in the course of a long speech, and usually at the beginning and end of quoted passages inside speeches—such as, for example, the statement by Beacon Hill in the first CHORUS speech.

A Prologue (1996)

THE OPERA:
    I am the Opera here to explain myself.
    Operas don't usually do this, but it seemed a good idea.
    The best understanding of a work is always to be gotten
        from the work
    Itself, so I have come out here on stage, personified,
        to give it to you.
    Most operas have a theme of love or vengeance
    But my theme is the construction of a city—
    The earth's best city perhaps—at least the coldest
    And the darkest at some moments of the year
    Which is, you've guessed it from my title, Boston.

Boston! the very word is like the bell
Of Old South Church that clangs in Copley Square!

Tonight, you'll see the city put together
As it was put together once before,
Not as in history it was, but as
It was on stage in 1962,
In New York, near where Forty-Second Street
Heads for the Hudson River.
A poet wrote the script.
Three artists built the town, and will tonight.
First Rauschenberg,
Who brings the city people and gives it weather;
Then Tinguely, who brings Boston architecture,
Streets, buildings, docks and landfill, all its shape
Finally, there is Niki de Saint Phalle
Who brings to Boston art, and beauty
With a magic pistol that she fires.
All this you'll see on stage; you'll see the city
Built by three artists in about an hour,
Which is not quite how it was built before
Then it was gradual, slower, and involved
So many complicated processes
That if you wished to see it thus again
You'd have to sit here for three hundred years.
I, and my artists, do it faster; this
Is true to our imaginings, as stars
Look small from where we are. One looks at things
As if they had just now been put together. When you see
A dazzling man or awe-inspiring woman
You don't say, Let me figure out what mixture
Of chemicals there must have been to make
That nose so beautiful, etcetera. Instead you think
Zowie! My God! Where did that beauty come from?
Are those eyes from the sea? And whence that hair?
What rainbow put the push to that complexion?
And what great compass made those shoulders square?

As William Blake, when looking at a Tyger,
Did not consult texts in zoology, but cried instead
"Where did you get those eyes, that heart, that head?"
Or "Who could dare to make you, tyger, so?"

This is how I see Boston.
Though later one may look to history books
To try to get some clue as to what happened,
One's first impulse is, mine at any rate,
To cry out, as at woman, man, or tyger,
"Boston! who put the dark in you, and light?
What slammed the buildings down, who made the sight
Of Beacon Hill so bending and so bright
When the sun rises? Place, where did you come from?
Did He who made Aix en Provence make thee?"
The answer is what you are going to see.
See me, the Opera, and in seeing me,
See Boston, see three artists build it up.
Inspired to madness by my harmony.

Two present-day Bostonians, Sam and Henry,
Are walking through and marveling at Boston,
At what it is and how it was before.
When suddenly—well, you will see what happens—
Thunder and darkness—Boston disappears.
Its dark, its stone, its noise, its freezing weather;
Its smoke, its people coming from all over;
You see it rise and hover
Then settle into place before your eyes
So quickly that you may not realize
You had been longing for it like a lover.

Now I begin!

(The scene is modern Boston. Backdrop of Boston buildings.)

HENRY:
Hello Sam.

SAM:
Hello Henry.
See where Boston stands so fair
And cruel. Have you ever thought
Once there was nothing there?

HENRY:
I never thought of that!
You mean there was mere space?
No Milk Street, S.S. Pierce, and no South End?
No place where the postman walks, no bend

To turn toward Needham, waiting for one's date
Or for one's fate, no building to sit in?

SAM:

Well—even more—before the first man came to pass
This site and called it "Boston," there was nothing—
Merely grass and sea: three high hills called Trimountain:
Beacon, Pemberton, Vernon,
And the salt sea—wallahhah!
And the cove.

HENRY:

And were there nymphs
Inhabiting this grove?
And demigods, and other treasure trove
Of ancient days?

SAM:

There were. They built this city.
Not ancient Botticelli
No sky-inspired Bellini
Ever trembled to
A sight more beautiful
Than Boston in her ancient days
And during her creation!
They say men came then who were more than men,
Who from one market reared a whole town up,
Made urban weather to give urban dreams
Built high brick walls where once there flowed fresh streams.

HENRY:
Ah, fair to tell!

SAM:
Yet none were satisfied
Until one greater Spirit came, who changed
What they had done and made it beautiful.

HENRY:
What kind of Spirit?

SAM:
A woman—

HENRY:
Beautiful?

SAM:

Incredibly so—But

HENRY:

What is happening?

SAM:

But now I feel faint

HENRY:

Everything is growing dark

A VOICE:

You speak of one men are not fit to know;
Such knowledge is not fit for mortal tongue.
Therefore this darkness. All must come again
As it has come before. You have undone
Three hundred years of building by your chatter
Of sacred things. This darkness signifies
Your crime; and your purgation shall be this:
You must see Boston built again
Just as it was before—perhaps, though, faster.
Oh tremble, mortals! Now, let there be nothing
But grass, Trimountain, and the answering sea!

(total darkness)

(Lights go on. Boston has vanished.)

CHORUS:

How strange! What freshness steals across my brow!
Delightful breezes, song of twittering birds,
And the faint smell of grass mixed with the spray.
See where the hawthorn blossoms, and the rose!
Ah in this wilderness let me remain
Forever! Here man's heart and brain find peace!
The year is 1630, peaceful year!
How lovely it is here!
And even nature seems to sing in joy!
Huge Beacon Hill cries out in gusty tones,
"How happy I am now, fat as a cow
And higher than a treetop's loftiest bough—
I'm made of mud and gravel
And squirrels up and down me travel
Which gladly I allow."

The light-blue summer day
Reflected in Back Bay   (*Enter* RAUSCHENBERG.)
Shines like an eye—but stop—who comes here now?
Who is he? oh, what kind of man is he?
This seems to me no man, but more than man!
Hail, Populator. . . .
What shall you to this barren coastland do?

RAUSCHENBERG:
  Bring people!
  And manufacture weather for the people.

CHORUS:
  He hopes to have a city here—
  At least a little town—that's clear—
  Or else why bring the people down?

RAUSCHENBERG:
  That's clear. Here!

(RAUSCHENBERG *brings people.*)

CHORUS:
  He's bringing people.

RAUSCHENBERG:
  And weather too.

CHORUS:
  There is already weather.

RAUSCHENBERG:
  I'm bringing more. Cities need different weather than the country.
  Otherwise why would people go to the country? I'm bringing city weather
    here. I need it for the city.

CHORUS:
  Dark afternoons in autumn he
  Brings to Boston peerlessly
  And in winter with the hush
  Of evening, miles of snow and slush!
  Springtime warmth, exploding late,
  Daisies 'mid the fish and freight;
  Sultry summer afternoons
  To make the Boston citizens
  Dressed in high style, dressed to the tens,

Uncomfortable as baboons—
Oh where has our lovely climate gone?
Ah Rauschenberg, have mercy!
Yet it's lovely,
And seems just right for Boston, I'll admit.
I'd almost swear that I can hear
The weather speaking as he brings it here
To be a part of Boston—
There is a deep gruff voice: "I am the storm!
I have a lovely loud mellifluous form
When I'm alone. Ah, but in the city
Bumped against the fire escape,
Mailbox and wall, I lose my shape,
And lightning rods poke into me—
Oh let me be a storm at sea!"
"No, no," says Rauschenberg.
And now we hear the summer noon
Whose voice is rather like a croon:
"Ah in the country let me be!
Tall buildings are the death of me!
They block my light and make me black
And humid: sweat runs down my back!"
But Rauschenberg says, "Noon, march on."
And we hear the summer dawn
Complaining now to Rauschenberg:
"Bob, this transfer is absurd!
In the country redbirds sing
When they see me: everything
Cries aloud for joy! But here amid
The stench of fish and people
Black roadway and black steeple
What function can I serve? I like to please."

RAUSCHENBERG:
   You shall, my tease,
   My love, my delectation!
   When you come
   The city's heart shall, like a muffled drum,
   Begin to beat, and as you go you'll see
   Proffered to you constantly
   Every single business day
   A great urban-souled bouquet

Of people and their actions!

CHORUS:

That sounds fine! And now he brings divine
And holy moonlight, which says, "I
Am interrupted here," but Rauschenberg replies:
"So by your interruption shall you shine
More brilliantly and wake a million dreams
Instead of one: besides which, we need moonlight in the city."

RAUSCHENBERG:

And now I have to stock
The city up with people!

PEOPLE: (*spoken by* CHORUS)

We are Irish, we're Italian,
We are British, why has he
Brought us here to stock this city
As if it were an aquarium,
As if we were human fish?

CHORUS:

Every city needs some people,
And a racial mixture functions
Very nicely in America.
You should be glad to be together—
Very exciting things will happen!
Ah I can hardly restrain myself
From singing praise to Rauschenberg
When I see this racial mixture
How enthralling! How exciting!
And, in the harbor, fish are biting!

RAUSCHENBERG:

Now I think I've done—

CHORUS:

All hail, great Rauschenberg!

RAUSCHENBERG:

And yet there's only one

CHORUS:

All hail to you!

RAUSCHENBERG:

Thing wrong. We have the weather and the people,
But they, the people, have no way to get
Out of the weather or back into it.
We need some BUILDINGS!

CHORUS:

Tinguely, spirit of the air,
Now descend, and kill despair!
Aid us with your mighty hands
Molding earth to your commands!
O spirit, come!

(TINGUELY *appears*.)

TINGUELY:

I am
Arrivèd!
Ah! what a lovely layout you have here!
What varied weather and what varied people!
What lovely mountains and what snappy sea!
I'll do it, Rauschenberg, for it inspires me!
Oh it sends great create-
Ive tremors all through me!

CHORUS:

All hail to Tinguely! We need houses to live in.

TINGUELY:

Peace, citizens—that's where I'll begin,
Quite naturally.

CHORUS:

Tinguely, we need public buildings.

TINGUELY:

Certainly! And ones with gildings—
That's my next endeavor!

CHORUS:

I have never
Seen such immense intense inflamed construction!
Oh like the beaver speeded at his work
Is Tinguely the great architectural Turk!
See how he functions! ah! ah!

TINGUELY:

But now we need more space!
How shall I solve this problem, tell,
For now we need more space!
Ha! Ha! I've got it! Now!

CHORUS:

Help, help!
My God, Tinguely, what are you doing? What are you trying to do? What are
   you going to do?

TINGUELY:

The city needs more land area. Thus I am going to fill the Mill Pond with
the top of Beacon Hill. Two, I am going to fill the Back Bay with sand, from
Needham, Mass. Thirdly, I am going to extend Boston out into the harbor
by means of docks.

CHORUS:

O brave ambition!
And see how he proceeds,
Ah mighty Tinguely!
Yet hear that cry
From Beacon Hill, which rends the sky,
"Oh do not dig me, Tinguely!
Oh Tinguely, leave me be!"
But he remorselessly
Goes digging on; and now he fills the Pond,
Which merely gasps, and now he smiles
To see poor Beacon Hill reduced by miles,
And now he turns another way
And contemplates the old Back Bay
And starts to fill it too.
At which the old Bay cries as to the skies:

"Boston, all that I can say
Is, it's grand to be a bay!
First you're full and then you're empty,
Then your friends go to the country—
They come back and fill you in:
All shall be as it has been.
Fill me up with sand and gravel,
No more boats across me travel—
And my chest where children play
Is black by night and brown by day.

Now I feel the buildings rising
Filled with chairs and advertising
Where was once a boat capsizing,
Splashes, and a frightened brow—
There is nothing like that now!
Oh the buildings are so heavy—
How they weigh me down!"

Now you're the *town,*
Back Bay—you mustn't complain!
It's wonderful to be a part
Of an existent urban heart
Where on hot summer days
The heat sings its own praise
By sheer cement!

"I know that true—
And I knew what you meant
Before you said it; still, my dear, do you
Know what it's like to feel upon your body
A seven-story home where there was only foam
Before? What used to be my shore
Ca ne l'est plus encore!"

TINGUELY:

Back Bay, you're lucky. You and Mill Pond are.
I am going to put
Sumptuous buildings on you that
Will make you lovely as a star.

CHORUS:

What? More?
What? More?

TINGUELY:

Come buildings, ah my airy darlings, come!

CHORUS:

They say he is a man, and yet he looks
Much like a woman to me. Yet he builds
Extremely like a man! They say his beard
Betrays his male identity, and yet—
And yet his skirt suggests he is a woman!
Perhaps this is an artist who combines
The sensitivity and strength of both

And is a whole man, such as Hesiod sung!
Oh man or woman, he can surely put
The buildings up! that noise of bumping fills
The atmosphere! and feel that weight upon us!

TINGUELY:
Now! now! I've done it! they are part of it!
Now to the seaside to fill in the sea!

CHORUS:
Fairest Tinguely, we the wharfs,
Splintery helpless wooden dwarfs,
Make appeal to you:
We love the water.
And if you'd be our friend, great building man,
O build us into her, thus let our natures
Sink down in her, oh let us fill the harbor
Till Boston's two times Boston's present size.

TINGUELY:
Sweet wharfs, I'm glad to see you are in love;
Your plan is just what I was thinking of.
Yes it's exactly what I thought about—
O bump bump bump throughout
The cove and harbor spread you out
Until we have a coastline that's in fact
A kind of wood and water pact,
A marriage of the forest to the sea!

CHORUS *as* WATER:
What do I feel sink into me?

CHORUS *as* WHARFS:
It's only we, dear harbor—
Oh sweetheart, sister, mother!

CHORUS *as* WATER:
O close-clutched ecstasy!

TINGUELY:
Well, wharf and water seem well satisfied—
I hope the city will be too. Now what have I to do
But plant a few more buildings here
And then rush back to Scollay Square
And, after, glance about

To see what things I have left out—
Ah, Commonwealth Avenue!
I must make you, and then I've finished!

CHORUS:
See how the smiling city takes its shape:
Fair Scollay shining like a stem of grape;
And Beacon Hill, though cut into,
Still like an orange to the view
Of one who sees it from Longfellow Bridge!
O Tinguely, Rauschenberg, it's fine
And yet I can't help feeling
Something sublime is gone: pure nature—roses; sparrows singing; redbird;
bluejay; twit-twit-twitter-twee!
It seems such a short time ago we had that here!
O tell me, how can we get back what's gone?
I miss the fresh air and the lovely feeling!

RAUSCHENBERG:
Don't you like cities? It's
A fine time to ask me,
A fine time to bring *that* up!
Why Tinguely is already underground
                                        (thump thump)
Building the subway, and you ask me how
To get back bubbling brooks?

CHORUS:
You don't know how?

(Enter NIKI.)

NIKI: *(sings)*
Well, I know how!
What this town needs is beauty, what Boston needs is art!
Let every heart rejoice,
Rejoice in every part
Of Boston!

(TINGUELY emerges from the subway.)

TINGUELY:
Well, the subway is finished.

NIKI:
But Boston is not quite.

CHORUS:

    Men say she has a magic pistol
    Which can turn plain glass to crystal
    And can change an apple cart
    To a splintery work of art!
    Shooting at a person she
    Makes him a celebrity!
    Everything she does
    Is not what it was—
    Niki, bring us beauty's virtue!
    Fire at that ancient statue—
    Perhaps it has retained some value.

NIKI:

    Here are streams—there are flowers
    For the Public Garden's bowers! Let the flowers fall!

CHORUS:

    O Niki de Saint Phalle!
    We knew that Boston could be beautiful,
    But it was not until you came along.
    Where were you, fairest of them all?

NIKI: *(sings)*

    Busy in Rome and Istanbul,
    In Florence and in Paris;
    Shooting landscapes in Shanghai
    And portraits in Peking;
    Shooting rainbows in the sky,
    Shooting the mosaics in
    Saint Apollinaris.
    I bring beauty and detail
    By the shots which cannot fail
    To delight the nation.
    I make ugly statues fall,
    And I give the palace wall
    Lovely rustication.
    I put features on the face
    That is much too solemn;
    I give a Corinthian grace
    To the Doric column.
    Why should I do anything
    But be glad to make you sing

Praises to my shooting?
In my hand I have a gun,
And it is the only one
That gives columns fluting!
It's the only pistol which
Makes an empty canvas twitch
And become a painting!
It's the only gun that fires
Answers to the soul's desires—

CHORUS: *(sings)*
Ah you are so pretty!

NIKI: *(sings)*
Therefore on this summer night,
Citizens, for your delight,
I'll shoot up your city!

CHORUS: *(sings)*
She'll shoot up the city.

(speaks)

There she goes!
From the top of old Beacon to the muddy Back Bay
There's a mumble of pleasure on this sunny day
As the shooting is heard to resound boom boom—
As the shooting is heard, like the cry of a bird,
And it's covering old Boston Ground
With love and pleasure.
Well, has she finished?

NIKI:
Yes.
And now, at last, my time is past, I must be drifting homeward—
I go to treat art's plastercast, both Parisward and Romeward!
Farewell, delicious citizens brought here
By Rauschen—Rauschen—what's his name? And dear
Great heavy streets of Tinguely, oh farewell!

CHORUS:
Now she drifts out to sea like a great bell!
How grand she is and fair!
We who feel our new creation
Run through us like syncopation

In the arms and tail
Praise her without fail!
Oh love which makes us new—
Newer than Rauschen—what his name?—
Oh Niki, love for you,
It is which makes us new!
And like a nightmare which does not come true
This Boston now, which seems so old, is new
As if we saw the place for the first time
From the sublimest view-
Point: Mystic River Bridge—
And here is what we see, and it is beautiful,
Niki de Saint Phalle, all because of you:
You have shot Boston full of love for you!
Ah, see how fair—
The outsize obelisk of Bunker Hill!

All hail to Tinguely for this masterpiece!
Below, on the left, the Boston Naval Shipyard,
Where Rauschenberg's creations slip
Beneath hot summer days he's given them
Up and down riggings of a full-rigged ship!
What sight so fair
As in this air
A seacoast made of ships!
To Rauschenberg then praise!
And there North Station, Beacon Hill,
Public Garden, swan with bill,
Restaurants where eat their fill
Fishermen and salesmen!
Here is Boston Latin tall,
There majestic Faneuil Hall,
Here's the Charles, and there's the Mall
And the Charles River Basin!
Who can count its beauties wholly?
Let us summarize them solely
Lest our praise proceed too slowly,
Niki dear, to you!

(TINGUELY *and* RAUSCHENBERG *kneel to* NIKI.)

TINGUELY:
    Niki, all this city's buildings

With their warm old-fashioned gildings
I dedicate to you.

RAUSCHENBERG:
Niki, all these sunlit people
Or in shadow of a steeple
I consign to you.

NIKI:
And yet without you two, what could I do?
We must have people and they have to live
Inside of something: therefore I shall praise
You equally, for fashioning this maze!
For I cannot exist without the rest
Of life, although I am perhaps what's best.
Now citizens, sunset cover you
Oh fairest sunset cover you
Now fairest Boston mother you and cover you and smother you, fair Boston
cover you,

(sings)

And until then, ADIEU!

FINAL CURTAIN

Editors' Note on GARIBALDI EN SICILE

Kenneth Koch conceived of *Garibaldi en Sicile* as a work in French, a language he knew well. Although he drafted some of the recitatives in English (and then translated them into French), he wrote all the sung passages in French; he never expressed an intention to have this work translated into English.

In a series of *tableaux vivants, Garibaldi en Sicile* takes pleasure in imitating the tone and language of romantic nineteenth-century French literature; Koch acknowledged that he drew directly on sources such as Alexandre Dumas's novel *The Garibaldians.* An early draft of the libretto even bears a subtitle that describes it as a melodrama. Its narrative portions could be translated without any loss, but not its arias, duets, and choruses, which are rhymed, often in short lines. For example, Garibaldi sings:

> *Maintenant le vent me crie*
> *"Cours, suis moi pour être là*
> *Quand ce bon temps arrivera*
> *Que je dise une dernière fois*
> *Deux paroles—l'une, ton nom; l'autre, Italie!*

> [Now the wind cries out to me,
> "Run, follow me to be there
> When the right time arrives
> For me to say for one last time
> Two words—one, your name; the other, Italy!]

This literal version gets lucky with "me/Italy," but rhyming or off-rhyming the other three lines would prove far more difficult, which is pretty much the case with all the songs. Turned into unrhymed English, they lose the fun of the old-fashioned and high-flown French rhetoric Koch enjoyed using in *Garibaldi en Sicile.*

Because of this, we decided to present the text in French only, which, by the way, benefitted from some corrections by Koch's friend, the poet Michel Deguy, and suggestions from the opera's composer, Marcello Panni. To aid the anglophone reader, we offer this plot summary:

> *Garibaldi en Sicile* begins in the city of Nice, where Alexandre Dumas gives us historical background to the events that follow, as Garibaldi sets sail for Italy. On the way Garibaldi thinks of his previous, unsuccessful assault on the south of Italy, of his military adventures in Uruguay, and of his beautiful wife Anita. We hear a chorus of Uruguayans singing a song of praise to Garibaldi and Anita. Meanwhile, at the

Piedmont court, Count Cavour and King Victor Emmanuel II decide that they can use this radical Garibaldi for their own purposes, letting him do the dirty work for them against the Bourbons, who control the Kingdom of the Two Sicilies. Arriving in Tuscany, Garibaldi's Colonel Turr cleverly convinces the governor of the fortress to turn over all his arms and munitions. Meanwhile, in Sicily, there is an underground movement preparing to rise up against the repressive Bourbon King Francis II, whose chief of police organizes a bloody pogrom against the inhabitants of Palermo. A chorus of police thugs sings a refrain about biting the inhabitants. There is a night of meteors and lightning. Garibaldi and his two ships arrive in the Sicilian port of Marsala, where he sees a vision of Anita. She addresses him with a fiery passion, abolishing his doubts and renewing his resolve. Finally he disembarks, proclaiming himself Dictator of Sicily even though he hasn't conquered it yet. The opposing forces are ten times the size of his, but he carries the day, at the battle of Calatafimi. Colonel Turr goes through every village, urging the population to rise up. Even a Franciscan monk joins, offering to fight with words and the Cross. Garibaldi now lays siege to Palermo, and after a night of intense combat the victory is his. Garibaldi's friend, Alexandre Dumas, arrives that morning, as the city of Palermo sings a song of jubilation. Dumas has brought with him 2,200 men, 10,000 rifles, and two steamships. The two friends are photographed, along with their officers. The courts of Europe tremble with the news of Garibaldi's successes in Sicily. Garibaldi marches on Messina, where he urges his countrymen to desert the Bourbons and join him, an Italian like them. They ignore his offer and, after a hotly contested siege, they surrender. Once again Anita appears to Garibaldi in a vision, and they sing about the possibility of continual peace and happiness in Sicily. The figure of History sings a song to Sicily, invoking its beauty and the unification of Italy, concluding with "O blessèd Sicily! And blessèd Garibaldi! And this beautiful destiny!"

This précis barely suggests the ironic humor that hovers over the entire opera, touching down occasionally, nor does it convey the pleasure Koch must have taken in writing a new opera, an art form he loved, in a language that he also loved.

Garibaldi en Sicile

OPÉRA LYRIQUE EN DEUX ACTES, EN VERS ET PROSE, EN SEIZE TABLEAUX VIVANTS

Livret: KENNETH KOCH, d'après *Les Garibaldiens* d'Alexandre Dumas

Musique: MARCELLO PANNI

Personnages: Alexandre Dumas père, Stefano Canzio, Joseph Garibaldi, la Ville de Nice, Emilie Cordier, le comte de Cavour, le Roi Victor-Emmanuel II, le Préfet Maniscalco, le fantôme d'Anita Garibaldi, la Voix de l'Histoire, Frère Jean Pantaleo, Gustave Le Gray, Napoleon III, l'Italie, le Général Bosco

Choeurs: des Chemises Rouges, d'Uruguayens, de Siciliens, de Malfaiteurs, et de Volon-taires Siciliens

ACTE I

Introduction

Choeur des Chemises Rouges en coulisse

LES CHEMISES ROUGES:
> Aux armes ! Aux armes!
> Le tombeau s'entrouvre, le martyr se lève
> Et l'on entend son cri vengeur qui s'élève:
> Il a la gloire au front, aux poings il a le glaive
> Et le nom d'Italie est gravé dans son coeur!
>
> Comme la tempête, en fureur
> Pour venger sa mémoire
> Levons notre drapeau vainqueur,
> Toujours à l'honneur.
> Courons à la victoire,
> Fidèles à l'histoire
> Par le fer, le feu, brisons l'envahisseur.
> Chassons d'Italie
> Cette race impie,
> Son glas tinté.
> Vive la Liberté!

1er Tableau Vivant

Récitatif et Cavatine d'Alexandre Dumas père

DUMAS:
> *"L'Histoire? C'est un clou auquel je suspends mes romans." Qui suis-je? Oui,*
> *vous m'avez reconnu: Alexandre Dumas, célèlbre écrivain français; pourtant*

mon sang est à moitié africain: ma mére, une esclave noire de Santo Domingo,
mon père le Général Dumas, qui des Antilles vint en Europe combattre pour la
Liberté. Il suivit Bonaparte en Egypte, puis, à son retour d'Orient, fut surpris
par la tempête et trahi par un infâme Bourbon de Naples. Enfermé dans un
cachot à Brindisi, il mourut dans le désarroi, tué par le poison.

Or, soixante ans plus tard, surgit un astre nouveau, un autre Général, qui
vengea mon offense et chassa l'indigne "Franceschiello" du trône des Deux-
Siciles. Garibaldi, mon ami, le Héros des Deux-Mondes, le Washington et le
Napoléon, le Kosciuzko, et le Bolivar de l'Italie, qui conquit un Royaume pour
le bon Roi de Savoie.

DUMAS:

Dès l'enfance avec ma plume
J'ai créé des héros qui
Fougueux et en costume
Ont conquis tout ennemi.
Et c'étaient de grandes affaires
Historiques, mes romans,
Célèbres mes Mousquetaires,
Très aimable d'Artagnan
Parmi d'autres, que fils et pères
Allaient tous admirant. Mais, mais . . .

Comment aurais-je pu imaginer
Un plus grand que tous ceux-là
De mon siècle et non pas du passé
Tel qu'était Garibaldi?
Un homme qui vivait comme moi
Ces années-là en Italie,
Et l'ayant retrouvé, comment ne pas
Le secourir dans son combat?

Comment ne pas me joindre à lui?
Et lui offrir mes armes à feu?
Comment ne pas devenir ami
Du héros vrai, et non imaginaire
Tel qu'était Garibaldi?

(De ce Chevalier de la Liberté je vous raconterai les aventures extraordinaires que
j'ai partagées et dont je fus témoin.)

Que sa flamme qui monte en moi
Dans des milliers de feuilletons résonne
Et puis aprés dans mes romans

Et que j'écrive, avec le temps
De merveilleuses fictions,

DUMAS *et* CHOEUR:
En feu autant que les canons
Et les chansons des échansons!
«Au vent la flamme,
Au Seigneur, l'âme!»

CHOEUR DES CHEMISES ROUGES:
Chassons d'Italie
Cette race impie,
Son glas a tinté.
Vive la Liberté!

Récitatif avant le 2è tableau

DUMAS:
A présent nous voici en mer, à bord du navire à vapeur "Piemonte" de l'armateur génois Rubattino. Droit sur le pont, vous voyez le Général Garibaldi en personne, le Colonel Stefano Türr à ses côtés. Un autre navire, le "Lombardo," le suit à trois ou quatres milles. Il est commandé par le Colonel Nino Boxio, le plus marin de la troupe après le Général.

CANZIO:
Garibaldi commande en réalité les deux bâtiments, le sien à la voix, celui de Bixio au moyen de signaux.

DUMAS:
Il n'y a à bord ni cartes, ni sextants, ni chronomètres.

CANZIO:
Ces mille quatre-vingts hommes sont partis de Gênes à sept heures et demie le dimanche 6 mai 1860, cap vers le sud, au cri de guerre lancé par Garibaldi: "Italie et Victor Emmanuel!"

DUMAS:
La mer est parfaitement calme, la lune encore resplendissante, le ciel d'azur. Si cette expédition réussit, elle sera avec le retour de Napoléon de l'île d'Elbe un des hauts faits de notre siècle si fécond en événements.

CANZIO:
Le Général est silencieux: revoit-il cette autre, lointaine nuit de vingt-six ans auparavant où il commença cette vie d'exil, de luttes et de persécutions, qu'il n'a pas encore entièrement parcourue?

DUMAS:

Quand il dut quitter sa mère chérie, ses frères, ses amis, abandonner sa ville natale bien-aimée que le Roi du Piémont venait de vendre lâchement à la France?

2è Tableau Vivant—Le Départ
Chanson d'adieu de Garibaldi à la Ville de Nice

GARIBALDI:

Ô Nice! Endroit béni de ma naissance!
Nice, ville de France!
Ville de jouissance,
Toi qui fais partie
De la seule Italie
Qui n'existe pas, l'Italie
Qui n'existe pas encore!

Ô Nice, avec ton port
En forme de corniche
Tu présentes à l'état pur
Les bleus célestes de la Côte d'Azur!
Nice-sur-mer, c'est toi la mère
De tout ce que je suis—
C'est moi ton fils, Joseph Garibaldi!
Tu m'aimes et je t'aime, mais
Comme le dicte la raison:
"Bien qu'elle te soit très chère
Il faut quitter ta maison"
Et la raison a raison, Nice, adieu!

NICE:

Adieu, mon fils chéri!
Adieu, Garibaldi!
Moi, ville vendue à la France
Je te souhaite la chance
De changer les circonstances
Et d'ajouter de la gloire
A l'Italie, et du territoire!

GARIBALDI:

Ô Nice! Endroit béni!
C'est moi ton fils . . .

NICE:

    Toi qui ne peux savoir qu'ici
    Un jour, sur la Place Garibaldi,
    Ta statue s'élèvera, pour que ton esprit
    M'anime toujours!

GARIBALDI:

    Ô Nice! Endroit béni!
    C'est moi ton fils, Garibaldi!

NICE:

    Adieu, enfant chéri!
    Adieu, Garibaldi!
    Adieu, adieu!

Récitatif avant le 3è tableau

CANZIO:

Appuyé au bastingage de son navire, Garibaldi pense à présent à Carlo Pisacane et à ses trois cents hommes, jeunes et forts, qui périrent, il y a à peine trois ans, alors qu'ils débarquaient en Calabre. Ils avaient tenté sans succès de soulever l'Italie du Sud—cette même entreprise qu'il veut reprende aujourd'hui.

EMILIE CORDIER:

Il se remémire alors d'autres combats: celui pour la liberté du peuple Uruguayen, là où il avait rencontré la belle Anita, son épouse, la maîtresse de son âme et de son corps, celle qui enflammait son être, celle qui lui ôtait la peur dans la bataille, le rendait invincible, inébranlable dans ses idéaux et tenace jusqu'au but.

Ils avaient tous deux combattu, l'un à côte de l'autre jusqu'à la victoire, et les Uruguayens les avaient remerciés en chantant:

3è Tableau Vivant—En Amerique du Sud
Choeur des Uruguayens reconnaissants

CHOEUR D'URUGUAYENS:

    Notre Pays est libre! Uruguayens!
    Gloire à Garibaldi!
    Ecoutez comme le vent vibre
    D'éloges qui disent comment
    Avec son coeur et ses deux mains

Ce formidable Italien
A sauvé notre Pays.

Avec des armes
A feu, avec l'esprit de feu
Et l'âme en feu
Garibaldi a mis à feu et à sang
Les ambitions des tyrans!
Que la joie aille de l'avant
Et que brille le diamant
Du coeur humain indépendant!
Tout a changé!
Vive la Liberté!

Ni les pampas, ni le Rio Négro,
Ni la belle Montévideo,
Ni Salto, ni Rocha,
Ni Mercédés, ni Paysandù,
Ne s'ouvraient vraiment à nous
Avant que cet Italien
Avec son coeur et ses deux mains
Nous rende notre Pays.
Louange à Garibaldi!

Récitatif avant le 4è tableau

EMILIE CORDIER:
Pendant que les navires Piemonte et Lombardo naviguent vers le Sud, avec leur mille hommes à bord . . .

STEFANO CANZIO:
. . . à la cour du Roi Victor-Emmanuel, à Turin, le comte de Cavour, son Premier-Ministre, tend ses filets d'embûches et de misérables difficultés à Garibaldi et à son expedition.

4è Tableau Vivant—À la cour du Piémont
Couplets entrecoupés du comte de Cavour et duettino

CAVOUR:
Je propose au roi François
Une Italie partagée
Entre lui et le vrai roi
Victor-Emmanuel—mais

Ce que je veux en fait
C'est que mon Souverain soit
Le roi du tout et non pas
Le roi de la moitié

J'ai écrit au gouvernement anglais: "Nous ne voulons pas l'expédition en Sicile.
La monarchie constitutionnelle italienne doit conserver la puissance morale
qu'elle a conquise par sa résolution de rendre la Nation Italienne indépen-
dante."

Tout de même j'autorise
L'escapade garibaldienne
Embarquée près de Gênes,
Cap du sud, qui croise par Pise
Passe par Rome, et atterrit
Avec mille hommes pour l'entreprise
En Sicile. Garibaldi . . .
L'homme, je le redoute un peu
Surtout à cause de son milieu
Plutôt républicain
Qui menace d'anarchie
Celle qui n'en a nul besoin
Ma chère, nouvelle Italie.

J'ai tout de même écrit: "Le gouvernement du Roi déplore cette entreprise; il ne
peut l'arrêter, il ne l'aide pas, il ne peut non plus la combattre."

CAVOUR:

Mais aurais-je d'autres choix?
Garibaldi mêle des armes
A feu aux mille charmes
De sa personne et de sa voix
Et de sa foi, honnête et pure!
Il constitue l'arme la plus sûre
Et sans faute il gagnera.

Embarque, va, ô grand soldat!
Que sur les eaux Tyrrhéniennes
Glissent tes bâtiments
Et que les vents rendent facile
Ton voyage en Sicile!

(Victor-Emmanuel entre.)

Mais patiente encore un moment . . .

Il faut que j'obtienne d'abord
De mon Roi son accord.

Je vous prie, Majesté,
D'accorder votre soutien
A l'idée d'expédier
Garibaldi en Sicile.

VICTOR-EMMANUEL:
  Nous ne savons pas, Cavour,
  S'il faut être pour:
  Un radical comme lui
  Nous menace d'anarchie.

CAVOUR:
  Majesté, c'est un radical
  Mais il est aussi loyal.
  Il vénère le sol que Vous foulez.

VICTOR-EMMANUEL:
  Ah bon. Si tel est le cas
  D'avis nous pourrions changer.
  S'il vénère ce sol, nous ne croyons pas
  Qu'il sera tenté de le dérober.

CAVOUR:
  Majesté! Soyez assuré
  Qu'il ne le fera pas.

VICTOR-EMMANUEL:
  Alors, qu'il aille et qu'il conquière
  Ce sol que pour nous il vénère
  Qui n'appartient qu'à nous d'ores et déjà.
  Alors, qu'il aille, ce loyal soldat,
  Qu'il conquière et nous donne
  Ce qu'il aura gagné.
  Qui n'appartient qu'à nous d'ores et déjà.

CAVOUR:
  Embarque, va, ô grand soldat
  Que sur les eaux Tyrrhéniennes
  Glissent tes bâtiments
  et que les vents rendent facile
  Ton voyage en Sicile!

A DEUX:
> Va, va, va!

Récitatif avant le 5è tableau

STEFANO CANZIO:
> *Entretemps les deux navires se sont arrêtés dans le port de Talamone en Toscane, pour faire des provisions. Le rusé Colonel Türr réussit a rallier le gouverneur de la forteresse de Orbetello, qui remet à Garibaldi—parti sans armes ni munitions—un millier de fusils à baïonette et cent-cinquante mille cartouches. Le lendemain 9 mai le Gouverneur est destitué de sa charge par le comte de Cavour, fou de rage. Mais Garibaldi et ses hommes ont déjà repris la mer.*

EMILIE CORDIER:
> *Dans la nuit, sous la voûte étoilée, le Général est secoué par une vague de tristesse. Revoit-il la mort tragique de son épouse Anita, il y a onze ans déjà, enceinte de son quatrième enfant, dans sa fuite désespérée dans les marécages de Ravenne? Et maintenant encore une fois il va se battre, mais sans elle hélas pour la liberté . . . pour l'Italie.*

5è Tableau Vivant—En Route pour la Sicile
Ricercare Nocturne de Garibaldi

GARIBALDI:
> Bien que seul et dévasté
> Par la mort de mon amie
> Je suis toujours emporté
> Par ce vent très fort qui crie
> Deux paroles—l'une, mon nom; l'autre, Italie!
>
> J'ai perdu et j'ai gagné
> Des combats pour la Patrie
> Et j'en ai d'autres à remporter
> En ta faveur, Italie,
> Par ce vent si fort qui crie
> Deux paroles—l'une, mon nom; l'autre, Italie!
>
> A mort déjà condamné
> Dès mes vingts ans, j'avais fui
> Par la mer, et gagné
> Des victoires pour d'autres Pays,
> Contre le Brésil, pour l'Uruguay,

Mais ici je suis rentré
Car un vent de Liberté
A travers la mer sifflait:
"C'est le moment où renaît
Toute possibilité!"

Maintenant le vent me crie
"Cours, suis moi pour être là
Quand ce bon temps arrivera
Que je dise une derniére fois
Deux paroles—l'une, ton nom; l'autre, Italie!

Récitatif avant le 6è tableau

DUMAS:

*En Sicile on se prépare à la révolte. Un comité dit "du bien public" s'organ-
ise: il est composé de chefs de la noblesse, de la bourgeoisie et du peuple. De
tous côtés, on ouvre des souscriptions qui ont pour but l'achat d'armes et de
munitions.*

*Désireux d'étouffer toute tentative d'insurrection, le roi bourbon François II a
nommé chef de la police Salvatore Maniscalco. Sous la férule de cet individu
brutal et sanguinaire, la Sicile souffre une répression inimaginable. Ni enfant
ni femme n'est à l'abri de sa fureur. C'est Narcisse sous Néron; c'est Olivier le
Daim sous Louis XI!*

*Maniscalco recrute des bandes de malfaiteurs. Ils tuent le père après avoir violé
la femme et la fille devant ses yeux. Cette horde de pillards et d'assassins est ré-
pandue par lui sur Palerme et ses environs:*

6è Tableau Vivant—Scènes de Cruauté en Sicile, Air de Fureur du Préfet Maniscalco

MANISCALCO:
Allez, allez, mes assassins
Contre ce peuple qui se croit
Au-dessus de la loi
Et qui prendrait dans ses mains
Les rênes de notre état!
Il faut les arrêter là,
Il faut tout arrêter là!
Allez, allez mes assassins.

Le mot même de Liberté
Je le trouve asphyxiant!

Moi, non, je n'ai pas le nez
D'inhaler un tel courant
De fétidité.

Allez donc mes durs!
Renversez les murs
Des maisons, pour chasser le poison!
N'hésitez pas à violer—
Femmes et filles, elles, sont à vous!
Tuez les hommes, ils sont à vous!

Allons! Allez! Mes chiens,
Mordons, mordons les Siciliens,
Mordons leur chair, elle est à vous!

CHOEURS DE MALFAITEURS:
Allons! Allons,
Mordons, mordons les Siciliens,
Mordons leur chair, elle est à nous!

7è *Tableau Vivant—L'attente*
Choeur des Siciliens invoquant l'arrivée de Garibaldi

DUMAS:
Ainsi Palerme, étouffant sous la main de Maniscalco, mais ferme et constante dans sa haine, se tourne vers tous les points de l'horizon pour demander à Dieu et aux hommes un appui quelconque qui la relève de sa chute.

CHOEUR DE SICILIENS:
Un astre nouveau
Se lève sur la Sicile
Et le nom, le nom de cet astre
C'est l'Espérance!

Brille, brille, étoile bénie
Céleste étoile, aimée amie,
Qui chassera la tyrannie
D'allure si vile, si peu civile
De tout endroit de la Sicile.

DUMAS:
Cependant, la ville est frémissante et anxieuse. Le soir, parents se réunissent et les portes se ferment. Les uns savent ce qui va arriver, les autres devinent qu'il doit arriver quelque chose. Malheureusement, le défaut d'armes, de munitions et d'ensemble empêche l'insurrection de devenir générale. Ce sont des météores, des éclairs, ce n'est pas encore une tempête.

CHOEUR DE SICILIENS:
 Car Garibaldi vient
 Il arrive dans cette île
 Ce héros qui détient
 Lui seul, notre espoir entier.
 Garibaldi vient!
 Garibaldi vient!

Récitatif avant le 8è tableau

EMILIE CORDIER:
 Garibaldi a jeté l'ancre dans le port de Marsala. Pourtant, en cette heure extrême—un silence attendu, une halte, un délai. Les troupes ne débarquent pas aussitôt. Alors que les navires sont là, qu'un millier de soldats, les Chemises Rouges, sont là, Garibaldi a une vision de l'amour de sa vie, de la belle Anita qui, quelque victoire qu'il obtienne, ne sera jamais plus à lui. Pendant quelques instants chargés de tension il titube à cause de la gravité de ce qu'il s'apprête à faire.

8è Tableau Vivant—Devant le Port de Marsala
Grande scène de Garibaldi évoquant le fantôme d'Anita et Cabalette

GARIBALDI:
 Nous voici arrivés, enfin
 Nous voici, enfin
 Soldats et marins
 En Sicile, le coeur gonflé!
 Et quoi. . . ? J'hésite, j'hésite à débarquer,
 Cette arrivée qui devait m'apporter du bonheur
 Me donne, hélas, une grande tristesse. Oh Anita!

LE FANTÔME D'ANITA:
 Sur le pont du navire immobilisé, Anita apparaît à Garibaldi en tous ses attraits et lui parle avec tout le feu de sa passion.

GARIBALDI:
 Je pense à toi—amour! Femme! Maîtresse!
 Oh, à quoi bon continuer
 Puisque de toi je suis privé?

LE FANTÔME D'ANITA:
 En avant, en avant, mon grand amour
 Regarde-moi, je suis ici

A tes côtes, Joseph Garibaldi,
Pour aujourd'hui et pour toujours.

GARIBALDI:
Oh Anita, oh amour!
Oui, je lutterai toujours
Ni pour le Roi, ni pour Cavour,
Mais pour toi et pour l'amour!

LE FANTÔME D'ANITA:
Débarque donc, et sois pour moi
L'homme que j'aime, et pour toujours
Celui qui unit cette désunie
Terre bénie d'Italie
Qui est pour toi ce que je suis.

GARIBALDI:
Oh, Anita! Maîtresse!
Oui, je lutterai toujours
Ni pour le Roi, ne pour Cavour,
Mais pour toi et pour l'amour!

LE FANTÔME D'ANITA:
Ce royaume tu l'auras conquis
Ni pour le Roi, ni pour Cavour
Mais pour moi et pour l'amour,
Joseph Garibaldi!

GARIBALDI:
Avançons, soldats de l'amour
Nous ne pourrons jamais faillir.
Avançons, soldats de ce grand jour
Jour de clarté d'où va jaillir
La source des coeurs unis.
Avançons, soldats, avançons!

CHOEUR DES CHEMISES ROUGES:
Avançons, soldats de l'amour,
Nous ne pourrons jamais faillir.

GARIBALDI:
Avec l'amour rien n'est difficile—
La bataille se gagne.
Si je veux, je deviens roi de Sicile
Empereur de Chine ou roi d'Espagne!
Avançons, soldats de l'amour!

CHOEUR DES CHEMISES ROUGES:
Avançons, soldats de l'amour!

GARIBALDI:
Eros ou héros c'est pour nous le même.
Vaincre la Nuit pour apporter le Jour
C'est de Garibaldi le stratagème!

GARIBALDI *et* CHOEUR:
Nous sommes peu, ils sont nombreux,
Mais nous sommes les plus amourex!
En avant, vers Salemi!

Fin de l'acte 1

ACTE II

Récitatif avant le 9è tableau

LA VOIX DE L'HISTOIRE:
Un matin, c'etait le 13 mai, un cri éclata dans toute l'île: "Garibaldi a débarqué à Marsala!" Le vengeur était venu. Arrivé devant Salemi, Garibaldi se proclama "Dictateur de Sicile"—mais il ne l'avait pas encore conquise! Le premier combat contre les forces napolitaines—dix fois plus nombreuses—fut engagé devant Calatafimi. La bataille fut d'abord incertaine, mais Garibaldi la remporta.

9è Tableau Vivant—La Bataille de Calatafimi
(orchestre seul)

Rècitatif avant le 10è tableau

LA VOIX DE L'HISTOIRE:
Après la victoire de Calatafimi, Garibaldi remarqua que, bien que chaque Sicilien fût d'enthousiasme et même de passion acquis à sa cause, presque personne ne s'offrait comme soldat dans son armée. Il fallait recruter.

Beaucoup, beaucoup de Siciliens répondirent à sa requête. Ils se rendaient en courant au campement des Chemises Rouges en chantant:

10è Tableau Vivant - Frère Jean s'enrole
Choeur des volontaires siciliens et Refrain de Frère Jean

CHOEUR DES VOLONTAIRES:
>Liberté ou mort!
>Nous n'avons pas de pistolets,
>Ni de mousquets, ni de canons,
>Mais nous avons des fourches et des râteaux
>Et de cuisine des couteaux.
>Avec des scies et des bâtons,
>Avec tout ce que nous avons,
>Pour la Patrie nous combattrons
>Jusqu'à ce qu'il fasse beau
>Sur toute la Sicile
>Notre Patrie, notre île!

CANZIO:
>*A présent, Garibaldi avait des volontaires siciliens en grand nombre. Le prochain jour arriva un autre signe de bonne fortune. Au moment où le Général faisait boire son cheval à une fontaine, un moine de l'ordre de Saint François réformé, à la figure intelligente, à l'oeil vif, aux cheveux courts et crépus, se fit jour et arriva jusqu'à lui.*

FRÈRE JEAN:
>Mon Dieu—

CANZIO:
>*. . . dit-il en tombant à genoux*

FRÈRE JEAN:
>—je te remercie de m'avoir fait vivre en ce temps où devait venir
>le messie de la liberté.

GARIBALDI:
>Jeune clerc, voulez-vous vous joindre à nous?

FRÈRE JEAN:
>C'est mon seul désir!

GARIBALDI:
>Fort bien! Alors, venez! Mais puisque vous voilà notre chapelain, frère Jean, il vous faut jeter le froc aux orties et prendre le mousquet!

FRÈRE JEAN:	CHOEUR DES VOLONTAIRES:
Je me battrai sans épée ni mousquet	
Mais avec la parole, avec la Croix!	
Qui porte haut le Christ sur sa poitrine	Nous n'avons pas de pistolets
N'a nul besoin de porter carabine!	Ni de mousquets, ni de canons

Mais nous avons des fourches, des rateaux.
Liberté ou mort!

A Palerme, Catane, Messine,
Qui m'aperçoit verra la Croix
Et non point le pistolet

Je me me battrai sans épée ni
mousquet

Liberté ou mort!
Avec des scies et des bâtons,

Mais avec la parole, avec la
Croix!

Avec tout ce que nous avons,

A Palerme, Catane, Messine,
Le Messenger du Christ, ce
sera moi
Et non pas le mousquet!

Pour la Patrie nous combattrons.
Liberté ou mort!

Liberté ou mort!

Récitatif avant le 11è tableau

LA VOIX DE L'HISTOIRE:

La bataille pour la Sicile se poursuit. Garibaldi, rendu plus fort par de nouveaux soldats, est prêt à livrer bataille devant Palerme. Toute la nuit le combat fait rage. Aux lueurs de l'aube, la bataille est gagnée. La ville de Palerme est en ruines, mais libérée.

11è Tableau Vivant—Dumas Debarque à Palerme
Ode à la Liberté

CANZIO:

C'est à ce moment qu'Alexandre Dumas arrive dans le port de Palerme sur sa propre goélette. Il saute à terre suivi par ses amis. Ils errent dans les ruelles de la ville, surpris et ravis de ce qu'ils voient. La ville est tout d'un coup joyeuse: une ville qui était morte revient à la vie.

LA VILLE DE PALERME (EMILIE CORDIER, FRÈRE JEAN, GUSTAVE LE GRAY):
Vous qui passez, regardez
Enfin: Palerme, l'heureuse!

DUMAS:
Je te salue, ô Liberté!
Déesse grande et sublime
Toi, seuele reine que l'on proscrit
Mais qu'on ne peut pas détrôner!

LA VILLE DE PALERME (LA VOIX DE L'HISTOIRE):
Endommagées, mes façades;

Dans mes rues, des barricades,
Mais victorieuse,
Libre et donc victorieuse.
A moi la Liberté!

CHOEURS MIXTES:
A moi la Liberté!

DUMAS:
Tous ces hommes, tes enfants
Qui sont si gais aujourd'hui,
Il y a huit jours, ô Liberté
Ils avaient la tête courbée,
Ils étaient dans l'abîme.
Tu les as relevés pourtant
Déesse, par ta majesté!
Ô Palerme, Palerme
Qui chantes victorieuse
C'est véritablement aujourd'hui
Que l'on peut t'appeler
Palerme l'heureuse!

LA VILLE DE PALERME: *(Tutti avec Choeur)*
Vous qui passez, regardez
Palerme, l'heureuse!

Récitatif avant le 12è tableau

DUMAS:
Je traverse Palerme, meurtrie par les bombardements. De nombreuses maisons fument encore, écroulées sur leurs habitants. Me frayant péniblement un chemin entre les barricades et sur les décombres, devant la Cathédrale criblée de balles, je retrouve Garibaldi. Dès que le Général m'aperçoit, il pousse un cri de joie qui me va droit au coeur.

12è Tableau Vivant—Devant la Cathédrale
Grand Duo de la rencontre entre Dumas et Garibaldi

GARIBALDI:
Cher Dumas, vous me manquiez!

DUMAS:
Ah, je vous avais promis
De vous chercher Garibaldi!

GARIBALDI:

    Vous voir ici, Dumas, me plaît,
    Mon grand ami français!

DUMAS:

    De ma goélette, en rade ancrée
    Je suis venu pour vous aider!

GARIBALDI:

    À propos, mes carabines?

DUMAS:

    Elles sont à bord, dans ma cabine.

GARIBALDI:

    Bon, je les enverrai chercher.

DUMAS:

    Et Nino Bixio? On l'a dit tué.

GARIBALDI:

    Non, ce fou est seulement blessé.
    Une balle morte dans la poitrine.

DUMAS:

    Et Manin?

GARIBALDI:

    Blessé deux fois, pauvre garçon.

DUMAS:

    Et vous? Qu'est-ce encore que cela?

GARIBALDI:

    Un maladroit, qui en causant avec moi
    Son revolver a laissé tomber,
    Il a brûlé mon pantalon.

DUMAS:

    En verité, vous êtes prédestiné.

GARIBALDI:

    Oui, je commence à le croire. Mais allons . . .

DUMAS:

    Que vois-je là, mon grand héros?
    Que font ces moines, ces cagots
    Ici, avec vous, dans cet endoit?

GARIBALDI:

    Mon camarade, n'en faites pas fi.
    Ce sont des prêtes, mais braves soldats
    Qui pour la cause ont souffert, et pour moi,
    Auxquels l'autre jour au combat
    Le feu ennemi brisa la croix.

DUMAS:

    Oh, la belle foi! Qu'ils viennent avec moi
    Je veux leur faire une photographie.

GARIBALDI:

    Quoi! Avec un photographe vous êtes venu ici?

DUMAS:

    Tout simplement Le Gray, le plus connu à Paris ...
    Et naturellement, je vous invite aussi,
    À figurer dans la photographie!

GARIBALDI:

    Dumas, vous m'êtes cher, bien qu'un peu fou,
    Je ferai très volontier cela pour vous.

GUSTAVE LE GRAY:

    Messieurs, regardez le petit oiseau.

Récitatif avant le 13è tableau

DUMAS:

    La nouvelle de la conquête de Palerme se propage comme le feu aux poudres;
    les cours d'Europe s'affolent. Monarques, politiciens, diplomates (que Garibaldi
    appelle avec mépris "les fourbes petits renards") sont très inquiets des succès de
    l'audacieuse entreprise des "Mille".

13è Tableau Vivant—En Europe
Ostinato / Galop des trois fourbes petits renards

CAVOUR:

    Passambleu,
    J'en ai assez de ce monsieur
    Moi qui suis un petit fourbe renard
    Je l'aurai à la fin—car
    Le talent qui a déchâiné
    Les révolutions
    Très souvent est écrasé.

Plus heureux celui qui suit
Le héroes et en tire profit.
Gare à toi, Garibaldi!

NAPOLEON III:
Il est vrai que je voudrais
Libérer l'Italie,
Mais seulement à ma façon! En vérité
A la possibilité
D'être débarrassé
De ce Garibaldi
Mon coeur s'envole
Et mon espirt s'affole.
Que le choléra
L'emporte sans délai
Et le monde exultera!

VICTOR-EMMANUEL:
De tous les rois du continent
C'est moi le plus intelligent
Le plus royal, le moins dément.
C'est moi qui commande
A Garibaldi et à sa bande.
Je leur dis: "Soyez prudents!
Ne mettez point pied sur le continent!"
Et les voilà obéissants.

A TROIS:
Tous trois dans nos coeurs
Nous avons peur.
Plus astucieux
Que glorieux,
Nous aurons les gros profits,
Toi la gloire, Garibaldi!

Récitatif avant le 14è tableau

CANZIO:
A présent une nouvelle tâche ardue reste à accomplir pour libérer toute l'île: la conquête de Messine.

Garibaldi pensait à l'absurdité de cette guerre où des Italiens combattaient contre des Italiens—lui et ses troupes contre leurs frères napolitains.

Pourquoi les Italiens devraient-ils être les ennemis des Italiens?

Pourquoi ne combattraient-ils pas, tous ensemble, pour l'unité et la liberté?

Il adressa ainsi une proclamation aux soldats de l'autre camp, leur parlant comme à ses frères—et l'Italie même lui en dictait les paroles.

14è Tableau Vivant
Fanfare de la Proclamation de Garibaldi et de l'Italie

GARIBALDI EN L'ITALIE:
Napolitains! Napolitains!
Vous êtes les fils d'Italie
Laquelle est terre
Qui s'étend du Mont Cenis
Aux eaux de la Sicile.

GARIBALDI:
Aujourd'hui rouges de sang!

A DEUX:
Napolitains! Napolitains!
Pourquoi combattez-vous contre vos frères?
De Varèse et de Côme les preux
Sont ici, sont avec vous
Hardis, vaillants, courageux
Et vous combattez contre eux!
Soulevez-vous donc
Au nom de l'Italie
Et que chaque frère soit
Avec son frère au combat!

GARIBALDI:
Le bon Dieu dit à Caïn:

L'ITALIE:
"Homme maudit! Qu'as-tu fait de ton frère?"

GARIBALDI:
Ainsi vous dit l'Italie:

L'ITALIE:
"Frères maudits! Qu'avez-vous fait de vos frères?"

A DEUX:
Frères napolitains

Ne soyez pas des Caïns,
L'Italie vous pardonne,

GARIBALDI:
Mais soulevez-vous, avec le feu
De vos volcans contre ceux

A DEUX:
Qui ne veulent pas l'Italie une!

LES CHEMISES ROUGES:
Soulevez-vous avec le feu
De vos volcans
Et revêtez la chemise rouge!

Suite du 14è et Récitatif avant le 15è tableau

FRÈRE JEAN *et* EMILIE CORDIER:
Hélas! Malgré la force de cette proclamation,

EMILIE CORDIER:
Le résultat fut presque nul.

FRÈRE JEAN:
L'armée napolitaine continua de se battre bravement.
Mais Garibaldi et ses Chemises Rouges

A DEUX:
étaient une force incontenable.

FRÈRE JEAN:
Garibaldi pénétra dans Messine

EMILIE CORDIER:
et les Napolitains se réfugièrent

A DEUX:
dans l'imprenable forteresse de Milazzo.

STEFANO CANZIO:
Cinq mille hommes s'y amassèrent sans possibilité de recevoir ni vivres ni boisson.

EMILIE CORDIER:
Après plusieurs jours de siège, Garibaldi depêcha un messager au Commandant de la fortesse, le Général Bosco.

STEFANO CANZIO:

Il y demandait la reddition de son armée, offrant en contrepartie un sauf-conduit pour lui et ses officiers.

DUMAS:

Après quelques réticences, Bosco décida de se rendre.

DUMAS, EMILIE CORDIER, FRÈRE JEAN:

*Il exprime dans une romance d'adieu ses raisons
et sa tristesse d'abandonner sa citadelle bien-aimée.*

*15è Tableau Vivant—Chute de Milazzo
Romance du Général Bosco*

LE GÉNÉNRAL BOSCO:

Dans un but d'humanité
Et désirant éviter
Des souffrances inutiles
Nous rendons la citadelle
Et quittons la Sicile
Nous quittons la Sicile.

Ô citadelle, avec tes gros canons
Tes lourds portails, ton ravelin,
Ton ordonnance, tes munitions,
Je te dis adieu!
Adieu généreux fossé
Qui nous tins en sûreté
Adieu gracieux pont-levis
Adieu à vous tous, je dis.

Moi qui aime la herse, la cour
Et les boulets de canon
Et la poudre de canon
Et le tonnerre des canons
Qui annonce la mort qui vient
A travers l'air sicilien
Au soldat comme au marin
Tonnerre, Adieu!

*16è Tableau Vivant—Finale:
Apothéose d'Anita, couronnée Reine de Sicile*

LA VOIX DE L'HISTOIRE:

C'est ainsi que prit fin la libération de la Sicile par le Général Garibaldi.

Elle prit fin, mais non la gloire de ces hauts faits, qui survécut, dans la mé-moire des gens de ces lieux.

CANZIO:

L'ultime bataille est remportée. Le soir, Garibaldi peut enfin dormir du som-meil du juste.

Il avait passé de nombreuses nuits à veiller, à réfléchir, à organiser, à décider, à ordonner: à présent il avait fort besoin de se reposer.

C'est alors qu'Anita lui apparait à nouveau:

LA VOIX DE L'HISTOIRE, *avec* CHOEUR DE FEMMES:

    Ô Sicile, île des Muses,
    Des prêtes, et de la pente
    Toute en marbre, d'Agrigente,
    Quelle histoire veux-tu qu'on invente
    Qui soit plus que celle-ci étonnante?
    Plus belle, plus étonnante?

GARIBALDI:

    Anita, je te couronne
    Reine de ce pays-ci
    La Sicile je te la donne
    Et en sus, Garibaldi—
        Tout est alors à toi.

LE FANTÔME D'ANITA:

    Je suis heureuse, puisque ici
    Je régne avec toi, mon ami,
    Sur cette Sicile qui
    A Garibaldi pour roi—
        Tout est alors à toi.

TUTTI, *avec* CHOEUR MIXTE:

    Ô Sicile, île bénie,
    Tout au sud de l'Italie
    Voici maintenant mille Muses
    D'une poésie unie
    (Le poème c'est l'Italie!)
    Qui avec des arquebuses
    Font sauter ceux qui refusent
    D'accéder à ce destin
    Qui met, à nos douleurs, fin.

The Banquet (Talking about Love)

To Marcello Panni

Prologo

*(The first scene is Paris streets, with two men—*JEAN-LUC *and* MICHEL*—walking along. The time is the present.)*

JEAN-LUC:

I think I know the story just about
By heart. I told it to Jean-Marc two days ago.
He came up to me saying, Ah, Jean-Luc!
I heard that you were present at the banquet
Given toward the end of the War—Picasso was there,
And Gertrude Stein, Marinetti, Satie, Cocteau,
And Marie Laurencin and Apollinaire—
Apollinaire's last banquet—and that everyone spoke of love.

MICHEL:

Yes, that's the one I want to hear about.

JEAN-LUC:

Well, it was very silly of Jean-Marc
To think I could have been at that banquet. I said, Look at me
Do you think I'm old enough to have been there?
It was in nineteen eighteen. No, I heard the story
From André Salmon, who *was* there. He said there were a whole
Lot of other people there, too—Max Jacob, Philippe Soupault,
Alice B. Toklas, Pablo's Fernande—but only seven of them spoke—
And how they spoke—and sang—of love!

MICHEL:

Tell me everything about it. That night seems certainly like the last night
Of something, and like the first night of something else. Tell me what the
    speeches were, and the songs.

JEAN-LUC:

Well, according to André Salmon, they were something like this—but I
    think it might be better
To show you what I saw, as if it were actually there in front of me,
When Salmon told me the story. He said he had gone with Picasso to the
    Closerie des Lilas
Which had been all set up for the occasion. He said "Everyone was excited.
I hadn't been planning to go, but Pablo talked me into it. He said Apollinaire
    would probably come.

However, when we got there, Guillaume was the only one not present—
    there were Jean Cocteau,
Erik Satie, who was in charge of it, Filippo Tomasso Marinetti, up
From Italy for the event, and Marie Laurencin, quite amazingly having
    traveled there from Spain,
Leaving her husband and everything, just to come and talk about love—
Or perhaps no, really, they didn't even know before they got there
That they were going to talk about love—I guess she came just for the
    company
And maybe to see Guillaume, though that part didn't turn out well.
In any case, she was there and looking beautiful, and Gertrude Stein was
There too, with Alice B. Toklas and some sheets of paper
As if *she* would be ready to speak about anything, and of course Picasso,
But no Guillaume. We knew, of course, about his injury
But Satie seemed confident anyway that he would come. It was Satie who
    proposed, after we got there,
The subject of what they'd say. We were, aside from Apollinaire, the last
    ones to get there."

Atto Unico

(The scene changes to the Closerie, the beginning of the Banquet. Drinking, merriment, and singing. The CHORUS, *or* EVERYONE *more or less, is singing The Banquet Song. Over the din of this song,* SATIE *welcomes the new arrivals,* PICASSO, FERNANDE, *and* SALMON.)

The Banquet Song

Ah, sweet Banquet, lovely Banquet
From your seats you get your name
From the bench, banchetto, banquette
But from love you get your fame
Love and drink and song and friendship
We extol you from our benches
Banquet, Banquet, holy Banquet
Here the spirit is transcendent
Joined by wine and wit and laughter
No one soul is independent
All are joined in one enormous
Vision of the life before us

Ah sweet banquet thank you thank you
Banquet hear our glasses ring

We shall do our best to make you
A fiesta'd everything
Such a banquet as has never
Been and which will last forever!

SATIE:

Welcome, Pablo and Fernande. Ah, André! How good that you could come!
Our party's just begun. Tonight
Each one of us is going to give a toast
And speak in praise of love.

PICASSO:

Splendid idea!

COCTEAU:

Pablo, welcome. Ah, Fernande. *Et toi, mon cher Salmon!*

PICASSO:

Cocteau, it's good to see you.
What a party!

SATIE:

From Italy we've drawn
This mighty Marinetti!

MARINETTI: *(imitating a racing-car engine on his rolled r's; he is wearing a racing-car helmet)*
Buona Sera, ovvero buooona serrrra to you all!

PICASSO:

Gertrude, you are on my wall, or rather you are on your wall—
I painted you, and you are on your wall—how nice to see you here!

STEIN:

Alice and I decided to walk out, is it? Is to visit
And get a little tremble from Paree.

PICASSO:

Dear Marie Laurencin!

MARIE LAURENICIN:

Pablo! Pablo!

SATIE:

Come, come, now let's sit down. And we'll begin.

(All the GUESTS now sit down at a big lavishly spread table with bottles of wine and all sorts of plates, glasses, etc. Waiters move in and out and there is much festive

serving and consuming of food and drink. There is silence, though, while the char-
acters speak and sing. After each speaker's song, the festive noise breaks out again.
SATIE, *who is a sort of master of the revels, is seated in the center; it is he who calls*
on the others to speak. In front of SATIE, *on or under the table, or perhaps to one*
side, is a very small piano keyboard, on which he may play notes to punctuate the
end of a speech or song, to call on a new speaker, to illustrate and accompany his
own speech and song, or for any other reason.)

SATIE:

I've told you my idea,
That each of us should speak in praise of love.
Perhaps the world can use new ways of looking
At love since Plato set the subject cooking
In Greece twenty-five hundred years ago—

PICASSO:

Ah, we do need Guillaume!
He is our living expert on the subject.

MARIE LAURENCIN: *(aside)*

Well, I don't know . . .

VARIOUS GUESTS:

Guillaume, what, not arrived yet? *Non. Non. Oui.*

(Now there is a sudden silence as everyone realizes that APOLLINAIRE *is not there.)*

VARIOUS GUESTS:

Where, where is Gui?
Where is Guillaume Apollinaire
Our reigning poet and great banqueteer?

(another silence)

COCTEAU:

He isn't here
I asked him but he isn't here

SATIE:

And I asked him—he isn't here

MARINETTI:

Is he too ill? Is his wound bad again?

MARIE LAURENCIN:

I heard that he was better—ill again?

PICASSO:

Past time and past loves do not come again
But something tells me Guillaume will appear—

MARIE LAURENCIN:

I did hear he was better—

PICASSO:

Before the evening's done—with us again.

SATIE:

I think you're right. He can speak later. He always likes, in any case, to play the most dramatic part in any street, café, or theatre. A late dramatic entrance suits him fine. If he does come . . . But let's begin! Silence! A toast: to Love!

(ALL *life their glasses, some saying or singing "Love"; others "Amore" or "Amour"*)

SATIE:

Picasso, I've decided. You are first.

PICASSO:

Thank you, Erik Satie. In love, as in painting, what is important is not to search but to find. I hate the search, I hate the concept of searching. What decent artist, what decent lover, ever spent his time in the search? Search is for ninnies. The point, if you are a serious man, is to find. I find a woman as I find a subject—here she is! Now to change her, to vary her, to cover the walls of my heart with her, that's it! And one day's work leads to another. It's tomorrow and it's time to begin again. It's constant action. I keep finding out who she is, who I am, what it is—such is Love. Love is finding and it is changes, and its changes are its seductions. It at last, it always adds up, it is a sum—but a sum of destructions. This is how I love and how I paint.

Aria

Love is a sum
Of destructions
A woman standing naked in the sun
Is not in need of introductions
You see her she sees you
What do you do? When I have no red, I use blue.

In love there is no one
Consummation
Assorted *demoiselles* of Avignon

Are made of color and sensation
You see them they see you
What do you do? When I have no red, I use blue.

Though in love there is perfection,
It is not what's in your mind
When you take your first direction—
But in what at last you find!

PICASSO: *(speaking again)*
And that is the beginning and the end of what I have to say. For this instant.
Let's drink!

SATIE: *(to* STEIN *who, it can now be seen, has a big pile of papers in front of her on the table)*
Fair lady of Fleurus, will you speak next
After this dark and barbarous man of Spain?

STEIN:
Will I will yes and thank you. I will use these papers I won't. Thank you. I won't use these papers because love is simple and yet to talk about love is simple and yet to talk about love is not is it not it is not simple. These papers are recipes. Sometimes recipes are simple. A cat and a dog in a pie is not simple. Love is simple.

(She hands the papers to ALICE B. TOKLAS *who puts them away in a big purse.)*

Love is as it is. In this way it is simple. But is it simple is it is it is it. Writing is simple it is less simple. Is it simple to write. To write is less simple. In writing one must begin again and again. Again and again and again and again and again. Again begin. Begin with a blue shovel. Again is simple it is not so simple. And include everything is this simple is this love. I say writing but it is also love. It is that simple. Is love simple is it simple. It is simple because it is not and we get used to it. I say love is simple because it is not and we get used to it. We get used to its being what it is not. I may say. And that is love is writing beginning and beginning without writing. Is it. It is simple to sing of love. And praise praise it.

Aria

What is love is it is it is it
Is it it is is it is it is it simple
There is is there blue sky above
Above roof above above roof
Not where I expect to be

The first time me you see
Love is Ladies' Voices
Act Three
Love is Four Saints
Ask me
Love is Lifting Belly
Thank you points to it

Thank you for love naturally
Which every single day I see
Act One The birds fly
Act Four You and I
Act Two Stay with me
Act Three is Act Five

SATIE:

Thank you, Lady of Sentences. Your prose is your prose is your prose. As for your poetry, I'm all envy for my songs. *Quelles delicieuses piecés froides!*

STEIN:

I thank you thank you.

SATIE: *(to* COCTEAU*)*

Jean. Can you speak next? By the way, happy birthday!

ALL:

Bonne anniversaire! bonne fête! and happy birthday!

(A cake, decorated with angels and motorcyclists and with twenty-nine candles, is brought in and set before COCTEAU.*)*

SATIE:

Do you, at the old age you reach today,
At twenty-nine, do you think, have something left to say?

COCTEAU:

Thanks for the cake. *Merci pour ce gateau.* As for my old age, Erik, it's not so funny. Well, you have almost twice my age. I guess it may be funny for you. But it's a sadness of life that we grow old. Love is something else. Love is always young, it's always new, and that, my dear teacher and funny man, and all the rest of you great talents around, is because it remains unknown—it is a mystery. That keeps it young. It is a mystery and it is a secret. Even when you find out the secret of love, you are left with the mystery. And of a mystery we can never have too much. It is always there, entreating us, to solve it, to be lost in it, to rejoice in it. From this, its eternal youth. Not paralleled, alas, by our own. We grow old, and love stays there the same, like an eternal sailor, or, rather, like a young one. And now he is transformed to an angel, that is the mystery, and he has wings made of wood, that is the secret, and he has an arm like the capital neck of a swan, and that is the beauty, and he is disheveled, and that is the chance occurrence, and he is in his shirtsleeves, and that is to be expected, and he looks like a sailboat when it is sinking, and that is the end, which is to say, it is the beginning of love. Its blue eyes go straight through my heart.

Aria

Love, love, composed
Of angels, of cyclists, of swans,
Of great marble statues with no clothes on,
And of the Virgin Mary and the soda-water siphon—
You fizz and you bubble in New York
And in Paris and where ships come into port.

In Dakar and in Marseilles
How you shine in each café!
You're a blue Negro who boxes
Equators as well as equinoxes.
You're the Little American Girl and the Sailor—
Beaux clowns vous êtes fox terriers!

And now you are an angel in shirtsleeves with the neck of a swan
On the Champs Elysées, at a café you're sitting down—
Is it too late, or will you give me the time of day?
For I'm twenty-nine, and time is almost gone!

SATIE:
Well, so! A toast to Jean! May he have many poetic returns of the day!

(*to* MARINETTI)

Marinetti, here you've been with your helmet on all this time. What news do you bring us from the future? Is it dangerous? Should we all be protecting our heads?

MARINETTI:
Basta l'umore. Et baste spaghetti et basta l'amore del passato. It is the FUTURE that determines the nature of love. Enough of the love of the past—all that useless paraphernalia! It is time to break through to the truth—of love and of everything else. In our factory-filled streets, with their sounds of machines, odor of smoke, in the distance noises of cannon,

(Noise of CANNON—*from the war—may be heard here.)*

with cars chasing by and airplanes overhead, look! who are these two, dressed in laces and frills, speaking to each other so plaintively, in measured verse, about *rondini* and *i piccini fiorini* and who knows what other *inininini*—and he plays—a mandolin! *Iddio mio,* and she, she lets fall her perfumed hankie to the street. The dump truck will pick it up! It is going to hit them, those two sappy lovers! They've crept here from another epoch, and they'll have to go back. Such lovers cannot be us. No! Love of the Future, you are a Love of steel. The man is a welder, and the woman is fire. You are violent and burning, and clear. No old sadness, no old treacheries, no secret meetings, no love notes—edged with tears! and with perfume! that silly poison—Pfui! Pfooah! It is *your* perfume, New Love, that impels us, propels us, drives us upward and outward into the air. You, perfume of the exhaust of a car, like the exhalations of angels, angels with wings like iron trenchers. I sing to the future, I sing my song of love to a car, to my *iddio di una razza d'acciaio,* to my racing car!

Aria

Veemente Dio d'una razza d'acciaio
Automobile ebbrrra di spazio
che scalpiti e Frremy d'angoscia
rodendo il morso con striduli denti
It is You that I love and who are Love!

Dieu véhément d'une race d'acier
Automobile ivre d'espace
qui piétines d'angoisse,
rongeant le mors aux dents stridentes
It is You that I love and who are Love!

Vehement God of a steel race
Automobile drunk on space
you pawing the road and breaking with anguish
champing at the bit with strident teeth
It's You that I love
and who are Love!

MARINETTI:

That's my song.

PICASSO: *(to* SATIE*)*

Satie, you speak next. I want to hear what *you* have to say, you who have been somewhat bossing us around.

SATIE:

Well, it seems more polite to me to let Marie—

MARINETTI:

I don't see why—

PICASSO: (*to* SATIE)

Erik, why don't you speak? And let Marie be later. We may yet see Gui.
Better if what she says is when he's here.

SATIE:

All right. So be it. I have mainly just one idea. It's about lightness. What if
love, truly, is light? Of course, love is supposed to be heavy and deep, and in
its heaviness and in its depths to bring sorrow and pain. Well, what if that is
all a mistake, and the truth about love is that like certain music, like the music
I am writing for my *Socrate,* love is essentially light and white—blank, *blanc.*
Listen, and you'll hear what I think love can be, what I think love is. Love
came in a shimmering white dress and gave this idea to me. Or so it seemed.
But in truth she was dressed very simply and said it to me as if it were a joke.

Aria

I have a girl in the form of a pear
She has thirty-two simple measures
In two/four time
And she is mine
Each morning when I sing to her, she's mine—
"Biqui," *je dis,* "ma poire!"—such simple pleasures!

When I sit down to write her an air
It is always full of syncopations
If love is blind,
It isn't mine
Each movement of it's in piano time—
Tink tank tunk tank tank tunk—such elations!

Run, run, my fingers, up and sideways,
Pedal here and silence there—
Love, and music, always finds ways
To be shaped and make a pear—
Love, like music, makes a pair!

SATIE:

Marie?

MARIE LAURENCIN:

Beautiful, Erik. But Love hasn't been light for me. It's been adventurous, but rather heavy and strong. *"Entre les fauves et les cubistes / Prise au piége, petite biche."* Between the Fauvists and the Cubists, that was me, caught in a trap, like a little deer. That's how Cocteau described me in a poem and I suppose it describes my artistic position pretty well. Guillaume was more flattering. He made me out to be some sort of delirious delectably eternally feminine painter, the female possessor of qualities not before present in the art of man. Well, that's how I seemed to be to them. Picasso ran into me in 1907 and he said to Apollinaire, "I think I've found you a fiancée!" Guillaume took him up on it, took *me* up on *him.* I hope my mother doesn't hear that! She's very proper. She didn't at all approve of Gui and my other bohemian friends. Gui says I broke his heart. He was all the time a little bit breaking mine. He's sometimes a rather cruel and eccentric man. I envisioned something else—

(At this moment the door opens and APOLLINAIRE *enters. He has a white bandage around his head.* MARIE LAURENCIN *stops speaking, as does everyone else. Then there is great excitement. Everyone at the banquet has been waiting for him to come.)*

SATIE:

Guillaume!

PICASSO:

Guillaume!

OTHERS:

Guillaume! Guillaume! Apollinaire!

APOLLINAIRE:

Hello! How much I've wanted to be here
In this last Banquet Year!

COCTEAU:

Your injury—from the war—?

APOLLINAIRE:

That hurts me much less than it did before.

SATIE:

How goes the war for France?

APOLLINAIRE:

Our troops and theirs advance
Our planes meet in explosions like great roses

Whose petals fall on Nancy and Coblentz!
I'm sorry to be late.

SATIE:

Sit down, sit down!
We have been waiting for you but you're not too late. Everyone is giving a little
talk about love. You'll be next, if you wish—after Marie.

(APOLLINAIRE *turns and sees* MARIE LAURENCIN.)

APOLLINAIRE: *(very agitatedly)*
Marie! Marie *ma* Laurencin!

SATIE:

Marie had just begun—

APOLLINAIRE:

Marie! You, here!

MARIE LAURENCIN:

Bonsoir, Guillaume!

APOLLINAIRE:

My Frizzy-head! my Standing-over-there!
My heart is broken like my head, Marie—
Oh my one only love, come back to me!

MARIE LAURENCIN:

I can't, Guillaume.

SATIE:

Gui, let her finish what she has to say, what she began to say—Then it's your
turn to speak. You can say—anything.

MARIE LAURENCIN:

It's, it's hard to talk of love when Gui is here. Well, well, I'll try. . . . The truth
is, when I think of Love, Love seems to have Gui's face, that extraordinary
face shaped like a pear. And Love has his lightness and his jokes. In other
ways, Love is not Gui at all. Gui is in love with change, and what he loved
in me was change. That's good for poetry, but not, for me, for love.

Aria

Under the Mirabeau Bridge flowed the Seine
I went away and I came back again
You loved me this way and you loved me that way

Nothing wholly made us happy
Like that river I can't go back again
Under the Mirabeau Bridge flowed the Seine.

You wrote, "Oh when will you come back Marie—
Quand donc reviendrez-vous Marie"
And wrote, "Ah when will this week ever end—
Quand donc finira la semaine"
You wrote when I was gone most beautifully
What had it, though, Guillaume, to do with me?

White days flow from us and light words from you
And from my brushes lines of red and blue.
I paint you with Picasso and Fernande—
I'm in it, too, a flower in my hand.
That moment's there, it cannot come again.
Under the Mirabeau Bridge flows the Seine.

APOLLINAIRE:

Marie, that's terrible! What you say about our love is terrible! Marie, it isn't true.

MARIE LAURENCIN:

Gui, I learned all of that from you—
Everything I said I got from you:
That nothing lasts and no one can be true—
It's all from you.

APOLLINAIRE:

Not fair, Marie, not true. I wrote that poem after I had lost you.
Having you was the truth of love for me.
I want that truth again!

MARIE LAURENCIN:

But I can't come back, Gui.

APOLLINAIRE:

Still, I have my chance to speak. Oh, Marie, let me persuade you! Let my speech and my poetry persuade you. That is, I suppose, what poetry is all about. But has it ever been more serious, more put to the test than this? And it's so hard for me to speak about love, quite aside from the fact that I have already done so much. It's hard for me to speak because love is almost everything I am. I don't exist apart from it. I am all kinds of it. I am made up of a thousand kinds of love. Do you know that there is no word for *horse* in the Arabic language? But that there are one hundred, at least, for different kinds of horses? That is how it is with love and me. I am love nostalgic, love sadistic, love longing, and love delicacy, I am love violent, love unbounded, I am love playful, I am love absconded, love with and without rhyme, I am love obscure, love clarity, I am love peculiarity. Do you remember making love in my bedroom, Marie? We couldn't use the bed, I'd only let us use the chair. We were happy there.

MARIE LAURENCIN: *(speaking aside)*
Yes, I was happy there
But can't be any longer.

APOLLINAIRE:
Oh, love
You've given me my best poetry and you
Have been best comfort when with women or alone.
You were my sweet companion all through *Zone*—
When I walked through Paris, Love, with you
And my fresh sense of Marie there too

MARIE LAURENCIN: *(to* APOLLINAIRE*)*
You were in love with losing me, and change.

APOLLINAIRE: *(to* MARIE LAURENCIN*)*
Marie . . . I feel change. That's not quite to say I love it. I look at the river flowing, and I feel love. But it's not for the river. A man can't simply attach himself to change. He needs a woman, a woman who embodies that change. To feel that flowing in one dear person one can hold in one's arms. Without that, I'm not a poet, I'm not anything!

Aria

Not war not aircraft guns not injury
Not time not change not age but just your leaving me
Deprives me of my self Marie
O Mona Lisa of Modernity
My love my luck my twentieth century
Marie Marie Marie come back to me

MARIE LAURENCIN:
I can't Guillaume.

Not that great shepherdess the Tour Eiffel
Not Notre Dame with its enormous bell

That praises heaven down as deep as hell
Not Botticelli's lady on the shell
Nor any other can give back to me
What you could if you wished me well Marie

MARIE LAURENCIN:
  I do, but can't, Guillaume.

  Marie I've seen the century turn and change
  I've seen this century's art become as strange
  As any ever was in history
  There never was so beautiful and strange
  A moment as this present century
  So found by me now lost in you Marie

MARIE LAURENCIN:
  In you and me!

(Now APOLLINAIRE *sings his aria again, and this time* MARIE LAURENCIN *joins in with hers—"Under the Mirabeau Bridge flowed the Seine," etc. So they are singing a duet of these two arias. Next,* APOLLINAIRE *sings the following aria. It may be sung as a duet with* MARIE LAURENCIN's *aria; or perhaps,* APOLLINAIRE *sings it alone first and then sings again the last stanza—"Let the days pass . . . Seine"—while* MARIE LAURENCIN *sings the first stanza of her aria.)*

  Apollinaire Aria #2

  Let us be hand in hand
  And face to face
  While underneath the bridge
  That our arms make passes
  The worn-out weary flow
  Of unending glances.

  L'amour s'en va
  Like that rushing water
  Love goes away
  Comme cette eau courante
  How slow life is *comme la vie est lente*
  How violent is hope *comme l'esperance est violente*

  Let the days pass let the weeks pass
  Neither time past

Nor loves come back again
Under the Mirabeau Bridge flows the Seine

APOLLINAIRE: *(crying out, at the end of the duet)*
  Unless———!

(Now there is loud knocking at the door of the café, and the sounds of an enormous festive Paris CROWD *outside.)*

KNOCK KNOCK

STEIN:
  What's all the noise outside?

COCTEAU:
  It's Paris—but Paris all excited. About what?

KNOCK KNOCK KNOCK KNOCK

*(*SATIE *goes to the door and opens it)*

SATIE:
  What is this all about?

THE CROWD OUTSIDE:
  There's good news of the war! It soon may be over! Let us in!

SATIE:
  Come in, come in!

(People throng into the Closerie. Recognizable among the new celebrants are JOSEPHINE BAKER, ANDRÉ BRETON, PAUL ÉLUARD, TRISTAN TZARA, DARIUS MILHAUD, ERNEST HEMINGWAY, SCOTT *and* ZELDA FITZGERALD, MAX ERNST, FRANCIS PICABIA, *and other notable participants in artistic life in Paris in the 1920s and 1930s. They are a sort of chorus representing the Times to Come, like the Chorus of Athenian Women at the end of Aeschylus's Oresteia.)*

MEMBERS OF THE NEW CROWD:
  Let's drink!
        We'll drink!
  Come on!
        We'll drink!

SATIE:
  Come in! Our revels now are ended.

ANDRÉ BRETON:
  No! Beginning.

PICABIA:
    Our revels now begin!

STEIN:
    Welcome well welcome.

MEMBERS OF THE CROWD:
    Well, we'll drink!

SATIE:
    Come in!

PICABIA:
    Let's sing of love!

(Now the CROWD, *led by* JOSEPHINE BAKER, *sings.)*

Song

Love is a flower
It lasts for an hour
Ah the sweet moment
So quickly over

VARIOUS VOICES:
    Love is a heart attack
    Love is an almanac
    Love is a breaking back
    Well, love is, obviously, anything you like

SATIE:
    I'd say not quite.
    Our talk tonight has been but a beginning.

PICASSO:
    Who knows as this young century goes spinning
    Through interstellar night
    If anything more new, or true, of love will come to light?

APOLLINAIRE: *(to* MARIE LAURENCIN)
    One chance, Marie!

SATIE: *(answering* PICASSO)
    That we must wait and see!

(Now all becomes quiet, and there is a last song, sung by PICASSO, STEIN, COCTEAU, MARINETTI, SATIE, MARIE LAURENCIN, *and* APOLLINAIRE.)

Last Song

When I have no red, I use blue

What is love is it is it is it
Is it is it it is is it simple
Is it too late?
I'm twenty-nine, and time is almost gone

Automobile drunk on space
Pawing the road and braking with anguish
It's you that I love

She has thirty-two simple measures
In two/four time—such simple pleasures!

Love is a sum of destructions

You wrote, "Oh when will you come back Marie"
And from my brushes lines of red and blue

And now you are an angel in shirtsleeves with the neck of a swan

Neither time past nor love comes back again
Under the Mirabeau Bridge flows the Seine

FINAL CURTAIN

THE APPLE (film) was directed and photographed by Rudy Burckhardt in 1967; music by Brad Burg; sung and played by Kim Brodey and Tony Ackerman.

THE BANQUET (opera) premiered June 28, 1998, at the Concordia Theater in Bremen, Germany, with the composer, Marcello Pannini, conducting. This opera had a series of Italian productions in Genoa, Rome, and Florence in the fall of 2001.

BERTHA (play) was first produced at the Living Theatre, New York, on December 28, 1959. Directed by Nicola Cernovich, with sets and costumes by Remy Charlip, music for solo trumpet by Virgil Thomson, and starring Sudie Bond.

BERTHA (opera), with music by Ned Rorem, had its first performance at Carnegie Recital Hall in 1972. Local subsequent performances include a 2003 production by the New York Festival of Song at Merkin Hall.

A CHANGE OF HEARTS (opera), with music by David Hollister, was performed by the Medicine Show Theatre Ensemble in New York in 1986.

THE CONSTRUCTION OF BOSTON (play) was first produced at the Maidman Playhouse, New York, on May 4, 1962. This collaboration with Niki de Saint Phalle, Jean Tinguely, and Robert Rauschenberg was directed by Merce Cunningham; the music was by John Dooley; the chorus was played by Richard Libertini and MacIntyre Dixon. This one-night performance had sets by the three artist/actors. During the performance Rauschenberg created a rain machine to bring weather to Boston; Tinguely, in charge of architecture, constructed a seven-foot wall between the stage and the audience; Saint Phalle "brought art to Boston" by shooting a rifle at a plaster copy of Venus de Milo, causing it to bleed paint.

THE CONSTRUCTION OF BOSTON (opera), with music by Scott Wheeler, premiered as a concert performance by the John Oliver Chorale in Boston in January, 1989. Koch and Wheeler added a prologue in 1990. Its first full staging, directed by Patricia Weinmann, was in February 2002 by the Boston Conservatory. It was recorded by Naxos by the Chorus and Orchestra of the Boston Cecilia in April 2007.

THE DEATH OF SIR BRIAN CAITSKILL (play) was first produced by the Medicine Show Theatre Ensemble, New York, in 1986, directed by Barbara Vann. A more recent production took place at Here, also in New York, in 1995, directed by John Michael Carley.

EDWARD AND CHRISTINE (play): Selections were performed at the Stella Adler School of Drama in New York in the winter of 2003.

GARIBALDI EN SICILE (opera), with music by Marcello Panni, premiered at the Naples Opera House in Naples, Italy. Panni conducted this semi-staged production in April 2005.

GEORGE WASHINGTON CROSSING THE DELAWARE (play) was first produced at the Maidman Playhouse, New York, in March, 1962. Directed by Arthur Storch, décor and costumes by Alex Katz, with Richard Libertini and MacIntyre Dixon as Washington and Cornwallis. This play has been produced many times by small companies and schools across America. The wooden cut-out figures by Alex Katz are at the National Portrait Gallery in Washington, DC.

THE GOLD STANDARD (play) was first produced at Saint Peter's Church Theater, New York in 1975, directed by Robert Gainer. In October 2007, the Verse Theater Manhattan produced the play at the Bowery Poetry Club; it was directed by Jim Milton.

THE GOLD STANDARD (opera) with music by Scott Wheeler, was commissioned and premiered by Sequitr, conducted by Paul Hostetter, February 2000 at Joe's Pub. Other performances include a 2003 performance at the Miller Theater conducted by Michael Barrett, and a Dinosaur Annex production conducted by Scott Wheeler at the 2008 Ditson Festival of Contemporary Music at the Institute of Contemporary Art in Boston.

GUINEVERE, OR THE DEATH OF THE KANGAROO (play) was first produced by the American Theatre for Poets in New York in May, 1964. Directed by John Herbert McDowell, sets and costumes by Red Grooms, music by John Herbert McDowell, and with Susan Kaufman as Guinevere.

THE ELECTION (play) was produced at the Living Theatre, New York, in November, 1960. Directed by Kenneth Koch, with masks by Alfred and Lisa Leslie, and with Arnold Weinstein as Richard Nixon, Bill Berkson as John F. Kennedy, Kenward Elmslie as Henry Cabot Lodge, Larry Rivers as Lyndon Johnson, Howard Kanovitz as the Bandleader and Garry Goodrow as Dwight D. Eisenhower and the Author.

LITTLE RED RIDING HOOD (play) was produced at the Theatre de Lys in New York, in 1953.

THE MOON BALLOON (play), commissioned by New York City's Department of Cultural Affairs, took place, in a slightly modified form, at Bethesda Fountain in Central Park, New York, on New Year's Eve 1969–70. Puppet parts were played by Larry Berthelson's Pickwick Puppets. Directed by Larry Berthelson, "Moon Balloon" designed by Kip Coburn, decorations by Barry Cohen, the song "The Moon Balloon" written by Bill Schwartz and Billy Tracy. Voice parts by Barbara Harris and Herb Gardner.

THE NEW DIANA (play) was produced at the New York Art Theatre Institute in April–May 1984, and later by the Latham Playhouse in the fall of 1984, also in New York. These productions were directed by Don Sanders.

ONE THOUSAND AVANT-GARDE PLAYS: Selections have been staged in many settings. A selection of about 70 of the 112 were produced by the Medicine Show Theatre Ensemble in New York in 1987. Other productions include selection at the Portland Stage Company in Portland, Maine, in 1990 and a broadcast production in Egypt through WorldNet (USIA) in the fall of 1990. Two weeks before Kenneth Koch's death in July 2002, the Oddfellows Playhouse had a large production at Guild Hall, Easthampton, New York, directed by Maria Pessino and featuring music by Roger Trefousse.

PERICLES (play) was first produced at the Cherry Lane Theatre, New York, on December 5, 1960. Directed by Nicola Cernovich, with sets and costumes by Robert Mitchell, music by Albert Fine, and with Athan Karras and Nicholas Crabbe in the roles of Pericles and his Friend.

POPEYE AMONG THE POLAR BEARS (play) was first produced by the Medicine Show in New York City, March–April 1986; directed by Barbara Vann; sets and visual direction by Christopher Cantwell; costumes by Janice Bridgers; with music written and performed by Butch Morris. Popeye was played by Kevin O'Connor; Olive Oyl by Susan Schader; and Swee'Pea by Paul Murphy. Nobles, citizens, bears, jewels, and others were played by James Barbosa, Melanie Demetri, David Frankel, Carl Frano, Steve Spicehandler, and Regan Vann.

THE RED ROBINS (play) was first produced at Guild Hall in East Hampton, New York, in August 1977; then, in a more ambitious production, in New York City, at St. Clement's Theatre in January 1978. Don Sanders directed and Vanessa James designed the costumes. Kyle Morris did the sets for East Hampton. For the New York production the sets were by a variety of artists: Jane Freilicher, Red Grooms, Vanessa James, Alex Katz, Katherine Koch, Roy Lichtenstein, and Rory McEwen. The New York City cast included Lynn Bowman, Kate Farrell, Steven Hall, Chris Hawthorne, Ken Kirschenbaum, James Lytras, and Martin Maniak as Red Robins; Don Schrader as the President, Christophe DeMenil as the Bird, Don Sanders as Santa Claus, Brian Glover as the Easter Bunny, and Taylor Mead as Mike the Tiger, Ni Shu, Jill's Father, Terrence, and the Captain. The lighting was by Alan Adelman and the choreography by Wendy Biller.

ROOSTER REDIVIVUS (play) was produced in Garnerville, New York, in 1975. It was on a double bill with *The Gold Standard*.

THE SCOTTY DOG (film) was directed and photographed by Keith Cohen in 1968; music by David Shapiro; voice-over by Norman Rose. The film starred Andrew Koch.

THE TINGUELY MACHINE MYSTERY, OR THE LOVE SUICIDES AT KALUKA (play) was presented at the Jewish Museum, New York, on December 22, 1965. Directed by Remy Charlip and Kenneth Koch, with machines by Jean Tinguely, music by Morton Feldman, and a cast consisting of Clarice Rivers, Syd Solomon, Jane Freilicher, Larry Rivers, Niki de Saint Phalle, Kenward Elmslie, Alexandre Iolas, Kiki Kogelnik, Howard Kanovitz, Arnold Weinstein, John Ashbery, Joe Brainard, and Frank Lima.

ACKNOWLEDGMENTS

Photo from *One Thousand Avant-Garde Plays* by Marisela Lagrave reprinted by the permission of the photographer.

Photo of artists, author, and cast of *The Construction of Boston* courtesy of the Center for Creative Photography, University of Arizona © 1962 Hans Namuth Estate.

Photo by Peter Moore of Jean Tinguely sculpture © Estate of Peter Moore/Licensed by VAGA, NYC.

Photo by Peter Moore of a scene from *Guinevere, or the Death of the Kangrooo* © Estate of Peter Moore/Licensed by VAGA, NYC.

Jean Tinguely sculpture © 2013 Artists Rights Society (ARS), New York/ADAGP, Paris.

Photos of *The Red Robins* and *The New Diana* used by permission of Donald Sanders.

Program drawing for *One Thousand Avant-Garde Plays* © Estate of Larry Rivers/Licensed by VAGA, New York, NY.

Photo of Guild Hall program for *One Thousand Avant-Garde Plays* by Phillipe Montant, used by permission of Guild Hall Museum, Christina Mossaides Strassfield, Director/Chief Curator.

Roy Lichtenstein set decoration for *One Thousand Avant-Garde Plays* reprinted by permission of the Estate of Roy Lichtenstein. Image and photo © The Estate of Roy Lichtenstein.

Alex Katz sets for *George Washington Crossing the Delaware*: Art © Alex Katz/Licensed by VAGA, New York, NY, and with the permission of the Smithsonian American Art Museum, Gift of Mr. and Mrs. David K. Anderson, Martha Jackson Memorial Collection. Photo by Karen Koch. Used by permission.

Photo of Kenneth Koch in Bremen by Karen Koch. Used by permission.

Kenneth Koch manuscript page and Cherry Lane Theatre Playbill page used by permission of the Henry W. and Albert A. Berg Collection of English and

American Literature, the New York Public Library, Astor, Lenox, and Tilden Foundations.

Cover and interior photo by Corrado Bonini of a scene from *The Banquet* by permission of the Fondazione Teatro Carlo Felice (Genoa), Franco Ripa di Meana, Director.

*   *   *

The editors of this volume are grateful to Isaac Gerwirtz, Neil Mann, and Rebecca Filner of the Berg Collection at the New York Public Library (the site of the Kenneth Koch Archive), to Donald Sanders and Vanessa James from the Massachusetts International Festival of the Arts, and to Marcello Panni for his help obtaining use of materials from the Teatro Carlo Felice and Casa Ricordi Music Publishing in Italy. For their generosity in the use of artwork, we thank Alex Katz, David Joel (the Larry Rivers Foundation), and Natasha Sigmund (the Roy Lichtenstein Estate). Finally, we would like to thank Ann Close, Kenneth Koch's editor at Knopf, and Maxine Groffsky, his friend and former literary agent.

COLOPHON

The Banquet was designed at Coffee House Press,
in the historic Grain Belt Brewery's Bottling House
near downtown Minneapolis.
The text is set in Minion.

FUNDER ACKNOWLEDGMENT

Coffee House Press is an independent, nonprofit literary publisher. Our books are made possible through the generous support of grants and gifts from many foundations, corporate giving programs, state and federal support, and through donations from individuals who believe in the transformational power of literature. Coffee House Press receives major operating support from Amazon, the Bush Foundation, the Jerome Foundation, the McKnight Foundation, from Target, and in part from a grant provided by the Minnesota State Arts Board through an appropriation by the Minnesota State Legislature from the State's general fund and its arts and cultural heritage fund with money from the vote of the people of Minnesota on November 4, 2008, and a grant from the Wells Fargo Foundation of Minnesota. Support for this title was received from the National Endowment for the Arts, a federal agency. Coffee House also receives support from: several anonymous donors; Suzanne Allen; Elmer L. and Eleanor J. Andersen Foundation; Around Town Agency; Patricia Beithon; Bill Berkson; the E. Thomas Binger and Rebecca Rand Fund of the Minneapolis Foundation; the Patrick and Aimee Butler Family Foundation; The Buuck Family Foundation, Ruth Dayton; Dorsey & Whitney, LLP; Mary Ebert and Paul Stembler; Chris Fischbach and Katie Dublinski; Fredrikson & Byron, P.A.; Sally French; Anselm Hollo and Jane Dalrymple-Hollo; Jeffrey Hom; Carl and Heidi Horsch; Alex and Ada Katz; Stephen and Isabel Keating; Kenneth Kahn, the Kenneth Koch Literary Estate; Kathy and Dean Koutsky; the Lenfestey Family Foundation; Carol and Aaron Mack; Mary McDermid; Sjur Midness and Briar Andresen; the Nash Foundation; the Rehael Fund of the Minneapolis Foundation; Schwegman, Lundberg & Woessner, P.A.; Kiki Smith; Jeffrey Sugerman and Sarah Schultz; Patricia Tilton; the Archie D. & Bertha H. Walker Foundation; Stu Wilson and Mel Barker; the Woessner Freeman Family Foundation; Margaret and Angus Wurtele; and many other generous individual donors.

   amazon.com

To you and our many readers across the country, we send our thanks for your continuing support.

COFFEE HOUSE PRESS

The mission of Coffee House Press is to publish exciting, vital, and enduring authors of our time; to delight and inspire readers; to contribute to the cultural life of our community; and to enrich our literary heritage. By building on the best traditions of publishing and the book arts, we produce books that celebrate imagination, innovation in the craft of writing, and the many authentic voices of the American experience.

Good books are brewing at coffeehousepress.org